SELF-AWARENESS AND ALTERITY

Northwestern University
Studies in Phenomenology
and
Existential Philosophy

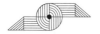

SELF-AWARENESS AND ALTERITY

A Phenomenological Investigation

Dan Zahavi

Northwestern University Press
Evanston, Illinois

Northwestern University Press
Evanston, Illinois 60208-4210

Printed in the United States of America

ISBN 0-8101-1700-2 cloth
ISBN 0-8101-1701-0 paper

Library of Congress Cataloging-in-Publication Data

Zahavi, Dan.
    Self-awareness and alterity : a phenomenological investigation /
Dan Zahavi.
        p.   cm. — (Northwestern University studies in phenomenology
and existential philosophy)
    Includes bibliographical references and index.
    ISBN 0–8101-1700–2 (alk. paper). — ISBN 0–8101-1701–0 (pbk. :
alk. paper)
    1. Self-perception. 2. Phenomenology. I. Title. II. Series:
Northwestern University studies in phenomenology & existential
philosophy.
BD222.Z34   1999
126—dc21   99–25952
                                                                CIP

The paper used in this publication meets the minimum requirements of the
American National Standard for Information Sciences—Permanence of Paper
for Printed Library Materials, ANSI Z39.48-1984.

[L]a question est toujours de savoir . . . *comment la présence à moi-même (Urpräsenz) qui me définit et conditionne toute présence étrangère est en même temps dé-présentation (Entgegenwärtigung) et me jette hors de moi.*
—*Maurice Merleau-Ponty*

In sensory experience I always experience myself *and* the world at the same time, not myself directly and the *Other* by inference, not myself before the *Other*, not myself without the *Other*, nor the *Other* without myself.
—*Erwin Straus*

Contents

Preface

The detailed investigation of *intentionality* stands as a major achievement in twentieth-century philosophy. This focus on subjectivity's ability to be directed toward and occupied with objects *different* from itself should, however, not obscure the fact that it has another important, but apparently antithetical feature, namely *self-awareness*. Obviously I can be aware of blooming trees, rainy mornings, or the cries of playing children, but I can also be aware that these are seen, smelled, and heard, that different perceptions are taking place, and furthermore that *I* am the one experiencing them, just as I may be aware that *I* am hungry, tired, or happy.

To say that consciousness is (or can become) aware of itself is, however, not in itself an important philosophical insight; it is rather to give name to a number of perplexing problems. This will become all too clear in a short while, but let me just mention one coming immediately to mind. If both intentionality and self-awareness are essential features of consciousness, what is their relation? Is self-awareness in reality a special higher-order intentional act, as when I reflect upon my act of perception, intending it and taking it as my intentional object, or is it rather a completely different mode of consciousness? In the latter case, is one then more fundamental than the other? Can the two exist in separation, i.e., are there intentional acts which are unconscious, or nonintentional experiences which are self-aware? Are they interdependent or perhaps, rather, as has also been suggested, mutually incompatible? Thus, it has occasionally been claimed that if consciousness is truly defined by intentionality, i.e., by its self-transcending reference to and occupation with something different from itself, then it cannot as well be pervaded by a fundamental self-presence and vice versa. In Ricoeur's formulation: "We frequently imagine reflection as a turning about of consciousness which is at first outside of itself, then returns into itself and suspends its outward orientation. This forces us to regard consciousness turned towards the other as unconscious of itself and self-consciousness as corroding the consciousness which is directed towards something other than itself. Re-reflection becomes retro-spection, disastrous for the pro-ject."[1]

The aim of this book is to clarify the issue of self-awareness and, as the title indicates, ultimately throw light on the relation between *self-awareness* and *alterity*. On closer inspection, however, self-awareness turns out to be a rather ambiguous concept. It is used in a number of different contexts to designate a number of different issues. Let me try to specify the topic I am concerned with by contrasting it to a number of related but alternative enterprises. Basically, I am interested in the *phenomenon* of self-awareness. I wish to clarify how consciousness is aware of itself, i.e., how it experiences itself, how it is given to itself. This specific question which deals with the phenomenological structure of *self-manifestation* should be distinguished from questions pertaining to the problem of personal identity, the relationship between mind and body, the empirical genesis of self-awareness, and the epistemic and foundational significance of self-awareness.

1. One obvious approach to the problem of self-awareness is psychological. To take one example, developmental psychology typically seeks to answer questions of the following type: When does the infant become able to discriminate between itself and the world? When does it recognize that it is the bearer of private mental states? When is it able to maintain some kind of detached perspective on itself? When does it recognize its own mirror image? And when does it master the use of the first-person pronoun? All of these questions are highly relevant, but none of them addresses the specific issue I wish to investigate: the self-manifestation of subjectivity. They all presuppose a specific understanding of what self-awareness amounts to, and they are generally concerned with far more complex and founded forms of self-awareness. They then seek to establish empirically when (and eventually how) self-awareness occurs for the first time in the development of the infant. Obviously, this enterprise differs from the traditional philosophical approaches to the problem of self-awareness. In fact, it is so different that one might even question whether it is at all the same topic under discussion. Despite this reservation, however, I do think it would be counterproductive for a philosophical analysis to exclude in advance the possibility of profiting from empirical research and, taking the direction of my own investigation into account, it will later on be quite natural to draw upon some recent research in developmental psychology.[2]

2. A substantial portion of the traditional philosophical discussion of self-awareness has been dominated by the Cartesian-Kantian paradigm. Self-awareness has not been analyzed for its own sake, but in connection with the attempt to locate an Archimedean point of departure, be it in the form of an indubitable epistemic foundation, or as a transcendental condition of possibility. Thus the central question has not been "What

is self-awareness?" but "How certain and/or fundamental is it?" I wish to reverse this priority. The following analysis will not per se pursue the traditional epistemological and transcendental aspects of the discussion, since this enterprise has had a tendency to divert the attention from the real issue, the understanding of the concrete phenomenon of self-awareness. Having said that, however, I have to add that it has in fact been difficult to separate the discussions completely, not only because my own investigation has led me to questions dealing with the relationship between self-awareness and intentionality, as well as between self-manifestation and hetero-manifestation, but also because at some point it will become necessary to distinguish different types of self-awareness, including the pure or transcendental self-awareness from the natural or mundane self-awareness. In itself this does not pose a problem, however, since I do not see any reason to renounce transcendental considerations altogether, as long as they do contribute to a clarification of the issue at hand.

3. Insofar as self-awareness has traditionally been taken to constitute a central and very fundamental feature of consciousness, there has often been a tendency to discuss it in connection with the mind-body problem. This is particularly the case in recent analytical philosophy of mind, where some have taken the irreducible first-person givenness of mental states to constitute an insuperable problem for naturalism. But, of course, it hardly needs to be pointed out that there is a difference between analyzing the structure of self-manifestation, on one hand, and clarifying the relation between the mind and the brain, on the other. It is one thing to investigate how my experiences (desires, perceptions, beliefs) are given to me, and a quite different thing to ask whether and to what extent they (and their givenness) might be conditioned by nonmental factors, such as neurophysiological processes. To put it differently, I am interested in a phenomenological and not in a neurological account of self-awareness. This is not to say, however, that the former investigation is of no relevance for the latter. As Nagel has pointed out, a necessary requirement for any successful reductionism is that that which is to be reduced is properly understood. But as long as a naturalistic account of consciousness ignores the subjective nature of the latter it has failed in advance.[3] My aim, however, is exactly to analyze the subjectivity of consciousness.

4. It might appear quite natural to broach the topic of personal identity in a discussion of self-awareness. But again I think these issues are better kept apart. On the one hand, I do not intend to investigate the type of self-awareness invoked by the Delphic *gnothi seauton* and articulated in the question "*Who* am I?" which is concerned with the specific

personality and narrative identity of a concrete subject. My topic is the kind of self-awareness exemplified above, the one which is traditionally associated with the *cogito* and with the first-personal givenness of our experiences, and which has recently been named "immediate epistemic self-awareness."[4] And although it has been claimed that it is only the first type of self-awareness which has a profound *existential* significance, I think it would be a grave fallacy to conclude that it is therefore also the only one really worth a philosophical investigation.[5] On the other hand, the specific first-personal givenness of our experiences can obviously be investigated in isolation from the classical problem of personal identity over time (particularly when this problem is examined from a third-person perspective, such as when one asks about the kinds of causal links required for P_2 at t_2 to be identical with P_1 at t_1).[6] When this is said, however, I would add that I take a clarification of the nature of self-awareness to be a prerequisite for a convincing analysis of personal identity in both of the above-mentioned senses. It hardly makes sense to strive for greater self-knowledge if there is nothing like immediate self-awareness. Nor does it seem to make much sense to speak of the separate problem of personal identity over time, in contrast to physical identity over time, unless there is something it is like to be a person, i.e., unless the creature in question is self-aware.

So far I have said something about *what* topic I wish to analyze. Let me add a few words about *how* I intend to proceed. As mentioned above, I am interested in the *phenomenon* of self-awareness, but I am also more specifically interested in the contribution to a clarification of self-awareness found within *phenomenology*, particularly within *Husserlian phenomenology*. Although I will draw freely upon the writings of most of the central phenomenological thinkers (Fink, Gurwitsch, Sartre, Merleau-Ponty, Ricoeur, Lévinas, Henry, and Derrida), my analysis will nevertheless focus specifically on Husserl's theory of self-awareness. I believe the phenomenological tradition has much more to offer when it comes to an understanding of self-awareness than has been conceded by most participants in the contemporary discussion.[7] Furthermore, phenomenology has traditionally focused on the dimension which speaks to my particular interest, namely, the relation between *self-awareness* and *alterity*, and it has asked the kind of questions which I wish to pursue, such as whether self-manifestation can obtain without hetero-manifestation, and without a relation to myself as an Other, and to the Other as a self.

That the problem of self-awareness has been of crucial importance for phenomenology should hardly come as a surprise. Phenomenology makes such extensive use of *reflection* that it has been forced to examine the nature of reflective self-awareness. (It should not be forgotten that a clarification of self-awareness is also an investigation into the conditions of possibility for a description of subjectivity.) Moreover, if—as Michel Henry has argued—the distinct task of phenomenology is to disclose the condition of possibility for manifestation, and if this condition were identified with transcendental subjectivity, phenomenology will eventually have to face the following questions: Does the condition of possibility for manifestation manifest itself? Can that which conditions all phenomena become a phenomenon itself? A traditional answer has been no. If the transcendental condition were to become a phenomenon itself, it would no longer be that which conditions, but something that is itself conditioned. But to deny that transcendental subjectivity can manifest itself would once and for all make a phenomenological examination of it impossible. Consequently, phenomenology has been forced to investigate the dimension of self-manifestation. Unless it was able to show that there is in fact a decisive and radical difference between the phenomenality of constituted objects and the phenomenality of constituting subjectivity, i.e., a radical difference between object-manifestation and self-manifestation, its entire project would be threatened.

My ambition has been to combine a systematic discussion with a careful interpretation of select authors. I do not think these two approaches are exclusive alternatives. On the contrary, I think that a fruitful interpretation must be guided by systematic interests, and that a systematic discussion can profit decisively from insights obtained through a careful reading of classical texts. To phrase it differently, my aim is threefold. I wish to present a systematic and comprehensive account of Husserl's theory of self-awareness; I wish to discuss and clarify some central topics in phenomenology; and finally, I wish to contribute to the current philosophical discussion of self-awareness.

This triple enterprise is reflected in the composition of the book. Although the central part will be devoted to an examination and discussion of a number of phenomenological insights pertaining to the problem of self-awareness, I will start elsewhere. In the first introductory section, I will summarize and systematize a number of recent nonphenomenological reflections on the nature of self-awareness. My exposition is divided into three chapters. In the first, I briefly account for the already classical contributions by Anscombe, Castañeda, and Shoemaker, all of them bearing in different ways on the irreducibility and nonsubstitutability of the first-person perspective. The main issue discussed will be the way in which "I" refers (or more precisely, the way in which "I" does *not* refer).[8] This presentation will then prepare the way for the second chapter, which contains my examination of what is arguably the most important contemporary theory of self-awareness, namely, the one offered by a group of German philosophers comprised by Henrich, Frank, Pothast, and Cramer. Employing insights mentioned in the first chapter, they shift and expand the framework of the discussion, drawing also on the philosophical resources of German idealism. The principal issue at stake here will be the relation between reflective and pre-reflective self-awareness. In the final introductory chapter, I will attempt to formulate a number of central questions that need to be (at least tentatively) answered if a theory of self-awareness is to prove convincing.

Part 2 will make use of the results already obtained and attempt to answer the questions by turning to phenomenology. Thus, my preliminary presentation will constitute the frame and background for my subsequent exploration of phenomenology. I believe that a phenomenological account of self-awareness can profit from the conceptual clarity and problem-oriented analyses to be found outside of phenomenology. But I also hope to show that the philosophical resources to be found within phenomenology allow for an increased understanding of the nature of self-awareness. The questions raised at the end of part 1 concern aspects of the problem of self-awareness in need of further elaboration and clarifications that can be provided by phenomenology. In this sense, the book is exactly also an attempt to show that phenomenology can contribute to current discussions of self-awareness.

Acknowledgments

This book was written in the years 1995 to 1997. In that period I had the opportunity and privilege to discuss it with a number of people in France, Belgium, Germany, Japan, the United States, and Denmark. I am very grateful for the philosophical generosity and encouragement I encountered.

First and foremost, I would like to thank Jim Hart, who has followed the work through its different stages with steady encouragement and valuable suggestions. I am also particularly indebted to Natalie Depraz and Luc Claesen for our discussions and their perceptive criticism. Finally, I would like to express my gratitude to Philippe Cabestan, Richard Cobb-Stevens, Klaus Held, Klemens Kappel, Kurt Keller, Søren Harnow Klausen, C. H. Koch, Shin Nagaï, Josef Parnas, Heiko Schulz, Frederik Stjernfelt, Toru Tani, and Yorihiro Yamagata, who have all contributed suggestions and helpful comments.

I am indebted to Jean-François Courtine, director of the Centre de recherches phénoménologiques et herméneutiques, for his kind permission to let me use the facilities at l'École normale supérieure (Paris).

I would like to thank the former director of the Husserl-Archieves in Leuven, Belgium, Samuel IJsseling, for the permission to consult Husserl's unpublished manuscripts, and the present director, Rudolf Bernet, for the permission to quote from them. I am grateful to the staff at the Husserl-Archieves in Leuven (Rudolf Bernet, Anne Montavont, Ullrich Melle, Roland Breeur) for our discussions and for their help with the manuscripts.

I wish to thank the Danish Research Council for the Humanities, which financed the first two years of the project, and Institutionen San Cataldo, which gave me a stay in Italy that allowed me to complete the book.

Finally, I would like to thank David Cockerham for having gone through the text and suggested numerous grammatical and linguistic improvements.

PART   1

PRELIMINARY
REFLECTIONS

1

"I"

L et me start my investigation by taking a brief look at the way in
which self-awareness is expressed linguistically, as in the sentences
"I am tired" or "I am looking at the Great Bear"—not because I
believe that this in itself will account for the phenomenon, nor because
I take this approach to be especially fundamental (I do not think that a
successful mastery of the first-person pronoun is a necessary precondition
for self-awareness), but because a *semantic* and *indexical* analysis of the self-
reference of "I" will reveal some of the peculiar features of self-awareness,
which will subsequently have to be explained. Drawing on considerations
to be found in analytical philosophy of language, I would like to start by
showing that self-awareness does in fact constitute a problem. It cannot be
accounted for by means of the standard models of object-intentionality
and object-reference. Ultimately, the first-personal self-reference owes its
uniqueness to the fact that we are acquainted with our own subjectivity
in a way that differs radically from the way in which we are acquainted
with objects.

"I" is used by a speaker to refer to himself or herself. But *how* does
it refer, and to *what* exactly does it refer? An indirect answer to these
questions might be given if one tries to replace "I" with a proper name, a
definite description, or a demonstrative pronoun, since this attempt will
expose its ineradicable difference.[1]

The Reference of "I"

That "I" does not refer or function in the same way as a proper name
or a definite description is relatively obvious. Whereas the reference of
the latter might misfire because there is either no object *or* more than
one object which bears the name or fits the description, this is not a
problem for "I." Correctly used, "I" cannot fail to refer to the object it

purports to refer to, and one can consequently speak of its *ontological and referential priority* over all names and descriptions.[2] Moreover, this infallible reference takes place even if the speaker is in complete ignorance or error concerning his own empirical identity and biography, i.e., in ignorance or error concerning the description which fits him and identifies him from a third-person perspective. Being in a state of complete amnesia does not entail losing self-awareness, nor the capability to refer infallibly to oneself using "I."[3] Conversely, if I falsely believed myself to be Neil Armstrong, I would still refer to myself saying "I," whereas the description "the first man on the moon" would surely refer to someone else.

Against this background the attempt to understand "I" as a demonstrative like "this" or "that" seems more promising, especially since demonstratives are often taken to refer not only directly to their object, i.e., independently of any description, but also unerringly. Both of these assumptions can be questioned, however. First of all, used correctly "this" can still refer to a number of things within a given context; consequently, it is necessary to know the answer to the question "This *what?*" if one is to intend anything specific.[4] Thus, whereas "I" (together with "here" and "now") is a *pure* indexical, the reference made by a demonstrative pronoun has to be specified by an ostensive or descriptive support, which also makes it vulnerable to a possible misinterpretation by the listener. Second, the referent of "this" does not have to be present and might not even exist. This can be illustrated with the following example. Finally arriving at the border, the refugee might give the soldier a jewel case, saying, "If you let me escape, *this* precious jewel will be your reward." Here the speaker refers not to the visible case, but to the gem inside. That is, the demonstrative pronoun refers to something not experientially present. Furthermore, though unknown to the speaker, the case might be empty. In this situation, as well as in every hallucination, the referent of the correctly used demonstrative does not really exist. With "I" it is different. The person who says "I" not only guarantees the *existence* but also the immediate experiential *presence* of its referent at the time "I" is uttered, a point which confirms *Cartesian* intuitions, for which reason the assertion "I don't exist now" is self-contradictory and internally inconsistent.[5]

Apart from having these fundamental characteristics, "I" also differs from "this" in a number of more trivial ways. If uttered by the same person, the referent of "this" changes from context to context, whereas the referent of "I" remains the same. If uttered by different persons, the referent of "this" might refer to the same object, whereas several people cannot refer to the same by saying "I." Thus, each speaker can only refer to one referent in saying "I," namely herself, and surely that is not the case with "this."

One of the conclusions that has been drawn against this background is that first-person statements are immune to the so-called *error of misidentification*. This insight presupposes, however, an initial distinction between two different uses of "I": the use as object, and the use as subject.[6] Examples of the first are "I am bleeding," "I have lost weight," and "I have dirty feet." Examples of the second are "I am sad," "I am looking at a canary," and "I believe the Earth to be flat." The first kind of statement, which articulates types of self-reference that do not differ from the way in which Others can also refer to me, presupposes perceptual observations and a subsequent recognition or identification of something as oneself, and it is consequently prone to the error of misidentification. Having been involved in an accident where my body is tangled up with other bodies, I may see a bleeding leg, which actually belongs to someone else, erroneously identify it as *mine* and infer that I am bleeding. This type of error is excluded when it comes to the subject-use of "I." When I say "I have an itch" or "I think so-and-so" or "I feel pain," it is not the case that I know this because I (introspectively) observe *somebody* feeling a pain and then identify that person as myself. Whenever we refer to or identify a particular object, we refer to or identify it *as* something. Whenever we identify *x* as being *y* we do so because *x* is taken to have a number of identifying properties which are true of *y*. This process of identification is criterial and fallible, whereas the subject-use of "I" is neither. It is impossible that I should be feeling pain and be mistaken about *who* is feeling pain.[7] Similarly, although I can be mistaken in saying "I see a canary," since I can be mistaken in thinking that what I see is a canary or (in the case of hallucination) that there is anything at all that I see, I cannot be mistaken in saying this because I have misidentified as myself the person I believe to see a canary.[8] It is nonsensical to ask whether I am sure that I am the one who is seeing it, or to demand a specification of the criteria which I use in order to determine whether the perception is in fact *mine*. Even serious doubt about *who* I am cannot entail a doubt about it being *me* who is entertaining the doubting.

If it is true that the subject-use of "I" never misfires, and that we consequently can never be mistaken when we claim to be self-aware, the central question is obviously "Why?" Part of the *negative* answer has already been given. In contrast to every fallible object-identification, the reference of "I" in first-person experience ascriptions is immediate, noncriterial, and noninferential.[9] In fact, when one is aware of one's thoughts, feelings, beliefs, and desires, one does not seem to be given to oneself as an *object* at all.[10] This highly significant insight can be supported by two further arguments which I will present in detail: (1) Self-awareness cannot come about as the result of a criterial self-identification, since this would lead to an infinite regress; and (2) self-awareness cannot be based on criterial self-identification, since the possession of identificatory knowledge is neither a necessary nor a sufficient condition for a successful use of "I."

1. Self-awareness cannot come about as the result of a criterial self-identification, since this would lead to an infinite regress. In order to identify something as oneself one obviously has to hold something true of it that one already knows to be true of oneself. This self-knowledge might in some cases be grounded on some further identification, but the supposition that *every* item of self-knowledge rests on identification leads to an infinite regress.[11] This even holds true for self-identification obtained through introspection. That is, it will not do to claim that introspection is distinguished by the fact that its object has a property which immediately identifies it as being me, since no other self could possibly have it, namely the property of being the private and exclusive object of exactly my introspection. This explanation will not do, since I will be unable to identify an introspected self as myself by the fact that it is introspectively observed by me unless I know it is the object of *my* introspection, i.e., unless I know that it is in fact *me* that undertakes this introspection, and this knowledge cannot itself be based on identification if one is to avoid an infinite regress.[12] More generally, one cannot account for the unique features of self-awareness by sticking to a traditional model of object-consciousness and then simply replacing the external object with an internal one. As Shoemaker writes:

> The reason one is not presented to oneself "as an object" in self-awareness
> is that self-awareness is not perceptual awareness, i.e., is not a sort
> of awareness in which objects are presented. It is awareness of facts
> unmediated by awareness of objects. But it is worth noting that if one were
> aware of oneself as an object in such cases (as one is in fact aware of oneself
> as an object when one sees oneself in a mirror), this would not help to
> explain one's self-knowledge. For awareness that the presented object was
> φ, would not tell one that one was oneself φ, unless one had identified the
> object as oneself; and one could not do this unless one already had some
> self-knowledge, namely the knowledge that one is the unique possessor
> of whatever set of properties of the presented object one took to show
> it to be oneself. Perceptual self-knowledge presupposes nonperceptual
> self-knowledge, so not all self-knowledge can be perceptual.[13]

This argument, which will be more fully elaborated in the following chapter, also shows that when one does in fact succeed in taking oneself as an object, one is dealing with a self-objectivation which in its turn presupposes a prior nonobjectifying self-awareness as its condition of possibility. This argument can gain additional support if we once more compare the subject-use and the object-use of "I." The object-use of "I," as in "I am bleeding," can be understood as ascribing a certain property to a body. Why, however, do we insist on speaking about *self*-reference in these cases? Obviously, because we are talking about *my* body. However, the moment we try to explain what is meant by calling a body "*my* body," we have to realize that this is impossible without making use of "I" as subject, as when saying that my body is the body with which *I* see, hear, speak, move, and act.[14] Consequently the object-use of "I," and more generally each and every type of (objectifying) self-reference, only counts as a case of *self*-ascription if it is supported by a prior nonobjectifying self-awareness.

2. That the possession of an identifying description is not a *necessary* condition for self-reference and self-acquaintance has already been indicated. Even if I am in a state of complete amnesia and being kept immobilized in a dark room, and consequently in ignorance of all those properties which identify me from a third-person perspective (including a perceptual awareness of my own physical appearance), I am not in a coma but remain in possession of self-awareness and can for instance have the thought "I feel weird." In this case "I" refers without attributing any specific property to the entity in question, and my awareness of myself is consequently not mediated by the awareness of any identifying property. I do not identify myself through criteria such as name, sex, physical appearance, family, nationality, profession, knowledge, or memories. Thus,

> there is no third-person special characteristic that one has to think that one possesses in order to think of oneself as *I*. Certainly, one *qua* I does not classify oneself as a self, a person, or a thinker—let alone as a human being, female, or whatever is true of all entities capable of *self*-consciousness. To illustrate, a small child at about the age of two can make perfect first-person references fully lacking knowledge involving those categories. . . . There is just no criterion one can apply to determine whether one is an *I* or not. One simply is an I. This primitive fact is primitively and immediately apprehended by a thinker who is an *I*.[15]

Nor is it a *sufficient* condition, however, since a person can be in possession of an identifying description of himself and still fail to realize that he himself is the person in question. Let us assume that the famous painter Quintus Lingens suffers from complete amnesia. By chance he walks into a bookstore where he happens to fall upon the new best-seller *Quintus Lingens: The True and Complete Story*. Even if he were to read and memorize the entire book nothing would force him to realize that he himself was the person in question.[16] Since there is always a gap between grasping that a certain third-person description applies to a person, and grasping that I am that person, i.e., since there is no third-person description such that grasping that it fits a certain person guarantees that I realize that I am that person, self-awareness cannot be regarded as involving the identification of an object by any third-person description.[17]

Castañeda is the one who has delivered the classical argument for the thesis that a person in order to be self-aware *can* not only dispense with every type of third-person reference, but *must* in fact do so, if she really is to think of herself as herself. In his article " 'He': A Study in the Logic of Self-Consciousness," Castañeda examines the third-person pronoun "he (him, his)" which is used to attribute self-awareness to someone, that is the "he" of self-consciousness, or to use Castañeda's notation the pronoun "he*," where "he*" stands for "he, himself." To say "X knows that he himself is ϕ" is to attribute to X knowledge that he can and *must* articulate by saying "I am ϕ."[18] Castañeda's central claim is that "he*" and "I" constitute unique logical categories, which are not analyzable in terms of any other type of referring mechanism.[19] As illustration let us compare the following statements:

1a. I know that I live in Copenhagen
1b. The author of *Intentionalität und Konstitution* knows that he* lives in Copenhagen
2. The author of *Intentionalität und Konstitution* knows that the author of *Intentionalität und Konstitution* lives in Copenhagen

These statements are not synonymous, since 1a and 1b can be true when 2 is false, and vice versa. The author of *Intentionalität und Konstitution* may know that he* lives in Copenhagen but may have forgotten that he* ever wrote a book entitled *Intentionalität und Konstitution*. And, conversely, the author of *Intentionalität und Konstitution*, suffering from amnesia, may know that the author of *Intentionalität und Konstitution* lives in Copenhagen, but fail to realize that it is true of himself*. Consequently "he*" (and "I") cannot be a proxy for "the author of *Intentionalität und Konstitution*," and more generally "he*" (and "I") cannot be replaced by any other name or description which does not already include a token of "he*" (or "I").[20] The relevance of this example for our understanding of the nature of self-awareness is immediately brought to light through Castañeda's conclusion: When N.N. asserts "The author of *Intentionalität und Konstitution* believes that he* lives in Copenhagen," then N.N. does not attribute to the author the possession of any way of referring to himself aside from the ability to use the pronoun "I" or the ability to be conscious of himself. The latter ability is the only way of referring to himself that N.N. must attribute to the author for his statement to be true.[21]

In other words, to attribute self-awareness to someone does not entail attributing a successful criterial self-identification to the person in question. Saying of the author of *Intentionalität und Konstitution* that he believes that he* lives in Copenhagen is not to imply that the person in question has successfully identified an object in the world by means of a definite description and is then attributing the predicate "lives in Copenhagen" to that object (as would have been the case if the author believed that the author lived in Copenhagen). Nor is it more generally to imply that the person in question is aware of himself* by being aware of any specific identifying third-person characteristic.

Whereas "he*" cannot be replaced by a description or a name, one might still wonder if it cannot be understood in terms of the demonstrative use of "he." One might, for instance, suggest that if a person X asserts "he is φ," using "he" purely demonstratively to refer to X, then X believes that he* is φ. This suggestion will not do, however, since it is entirely possible to point to one's own bleeding legs, saying "he is bleeding" without realizing that it is oneself who is bleeding. Similarly, X may see a person and point at him, exclaiming "he looks dreadful," without realizing that he is looking in a mirror and thus referring to himself.[22]

This argument bears directly on the use of "I." To say "I" is not merely for the speaker to single a specific person out in a given context; the speaker must also be aware that it is he himself who is referred to. Since the use of "I" implies self-awareness, "I" cannot simply be defined as the word each one uses in speaking of himself, since it is possible to speak and refer to oneself (by way of a proper name, a definite description, or a demonstrative) without realizing that it is oneself, and this ignorance is incompatible with the proper use of "I."[23] To quote Nozick:

> For a person X to reflexively self-refer is not merely for X to use a term that actually refers to X; this omits as internal to the act of referring that it is *himself* to which he refers. When Oedipus sets out to find "the person whose acts have brought trouble to Thebes," he is referring to Oedipus but he is not referring to himself in the requisite reflexive way. He does not know that he himself is the culprit. To do that, he would have to think or know some suitable first-person statement using "I," "me," "my."[24]

A well-known example by Perry can also illustrate this conclusion. Let us assume that I suddenly discover a trail of sugar on a supermarket floor. Pushing my cart down the aisle on one side of a tall counter and back the aisle on the other, I try to catch up with the shopper with the torn sack in order to tell him that he is making a mess. With each trip around the counter, the trail becomes thicker and thicker, but I seem unable to catch up. Suddenly I realize that the shopper I am trying to catch is myself, and I consequently stop my cart and rearrange the sack.[25] When I started my search, I was looking for the shopper with the torn sack of sugar. I was referring to myself all the time, but it was only at the end that I realized this. The significant thing is that if the belief I came to hold, namely "*I am the one who is making this mess*," is replaced with a third-person description of myself, we will no longer have an explanation of why *I* stopped my shopping cart. If, for instance, we describe my realization as "I realized that Dan Zahavi was making the mess," or "I realized that the author of *Intentionalität und Konstitution* was making the mess," or "I realized that *he*"—pointing at someone in the mirror—"was making the mess," we still have not got an explanation, unless we add "and I believe that *I* am Dan Zahavi," " . . . the author of *Intentionalität und Konstitution*," or " . . . the man in the mirror," i.e., unless we capture the fact that I am thinking of the messy shopper as *me*.[26] No description of myself not entailing "I" (me, my, mine) requires me to realize that *I* am that person. No matter how detailed a third-person description I give of a person, this description cannot entail that *I* am that person.[27] Incidentally, Perry's example also illustrates that it is a distinctive feature of first-person beliefs that they play a decisive role in practical reasoning. Agency requires a subjective point of view. Since the change from a third-person to a first-person perspective can make us change our behavior, self-awareness cannot be a mere epiphenomenon.

To recapitulate, whereas Others refer to me using identifying and discriminatory means such as proper names, demonstratives, or definite descriptions, these third-person references are not merely unnecessary but ultimately insufficient if I am to think of myself *as* myself, that is, in the proper first-person way.

The Referent of "I"

So far it has been shown *how* "I" does *not* refer. Is it possible to reach some conclusions concerning *what* "I" does refer to? Three options seem possible.

1. "I" does not refer at all. This is the radical (if not to say extreme) conclusion drawn by Anscombe. Although she has certain sympathies toward a Cartesian interpretation, she also emphasizes that Descartes would only have been right about the character and nature of the referent *if* in fact "I" was a referring expression. According to Anscombe, Descartes's position has, however, the intolerable difficulty of requiring an identification of the same referent in different "I"-thoughts. She believes this difficulty to be so insurmountable that she finally opts for a different solution: "Getting hold of the wrong object *is* excluded, and that makes us think that getting hold of the right object is guaranteed. But the reason is that there is no getting hold of any object at all. With names, or denoting expressions (in Russell's sense) there are two things to grasp: the kind of use, and what to apply them to from time to time. With 'I' there is only the use. . . . 'I' is neither a name nor another kind of expression whose logical role is to make a reference, *at all.*"[28] Consequently, Anscombe ends by adopting a Wittgensteinian conclusion— "To say 'I have pain' is no more a statement *about* a particular person than moaning is"[29]—and claims that our belief in the existence of a subject-I is due to our having fallen victim to a language-image. This conclusion is, however, confronted with several problems. First of all, the assertion "I feel pain" cannot be substituted with the assertion "Nobody feels pain,"[30] and one might wonder if it would not have been more fruitful to attempt to solve the difficulties confronting Descartes rather than to simply dissolve the problem, especially since Anscombe never provides any more detailed arguments for her claim that his position is aporetical.[31] Second, the genuine indexical uses of "here" and "now" share the immunity to the error of misidentification with "I." But nobody would conclude that "here" and "now" for that very reason do not refer at all, and one might consequently question whether that conclusion is appropriate in the case of "I."[32]

Anscombe's position has a certain affinity to the so-called *no-ownership* view according to which experiences are subjectless or egoless.[33] They are not states or properties of anyone, but mental events which simply occur, wherefore self-awareness properly speaking must be understood as the anonymous acquaintance which consciousness has of itself, and *not* as an awareness of one*self* as the one who thinks, deliberates, resolves, acts, and suffers. A classical version of this position can be found in Hume, who is famous for the following statement: "For my part, when I enter intimately into what I call *myself*, I always stumble on some particular perception or other, of heat or cold, light or shade, love or hatred, pain or pleasure. I never can catch *myself* at any time without a perception, and never can observe any thing but the perception."[34] More recently, it has been claimed that it is possible to have strictly *impersonal* experiences, which do not include any (implicit) reference to oneself as the subject of the experience.[35] Thus, even if one had to concede that two persons who had two simultaneous and qualitatively identical experiences would still have two numerical distinct experiences, this would not be the case because each of the experiences had a different *subject*, but simply because "one of these experiences is *this* experience, occurring in *this* particular mental life, and the other is *that* experience, occurring in *that* other particular mental life."[36]

An objection to this position comes to mind, however, the moment one adopts a first-person perspective. Is it really true that the primary difference between my perception and my friend's perception is that my perception is *this* one and his *that* one? Is this not, as Klawonn has argued, a parasitic and derived characterization? Is it not rather the case that my experience is *this* one exactly because it is *mine*, i.e., given in an irreducible *first-personal mode of presentation*, whereas the Other's experience is not given in a first-person mode for *me*, and therefore no part of *my* mental life?[37] Thus, it has been suggested that it is exactly the primary presence or first-personal givenness of a group of experiences which makes them *mine*, makes them belong to a particular subject. If this were the case, Hume did in fact overlook something in his analysis, namely, the specific givenness of his own experiences. He was looking for the self in the wrong place, so to speak. To be self-aware is not to apprehend a pure self apart from the experience, but to be acquainted with an experience in its first-personal mode of givenness, that is, from "within." The subject or self referred to in *self*-awareness is not something apart from or beyond the experience, nor is it a new and further experience, but simply a feature or function of its givenness. If the experience is given to me originarily, in a first-personal mode of presentation, it is experienced as my experience, otherwise not. In short, all the experiences of which I am self-aware are necessarily *my* experiences.[38] This argument is only intended as provisional. It anticipates a more detailed analysis in part 2, and for the moment it must consequently remain undecided whether there are other forms of self-awareness (such as time-consciousness or recollection) which either lack an ego or have an act-transcending ego.

2. *"I" refers to an object.* "I" can be used to single out and identify a specific object (or objective property). But this identification, which is based on the same kind of evidence that is accessible from a third-person perspective, hardly captures the unique and irreducible features of "I." If the referent of "I" were simply to be equated with the set of properties identifying me from a third-person perspective (or perhaps rather with the X, which is their common referent), we would be faced with familiar problems: I am able to use "I" infallibly even when I am in complete ignorance, doubt, or error concerning these properties, and

since I remain self-aware even when in a state of complete amnesia, it seems highly paradoxical to suggest that it should be (the sum or the bearer of) my identifying properties of which I was self-aware.

3. "I" refers to a subject. An analysis of the subject-use of "I" reveals that we are dealing with a unique, immediate, noncriterial, and infallible first-person reference. Although it still remains open what precisely "I" refers to, it seems reasonable to conclude that we are dealing with something which in an emphatic sense has to do with our subjectivity. The reference of "I" differs significantly from the well-known types of reference available from a third-person perspective, and it seems natural to assume that it owes its peculiar features exactly to the phenomenon which it is used to articulate, namely, self-awareness. We are not acquainted with our own subjective experiences in the same way that we are acquainted with objects, and the task facing us in the following is to reach a better understanding of their unique self-manifestation and first-personal givenness.

Although the outcome of the first chapter is mainly critical (telling us how "I" does not function and why self-awareness cannot simply be accounted for by means of the standard modes of object-consciousness), it also enables us to make the following minimal demand to any proper theory of self-awareness. It has to be able to explain the peculiar features characterizing the subject-use of "I"; that is, no matter how complex or differentiated the structure of self-awareness is ultimately shown to be, if the account given is unable to preserve the difference between the first-person and third-person perspectives, unable to capture its referential uniqueness, it has failed as an explanation of self-awareness.

2

Reflective versus Prereflective Self-Awareness

I n chapter 1, I argued that it is necessary to distinguish sharply between two different kinds of self-reference, one external and the other internal. The external kind of self-reference is the one available from the third-person perspective. I can refer to an object by way of a proper name, a demonstrative, or a definite description, and occasionally this object is myself. When I refer to myself in this way, I am referring to myself in exactly the same way that I can refer to Others and Others can refer to me (the only difference being that I am the one doing it, thus making the reference a self-reference). Apart from being *external* and *contingent,* this kind of self-reference is also *nonemphatic,* since it can occur without my knowledge of it, that is, I can refer to myself from the third-person perspective without realizing that I myself am the referent. In contrast, the self-reference available from the first-person perspective—the one expressed in the subject-use of "I"—is of an internal kind. Not only is it impossible to refer to anybody and anything beside oneself in the first-person way, but it also belongs to the proper use of "I" that one knows that one is referring to oneself. That is, apart from being *internal* and *necessary,* the self-reference in question is also of an *emphatic* nature.[1]

At this point, I will leave the issue of self-reference and begin a more traditional investigation of self-awareness. What is it exactly? To start with, it must be emphasized that it is not only legitimate to speak of self-awareness when I realize that *I* am perceiving a candle, but also when I am aware of my feeling of sorrow, or my burning pain, or my perception of a candle, i.e., whenever I am acquainted with an experience in its first-personal mode of givenness. I am entitled to speak of self-awareness the moment I am no longer simply conscious of a foreign object, but of my experience of the object as well, for in this case my subjectivity reveals itself to me. On this account, any experience of which I was not self-aware would be an experience I am not conscious of, i.e., an unconscious experience.

The Reflection Theory of Self-Awareness

If we are to understand what it means to be self-aware, it might be useful to point to the contrast between *intentionality*, which is characterized by a *difference* between the subject and the object of experience, and *self-awareness*, which implies some form of *identity*.[2] Any convincing theory of self-awareness has to be able to explain this distinction, and the most natural explanation seems to be that consciousness is self-aware, insofar as it has itself rather than anything else as its *object*. Of course, in order to retain the important difference between the internal and external kinds of self-reference, it is necessary to specify that this *object* must be given in a peculiar irreducible first-person way. In *An Essay concerning Human Understanding*, Locke used the term "reflection" to designate our mind's ability to turn its view inward upon itself, making its own operations the object of its contemplation.[3] Thus we can describe a theory stating that self-awareness is the result of consciousness directing its "gaze" at itself, taking itself as its object, and thus becoming aware of itself, as a *reflection theory of self-awareness*.

It is not difficult to find contemporary defenders of some version of this theory. In *A Materialist Theory of the Mind*, Armstrong argues that there is a close analogy between perception and introspection. A perception is a mental event whose intentional object is a situation in the physical world. Introspection is a mental event whose intentional object is other mental happenings occurring in the *same* mind. It is only by becoming the object of an introspection that a mental state can be conscious. Just as there are many features of our physical environment which we do not perceive, there are many mental states of which we are *unconscious*, namely all those which we do not currently introspect. Just as one must distinguish between the perception and that which is perceived, one must distinguish between the introspection and that which is introspected. A mental state cannot be aware of itself, any more than a man can eat himself up. But of course, the introspection may itself be the object of a further introspective awareness, and so on.[4]

The reflection theory gives priority to intentionality. Not only is self-awareness itself qua reflection an intentional act, but often the theory also claims that self-awareness presupposes a prior intentional act as its point of departure: No self-awareness would be possible unless there were an intentional act to reflect upon and be self-aware of. However, the reflection theory of self-awareness is not the name of a single doctrine, but rather the label for several related positions. It is not only possible to claim that self-awareness is the result of the primary intentional act being taken as an object by a higher-order intentional act called the act of reflection. In this case self-awareness is a subject-object relation between two different acts. It is also possible to claim that self-awareness comes about when the intentional act literally re-flexes and takes itself as its own (secondary) object. In this case self-awareness would be a subject-object relation between the act and itself.

Although at first sight it might seem obvious and unavoidable to say that self-awareness is exactly characterized by the subject having itself, rather than anything else, as its object, this approach ultimately generates such severe difficulties that even its advocates have occasionally admitted that self-awareness on this account remains either incomprehensible or plainly impossible. In a late publication Kant writes: "That I am conscious of myself is a thought that already contains a twofold self, the I as subject and the I as object. How it might be possible for the I that I think to be an object (of intuition) for me, one that enables me to distinguish me from myself, is absolutely impossible to explain, even though it is an indubitable fact."[5]

It is easy to increase this incomprehensibility:

1. Awareness is a relation between a subject (qua experiencing) and an object (qua experienced).
2. If the subject is to be aware of itself, it must take itself as an object.
3. If the subject is aware of an object, it is not aware of itself.
4. Real self-awareness is impossible.

In other words, if awareness is a relation between a subject and an object, real self-awareness is impossible, since the subject of experience can never truly be its own object, insofar as this would imply both a negation of its subjectivity, as well as a violation of the principle of identity. Consequently, that which we experience in so-called states of self-awareness cannot be identical with the original subject of that experience, which always remains in the dark, but is at most a derived objectified representation.[6]

It is obvious that the reason for this impasse is to be found in premise 1, i.e., in the reflection theory's assumption that all awareness implies a subject-object structure. It is not necessary to expound on the traditional domination of this often tacit premise, but it should be noted that the temptation to ascribe a subject-object structure to self-awareness has frequently found support in language and in seemingly innocent phrases, such as "I feel pain" or "I feel happy" (both of which obviously has the structure "x perceives y").[7]

The most thorough examination and refutation of the reflection theory of self-awareness can be found in the writings of a group of German philosophers comprised by Henrich, Frank, Pothast, and Cramer, and recently named the *Heidelberg School* (since they originate from Henrich's seminars in Heidelberg and from his early study "*Fichtes ursprüngliche Einsicht*").[8] The approach of the Heidelberg School is unusually broad, since it draws on the resources of several different philosophical traditions, including German idealism, neo-Kantianism, analytical philosophy, and phenomenology. Since it also represents one of the most persistent attempts to clarify the problem of self-awareness in contemporary thought, I wish to examine its arguments more carefully. Let me start by presenting its criticism of the reflection theory.

The reflection model of self-awareness always operates with a duality of moments. Regardless of whether it comes about by one act taking another act as its object, or one act taking itself as its object, we are dealing with a kind of self-division, and so we have to *distinguish* the reflecting from the reflected.[9] Of course, the aim of reflection is then to overcome or negate this division or difference and to posit both moments as identical—otherwise we would not have a case of *self*-awareness. However, this strategy is confronted with fundamental problems, such as how an awareness of something *different* can generate self-awareness (or, vice versa, how the primary intentional act can become *self*-aware by being made the object of a different act); how the identity of the two relata can be certified without presupposing that which it is meant to explain, namely, self-awareness; and why the fact of being the intentional object of an unconscious higher-order act should confer consciousness or subjectivity on an otherwise unconscious first-order experience.

The reflection theory claims that self-awareness is the result of a reflection, i.e., in order to become self-aware (and not merely remain *unconscious*) an act of perception must await its thematization by a subsequent act of reflection. In order to speak of *self*-awareness, however, it is not sufficient that the act in question is reflexively thematized and made into an object. It must be grasped as being *identical* with the thematizing act. As the previous distinction between emphatic and nonemphatic self-reference illustrated, there is a difference between being aware of a self and being aware of oneself. In order to have *self*-awareness, it is not enough that I am *de facto* thinking of myself; I also need to know or realize that it is my*self* that I am aware of. In order to be a case of self-awareness, it is not sufficient that A is conscious of B; in addition, A must be conscious of B as being identical with A. In other words, in order to count as a case of self-awareness the act of perception must be grasped as being identical with the act of reflection (and since a *numerical identity* is excluded in advance, the identity in question must be that of belonging to the same subject or being part of the same stream of consciousness).[10] This poses a difficulty, however, for how can the act of reflection (itself lacking self-awareness) be in a position to realize that the act of perception belongs to the same subjectivity as itself? If it is to encounter something as itself, if it is to recognize or identify something as itself, it obviously needs a prior acquaintance with itself.

> Wie aber soll das Subjekt in der Reflexion wissen können, daß es sich selbst als Objekt hat? Offenbar einzig dadurch, daß das Ich sich mit dem, was es als Objekt hat, identisch weiß. Nun ist es aber unmöglich, dies Wissen der *Reflexion* zuzuschreiben und aus ihr zu *begründen*. Denn für den Akt der Reflexion ist vorausgesetzt, daß das Ich sich *schon kennt*, um zu wissen, daß dasjenige, was es kennt, wenn es sich selbst zum Objekt hat, mit dem identisch ist, was den Akt reflektiver Rückwendung auf sich vollzieht. Die *Theorie*, die den *Ursprung* von Selbstbewußtsein aus der Reflexion verständlich machen will, endet daher notwendig in dem Zirkel, diejenige Kenntnis schon voraussetzen zu müssen, die sie erklären will.[11]

Self-awareness cannot come about as the result of the encounter between two unconscious acts. Consequently, the act of reflection must either await a further act of reflection in order to become self-aware, in which case we are confronted with a vicious infinite regress, *or* it must be admitted that it is itself already in a state of self-awareness *prior to reflection*, and that would of course involve us in a circular explanation, presupposing that which was meant to be explained, and implicitly rejecting the thesis of the reflection model of self-awareness, namely, that *all* self-awareness is brought about by reflection.[12]

The act of reflection is a secondary act, and if this is taken not only in the logical, but also in the temporal sense, it poses additional problems. If the act of reflection always succeeds the act that is reflected upon, or at least precedes part of it (after all I can be aware of listening to a piece by Bach while still listening to it), then self-awareness turns out to be an awareness of a past experience, and reflection therefore is in reality a peculiar (if not to say unintelligible) kind of retrospection or recollection. It would be peculiar, insofar as I would be *remembering* something which I had never before been aware of. Moreover, the temporal distance would imply that it takes time to become aware of oneself, and this does not seem to correspond with the *immediate* and *instantaneous* character of our self-awareness. To be in pain is to be (self-)aware of it. It is so to speak both a way of being and a way of being aware.[13] If somebody asks us whether we are in pain, we know so immediately, and do not have to check it out first.[14]

The aim of reflection is to disclose and thematize the primary act of perception. In order to explain the occurrence of reflection, however, it is necessary that that which is to be disclosed and thematized is to some extent (unthematically) present. Otherwise there would be nothing to motivate and call forth the act of reflection. Thus there must be an awareness of the act of perception prior to reflection, and consequently the reflection theory can at most explain *explicit* experience of self, but not the origin of self-consciousness as such.[15]

Finally, we can profit from the results of the first chapter. Self-awareness cannot be the result of reflection understood as a procedure of introspective object-identification, that is, I do not first scrutinize a specific pain and subsequently identify it as being mine, since that kind of criterial identification implies the possibility of misidentification, and self-awareness is not subject to that error. If I am dizzy, I cannot be mistaken about who the subject of that experience is, and it is nonsensical to ask whether I am sure that I am the one who is dizzy, or to demand a specification of the criteria being used by me in determining whether or not the felt dizziness is really mine.

Let me repeat that it is relatively easy to find contemporary defenders of some version of the reflection theory (although its advocates often claim that they are clarifying the nature of phenomenal consciousness and not self-awareness as such; since I interpret the first-personal givenness of phenomenal consciousness as a primitive type of self-awareness, their analyses remain, however, of pertinence for my topic). Recently, Rosenthal has argued in favor of refining Armstrong's higher-order perception (HOP) theory with a higher-order thought (HOT) theory. As Rosenthal points out, there is more to the fact of being a conscious mental state than being the thematic object of introspection. A state can be nonintrospectively conscious, and in fact introspective conscious states presuppose nonintrospective conscious states. On the face of it, the claim that a mental state can be conscious even when we do not pay explicit and thematic attention to it seems quite reasonable, and Rosenthal's distinction between introspective and nonintrospective conscious states might at first be taken to mirror our distinction between the thematic and reflective type of self-awareness, on the one hand, and the tacit and unthematic kind of prereflective self-awareness, on the other. The moment Rosenthal starts to analyze the nature of this nonintrospective consciousness it becomes clear, however, that he has something quite different in mind. In fact, Rosenthal argues that if one wishes to come up with a nontrival and informative account of consciousness one must at any price avoid the claim that consciousness is an intrinsic property of our mental states. To call something intrinsic is to imply that it is simple and unanalyzable and mysterious, and consequently beyond the reach of scientific and theoretical study: "We would insist that being conscious is an intrinsic property of mental states only if we were convinced that it lacked articulated structure, and thus defied explanation."[16] Although Rosenthal acknowledges that there is something intuitively appealing about taking consciousness to be an intrinsic property, he still thinks that this approach must be avoided, since it will stand in the way for a naturalistic (and reductionistic) account, which seeks to explain consciousness by appeal to nonconscious mental states, and nonconscious mental states in nonmental terms. For Rosenthal, the property of being conscious is not an *intrinsic* property, but a *relational* property; that is, a mental state is conscious only if it stands in the appropriate relation to something else. More precisely, for a state to be conscious is for it to be accompanied by a suitable higher-order thought, namely, a higher-order thought *about* that state. Thus, consciousness is a kind of higher-order representing of lower-level mental states and processes. The higher-order thought confers intransitive consciousness on the mental state it is about. In fact, a mental state is intransitively conscious exactly insofar as there is a higher-order thought that is transitively conscious *of* it. This model does not lead to an infinite regress, however, since the higher-order thought does not itself have to be conscious. This will only be the case if it is accompanied by a third-order thought. It is this construction which then allows Rosenthal to make his distinction between nonintrospective conscious thoughts and introspective conscious thoughts. A mental state is nonintrospectively conscious when accompanied by a second-order thought. Introspection occurs when the second-order thought is accompanied by a third-order thought that makes the second-order thought conscious.[17] Obviously, Rosenthal has to answer the following question: Why is the second-order thought, B, directed at the first-order mental state, A? What is it that makes B conscious of A? Rosenthal writes that a "higher-order thought, B, is an awareness of the mental-state token, A, simply because A is the intentional object of B."[18] At the same time, however, Rosenthal is well aware that the relation between the mental state and the higher-order state that makes it conscious is unlike ordinary intentional relations. On the one hand, we only regard mental states as being conscious if we are conscious of them in some suitably unmediated way, namely, directly and noninferentially—otherwise, even an unconscious mental process would qualify as conscious, if we could *infer* that we were having it. On the other hand, Rosenthal argues that for a mental state to be conscious is not simply for us to be directly conscious of it; we must be directly conscious of being *ourselves* in that very state: "Only if one's thought is about oneself as such, and not just about someone that happens to be oneself, will the mental state be a conscious state. Otherwise it might turn out in any particular case that the state was a state of somebody else instead."[19] That Rosenthal thereby makes himself vulnerable to the criticism presented above should be fairly obvious.

Subjectivity and Indexicality

What is the outcome of our considerations so far? We have seen that the reflection theory faces a series of difficulties. Since its attempt to account for self-awareness is aporetical, leading either to a vicious infinite regress or to circularity, one is confronted with the following choice. Either one denies the existence of self-awareness or one rejects the reflection theory. Since it is the theory and not the phenomenon which is inconsistent, one must choose the second option, and consequently accept the existence of an immediate, tacit, and nonthematic kind of self-awareness. This rather indirect argumentation—reflective self-awareness presupposes a more basic kind of self-awareness, and since our experiences are reflectively accessible they must already have been self-aware—is at the heart of Henrich's and Frank's theory. But let me also briefly outline two complementary arguments for the existence of a nonthematic self-awareness, which Frank has also made use of in his recent discussion of analytical philosophy of mind.[20]

The most direct and perhaps also most natural way to argue for the existence of a tacit or nonthematic self-awareness is in the following way. Whereas the object of my perceptual experience is intersubjectively accessible in the sense that it can in principle be given to Others in the same way that it is given for me, my perceptual experience itself is only given directly to me. It is this first-personal givenness of the experience which makes it *subjective*. In contrast to physical objects, which can exist regardless of whether or not they *de facto* appear for a subject, experiences are essentially characterized by having a subjective "feel" to them, i.e., a certain (phenomenal) quality of "what it is like" or what it "feels" like to have them.[21] Whereas we cannot ask what it feels like to be a piece of soap or a radiator, we can ask what it is like to be a chicken, an alligator, or a human being, because we take them to be conscious, i.e., to have experiences. To undergo an experience necessarily means that there is something it is like for the subject to have that experience.[22] This is obviously true of bodily sensations like pain or nausea and pervasive moods such as depression or happiness. But it has also been taken to be the case with, for instance, perceptual experiences such as tasting an omelet, feeling an ice cube, or seeing a bumblebee, and for intentional feelings such as having a desire for chocolate. Ultimately it has been argued that it is a serious mistake to limit the phenomenal dimension of experience to *sensory* qualia.[23] There is also something it is like for the subject to entertain abstract beliefs; yes, there is even something it is like to contemplate the problem of self-awareness. But insofar as there is something it is like for the subject to have experiences, there must be some awareness of these experiences themselves; in short, there must be self-awareness. And obviously, this self-awareness is not of the reflective kind. Even prior to reflection, there is something it is like to smell honey or watch the full moon. There is something it is like to taste water or be scared even for creatures such as cows or chickens, which are (presumably) incapable of reflection.[24]

Now the moment one claims that there is a "what it is like" quality to all experiences, and not only to different types of emotions or bodily sensations, one must be able to exemplify this quality. In the discussion, one often finds references to what has traditionally been called secondary sense qualities, such as the smell of coffee, the color of red silk, or the taste of a lemon. But this is misleading. If our experiences are to have intrinsic qualities, they must be qualities over and above whatever qualities the intentional object has. But it is exactly the silk which is red, and not my perception of it. Likewise it is the lemon which is bitter and not my experience of it. The *taste* of the lemon is a qualitative feature of the lemon, and must be distinguished from whatever qualities my *tasting* of the lemon has. Even if there is no other way to gain access to the gustatory quality of the lemon than by tasting it, this will not turn the quality of the object into a quality of the experience.[25] But in this case a certain problem arises. There is definitely something it is like to taste coffee, just as there is an experienced difference between tasting wine and water. But when one asks for this quality and for this qualitative difference it seems hard to point to anything besides the taste of coffee, wine, and water, though this is not what we are looking for. Should we consequently conclude that there is in fact nothing in the tasting of the lemon apart from the taste of the lemon itself, and that the only thing which appears when we experience a lemon is the lemon itself, but not our experience of it?

However, this reasoning is based upon a certain confusion. Although the taste or color of the lemon is an objective property of the lemon, the manifestation or appearance of the taste or color of the lemon is not. In fact, the "what it is like" to taste or see a lemon is a question of how the lemon *seems* or *appears* to me, that is, a question of how it is given to and experienced by me. If there had been no awareness of the experience, there would have been no "what it is like" to perceive the object. Thus, the only type of "experience" which would lack a "what it is like" quality would be an "unconscious experience." There is nothing it is like for the subject to have such an experience, since it is exactly unconscious, i.e., without self-awareness.[26] And vice versa, to be self-aware is not somehow to withdraw to a self-enclosed interiority, it is simply to be aware of "what it is like" to perceive the object, that is, it is simply to be *conscious* of whatever object is given. This suggests that there is a close interconnection between *intentionality* and *phenomenality*. To quote McGinn: "Thus perceptual experiences are Janus-faced: they point outward to the external world but they also present a subjective face to their subject: they are of something other than the subject and they are like something for the subject. But these two faces do not wear different expressions: for what the experience is like is a function of what it is of, and what it is of is a function of what it is like. . . . The two faces are, as it were, locked together. The subjective and the semantic are chained to each other."[27] This interconnection questions the adequacy of a purely functional analysis of intentional consciousness. If we wish to understand what intentional acts, like imagining a unicorn, desiring an ice cream, anticipating a holiday, or reflecting on a economic crisis, are, we have to take the first-person perspective and the problem of phenomenal consciousness seriously. After all, all of these intentional "relations" bring us into the presence of specific intentional objects, and this presence, this mode of presentation, the fact that the object is there *for me*, does not seem to be explicable in terms of mere functional relations.

To rephrase the idea in more phenomenological terms, we are never conscious of an object simpliciter, but always of the object as appearing in a certain way (judged, seen, feared, remembered, smelled, anticipated, tasted, etc.). However, I cannot be conscious of an intentional object (a tasted lemon, a smelled rose, a seen table, a touched piece of silk) unless I am aware of the experience through which this object is made to appear (the tasting, smelling, seeing, touching). But this is not to say that our access to, say, the lemon is *indirect*, namely mediated, contaminated, or blocked by our awareness of the experience, since the given experience is not itself an object on a par with the lemon, but instead constitutes the very access to the lemon. The object is given through the act, and if there is no awareness of the act, the object does not appear at all. If I lose consciousness, I (or more precisely *a* body) will remain causally connected to a number of different objects, but none of these objects will appear. Nothing will manifest itself unless it is encountered by a wakeful mind. As Henrich writes, "in consciousness there is no appearance of anything without something like an appearance of consciousness itself."[28] To phrase the point in a more metaphorical way, the intentional object is given in a phenomenal light. This light does not only exist as a formal condition of possibility for the givenness of the object. It is because it is self-luminous that it can illuminate the object for *me*. Let me add that this line of thought is merely anticipatory. It raises a number of intriguing phenomenological questions, particularly concerning the difference and interdependency between self-manifestation and hetero-manifestation, which will be pursued more systematically in part 2.

The moment it is realized that the "what it is like" has more to do with the very *aspectual givenness* of our intentional objects than with the grasping of some evanescent qualia, a different but related argumentation for the existence of prereflective self-awareness becomes discernible. For instance, one classical transcendental philosophical argument to be found in Fichte runs as follows: "When you are conscious of any object whatsoever—of the wall over there, let us say—then . . . what you are really conscious of is your own act of thinking of this wall, and only insofar as you are conscious of this act of thinking is any consciousness of this wall possible."[29] If it could be shown that object-consciousness presupposes self-awareness as its condition of possibility, and if we are able to intend objects even without reflecting, there must be another, more basic type of self-awareness at play. Different indexical variants of this argumentation have recently been proposed. It has been suggested that the subject-use of "I" is not only a condition of possibility for the object-use of "I," but is in an important sense the anchoring point of the person's entire system of reference, since one can only refer demonstratively (and perceptually) to something in the world if one knows its position vis-à-vis oneself, and consequently is in possession of an implicit awareness of oneself. Let me try to spell this argument out in more detail.[30]

Indexical reference is often taken to be a perspectival mode of presentation. It embodies a subjective point of view on the world. Whereas an object might be intrinsically heavy, soluble, or green, it cannot be intrinsically "this," "mine," or "here"; it only becomes so relative to the confronting subject. To think of something indexically is to think of it in relation to oneself. Our indexical reference reveals the object's relation to the referring subject, and it consequently implies a kind of self-reference.[31] This is why indexicality has been claimed to be egocentric, why it has been said to be anchored in some kind of self-presentation.[32]

Indexical reference is by no means an infrequent type of reference. It is on the contrary an essential element in the most common form of intentionality: perception. To perceive an object is not simply to perceive a certain type of object, that is, any object with some specific properties; rather it is to perceive *this* particular object. Thus, perception is itself an indexical form of experience. It presents me with an object which, to use Smith's phrase, is "actually now here sensuously before me."[33] But to be acquainted with an object in this mode of presentation entails a minimal form of self-awareness. It is only by being tacitly aware of our own subjective perspective that we can refer indexically to objects and consequently perceive them. In itself this is sufficient in order to argue for the existence of prereflective self-awareness. I am obviously able to perceive this chair without reflecting on the experience, and since my perception involves a sort of self-awareness, it must be of a prereflective kind.

To show that indexical reference presupposes a tacit, unthematic self-awareness is sufficient as an argument for the existence of the latter. But it is fairly obvious that this line of thought lends itself to a radicalization, insofar as it could be claimed that every singular reference whatsoever implies a type of self-presentation. I will not attempt to argue in detail for this more ambitious thesis, but let me just outline a possible strategy of argumentation. A necessary condition for any successful definite reference is that it refers to one and only one object. It is not difficult to see how this condition might be satisfied when it concerns indexical references, but what about our reference to particulars not sensibly present? In this case we have to rely on reference by means of proper names or definite descriptions. It could be argued that whenever we refer by means of a name or a definite description we can never be sure that we do in fact succeed in making an identifying reference, since there might be either no object or more than one object which bears the name or fits the description. However, this skepticism can be overcome the moment it is realized that our identifying reference to one particular might be mediated through the identification of another particular; i.e., although a particular not sensibly present "cannot itself be demonstratively identified, it may be identified by a description which relates it uniquely to another particular which can be demonstratively identified."[34] In this sense all identifying reference to particulars may include, ultimately, a demonstrative element. But if a demonstrative reference implies self-awareness, all other types of reference depending upon a demonstrative reference must imply self-awareness as well. Now, it might be suggested that it is possible to refer nondemonstratively and unequivocally by means of pure individuating descriptions, such as "the tallest president," etc. But not only might such a description fail to refer because there are in fact two or more candidates which fit the description equally well, it is also doubtful whether such a description is in fact completely free from indexical components. Presumably the description "the tallest president" is meant to refer to "the tallest president presently existing" or "the tallest president in our (actual) world," etc. And these specifications entail indexical components.[35] Thus each and every reference to particulars in the actual world is ultimately anchored either directly or indirectly in an unthematic self-awareness.

But perhaps a certain caution is appropriate. In his criticism of Chisholm, Castañeda argues that although all singular references to objects in the world involve some kind of self-reference—they are after all references to objects in the *actual* world, i.e., to objects in one's own world—it does not in any way presuppose an explicit self-reference. It is my point of view which anchors my indexical reference, and to this extent it is contained implicitly in the reference, but this does not imply that it is itself singled out and referred to. Nor does my perspective have to be apprehended as such, or be grasped as being specifically mine. We are merely dealing with the *implicit* self-reference of unreflective consciousness. This implicit reference is not spelled out every time an object-identification takes place, but is holistically built into the very contents of experience.[36] Obviously, the central question is to understand what is meant by the expression "the implicit self-reference of unreflective consciousness." And as Hart has argued, Castañeda is probably not speaking of an unthematic experiential dimension but of a mere logical implication.[37] This is why Castañeda can ultimately *deny* that every indexical reference presents us with a type of self-awareness. In his view, self-awareness is essentially egological. Thus Castañeda takes self-awareness to be executed in episodes of thinking about oneself qua oneself. It is a confrontation with oneself, where one refers to oneself in an explicit and irreducible first-person way. Thus, for an experience to be self-aware is for it to be experienced as being owned by or belonging to an "I."[38] Needless to say, not all our experiences are of such a nature, and Castañeda consequently claims that *self*-consciousness is built up on layers of self-*less* consciousness.[39] In the article "Self-Consciousness, I-Structures, and Physiology," this point is illustrated with the following story:

> At a park Friedrich is fully absorbed watching the birds and the bees carrying on their usual affairs. He is then having an *I*-less experience, of the sort of thing Sartre made a big fuss as irreflexive consciousness. He even feels some pressure on his bent knees, and without jumping to an I-owned experience he simply stands up and then sits on the grass. Then

he becomes aware of himself. A thought that the experience was pleasant made him think that he himSELF was enjoying it.[40]

This line of thought is then further developed in Castañeda's differentiation between the following hierarchically structured forms of consciousness:

1. sensory content, conceptually inarticulated
    a. bodily
    b. worldly
2. I-less articulated content pertaining to
    a. external objects
    b. bodily content
    c. occurring mental acts
3. I-less focal consciousness, the core of which is a complex of perceptual judgments
4. I-owned content articulating the contrast between Self and Object
5. I-owned content articulating intentional agency
6. I-owned content articulating the contrast between Self and others
7. I-owned content articulating an interaction between Self and *you* as well as absent persons[41]

I think the error in Castañeda's reasoning is obvious. Castañeda identifies self-awareness with I-consciousness, and I-consciousness with an explicit awareness of the experience as being owned by or belonging to an "I." But this is not only a very narrow definition of self-awareness, it is also an unacceptable definition since it overlooks the more basic and tacit *self-givenness* of our experiences. Thus, whereas Sartre is in perfect agreement with Castañeda when it comes to the criticism of an egological conception of consciousness, he would insist, as we shall soon see, that even the nonegological or egoless experiences are *prereflectively* self-aware—something like when one runs after a streetcar, even if there is no time for reflection and no room for a separate ego.

Brentano on Inner Consciousness

Although we have just encountered two additional arguments for the existence of an immediate, tacit, and nonthematic form of self-awareness, neither tells us much about the more precise nature or structure of this kind of self-awareness. However, it is possible to find an influential attempt to do exactly that in the account of self-awareness offered by Brentano in his *Psychologie vom empirischen Standpunkt.*

After his famous analysis of *intentionality* in book 2, chapter 1, Brentano turns to the problem of *inner consciousness.*[42] Equating consciousness with the psychical phenomenon or act, Brentano takes consciousness to be characterized by a reference to an object, namely, to the object that consciousness is exactly conscious of. The term "conscious," however, can be used in a twofold sense. On the one hand, we say of an act that it is conscious insofar as it is aware of an object. On the other hand, we say of an object that it is conscious insofar as one is aware of it. All psychical acts are characterized by their being conscious of something. The question is whether they are also conscious in the second sense, i.e., whether one is also aware of them, or whether one must deny this and consequently admit the existence of *unconscious* psychical acts.[43]

Brentano examines four different reasons for accepting the existence of an *unconscious* consciousness (that is, a consciousness which is intentionally directed toward an object, but which lacks self-awareness), but it is only the last one which is of relevance in this context. It has been claimed that *if* all psychical acts were conscious, i.e., themselves something one were aware of, one would be faced with a vicious infinite regress. In order to avoid this, one has to deny the premise and consequently accept unconscious psychical acts. What is the argument? Let us take as an example the simple act of perceiving (*Vorstellen*) a tone. If no psychical phenomenon were possible without being itself conscious, i.e., the object of a higher-order consciousness, then one would have two different perceptions when perceiving a tone: (1) the perception of a tone, and (2) the perception of the perception of the tone. However, the multiplication would not stop here, since the perception of the perception of the tone would also have to be conscious. Thus, we would also have (3) the perception of the perception of the perception of the tone, and so forth ad infinitum. Furthermore, as Brentano points out, this would not be the only problem. If the perception of the tone was really the object of a higher-order perception, it would imply that the tone would be perceived twice. And in the perception of the perception of the perception of the tone, we would thrice have the tone as object, whereas the original perception would be perceived twice, and so forth. Thus the regress would be of an exceedingly vicious kind, implying in addition to the simple infinite iteration a simultaneous complication of its single members.[44] Since this consequence is absurd, i.e., since it is absurd that even as simple an act as the perception of a tone should involve an infinite complex series of psychical acts, one has to close the regress by accepting the existence of unconscious psychical acts, i.e., one must accept the existence of intentional acts which lack self-awareness.[45]

Brentano, however, will not accept this conclusion, since it would imply that the self-awareness which we do after all have originates out of the unconscious, and he consequently has to propose an alternative model of self-awareness which avoids the regress, and which furthermore avoids being incompatible with the basic facts. As Brentano points out, we need a theory of self-awareness which does not render its certainty and immediate evidence impossible, and this is exactly what happens if we take self-awareness to be an intentional relation between two different intentional acts; i.e., this approach makes it impossible to account for the infallibility of self-awareness.[46]

If we examine the phenomena once more, nobody will deny that we are occasionally aware of a psychical act while it happens. While hearing a tone, we can be aware of hearing it. What is the structure of our consciousness in this case? We have a perception of a tone, and an awareness of the perception, and consequently two objects: the tone and its perception. However, contrary to the account first offered, we do not have two psychical acts! As Brentano points out, the perception of the tone is so intrinsically and intimately united with the awareness of the perception of the tone that they only constitute one single act, only one single psychical phenomenon. Their apparent separation is merely due to a conceptual differentiation:

> In the same mental phenomenon in which the sound is present to our minds we simultaneously apprehend the mental phenomenon itself. What is more, we apprehend it in accordance with its dual nature insofar as it has the sound as content within it, and insofar as it has itself as content at the same time. We can say that the sound is the *primary object* of the *act* of hearing, and that the act of hearing itself is the *secondary object*. Temporally they both occur at the same time, but in the nature of the case, the sound is prior. A presentation of the sound without a presentation of the act of hearing would not be inconceivable, at least *a priori*, but a presentation of the act of hearing without a presentation of the sound would be an obvious contradiction. The act of hearing appears to be directed toward sound in the most proper sense of the term, and because of this it seems to apprehend itself incidentally and as something additional.[47]

Brentano consequently avoids the regress by claiming that every psychical act is conscious, insofar as it has itself as object. Thus, even as simple an act as hearing a tone has a double object, one primary, the other secondary. The primary and thematic object is the tone, the secondary and unthematic object is the hearing.[48] It is important to notice, however, that the secondary object of the act, although conscious, is not thematically observed (*beobachtet*). To observe something thematically is to take it as one's primary object, and for the act to do this with itself is strictly impossible. The tone which we hear is observed, whereas the hearing of the tone is not, since it is only by observing the tone that we are aware of the hearing, i.e., it is only by intending the primary object that we are aware of the secondary object. Thus Brentano gives priority to intentionality, describing it as a precondition for self-awareness, rather than the other way around. The outcome of this is that Brentano actually denies the possibility (and not merely the primacy) of a thematic reflective relation between *two* simultaneously existing acts, operating instead (1) with the unthematic self-awareness of a *self-reflexive* act; and (2) with a thematic *retrospective* self-awareness, since we can observe a past act and take it as our primary object (in this case the present act of retrospection would be our secondary object).[49]

The only remaining question which has to be answered is one which Brentano raises himself. If I hear a tone, I am coconscious of my hearing, but am I also conscious of this peculiar coconsciousness? Brentano answers the question by saying that his analysis has exactly shown that the awareness of the hearing of the tone coincides with the awareness of this awareness. Thus, the awareness which accompanies the hearing of the tone is after all an awareness of not only the hearing of the tone, but of the entire psychical act (including itself).[50]

Is this account of self-awareness acceptable? Brentano is certainly right in claiming that our intentional act does not need to await a secondary act of reflection in order to become self-aware. But although his account of how this self-awareness is to be explained avoids the problem confronting the version of the reflection theory which takes reflection to be a relation between two different acts, his own proposal is, as Cramer and Pothast have shown, faced with an equally disastrous problem. An act which has a tone as its primary object is to be conscious by having itself as its secondary object. But if the latter is really to result in self-awareness, it has to comprise the entire act, and not only the part of it which is conscious of the tone. That is, the secondary object of the perception should not merely be the perception of the tone, but the perception which is aware of both the tone and of itself. As I have just quoted: "In the same mental phenomenon in which the sound is present to our minds we simultaneously apprehend the mental phenomenon itself. What is more, we apprehend it in accordance with its dual nature insofar as it has the sound as content within it, and insofar as it has itself as content at the same time." But in this case, self-awareness is interpreted as an awareness of a secondary object, which is already in possession of self-awareness, and as an explanation this circularity will not do (see figure 2.1).[51]

If it is acknowledged that part of the reason for the failure of the reflection theory is due to its attempt to understand and explain self-awareness through the subject-object model, one might reasonably ask if Brentano's failure was not due to a lack of radicality. Despite his criticism of the reflection theory, he continues to speak of consciousness taking itself as its own object, and thus of self-awareness as a (secondary) *object*-awareness.[52] However, as Henrich points out, it will not solve the problem simply to speak of consciousness being per se furnished with a reflective relation, which does not need to be brought forth by a separate act, for the circularity in the concept of such a self-related knowledge is not removed by attributing to it a quality of immediacy.[53] Thus, although Brentano's theory has occasionally been described as a genuine theory of prereflective self-awareness, I think it must be realized that it is in fact merely a more unusual version of the reflection theory.

The Position of the Heidelberg School

Let me return to the Heidelberg School. So far its contribution to a clarification of self-awareness has mainly consisted in its thorough criticism

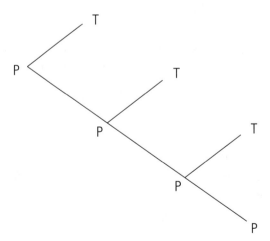

Figure 2.1. This is yet another way to illustrate the problem in Brentano's account.

of the reflection theory. But if it could offer nothing more than these negative observations, it would hardly qualify as an alternative theory of self-awareness. Henrich readily acknowledges that it is essential to transcend a mere disclosure of the aporetical implications of the reflection theory and offer a more substantial account, but, as he continues, one has to realize that the difficulty in interpreting the familiar phenomenon "consciousness" by direct description is so extreme that it is practically impossible to overcome.[54] The difficulty Henrich has in mind is simple but acute, and touches upon the difference between being self-aware and explaining self-awareness. Whereas the self-givenness of lived consciousness is characterized by immediacy, this is certainly not the case with our philosophical understanding of it. In order to examine (reflect upon) the structure of self-awareness we have to direct our attention to it, and since this inevitably implies its objectivation, the original subjective dimension will always evade our theoretical gaze and remain inaccessible for direct description and investigation.[55] This does not imply that its existence is merely postulated, since, after all, not only are we acquainted directly (and nontheoretically) with the original state of being conscious (e.g., we all know the difference between wakefulness and sleep), but we are also in a position to ascertain that we are self-aware through reflection, and by analyzing reflection regressively infer that it has an original pre-reflective self-acquaintance as its condition of possibility. Nevertheless, a direct examination of this dimension seems impossible, and the following four features which constitute the core of Henrich's own theory of self-awareness have consequently been disclosed indirectly, *ex negativo*, through a criticism of the reflection theory:[56]

1. Consciousness is a dimension which contains knowledge of itself, for there is no consciousness of anything which is not implicitly acquainted with itself. "Implicitly" is not here used in the sense of being a mere potential acquaintance, but in the sense of existing even prior to reflection and explicit thematization.

2. Original self-awareness is not a performance, but an irrelational occurrence (*Ereignis*). That is, self-awareness is not only irrelational, it is also something which is given rather than voluntarily brought about.

3. Self-aware consciousness is an *egoless* dimension within which intentional acts and mental states take place.

4. It is a private or exclusive dimension, in the sense that each consciousness has special access to itself.

Let me add a few clarifying comments. We have seen that *original* self-awareness cannot be understood either as a relation between two acts or as a relation between the act and itself. The lesson seems to be that it is necessary to avoid theories that describe self-awareness as a kind of *relation*, since every relation—especially the subject-object relation—presupposes a *distinction* between two (or more) relata, and this is exactly what generates all the problems. Thus, if the specific *immediacy, unity,* and *infallibility* of original self-awareness are to be preserved, self-awareness cannot come about as the result of a criterial self-identification, nor can it be a kind of reflection, introspection, object-intentionality, or conceptually mediated propositional attitude, all of which entail the distinction between two or more relata. The basic self-awareness of an experience is not mediated by foreign elements such as concepts or classificatory criteria, nor by any internal difference or distance. It is an immediate and direct self-acquaintance, which is characterized by being completely and absolutely *irrelational* (and consequently best described as a purely immanent self-presence).[57]

The criticism directed at the reflection theory has generally not been meant to imply that reflective self-awareness is impossible, but merely that it always presupposes a prior unthematic and prereflective self-awareness as its condition of possibility. We are not merely aware of ourselves when we explicitly direct our attention at our conscious life. Thus, it is necessary to differentiate *prereflective* self-awareness, which is an immediate, implicit, irrelational, nonobjectifying, nonconceptual, and nonpropositional self-acquaintance, from *reflective* self-awareness, which is an explicit, relational, mediated, conceptual, and objectifying thematization of consciousness: "Reflexionen können mittelbar an unmittelbares Bewußtsein anschließen und es in den Status eines Wissens erheben. Die ursprüngliche Gegebenheit ist aber das Bewußtsein selbst, welches offensichtlich einstellig auftritt und nicht als Objektpol eines sich darauf richtenden Bewußtseinssubjektes."[58]

If reflection always presupposes prereflective self-awareness, and if we are capable of reflecting on all our intentional acts and mental states, the conclusion seems obvious: Consciousness as such must originally imply self-awareness since it is impossible to acquire it afterward, be it through reflection or through a study of external types of self-reference: If I see, remember, know, think, hope, feel, or will something, I am *eo ipso* aware of it. Thus the second of the two following accounts of the relation between consciousness and self-awareness is the adequate one:

1. Consciousness is strictly and exclusively conscious of the intentional object. There is no simultaneous self-awareness. Thus the act itself is unconscious, but it can be made conscious through a subsequent, higher-order intentional act, which takes the first act as its object. In this way consciousness can be compared to a knife, which is able to cut other things, but not itself.

2. Consciousness is self-luminous. It is characterized by intentionality, but being intentionally aware of objects, it is simultaneously self-aware through and in itself. Its self-awareness is not due to a secondary act or reflex but is a constitutive moment of the experience itself, and consciousness can consequently be compared to a flame, which illuminates other things, and itself as well.[59]

In accepting 2, one has to be careful, however, not to commit the error of the reflection theory:

If

(1) I know that p
   or (1a) my awareness of blue

implies

(2) I know that (I know that p)
   or (2a) my awareness of (my awareness of blue)

then

(2) I know that (I know that p)
   or (2a) my awareness of (my awareness of blue)

must imply

(3) I know that (I know that [I know that p])
   or (3a) my awareness of (my awareness of [my awareness of blue])

And so forth.

It is impossible to avoid this regress as long as one takes self-awareness to be a higher-order intentional act or propositional attitude, i.e., as long as one conceives of it as a higher-order "awareness of" or "knowing that." To have an experience, e.g., a perception of a burning bush, is to be aware of it. But this self-awareness is not itself a separate experience in need of yet another awareness. The self-awareness of the experience is an internal, nonreflective, irrelational feature of the experience itself, and thus the regress is stopped.

Henrich's third feature also calls for a clarification. The question whether it makes sense to speak of a subjectless or egoless self-awareness, i.e., of a self-awareness without anybody being self-aware, ultimately depends upon whether one opts for an *egological* or a *nonegological* theory of consciousness. An egological theory would claim that whenever I taste a Calvados, then I am not only intentionally directed at the *Calvados*, nor merely aware of the Calvados being *tasted*, but also aware that it is being tasted by *me*, i.e., that *I* am *tasting* a *Calvados*. It would claim that it is a conceptual and experiential truth that any episode of experiencing necessarily includes a subject of experience.[60] Thus, to be conscious (at least if we are dealing with fully fledged intentional acts) includes consciousness of the entire structure *ego-cogito-cogitatum*. This account, which identifies self-awareness with *I-consciousness*, is, however, regarded by the Heidelberg School as having fallen victim to the language of reflection—*the use of "I" seems exactly to articulate a self-reflection*—and is rejected for the following reasons: Whereas reflection is described as the accomplishment of an active principle, as an act initiated by a subject, prereflective self-awareness must precede all performances, and can consequently not be attributed to the ego, but must be characterized as a subjectless or egoless awareness.[61] Moreover, an egological theory claiming that self-awareness is properly speaking an original awareness of my*self*, as a self, subject, or ego seems in an eminent way to take self-awareness as a kind of object-awareness, and thus to be prone to all the problems confronting this approach.[62] Finally, if one conceives of the ego qua subject of experience as that which *has* the experience, one obviously makes a distinction between the ego and the experience. They are not identical. In this case, however, it is difficult to understand why the ego's awareness of the experience should be classified as a case of *self*-awareness. Thus, "Die Forderung, alles, was weiß, müsse auch selbst bewußt sein, ist nicht so zu verstehen, daß im Bewußtsein noch zu den Vollzügen des Wissens ein besonderes Wissendes auftreten muß, sondern so, daß die Daten der Erlebnisse alles sind, was Wissen ausmachen kann, und es nicht noch darüberhinaus eines geben darf, das nicht selbst Erlebnis ist, sondern das Erlebnis nur hat."[63] Against this background Pothast somewhat paradoxically concludes that consciousness, insofar as it is subjectless, must be conceived as a thoroughly *objective* process.[64]

This criticism does not imply, however, that the ego is a completely superfluous and dispensable notion. As Henrich points out, it is impossible to understand phenomena such as concentrating on a task, making a decision, solving a problem, expecting an event, or initiating a reflection, without assuming the existence of an active principle of organization in the field of consciousness, i.e., without accepting the existence of an ego or a self. But this egological structure is not a fundamental feature of consciousness; rather, it is merely a mode of its organization. Originally, consciousness is egoless and anonymous.[65]

An Internal Complexity

Is the position of the Heidelberg School convincing? Surprisingly enough, both Henrich and Frank have later expressed reservations about the adequacy of the central and, at first glance, most convincing and unproblematic claim, namely, that original self-awareness is strictly *irrelational*. Both explicitly acknowledge that the phenomenon of self-awareness has an internal structural *complexity* that manifests itself in a plurality of ways.

We have just seen that the anonymous dimension of *consciousness* is characterized by a prereflective *self-acquaintance*. These two moments are not the only ones, however. There is also the element of (egological) spontaneity, which is needed in order to explain reflection, concentration, and conceptual thought. Although this egological element might be secondary, it still has to be accounted for. Thus we are faced with *three* moments which together make up the unity of self-awareness: the anonymous dimension of subjectivity, the epistemic self-acquaintance, and the egological organization. All features have to coexist in a structural unity, and this seems to contradict the claim that self-awareness per se lacks internal differentiation.[66]

A similar conclusion must be reached the moment one pays attention to the *temporal* structure of self-awareness. As Frank has pointed out, it is necessary to combine a plausible theory of self-awareness with an account of temporality. After all, I am not only aware of my current perception, but also able to remember my past experiences as *mine*.[67] This observation shows unequivocally that any theory of self-awareness which neglects the temporal dimension is deficient. This is not because a theory of self-awareness must necessarily develop into a theory of personal identity (the latter analyzing the necessary and sufficient conditions for the continued existence of a person over time), but because a theory of self-awareness which is only able to explain the isolated experience's prereflective acquaintance with itself, and not how I can have self-awareness across temporal distance, not how I can bridge the numerical difference of the experiences, and remember my past experiences as *mine*, is not worth much as a theory.[68] Ultimately, it could even be argued that consciousness is so intrinsically temporal that even a clarification of instantaneous self-awareness would have to take it into account. And in this case self-awareness would not only entail a certain inner articulation and differentiation, it would also include an awareness of its own temporality.[69]

In short, it seems as if one has been too hasty in banning every kind of internal differentiation and structure from prereflective self-awareness. This is not to say that the arguments presented against the reflection theory and against the attempt to understand self-awareness as a kind of relation have suddenly lost their validity, and one still has to display the utmost caution not to become vulnerable once more to that criticism. But as Frank suggests, it is possible to escape the previously outlined difficulties if one conceives of the moments as conceptually differentiable, but factually inseparable:[70] "Es mag aber genügen, die von der Tradition immer aufs neue entdeckten und geltend gemachten Elemente in die volle Struktur des Selbstbewußtseins wieder einzutragen, sofern man nur sicherstellt, daß sich das Gesamtphänomen nicht aus einer abstrakten Interaktion der Elemente (gleichsam nach und nach) aufbaut, sondern wie eine 'Gestalt' im Nu und als integrales Phänomen sich präsentiert."[71] Thus, when all is said and done, self-awareness is primitive in the sense of being irreducible, but it is neither simple nor unstructured. We are ultimately dealing with a unitary phenomenon which is composed of connected elements that can neither be subsumed under nor deduced from a higher principle. Frank speaks of a unity of identity and difference, in the sense that each of the elements is irreducible, but nevertheless unable to exist in separation from the others.[72]

At this point, however, the clarification and analysis terminate. According to Henrich we do not possess an *adequate* understanding of either the structure of self-awareness or the connection between its different elements. We can ascertain that it is complex, but we cannot analyze it any further. Why the elements are inseparable, and how they manage to constitute the unity of self-awareness, are questions which cannot be answered: "So ist also beides anzunehmen notwendig: Daß Selbstbewußtsein in sich komplex ist und daß der Komplex von uns nicht aufgelöst oder in seiner inneren Konstitution verstanden werden kann."[73] Thus, it is claimed that the unitary phenomenon of self-awareness is conditioned by something which it can neither control nor comprehend. As a phenomenon it is characterized by a profound obscurity, and self-awareness therefore ultimately remains incomprehensible (*unverständlich*).[74] This conclusion, which reminds one of Henrich's own description of Fichte's theory as taking self-awareness to be an inner unity of inaccessible and unfathomable ground,[75] is hardly satisfying. Although Frank admits that it conceals rather than solves the problem—if the different moments are not only to be different, but in fact moments of one phenomenon, it is essential to explain and clarify their connection and interaction—he is ultimately unable to contribute with a more satisfying solution himself, and he as well must in the end admit that the way in which the elements of self-awareness are united remains obscure.[76]

3

Some Essential Questions

My presentation in the first chapter closed with the observation that we had by and large learned how "I" did *not* function. In a similar manner it can be concluded that the account given by the Heidelberg School is significant and illuminating because of its focus upon the aporetical character of the reflection theory of self-awareness, and because of its systematic and instructive analysis of how *not* to conceive of self-awareness. However, despite its insights, it still remains a critical *introduction*.[1] Although both Henrich and Frank acknowledge that prereflective, irrelational self-awareness is characterized by a certain internal differentiation and complexity, they never offer a more detailed analysis of this complex structure. That is, when it comes to a positive description of the structure of original prereflective self-awareness they are remarkably silent, claiming by turns that it is unanalyzable, or that the unity of its complex structure is incomprehensible. That this outcome represents a shortcoming is obvious. But it is not the only one. Ultimately the negative, formalistic, and overly regressive account offered by the Heidelberg School is confronted with a number of interrelated deficiencies, not in the sense that its account is internally incoherent or aporetic (as is, for instance, the reflection theory), but in the sense that there remain a number of essential aspects of the problem of self-awareness which it either ignores completely or only analyzes inadequately.

As I mentioned in the preface, the aim of this first part is not only to present some recent attempts to come to grips with the problem of self-awareness, but also to call attention to a number of urgent problems that any *philosophical* investigation of self-awareness has to deal with. Let me conclude my introduction by specifying eight problems which I believe the Heidelberg School failed to take into sufficient consideration, but which have to be examined if a theory of self-awareness is to prove convincing.

1. The following methodological problem has to be considered far more explicitly and in more detail: Can subjectivity be made accessible for

direct theoretical examination, or does its examination necessarily imply an objectivation and consequently a falsification? In other words, can subjectivity be described phenomenologically, or is it only approachable *ex negativo*?

2. Obviously, it will also be necessary to examine the exact nature and structure of self-awareness. This will call not only for a distinction between several different forms of self-awareness, as well as for an analysis of their mutual relation and interdependency, but also for a clarification of their internal differentiation and complexity. We have already seen that the Heidelberg School failed to do the latter, and although it has offered a convincing criticism of the reflection theory, it has in fact also said rather little about *reflection* itself. One should not forget that reflection remains an irreducible and emphatic self-awareness. It can never be replaced by any third-person reference. As Castañeda points out, "I know that I know that *p*," is quite different from "A knows that A knows that *p*" where "A" stands for any name or description of a person.[2] For the very same reason it might be problematic simply to identify reflection with a higher-order objectifying intentional act. Second, if reflection does in fact contain a kind of internal self-division or self-detachment, it is of paramount importance to understand how prereflective self-awareness can give rise to such a fracture. That is, it will not do to conceive of prereflective self-awareness in a manner that makes reflective self-awareness incomprehensible.

3. As was pointed out above, any convincing theory of self-awareness should not only be able to account for the prereflective self-awareness of a single experience, but also explain how I can have self-awareness across temporal distance; that is, it should be able to explain why I remember a past experience as *mine*. (This demand, obviously, constitutes a particularly serious problem for any nonegological theory of consciousness. If there are forms of self-awareness which bridge the numerical difference of the isolated acts, these forms must be accounted for, and this appears impossible unless one recurs to an act-transcending principle).[3] Thus, at the same time, the *temporality* of consciousness has to be accounted for, and in far more detail than the Heidelberg School has done. It will not only prove necessary to account for the structure of inner time-consciousness, and to explain the possibility of temporal self-manifestation. Ultimately, it will also be necessary to correlate the different forms of self-awareness with different forms of temporality.

4. The question concerning the egological and/or nonegological character of self-awareness also has to be clarified. Does self-awareness necessarily have an egocentric structure, or is self-awareness rather the anonymous acquaintance of consciousness with itself? Since an answer

to this question can only be given after it has been established what exactly an ego is, this must also be done, and ultimately it will prove necessary to determine the relation between the isolated act, the stream of consciousness, and the ego, and to differentiate between different concepts of the ego and different egological levels. However, the analysis of the ego offered by the Heidelberg School is clearly inadequate. The validity of their rejection of the egological theory of consciousness is tied to their very narrow definition of the ego. It is either understood as a principle of activity[4] or as something which must necessarily be conceived as standing opposed to consciousness "having" it.[5] But as I have already indicated, there might be other ways to conceive of the ego (see page 12).

5. Although the subject-use of "I" cannot be substituted by any physical self-description, this does not imply that the self-awareness it articulates is the self-awareness of a disembodied subject.[6] The difference between a first-person and a third-person perspective does not coincide with a traditional difference between mind and body. As an analysis of our *kinaesthetic* experiencing reveals, the body itself can appear in a first-person perspective, and the investigation of the different types of bodily self-appearance must be integrated into a general analysis of self-awareness. This investigation of the body is indispensable if one is eventually to understand how one can appear to oneself as a mundane object, i.e., if one is to understand the relation between one's awareness of oneself as an elusive subjective dimension, i.e., something which is neither a mental nor a worldly object,[7] and one's awareness of oneself as an intersubjectively accessible entity in the world. To put it differently, regardless of whether one conceives of prereflective self-awareness as being essentially a bodily self-awareness, or rather conceives of the latter as being a form of subsequent self-objectivation, any convincing theory of self-awareness cannot allow itself to ignore the *body*. But this is exactly what the Heidelberg School does.[8]

6. Not only can I be aware of my own subjectivity, I can also be aware of other subjects, and so an analysis of self-awareness must also deal with the problem of *intersubjectivity*. It must do so not because every type of self-awareness is intersubjectively mediated, nor because the analysis must necessarily account for the types of self-awareness which are in fact intersubjectively constituted, but because a theory of self-awareness must avoid conceiving of self-awareness in such a fashion that intersubjectivity becomes impossible. That is, it will not do to conceive of the manifestation of subjectivity in such exclusive terms that it becomes incomprehensible how I should ever be able to recognize a foreign body as being in fact a foreign-embodied subjectivity.

7. It will not do to conceive of self-awareness in strict isolation from *intentionality*. As Henrich himself acknowledges, consciousness is simultaneously and co-originally aware of itself and related to the world.[9] But this connection obviously has to be explored and clarified. Self-manifestation might not itself be a type of intentionality, but should it turn out that it is always accompanied by and inseparable from hetero-manifestation, and that it cannot take place on its own, it is necessary to question its strict self-sufficiency and irrelationality.

8. Finally, I think that a theory of self-awareness will eventually have to confront the problem of the *unconscious*. Are all of our experiences characterized by a fundamental self-manifestation and is the notion of an "unconscious consciousness" a contradiction in terms, or is it possible to reconcile a strong thesis concerning self-awareness with a recognition of the unconscious?

Naturally, these questions can be approached in a number of different ways and with a number of different objectives in mind. As I have stated in the preface, my approach will be phenomenological, and I am especially interested in pursuing the relation between *self-awareness* and *alterity* and to clarify the following question: *To what extent does the self-awareness of subjectivity depend upon its relation to something foreign, be it worldly objects, another subject, or itself as Other?* I do not take this to be merely an additional problem, but rather to be a productive angle or perspective through which one might investigate and, one hopes, answer the other questions.

It is important not to misunderstand my criticism. Obviously, I am not claiming that a theory of self-awareness, in order to be convincing, must necessarily account for intentionality, intersubjectivity, temporality, etc., as well. Although a full and comprehensive theory of conscious-ness would have to tackle all of these issues, it is certainly possible and legitimate to focus on and isolate certain specific topics, including the nature of self-awareness. The point I wish to make is that the account of self-awareness offered by the Heidelberg School is problematic because it focuses on self-awareness *in abstracto* rather than accounting for the self-awareness of the *self-transcending* temporal, intentional, reflexive, corporeal, and intersubjective experiences, experiences which all contain a dimension of alterity. Ultimately their account fails to clarify the relation between the self-presence and the self-transcendence of subjectivity. And this must be the task. As Merleau-Ponty formulates it, "the question is always . . . *how the presence to myself [Urpräsenz] which establishes my own limits and conditions every alien presence is at the same time depresentation [Entgegenwärtigung] and throws me outside myself.*"[10] The account offered by the Heidelberg School is insufficient, since it never explains how a subject essentially characterized by a kind of complete irrelational self-presence can simultaneously be in possession of an inner temporal articulation; how it can simultaneously be directed intentionally toward something different from itself; how it can be capable of recognizing other subjects (being acquainted with subjectivity as it is through a completely unique self-presence); how it can be in possession of a bodily exteriority; and finally how it can give rise to the self-division found in reflection. Basically, my claim is that an investigation which attempts to provide answers to these questions will not only increase our understanding of self-awareness decisively, it will also show why it is problematic to claim that the self-manifestation of subjectivity is to be characterized as a pure, independent, and self-sufficient self-presence.

But although the contribution of the Heidelberg School is mainly negative, it remains of decisive importance, and it enables one to make the following demand to any consistent theory of self-awareness: No matter how differentiated the structure of self-awareness is ultimately shown to be, if the account given reintroduces a duality in the core of self-awareness or if it is unable to preserve the difference between self and Other, it has failed.

Tugendhat's Criticism

Before I continue to part 2, it is necessary to mention one critical reservation. The questions I have raised are all part of an attempt to throw light upon the nature and structure of self-awareness, and they consequently take it for granted that there is in fact something like self-awareness, and that it has a perplexing structure which calls for a philosophical elucidation. It has been claimed, however, that there is in fact no such phenomenon at all, at least not as it is described by the Heidelberg School, and that all the difficulties confronting the attempt to understand and explicate its structure are in reality the result of an improper inquiry, and ultimately based on a misinterpretation of a banality.

I have earlier mentioned that the examination of the subject-use of "I" seemed to confirm a number of *Cartesian* intuitions, and it is to a certain extent possible to classify the discussions of self-awareness examined in chapters 1 and 2 as representing a Cartesian revival.[11] This has also been pointed out by the critics, however,[12] and Tugendhat has gone so far as to claim that the reflections of the Heidelberg School represent the culmination *and* termination of the traditional discussion of self-awareness since, after having pointed to the aporias of previous theories of self-awareness, they fail to provide a less aporetical solution and description themselves, instead ultimately choosing to forsake the very phenomenon which was to be explained. Thus Tugendhat claims that Henrich in particular has unwittingly led the traditional concept of self-awareness *ad absurdum,* and that it is consequently necessary to undertake a fundamental revision of the notion of consciousness which the entire classical tradition has uncritically made use of.

Tugendhat's own alternative is based upon more general language-philosophical reflections. According to Tugendhat, one cannot know or be conscious of an object. One can only be intentionally related to states of affairs. I do not know a table; I know *that* a table has such and such properties. Self-awareness should be interpreted in a similar way: "I suggested that we should first make the general structure of consciousness of something clear; on this basis we were to acquire a concept of what consciousness of oneself means by replacing the variable 'something' accordingly."[13] Thus, self-awareness is a kind of knowledge. It is not knowledge about an (internal) object, about a self or an experience; rather it is propositional knowledge expressed in the form "I know that I ϕ," where ϕ stands for a mental or psychic state.[14] In contrast to Henrich and Frank, Tugendhat consequently takes immediate self-awareness to be an epistemic relation between an empirical person and a proposition. Self-awareness is a *propositional attitude.*[15]

It is against this background that Tugendhat claims that the problem discussed by the Heidelberg School is a pseudoproblem. In the phrase "I know that I ϕ" the word "I" appears twice, and one could then wonder how we know that both uses refer to the same subject. How do we account for the identity between the one who knows and the one who is in the mental state? It is true that I cannot be aware that I am in pain or that I am seeing a canary and be mistaken about who the subject of that experience is. But the fact that first-person experience ascriptions are not subject to the error of misidentification is not in need of any further explanation and is particularly not due to some mysterious self-transparency or self-acquaintance, since no infallible identification or informative reference has taken place. The identity in question is of the purely tautological sort. That my awareness of an experience does not leave open whose experience it is, is just as unproblematically true as that A=A or I=I.[16]

Tugendhat attempts to transform the problem of self-awareness into a semantical problem. But rather than clarifying and solving the problem, this transformation merely covers it.[17] Despite his criticism of the traditional subject-object model, Tugendhat remains convinced that self-awareness is to be understood as a relation between two different entities, a person and a proposition. But he never explains why such a relation should establish *self*-awareness. Nor does he seem to realize that the principal task facing a clarification of immediate epistemic self-awareness is to account for the unique first-personal givenness of our experiences rather than to explain the identity between the knower and the known.

Tugendhat continues his analysis by claiming that the very proposition which we are aware of when we are self-aware is intersubjectively accessible. It is possible to refer to the same state of affairs from a third-person perspective. And according to Tugendhat this possibility is essential for the very existence of self-awareness. If we are to be aware of anything at all, that which we are aware of must in principle be accessible to Others as well. Thus, Tugendhat claims that a proper use of "I" implies that the speaker knows that Others can refer to the same using a third-person pronoun.[18] Against this background he can conclude that the self-reference of "I" is neither unconditioned nor self-sufficient but incorporated into and conditioned by its relation to the entire network of personal pronouns.[19]

Insofar as Tugendhat claims that self-awareness is a propositional attitude, he is confronted with an obvious question. Does self-awareness presuppose language use? Is a person only in possession of self-awareness when it has acquired a sufficient mastery of language to be able to refer to itself with "I"? If it does, are we then to deny self-awareness in children and animals? Tugendhat's reply is remarkably vague. He says that it remains unclarified whether we can refer to propositions nonlinguistically, but suggests that self-awareness only becomes conscious when it is linguistically articulated![20] That this claim is rejected by dominant positions within current developmental psychology will be shown in part 2.

But more fundamentally, one must criticize the attempt to explain self-awareness as a result of an internalization of a third-person perspective on oneself. If Tugendhat is actually claiming that I only attain self-awareness the moment I realize that Others are able to refer to me as well, he is presumably wrong. How should I know that I am the one the Other is referring to unless I am already in possession of self-awareness? As Castañeda has shown, the only third-person pronoun which mirrors and captures the use of "I" in "I am ϕ," is the "he*", i.e., the "he" of self-consciousness. Thus, even if the semantical rules governing the use of "I" in "I know that I am ϕ" implies that the speaker must know that Others can express the same by saying "x knows that he himself is ϕ," this would not lead to an explanation of self-awareness, since the use of "I" would then be tied up with a use of "he," which ascribes self-awareness to the person in question, i.e., which presupposes the existence of self-awareness in the person referred to. As an explanation of self-awareness, this account is obviously circular.

I have already indicated that I take an examination of the *use* of "I" to be illuminating but by no means sufficient for a real understanding of the structure of self-awareness. The use of "I" articulates reflective self-awareness, and it consequently presupposes a more fundamental form of self-acquaintance. This is why the investigation of the Heidelberg School is after all a spit deeper than the indexical analysis of linguistic self-reference. I do not think that Tugendhat's own alternative is convincing, but he has touched upon a tender spot: It must be admitted that *if* it in fact proved impossible to give a coherent and intelligible account of the structure of self-awareness using the categorial means of the *Bewußtseinsphilosophie,* the latter would face a very serious problem. Thus, at no point should one forget that an analysis of the structure of self-awareness is also an investigation into the more general conditions of possibility for an examination of subjectivity. At the end of part 2, we will be in a position to judge whether Tugendhat's assessment is correct.

PART   2

THE
SELF-MANIFESTATION
OF SUBJECTIVITY

4

Some Initial Distinctions

The time has come to commence the central task, an analysis of the contribution to a clarification of self-awareness found within phenomenology. As I pointed out in the preface, I hope to show not only that there are insights to be gained from this tradition which will allow for an increased understanding of the nature of self-awareness, but also more specifically that this tradition can provide answers to the questions raised at the end of part 1.

Although I will draw freely on the writings of most of the central phenomenological thinkers, my analysis will—as I have already indicated —nevertheless focus particularly on the theory of self-awareness developed within Husserlian phenomenology. At first glance this might appear as a slightly surprising decision, since one only infrequently finds analyses dedicated explicitly and exclusively to the problem of self-awareness in Husserl's writings. However, this is not because the topic is absent, but rather because his reflections on this problem are usually integrated into his analysis of a number of related issues, such as the nature of intentionality, spatiality, the body, temporality, attention, intersubjectivity, etc. This fact makes any attempt at a more systematic account both challenging and rewarding. Rewarding because Husserl's phenomenological analysis of self-awareness is often of a far more concrete and substantial nature than the more formal considerations to be found in, for instance, the Heidelberg School. Challenging because although there is a profound and complex theory of self-awareness to be found in Husserl's writings, it is a theory that will first have to be pieced together, and simply to isolate the relevant elements and avoid getting lost in the adjacent discussions will demand a distinct effort. But it is exactly at this point that my preparatory discussion in part 1 proves helpful. Not only does it provide additional arguments in support of a number of central phenomenological theses, but it will also facilitate the maintenance of a problem-oriented and systematic perspective.

The Ontological Monism

Most of Husserl's reflections on self-awareness are not contained in the writings published during his lifetime, but are rather to be found in the posthumously published volumes of *Husserliana* as well as in manuscripts still unpublished. This has not prevented subsequent phenomenologists from developing Husserl's insights, however, and to a certain extent, the most intensive and explicit Husserlian discussion of self-awareness is not to be found in Husserl's own writings, but in the writings *on* Husserl. But why have Husserl's reflections on self-awareness given rise to such an intense and often highly technical discussion?[1] One answer is that self-awareness is not simply *a* but rather *the* fundamental problem of phenomenology. As Michel Henry has convincingly shown, the task of transcendental phenomenology is by no means to describe objects as precisely and meticulously as possible, nor to investigate the phenomena in all their ontic diversity, but to examine their very manifestation and its condition of possibility.[2] The whole point in executing the epoché and the transcendental reduction is exactly to break loose from the natural attitude which remains spellbound by mundane affairs, and to carry out an unnatural reflection that permits us to analyze something which has always been there but to which we have never (systematically) paid attention, namely, *appearance.* When we start examining the appearance we discover that it is characterized by a *dyadic* structure: An appearance is an appearance of something for somebody, and at this point a central question emerges with which Kant, Husserl, and Heidegger fought. If it is acknowledged that the manifestations of, say, penknives and orchards have a dyadic structure, what about transcendental subjectivity itself? Does the condition of possibility for manifestation manifest itself? Can that which conditions all phenomena become a phenomenon itself?[3] And if the answer is yes, does the appearance of this condition also have a dyadic structure, i.e., is it an appearance of something for somebody? The answer to the last question presumably must be negative. If the appearance of subjectivity were dyadic, it would not only involve us in an infinite regress, insofar as there would always be yet another dative of manifestation. It would also be difficult to understand why we should be dealing with a case of *self*-awareness. Self-awareness does not seem to allow for any distinction or separation between the dative and genitive of manifestation. That which appears and that to whom it appears must be one and the same. Against this background it is tempting to answer no to the first question as well. If the transcendental condition were to become a phenomenon itself, it would no longer be that which conditions, but something that was itself conditioned. But although this option might have been available to Kant, it is not available to the phenomenologists. To deny that transcendental subjectivity manifests itself is to deny the possibility of a *phenomenological* analysis of transcendental subjectivity. And to deny that is to deny the possibility of transcendental phenomenology altogether.

Normally, the term "constitution" has been used to designate the process of bringing to appearance. More specifically, something (an object) is said to be *constituted* if it is brought to appearance by something else, that is, if it owes its manifestation to something different from itself, whereas something (transcendental subjectivity) is said to be *constituting* if it is itself the condition for manifestation. To speak in this way obviously raises a question concerning whether or not that which constitutes does itself appear or not. Traditionally, one has then had the choice between two formulations, both of which were ambiguous. Either one could say that transcendental subjectivity is itself unconstituted, or one could say that it is self-constituting. The first formulation might suggest that transcendental subjectivity does not at all manifest itself, the second that it manifests itself in the same way as objects do.

According to Michel Henry, the entire history of Western thought has been dominated by what he calls an *ontological monism*, that is, by the assumption that there is only one kind of manifestation, only one kind of phenomenality. It has thus been taken for granted that to be given is always to be given as an object. Needless to say, this principle of *ontological monism* has also infiltrated the traditional understanding of self-awareness. Self-awareness has been interpreted as being the product of a reflection or introspection, i.e., the result of an objectifying activity. It was thus taken for granted that self-manifestation was simply an unusual type of object-manifestation.[4]

This assumption must be questioned. Unless phenomenology can prove that there is in fact a decisive and radical difference between the phenomenality of constituted objects, on one hand, and the phenomenality of constituting subjectivity, on the other, that is, a radical difference between object-manifestation and self-manifestation, its entire project is threatened.[5]

Henry himself has confronted the problem and dedicated most of his oeuvre to a phenomenological investigation of self-awareness. He makes it clear that it is not the reflective knowledge of self which holds his particular interest, but rather the dimension which makes reflection possible in the first place.[6] Nevertheless, phenomenology cannot afford to ignore the problem of reflection either, since its own methodology is so heavily dependent upon it. We consequently end up with two issues that phenomenology is bound to clarify: What is the nature of the *self-manifestation* and the *self-comprehension* of subjectivity, respectively?

Prereflective Self-Awareness in Sartre and Husserl

Sartre's account of self-awareness is probably the best known phenomeno-logical theory of self-awareness. It is definitely the one most often referred to when philosophers coming from other traditions are discussing phe-nomenological insights pertaining to the problem of self-awareness. I will return to Sartre's theory in more detail later on, but let me already at this stage briefly mention his most influential thesis. According to Sartre, consciousness is essentially characterized by intentionality. It is as such consciousness *of* something. He also claims, however, that each and every intentional act is characterized by self-awareness. What kind of justification does Sartre present in support of such a strong thesis? Sartre takes self-awareness to constitute a necessary condition for being conscious of something. If I were conscious of a scratch in my record, an uncomfortable chair, or a burning pain without being aware of it, it would be a consciousness oblivious of itself, an unconscious consciousness, and Sartre takes this suggestion to be a manifest absurdity.[7]

This line of thought is elaborated in the important introduction to *L'Être et le néant*, where Sartre claims that an ontological analysis of intentionality leads to self-awareness since the *mode of being* of intentional consciousness is to be *for-itself* (*pour-soi*), that is, self-aware. The conscious givenness of an experience is not simply a quality added to the experience, a mere varnish, but the very mode of being of the experience. Just as an extended object can only exist three-dimensionally, an experience can only exist as self-aware. As Malcolm once put it, pain is painful.[8] Pain can only exist consciously, that is, to be in pain and to feel the pain is one and the same and cannot be separated, not even conceptually.[9]

This reasoning might appear especially convincing when it comes to feelings like pain or pleasure, but Sartre insists that it holds true for all intentional acts: "This self-consciousness we ought to consider not as a new consciousness, but as *the only mode of existence which is possible for a consciousness of something.*"[10] Originally, my intentions are not (possible) objects for consciousness, but (actual) modes of consciousness, and as such are self-aware.

When speaking of self-awareness as a permanent feature of our consciousness rather than as a mere addendum to the intentional act, Sartre is not referring to reflective self-awareness, however. Reflection operates with an epistemic duality, and to introduce that duality into the core of consciousness has aporetical consequences. We would either have to face an infinite regress or accept an unconscious starting point, i.e., an act of reflection which itself remained unconscious. Since both options fail to explain how self-awareness is brought about, they must be rejected, and Sartre speaks instead of the original self-awareness as an immediate and noncognitive "relation" of the self to itself.[11] The Cartesian *cogito* presupposes a prereflective *cogito* as its condition of possibility:

> If anyone questioned me, indeed, if anyone should ask, "What are you doing there?" I should reply at once, "I am counting." This reply aims not only at the instantaneous consciousness which I can achieve by reflection but at those fleeting consciousnesses which have passed without being reflected-on, those which are forever not-reflected-on in my immediate past. Thus reflection has no kind of primacy over the consciousness reflected-on. It is not reflection which reveals the consciousness reflected-on to itself. Quite the contrary, it is the nonreflective consciousness which renders the reflection possible; there is a prereflective cogito which is the condition of the Cartesian cogito.[12]

To put it differently, consciousness has two different modes of existence, a prereflective and a reflective. The first has ontological priority since it can prevail independently of the latter, whereas reflective consciousness always presupposes prereflective consciousness.

Sartre's theory of self-awareness, particularly his notion of prereflective self-awareness, has often been taken to constitute a major breakthrough when compared to the theory found in Husserl. Thus Henrich, Frank, and Tugendhat all accuse Husserl of defending a reflection theory of self-awareness, of taking object-intentionality as the paradigm of every kind of awareness. This criticism must be rejected, however. The notion of prereflective self-awareness is not only to be found in Husserl; in addition he subjects it to a highly illuminating analysis.[13]

It is in particular Frank who has claimed that Husserl's entire investigation of consciousness is based on the tacit assumption that consciousness is conscious of something different from itself. Due to this fixation on *intentionality* Husserl never managed to escape the reflection theory of self-awareness. He persistently operated with a model of self-awareness based upon the subject-object dichotomy, with its entailed *difference* between the intending and the intended, and therefore, according to Frank, never discovered the existence of a prereflective self-awareness.[14] As anyone familiar with Husserl's writings will know, Husserl already in *Logische Untersuchungen* distanced himself from Brentano's characterization of the psychical phenomena as being essentially intentional, by claiming that there are experiences which lack intentionality.[15] And when Husserl was later to investigate the entire realm of passivity and temporality, he also disclosed dimensions of subjectivity not characterized by object-intentionality. Frank's critique is marked by a rather unfortunate tendency to simply presuppose a certain (faulty) interpretation of Husserl's thinking, and every time Frank then encounters passages where Husserl says otherwise, he either misinterprets them or rejects them as being "aporetical" or "mystical."[16] In contrast, one might point out that already Sartre acknowledged that Husserl had decribed the prereflective being of consciousness.[17]

Let us turn to a simple act of reflection, e.g., a thematic consciousness of a perception of a black billiard ball. According to Husserl, this reflection is *founded* in a twofold sense. It does not present us with a self-enclosed subjectivity, but with a self-transcending subjectivity directed at an object, and it consequently presupposes the preceding act of object-intentionality.[18] Moreover, as an explicit self-awareness, the reflection also relies on a prior prereflective self-awareness. To utilize a distinction between perceiving (*Wahrnehmen*) and experiencing (*Erleben*) dating back from the *Logical Investigations*, prior to reflection one *perceives* the intentional object, but one *experiences* the intentional act. Although I am not intentionally directed at the act (this only happens in the subsequent reflection, where the act is thematized), it is not unconscious but conscious,[19] that is, prereflectively self-aware. In Husserl's words:

> Das Wort Erlebnis drückt dabei eben dieses Erlebtsein, nämlich Bewussthaben im inneren Bewusstsein aus, wodurch es für das Ich jederzeit vorgegeben ist.[20]

> [E]very experience is "consciousness," and consciousness is consciousness *of.* . . . But every experience is *itself experienced* [*erlebt*], and *to that extent* also "conscious" [*bewußt*].[21]

> Every act is consciousness of something, but there is also consciousness of every act. Every act is "sensed," is immanently "perceived" (internal consciousness), although naturally not posited, meant (to perceive here does not mean to grasp something and to be turned toward it in an act of meaning). . . . To be sure, this seems to lead back to an infinite regress. For is not the internal consciousness, the perceiving of the act (of judging, of perceiving something external, of rejoicing, and so forth), again an act and therefore itself something internally perceived, and so on? On the contrary, we must say: Every "experience" in the strict sense is internally perceived. But the internal perceiving is not an "experience" in the same sense. It is not itself again internally perceived.[22]

In a moment, I will return to Husserl's use of the term "perception" when it comes to prereflective self-awareness, but it is quite obvious that he has seen the aporetic implications of the reflection theory. The claim that self-awareness only comes about when the act is apprehended by a further act ultimately leads to an infinite regress.[23]

As far as the interpretation of Henrich, Tugendhat, and Frank is concerned, it must be acknowledged that Husserl occasionally writes that we do not *perceive* our own subjectivity prior to reflection, but live in a state of self-oblivion and self-forfeiture (*Selbstverlorenheit*). But when he then adds that we only *know* of our acts reflectively, that is, that we only gain *knowledge* of our conscious life through reflection,[24] it becomes clear that he is using the term "perception" to denote a thematic examination. Husserl does not deny the existence of a prereflective self-awareness. But he does deny that this self-awareness can provide us with more than awareness. It cannot give us knowledge of subjectivity.

As just mentioned, however, it is also possible to unearth passages where Husserl in fact describes the pervasive prereflective self-awareness as a type of *inner perception*,[25] but a closer examination of these texts does not substantiate the claim that Husserl is trying to reduce self-awareness to a type of object-intentionality. On the one hand, Husserl's terminology is taken from his classical investigation of the hierarchy of foundation existing between different types of acts. In contrast to various kinds of presentiating (*vergegenwärtigende*) acts, such as recollection, fantasy, or empathy, perception is characterized by bringing its object to an originary kind of presentation. That which appears in perception is given *leibhaftig*, and it is exactly this feature which Husserl focuses upon in his discussion of prereflective self-awareness. This is brought to light in a passage from *Erste Philosophie* II, where Husserl writes that the life of the subject is a life in the form of original self-awareness. He then equates this self-awareness with an *innermost* perception, but adds that it is a perception, not in the sense of being an active self-apprehension, but in the sense of being an *originary* self-appearance.[26] On the other hand, Husserl's at times rather misleading terminology can also be taken to illustrate an often-noticed tension in his writings, the tension, namely, between his actual and innovative analysis and the more traditional systematic or methodical reflection accompanying it. It was the latter (representing Husserl's self-interpretation) that determined the terminology used, but Husserl's analyses were often more radical than he himself knew and more than his nomenclature suggested.[27] In the above quoted passage from *Vorlesungen zur Phänomenologie des inneren Zeitbewußtseins*, Husserl speaks alternately of prereflective self-awareness as an inner or immanent perception and as an inner consciousness (*inneres Bewußtsein*—one feels the influence from Brentano).[28] As will gradually become clear, Husserl ultimately opts for the latter expression, and much misunderstanding might have been avoided if he had done that from the very start.[29]

Our acts are prereflectively self-aware, but they are also accessible for reflection. They can be reflected upon and thereby brought to our attention,[30] and an examination of the particular intentional structure of reflection can substantiate the thesis concerning the existence of a prereflective self-awareness. As Husserl points out, it is in the nature of reflection to grasp something which was already there prior to the grasping. Reflection is characterized by disclosing and not by producing its theme: "Sage ich 'ich', so erfasse ich mich in schlichter Reflexion; aber diese Selbsterfahrung ist wie jede Erfahrung, und zunächst jede Wahrnehmung, bloss Hin-mich-richten auf etwas, das schon für mich da ist, schon bewusst ist und nur nicht thematisch erfahren ist, nicht Aufgemerktes."[31]

In a regular intentional act, I am directed at and preoccupied with my intentional object. Whenever I am intentionally directed at objects I am also self-aware. But when I am directed at and occupied with objects, I am not thematically conscious of myself. And when I do thematize myself in a reflection, the very act of thematization remains unthematic. However, one should not forget that the act of reflection is itself a prereflectively self-given act. Thematic self-awareness presupposes a double prereflective self-awareness. The reflected act must already be self-aware, since it is the fact of its being already mine, already being given in the first-personal mode of presentation that allows me to reflect upon it. And the act of reflection must also already be prereflectively self-aware, since it is this that permits it to recognize the reflected act as belonging to the same subjectivity as it *self*.[32]

Naturally, the unthematic act of reflection can be thematized in a higher-order reflection, wherein we then ascertain the identity between the perceiving and the reflecting subject, but ultimately this will merely reiterate the dual structure reflecting (unthematic)–reflected (thematic), although the structural complexity of the reflected pole will keep increasing.[33] In *Erste Philosophie* II, Husserl struggles to find an accurate description of this situation. At one point he describes the reflecting ego as being in a state of self-oblivion, but later backtracks since forgetfulness presupposes a prior state of thematic experience. I can only forget something that I have already known. For a number of reasons, it is also highly awkward to call the reflecting ego unconscious, and for a while Husserl then uses the terms "*latent*" and "*patent*": An act is made patent or thematized through an act of reflection, which is itself latent, but which in its turn can be made patent through a latent higher-order reflection.[34] This terminology is then finally superseded by the more frequently used distinction between the anonymously functioning subjectivity (in short, the *Ur-Ich*) and the thematized, ontified subjectivity. When subjectivity functions, it is self-aware, but it is not thematically conscious of itself, and it therefore lives in *anonymity*.

Somit haben wir immerfort die Scheidung zwischen dem Ich und *cogito* als fungierendem, aber nicht erfasstem (fungierende Subjektivität), und dem evtl. thematisierten, direkt oder selbsterfassten Ich und seinem *cogito*, oder kurzweg, fungierende Subjektivität und objektive Subjektivität (vergegenständlichte, thematisch erfahrene, vorgestellte, gedachte, prädizierte) sind zu unterscheiden, und, wenn immer ich mich und was immer sonst als Objekt habe, bin ich zugleich notwendig als fungierendes Ich ausserthematisch dabei, mir zugänglich als das durch Reflexion als einer neuen, nun wieder nicht thematischen Aktivität des fungierenden Ich.[35]

When I start reflecting, that which motivates the reflection and which is then grasped has already been going on for a while. The reflected experience did not commence the moment I started paying attention to it, and it is not only given as still existing, but also and mainly as having already been. It is the *same* act which is now given reflectively, and it is given to me as enduring in time, that is, as a temporal act.[36] Let me try to be a bit more specific. When reflection sets in, it initially grasps something that has just elapsed, namely the motivating prereflective phase of the act. The reason why this phase can still be thematized by the subsequent reflection is that it does not disappear, but is retained in the retention, wherefore Husserl can claim that retention is a condition of possibility for reflection. It is due to the retention that consciousness can be made into an object.[37] Or to rephrase, reflection can only take place if a temporal horizon has been established.

I will return to the relationship between retention and self-awareness shortly, but it can already now be ˙established that reflective self-awareness does not only presuppose temporality, it also brings it into focus, in the sense of making me aware of my own temporal existence.[38] This is because reflection is by no means an instantaneous fixation of, e.g., a perception of a house, but is itself a streaming act, and because reflection temporally viewed is initially a grasping of something that has just elapsed, namely, the motivating phase of the perception. Of course the perception might continue as a reflectively given perception of the house, and in this case there will no longer be any temporal distance between the reflecting and the reflected.[39] But although the distance might be bridged, it remains incorporated into the structure of reflective self-awareness.

The temporal nature of reflection is particularly striking if one accepts Husserl's distinction between the following two kinds of reflection. We are not only able to reflect upon our present intentional consciousness, be it a perception, a fantasy, or a recollection. We can also reflect upon our past consciousness. In Husserl's words, it is not only possible to reflect upon the recollection, it is also possible to reflect *in* the recollection. When I remember a past promenade, I am thematically concerned with the promenade, i.e., with how the world was, and not with my former experience of it. But I always have the opportunity to reflect. I can reflect upon my present recollection of the past promenade, but I can also reflect upon my past experience of the promenade.[40]

> Die von der geraden Erinnerung, etwa eines Hauses, abbiegende Selbsterinnerung enthüllt nicht das gegenwärtige Ich, das der aktuellen Wahrnehmungen (darunter der jetzigen Wiedererinnerung selbst als Gegenwartserleben), sondern das vergangene Ich, das zu dem eigenen intentionalen Wesen des erinnerten Hauses gehört, als das, für das es dawar, und dawar in den und den subjektiven Bewußtseinsmodis. Erinnerung ist ihrem Wesen nach nicht nur In-Geltung-haben eines Vergangenen, sondern dieses Vergangenen als eines von mir Wahrgenommenen und eines sonstwie Bewußtgewesenen; und eben dieses in gerader Erinnerung anonyme vergangene Ich und Bewußtsein kommt in einer Reflexion (Reflexion nicht auf das jetzige Erinnern, sondern "in" ihm) zur Enthüllung.[41]

In ordinary reflection we thematize an act we are still living through, whereas we in the retrospective type of reflection presentiate an absent, past act. If it is merely the backward sinking phase of an ongoing perception which is grasped, we are dealing with an ordinary reflective self-awareness. But if the entire perception has come to an end and is then grasped, we are dealing with a retrospective type of reflection.[42]

Insofar as a theoretical examination of the acts depends upon their being accessible for reflection, it is no wonder that Husserl often stresses this aspect. Occasionally, however, it gains dominance, since the most significant feature of the prereflectively self-aware act appears to be its accessibility for a subsequent reflection. Thus, from time to time, Husserl seems to suggest that for an experience to be prereflectively self-aware is for the experience to be nothing but a possible object of reflection.[43] Recalling Brentano's description of the self as the secondary object of the intentional act, Bernet remarks: "Plutôt qu'un 'objet secondaire', le soi préréflexif est pour Husserl un pré-objet, c'est-à-dire une donnée qui attend de devenir l'objet d'un acte réflexif."[44] But as Bernet also adds, this is not Husserl's final word on the issue. To get to that, I have to shift the focus to the place where Husserl's most explicit investigation of the structure of prereflective self-awareness can be found, in his analysis of *inner time-consciousness.*[45]

Marginal Consciousness

Before I do that, however, I wish to take a brief look at Husserl's notion of *horizontal intentionality,* since this will allow for a double clarification. On the one hand, it will permit a dismissal of any narrow conception of consciousness which equates consciousness with attention and consequently claims that we are only conscious of that to which we pay attention. On the other hand, it will make it clear why prereflective self-awareness cannot be understood as a kind of *marginal consciousness.*

   When we perceive an object, it is necessary to distinguish that which appears from the appearance, since the object is never given in its totality (front, back, sides, top, bottom) but always present itself from a certain restricted perspective. Despite this, the object of perception is exactly the appearing object and not its intuitively given profile. That is, perception furnishes us with a full object-consciousness, even though only part of the perceived object is intuitively given.[46] In order to clarify how this is possible, Husserl describes a kind of intentional consciousness which we possess of the absent profiles of the object, i.e., of the object's inner horizon.[47] The meaning of the present profile is dependent upon its relation to the absent profiles of the object, and no perceptual consciousness of the *object* would be possible if our consciousness were strictly restricted to the intuitively and attentively given. Whenever I see a die, I am also conscious of its back. I am conscious of the die as seen from the front, and although I neither *perceive* its back nor pay attention to it, I am still conscious of it. Otherwise I would not be able to see the die at all: "The improperly appearing objective determinations are co-apprehended, but they are not 'sensibilized,' not presented through what is sensible, i.e., through the material of sensation. It is evident that they are co-apprehended, for otherwise we would have no objects at all before our eyes, not even a side, since this can indeed be a side only through the object."[48] In other words, in order for a perception to be a perception-of-an-object, it must be permeated by a horizontal intentionality which intends the absent profiles,[49] bringing them to a certain *appresentation.*

However, the object is not only given with an inner horizon but also with a far more extensive outer horizon.[50] To perceive an object is always to perceive an object situated in a perceptual field, and whenever we pay attention to something, we single it out from its surroundings. Thus one might describe the appearance of a thematic object as an appearance out of a field or background. This field is neither unconscious nor totally undifferentiated. Whenever we focus on an object, we are conscious of an object in a particular setting, and the way it is given to us is influenced by that which is cogiven with it, as Gestalt psychology has persistently and convincingly pointed out. The significance of a given object partially depends on its cogiven context, and it is absurd to suppose that the ties between the thematic object and its background should be cut through an attentional modification.

Within the sum total of all that is cogiven with the thematic object, there is also a particular domain of components of special relevance for the theme and, following Gurwitsch, we might call this domain the "thematic field."[51] The items in the thematic field are not only cogiven with the thematic object, they are of relevance for it, and it refers to them. I am primarily concerned with and absorbed by the thematic object, and incidentally concerned with the items pertaining to the thematic field. Apart from the thematic field, however, our occupation with a particular theme is also accompanied by a number of marginal components which are merely copresent, without having any internal connection to the theme in question. Let me provide a concrete example. I am standing in my kitchen slicing a tomato. The tomato, which is my thematic object, is lying on the kitchen counter surrounded by different utensils which make up part of its thematic field. Whether something belongs to the thematic field or not is not a question of physical distance, however. While I slice the tomato, I feel the knife in my hand and the hardness of the carving board, but I am also reminded of a commercial for tomato juice, and if this commercial makes me pay attention to the juicy quality of the tomato, it too belongs to the thematic field. At the same time, however, I might also hear the hum of the refrigerator, or feel the trousers rubbing against my legs. Although I do not pay attention to any of these components, they are not unconscious, but cogiven. They belong to the margin of my field of consciousness. And their marginal position is due to their irrelevance for the theme in question: "The total field of consciousness can be symbolized by a circle. The theme with which we are dealing occupies the center of this circle; it stands in the thematic field, which—to abide by the metaphor—forms the area of the circle; and around the thematic field, at the periphery as it were, the objects of marginal consciousness are arranged."[52] When I am absorbed in my tomato-slicing, I do not pay

attention to its surroundings. But I do not cease to be conscious of the
kitchen counter, the dripping tap, the hum of the refrigerator, etc. I
am merely conscious of them as ground, i.e., they are parts of the totality
which serves as the background of my slicing. And although none of these
objects are thematically given, they can easily become themes through a
mere change of attention. The possibility of this thematic modification
is exactly grounded in the fact that my theme is always situated in a field
that is cogiven with it, i.e., whenever I am paying attention to something,
I am affected by and coconscious of its surroundings, and can therefore
change my attention. The field is, as Fink puts it, a "Spielraum möglicher
Zuwendungen."[53]

All this is simply to say that it is a mistake to overlook the variety
of different modes of consciousness and to identify the realm of the
conscious with the realm of the thematically given. In other words, it
will obviously not do to deny the existence of prereflective self-awareness
on the ground that our consciousness is not given thematically prior to
reflection. But at this point the following question arises: Is the distinction
between thematic and marginal consciousness pertinent when it comes
to self-awareness? It can hardly be denied that I do not pay attention to
the experience as long as I am occupied with the objects. But this is not
the current issue. The question is whether the experience remains in
the background as a potential theme in the same way as the hum of the
refrigerator. In short, is prereflective self-awareness a kind of marginal,
inattentive, object-consciousness? The answer is obviously no. Prior to
reflection, consciousness is not given as a marginal *object*. (It is interesting that Gurwitsch, in his noematically oriented analysis, apparently
commits this error and consequently claims that the self-awareness which
accompanies every act of consciousness is a marginal datum.)[54] The entire
analogy is misleading since it remains stuck in the subject-object model.
In a text from 1906–7 Husserl reached a similar conclusion:

> Nicht verwechseln darf man das Bewußtsein vom gegenständlichen
> Hintergrund und das Bewußtsein im Sinn des Erlebtseins. Erlebnisse
> als solche haben ihr Sein, aber sie sind nicht Gegenstände von
> Apperzeptionen (wir kämen ja sonst auf einen unendlichen Regreß). Der
> Hintergrund aber ist uns gegenständlich, er ist es durch den Komplex
> von apperzeptiven Erlebnissen, die ihn gleichsam konstituieren. Diese
> Gegenstände sind unbeachtet, im dritten Sinn unbewußt, aber etwas ganz
> anderes für uns als die bloßen Erlebnisse, z.B. die sie objektivierenden
> Apperzeptionen und Akterlebnisse selbst. (Das Bloß-Erlebtsein, können
> wir auch sagen, ist nicht ein Bloß-unbemerkt-Sein oder Unbewußt-Sein
> im Sinn des Unbemerkt-Seins des gegenständlichen Hintergrunds.) Das

attentionale Bewußtseins des Hintergrunds und das Bewußtsein als bloßes Erlebtseins ist ganz zu scheiden.[55]

After this clarification, which will prove of value later on, it is time to take a closer look at Husserl's notion of prereflective self-awareness. Ultimately, Husserl's thesis concerning the existence of a prereflective self-awareness is connected to a general claim concerning the *being* of subjectivity. To be a subject is to exist for-itself, that is, to be self-aware. No matter what worldly entities subjectivity might be conscious of and otherwise occupied with, it is thus also self-aware.[56] "*An absolute existent* is existent in the form, an intentional life—which, no matter what else it may be intrinsically conscious of, is, at the same time, consciousness of itself. Precisely for that reason (as we can see when we consider more profoundly) it has at all times an essential ability to *reflect* on itself, on all its structures that stand out for it—an essential ability to make itself thematic and produce judgments, and evidences, relating to itself."[57] Husserl's attempt to elucidate this pervasive self-awareness, which by no means is to be understood as a particular intentional act but as a dimension of basic self-manifestation that precedes and founds reflection, leads in two different but nevertheless intrinsically intertwined directions: to *temporality* and to *embodiment*.[58] As Castañeda has formulated it: "The true transcendental prefix is, it seems, the extended one: *I think here now.*"[59]

5

The Temporality of
Self-Awareness

L et me turn first to Husserl's analysis of *inner time-consciousness*, and thereby to a nest of problems which has often and rightly been characterized as being among the most important and difficult ones in the whole of phenomenology.[1] Due to what can only be described as the extraordinary complexity of Husserl's analysis, I think it might be useful to start with a brief presentation of some of his more elementary considerations.

The Constitution of Temporal Objects

In *Vorlesungen zur Phänomenologie des inneren Zeitbewußtseins,* Husserl asks how it is possible for us to be conscious of temporal objects, objects with a temporal extension. How is it possible to be conscious of objects such as melodies, which cannot appear all at once, but only unfold themselves over time? Husserl's well-known thesis is that a perception of a temporal object (as well as the perception of succession and change) would be impossible if consciousness merely provided us with the givenness of the pure now-phase of the object, and if the stream of consciousness were a series of unconnected points of experiencing, like a string of pearls. If our perception had been restricted to being conscious of that which exists right now, it would have been impossible to perceive anything with a temporal extension and duration, for a succession of isolated, punctual, conscious states does not as such enable us to be conscious of succession and duration. But this consequence is absurd. Thus, consciousness must in some way or another transcend the punctual now, and be conscious of that which has just been and is just about to occur. But how is this possible? How can consciousness be conscious of that which is no longer or not yet present?

According to Husserl, Brentano held the position that it is our presentiating (*vergegenwärtigende*) acts which permit us to transcend the now-point. We perceive that which is now, and we imagine, remember, or anticipate that which does not yet or no longer exists.[2] Husserl rejects this explanation, however, since it implies that we cannot *perceive* objects with temporal duration. Basically, his alternative is to point out that the basic unit of perceived time is not a "knife-edge" present, but a "duration-block," i.e., a temporal field which contains all three temporal modes—present, past, and future.[3] Let us assume that I am hearing a triad consisting of the tonal sequence C, D, and E. If we pay attention to the perception the instant the tone E sounds, we will not find a consciousness occupied exclusively with this tone alone, but a consciousness of both E, D, and C. When I hear the tone E, I am still conscious of the tones D and C, but not only that. I am still *hearing* these two tones (and neither remembering nor imagining them). This is not to say that there is no difference between our consciousness of the present tone E and our consciousness of the tones D and C. D and C are not simultaneous with E; they are past tones, but they are *intuited as past*, and it is exactly for this reason that we can say that we *hear* the triad in its temporal duration and not merely isolated tones replacing each other abruptly.[4]

Husserl does in fact have a name for our consciousness of the narrow now-phase of the object. He calls this consciousness the *primal impression*, but it alone cannot provide us with consciousness of anything with a temporal duration, and it is in fact only the abstract core-component of the full structure of experiencing. The primal impression is embedded in a twofold temporal horizon. On the one hand, it is accompanied by a *retention* which provides us with consciousness of the phase of the object which has just been, i.e., which allows us to be aware of the phase as it sinks into the past and, on the other hand, by a *protention* which in a more or less indeterminate fashion anticipates the phase of the object yet to come.[5]

> In this way, it becomes evident that concrete perception as original consciousness (original givenness) of a temporally extended object is structured internally as itself a streaming system of momentary perceptions (so-called primal impressions). But each such momentary perception is the nuclear phase of a continuity, a continuity of momentary gradated retentions on the one side, and a horizon of what is coming on the other side: a horizon of "protention," which is disclosed to be characterized as a constantly gradated coming.[6]

It is important to realize that "primal impression" is Husserl's name for the consciousness of the now-phase of the object, and not the name for this now-phase itself, and it is essential to distinguish the phases of the object from time-consciousness itself, with its full structure primal impression–retention–protention.[7] The retention (B) and protention (C) are not past or future in regard to the primal impression (A). They are "together" with it.[8] The correlates of this tripartite *ecstatic-centered* structure of inner time-consciousness will be the phases of the *object* given in the temporal modes *now* (O2), *past* (O1), and *future* (O3). The now-phase of the object has a horizon, but it is not made up of the retention and the protention, but exactly of the past and future phases of the object (see fig. 5.1).[9]

Since the constitutive function of perception depends upon the contribution of retention, and upon its retaining of that which is no longer, it would be wrong to restrict the evidence of our perception to that which in a narrow sense is present, namely, that which is given in the primal impression. For this reason Husserl often remarked that the analysis of the retention led to a significant widening of the phenomenological field.[10]

Both retention and protention have to be distinguished from the proper (thematic) recollection and anticipation. There is an obvious difference between retaining and protending the tone which has just passed and is just about to occur, on one hand, and remembering one's tenth

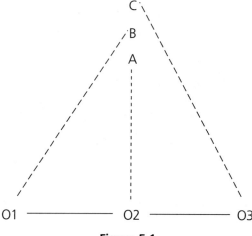

Figure 5.1

birthday or looking forward to next Christmas, on the other. Whereas the latter are independent intentional acts which presuppose the work of the retention and the protention, the retention and the protention are dependent moments of experiencing. They do not provide us with new intentional objects, but with a consciousness of the present object's temporal horizon. Whereas the retention and protention occur passively without any active contribution from our side, the thematic anticipation and recollection are acts which we can initiate voluntarily. If we compare the retention and the recollection, the retention is an intuition, but an intuition of something absent, of something which has just been, whereas the recollection is a presentiating act, which gives us a completed *past* event as our intentional object.[11] When I recollect, the past event is reproduced in my present experience, but it does not become a part of it. It is exactly given as past and absent—in relation to the present. If it is to be experienced as past, it must be given as past together with and in contrast to that which is now present. The experience of this distance or difference is essential for recollection. If it is missing, if the past event is relived as if it were present, we would not be recollecting, but hallucinating.[12]

Let me return to the triad C, D, and E. When C is first heard, it is presenced in the primal impression. When it is succeeded by D, D is given in the primal impression, whereas C is retained in the retention, and when finally E sounds, it replaces D in the primal impression, whereas D is retained in the retention. However, the retention is not merely a

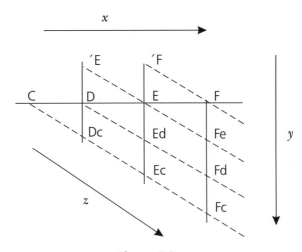

Figure 5.2

retention of the tone which has just passed. Every time a new tone is presenced in a primal impression, the entire retentional sequence is recapitulated and modified. When the tone C is succeeded by the tone D, our impressional consciousness of D is accompanied by a retention of C (Dc). When D is succeeded by the tone E, our impressional consciousness of E is accompanied both by a retention of D (Ed) and by a retention of the tone retained in D (Ec), and so forth.[13] This is shown in fig 5.2,[14] where the horizontal line x denotes the sequence of tones (C, D, E, F); where the vertical line y designates our consciousness of this sequence with its structure of protention, primal impression, and retention$s$ (for instance, 'F, E, Ed, Ec); and where the diagonal line z illustrates how a single tone retains its identity and position vis-à-vis the other tones when it sinks into the past, although its mode of givenness changes, i.e., although it is constantly given in new temporal perspectives (for instance, C, Dc, Ec, Fc). It is important to emphasize that although the sequence of tones (x) is a sequence of temporally distinct tones, our awareness of this sequence (y) is not itself sequential. The primal impression is "together" with the entire series of retentions. But that which is given in the primal impression is not simultaneous with that which is given in the retention, nor is that which is retained in the first retention simultaneous with that which is retained in the retention of the retention. The order of the tones is preserved. They are not given as simultaneous, but as succeeding each other.

The Self-Manifestation of the Flow

So far I have dealt with the constitution of temporally extended objects, such as tones and melodies. This type of constitution has been classified as a *noematic temporalization*, and it must now be complemented by an account of the *noetic temporalization*.[15] That is, the analysis of time-consciousness is by no means a mere investigation of the temporal givenness of objects. It is also an account of the temporal manifestation of consciousness itself. In fact, the reason why Husserl attributes such an immense importance to his analysis of inner time-consciousness is exactly because there is far more at stake than a mere clarification of the constitution of the temporality of the intentional object. Ultimately, Husserl is struggling with the very problem concerning the condition of possibility for manifestation as such, and it is this problem which leads him to the question concerning the temporal self-manifestation of consciousness.

Our perceptual objects are temporal, but what about our very perceptions of these objects? Are they also subjugated to the strict laws of temporal constitution? Are they also temporal unities which arise, endure, and perish? Husserl often speaks of the acts themselves as being constituted in the structure primal impression–retention–protention. They are only given, only self-aware, within this framework.[16]

How is this self-awareness to be understood? And how do we avoid an infinite regress? If the duration and unity of a tonal sequence is constituted by consciousness, and if our consciousness of the tonal sequence is itself given with duration and unity, are we then not forced to posit yet another consciousness to account for the givenness of this duration and unity, and so forth *ad infinitum*?[17]

Although Husserl in the beginning seemed to advocate such a view, for instance, when he wrote that the perception of duration presupposes the duration of the perception,[18] he eventually became aware of its problematic nature:

> Is it inherently absurd to regard the flow of time as an *objective movement*? *Certainly!* On the other hand, memory is surely something that itself has *its now*, and the same now as a tone, for example. *No.* There lurks the fundamental mistake. *The flow of the modes of consciousness is not a process; the consciousness of the now is not itself now.* The retention that exists "together" with the consciousness of the now is not "now," is *not simultaneous* with the now, and it would make no sense to say that it is.[19]

Just as my experience of a red circle is neither circular nor red, there is a difference between the temporal givenness of the intentional object and the temporal givenness of the intentional act. They are not temporal, given, or constituted in the same manner. It was against this background that Husserl eventually came to distinguish three different layers of temporality: the objective time of the appearing objects, the subjective, immanent or preempirical time of the acts, sensa, and appearances, and the absolute, prephenomenal flow of time-constituting consciousness.[20] In *Ideen* I, Husserl confined himself to an analysis of the first two levels. But from a phenomenological perspective this is an unacceptable limitation. The very condition of possibility for the temporal manifestation of the acts has to be investigated as well, and it consequently proved necessary to subject the results achieved by the reduction to further investigations, i.e., it proved necessary to carry out an even more radical reduction within the transcendental reduction, a reduction that led from subjective time to the absolute flow.[21] This is why Husserl, after he has described the relation between the constituting subject and the constituted objects in *Ideen* I, writes that he has quite deliberately left out the most important and difficult problems, namely, those concerning inner time-consciousness, and that only this analysis would be able to disclose the truly absolute dimension.[22] To explicate the structure of inner time-consciousness (primal impression–retention–protention) is a different and more fundamental enterprise than to distinguish and analyze different types of object-intentionality, such as memory, perception, and imagination. Needless to say, the decisive problem is then to clarify the relation between the absolute flow or flowing experiencing (*das strömende Erleben*),[23] on the one hand, and the constituted act, on the other.

Unfortunately, however, I do not think that Husserl ever managed to achieve complete clarity on this issue. Both his published and unpublished analyses remain characterized by fundamental ambiguities, and it is ultimately possible to find textual evidence in support of several different interpretations. Needless to say, this is not a very satisfying situation, but at this point it is important to keep the overall topic in mind. The explicit aim of this particular investigation is to unearth a Husserlian theory of self-awareness. As a consequence, and in opposition to some of the more established readings, I will specifically opt for the interpretation of Husserl's analysis of time-consciousness which will contribute the most to our understanding of self-awareness. Although this will imply that there are aspects of Husserl's reflections on time which I will have to bypass, I still tend to believe that my particular perspective can throw new light upon Husserl's theory as a whole.

On one dominant interpretation, Husserl is taken to argue in the following way: Just as we must distinguish between the constituted dimension in which transcendent objects exist and the constituting dimension that permits them to appear, we must distinguish between the constituted dimension in which the acts exist and the constituting dimension that permits them to appear. The acts are temporal objects existing in subjective time, but they are constituted by a deeper dimension of subjectivity, namely, the absolute flow of inner time-consciousness.[24] Let me quote a few passages that could be read in support of this interpretation:

Jedes Erlebnis als innerer Zeitgegenstand konstituiert sich zunächst und ursprünglich aber für das innere Bewußtsein, durch das er bewußt wird vermöge eines Flusses von Urimpression, Retentionen und Protentionen als durchgehende Einheit.[25]

Every concrete lived experience is a unity of becoming and is constituted as an object in internal consciousness in the form of temporality.[26]

> Das Erlebnis: "Wahrnehmung von irgendwelchen körperlichen Dingen"
> ist ein immanenter Gegenstand, in der inneren Zeit bewußt wie ein
> sonstiges Erlebnis.[27]

On closer examination, however, this account is deeply problematic. To say that the acts are originally given as *objects* for an inner consciousness, or to interpret their primal givenness as an object-manifestation, leads us right back into a version of the reflection theory. Not only is act-manifestation understood on the basis of a subject-object model, but it is even suggested that the act is not at all self-given but is brought to givenness by something other than itself, namely, by inner time-consciousness. This account does not explain self-awareness; it merely defers the problem. Obviously one is forced to ask whether inner time-consciousness is itself in possession of self-awareness or not. If it is denied that this consciousness is itself self-aware, the regress is indeed halted, but as was repeatedly pointed out in chapter 2, this account cannot explain why the relation between inner time-consciousness and the act should result in *self*-awareness. If the answer is yes, one must ask how the self-awareness of inner time-consciousness is established. Two possibilities seem open. First, it could come about in the same way in which the act is brought to givenness. In this case we are confronted with an infinite regress. The second possibility is that inner time-consciousness is in possession of an implicit or intrinsic self-manifestation. But if it is acknowledged that such a type of self-awareness exists, one might reasonably ask why it should be reserved to the deepest level of subjectivity, and not already be a feature of the act itself. Furthermore, to claim that the absolute flow of inner time-consciousness is itself self-aware, and to claim that this is something apart from and beyond the givenness of the acts, is to operate with an unnecessary multiplication of self-awareness. Nevertheless, this is exactly the position that Sokolowski and Brough take Husserl to hold. In their reading, Husserl takes the acts to be *full-blown inner objects* which are immediately given as such, even prior to reflection. Apart from this, however, the flow is also given to itself. Thus, if we examine a reflection on a perception of a black billiard ball, the following should be the case: (1) the black billiard ball is given as a transcendent object; (2) the act of reflection is prereflectively given as an inner object; (3) the act of perception is reflectively given as an inner object; and finally (4) the flow for whom all of these objects are given also reveals itself in a fundamental *shining*. Reflection should consequently present us with a threefold self-awareness with one transcendent object and two inner objects.[28] That seems too excessive. Not only is the distinction between 2 and 4 hard to fathom, but the characterization of 2 also seems misleading.

Even if one takes prereflective self-awareness to be a "marginal form of consciousness" and consequently distinguishes the prereflectively given inner object from the reflectively given inner object by emphasizing that the first is merely a marginal object,[29] this will not solve the problem, and as we have already seen, Husserl himself rejects the suggestion quite explicitly (see page 61).

I would like to propose a different interpretation, an interpretation which will ultimately permit one to link Husserl's distinction between the absolute flow and the temporally constituted act to his respective differentiations between functioning and thematized subjectivity, and prereflective and reflective self-awareness. I believe this linkage to be indispensable if one is to understand Husserl's analysis of time.

To speak phenomenologically of the temporality of consciousness is to speak of the temporal givenness of consciousness. But to speak of the temporal givenness of consciousness is to speak of its temporal self-manifestation. To suggest otherwise is to reify consciousness. Of course, it might be necessary to distinguish different types of self-manifestation, and different types of subjective temporality, but from the outset it should be realized that Husserl's investigation of inner time-consciousness is nothing apart from an investigation into the temporality of prereflective self-awareness.

One of the problems confronting Husserl's analysis was how to avoid an infinite regress. However, one should not conceive of the relation between the absolute flow (or inner time-consciousness) and the intentional act as if it were a relation between two radically different dimensions in subjectivity. When Husserl claims that the intentional act is constituted in inner time-consciousness, he is not saying that the act is brought to givenness by some other part of subjectivity. Inner time-consciousness is the prereflective self-awareness of the act, and to say that the act is constituted in inner time-consciousness simply means that it is brought to givenness thanks to itself. It is called *inner* consciousness because it belongs *intrinsically* to the very structure of the act itself. To phrase it differently, Husserl's description of the structure of inner time-consciousness, his analysis of the primary-showing-together-with-retention-and-protention (to use Prufer's formulation)[30] is an analysis of the structure of the prereflective self-manifestation of our acts and experiences. Thus, Husserl's position is relatively unequivocal. The intentional act is conscious of something different from itself, namely, the intentional object. The act is intentional exactly because it permits hetero-manifestation. But the act also manifests itself. The object is given through the act, and if there were no awareness of the act, the object could not appear. Thus, apart from being intentional, the act is also characterized by its "inner consciousness," "*Urbewußtsein,*" or "impressional conscious-ness," to mention three different terms for one and the same.[31] We are not dealing with a particular intentional act, but with a pervasive dimension of self-manifestation, and it is exactly this which precedes and founds reflective self-awareness.[32]

Is it possible to specify the nature of this primary self-manifestation, this absolute experiencing, any further? The terminology used, and the fact that we are confronted with an unthematic, implicit, immediate, and passive occurrence, which is by no means initiated, regulated or controlled by the ego, suggests that we are dealing with a type of passive *self-affection.*[33] This interpretation is occasionally adopted by Husserl, for instance, in the manuscript C 10 (1931), where he speaks of self-affection as an essential, pervasive, and necessary feature of the functioning ego, and in the manuscript C 16 (1931–33), where he adds that I am ceaselessly (*unaufhörlich*) affected by myself.[34]

I will return more explicitly to the problem of self-affection later on, but now it should be stressed that we are dealing with a kind of self-manifestation which lacks the ordinary structure of appearance. There is no distinction between subject and object, nor between the dative and genitive of appearing. On the contrary, it is a kind of self-manifestation, a fundamental *shining*, without which it would be meaningless to speak of the dative of appearance. Nothing can be present *to me* unless I am *self*-aware.[35]

The analysis of the structure of this self-manifestation is further elaborated in Husserl's renowned analysis of the double intentionality of the retention, its so-called *Quer-* and *Längsintentionalität* (transverse and longitudinal intentionality). If $P(t)$ is the primal impression of a tone, then $P(t)$ is retained in a retention $Rp_{(t)}$ when a new primal impression appears. As the notation makes clear, however, it is not only the conscious tone which is retained, but also the primal impression. Each retention is not only retaining the preceding tone, but also the preceding primal impression. That is, the actual phase of the flow is not only retaining the tone which has just been, but also the elapsing phase of the flow.[36] Whereas the first permits us to experience an enduring temporal object, that is, accounts for the constitution of the identity of the object in a manifold of temporal phases, the latter provides us with temporal self-awareness:

> Our regard can be directed, in the one case, *through* the phases that "coincide" in the continuous progression of the flow and that function as intentionalities of the tone. But our regard can also be aimed *at* the flow, at a section of the flow, at the passage of the flowing consciousness from

the beginning of the tone to its end. Every adumbration of consciousness of the species "retention" possesses a double intentionality: one serves for the constitution of the immanent object, of the tone; it is this intentionality that we call "primary memory" of the (just sensed) tone, or more precisely, just retention of the tone. The other intentionality is constitutive of the unity of this primary memory in the flow; namely, retention, because it is a still-being-conscious, a consciousness that holds back—because it is, precisely, retention—is also retention of the elapsed tone-retention: in its process of being continuously adumbrated in the flow, it is continuous retention of the continuously preceding phases.[37]

Whereas the flow's constitution of the duration of its object is called its *Querintentionalität*, the flow's awareness (of) its own streaming unity is called its *Längsintentionalität*[38] and, although the latter carries the name intentionality, it would be tantamount to a decisive misunderstanding of Husserl's theory if one were to identify it with a type of object-intentionality.[39] Husserl's account of the *Längsintentionalität* does not succumb to the lure of the reflection theory, but is in fact an analysis of the prereflective self-manifestation of consciousness. It is because consciousness is characterized by this self-manifestation that it is possible to escape the infinite regress of the reflection theory: "The flow of the consciousness that constitutes immanent time not only *exists* but is so remarkably and yet intelligibly fashioned that a self-appearance of the flow necessarily exists in it, and therefore the flow itself must necessarily be apprehensible in the flowing. The self-appearance of the flow does not require a second flow; on the contrary, it constitutes itself as a phenomenon in itself."[40]

This central passage from *Zur Phänomenologie des inneren Zeitbewußtseins* has not been overlooked by Husserl's critics, but it has for instance been met with the argument that it simply reproduces the mistakes inherent in Brentano's account.[41] Cramer argues that if one claims that the stream of consciousness is characterized by self-appearance, then one must necessarily ask a further question, namely, what it is that appears when the stream appears to itself. According to Cramer the only answer possible is that the stream appears to itself as a self-appearing stream, and on that background he claims that the notion of self-appearance is redundant, and its explication circular. Whereas a variant of this criticism seemed appropriate when it came to Brentano's theory, since it conceived of self-awareness as a (secondary) object-awareness, I am not convinced of its pertinence when it comes to Husserl. On the one hand, Cramer explicitly identifies Husserl's notion of self-appearance with a kind of "quasi-perception,"[42] but he thereby overlooks one of the decisive differences between Husserl's and Brentano's accounts. On the other hand, Cramer seems to expect something from a theory of self-awareness that it qua explication of a fundamental phenomenon *sui generis* will ever be prevented from providing—namely, a decomposition of the phenomenon into more basic elements without self-awareness.

If we compare the two interpretations, it is undisputed that Husserl's analysis of time-consciousness takes its point of departure in the analysis of our consciousness of an immanent temporal object. But then the interpretations already diverge. The standard interpretation claims that Husserl's analysis of our consciousness of an immanent tone is an investigation of our consciousness of a subjective experience, namely, the sensing of the tone, and not an investigation of our consciousness of the sensed tone itself. Thus, Husserl from the very start is investigating *temporal self-awareness*. Husserl's analysis of *Querintentionalität* is consequently taken to be an analysis of the way in which we are (prereflectively) aware of our enduring experiences and intentional acts, whereas his analysis of the *Längsintentionalität* is an analysis of the self-givenness of the absolute flow.[43] That is, Husserl's analysis of the shining of the absolute flow is taken to be an analysis of an additional, deeper, and more basic form of self-manifestation.

Since I am incapable of making any sense out of the distinction between the prereflective givenness of our experiences, and the deeper self-givenness of the flow, I am suggesting a different reading. As I see it, Husserl's analysis of the immanent tone is an analysis of the temporal givenness of an intentional correlate, that is, of the sensed rather than of the sensing.[44] The reason why Husserl chooses to speak of an immanent tone rather than of a transcendent tone, such as the whistle of a locomotive, is not because he wishes to shift the focus from the temporal givenness of the (proto-)object to the temporal givenness of the experience of the object, but simply because he wishes to focus strictly on the temporal dimension of the object. If he had started out with an analysis of the givenness of a note of a violin, he would straightaway have had to account for the constitution of an intersubjectively given spatiotemporal object, and although his analysis ultimately aims at doing exactly that, it would have been too complex a point of departure. Thus, Husserl's first question is: How do we experience an enduring (proto-)object? Through his analysis of this problem he is led to a more fundamental question: How is our experience of a temporal object itself given? It is only at this point that the issue of self-awareness is introduced. And Husserl's investigation of the self-givenness of the flow is exactly an investigation into the prereflective self-manifestation of the act, and not an analysis of some further, additional self-awareness. Thus, I think that Husserl's analysis of the *Querintentionalität* is intended as an analysis of the way in which we experience enduring intentional (proto-)objects, whereas his analysis of the *Längsintentionalität* is intended as an account of the primary self-manifestation of the experiences of these intentional objects.

Different Forms of Temporality

So far I have argued that the prereflective self-awareness of the act and the nonobjectifying self-manifestation of the absolute flow are one and the same. Occasionally, however, Husserl does in fact claim that the act is given as a temporal object in subjective time. But how is this assertion to be understood? When does consciousness appear to itself as a *temporal object*? Perhaps one can clarify the issue by asking the following question: When are we entitled to call something an object, i.e., when do we experience something as an object? According to Husserl, it is only when something is experienced as being in possession of a minimal sort of transcendence that it is experienced as an object. It is only when we experience something as a unity in a multiplicity of adumbrations, as an identity across differences, that is, as something that transcends its actual appearance, that we are dealing with objects. It is when we recognize that what we are now experiencing is something we have experienced before that we recognize we are confronted with something transcendent that retained its identity through changing experiences.[45]

This definition does not exclude the existence of immanent objects. Although an immanent tone-data in contrast to a spatiotemporal object does not have a multiplicity of coexisting profiles—at each moment it has only one—it has a temporal extension, and can consequently appear in a series of changing temporal phases.[46] This permits us to distinguish between the appearance and that which appears, and consequently to experience the immanent tone as a unity in the flow of its temporal phases, as an identity across differences, that is, as an object.

Occasionally Husserl argues that we are only confronted with objects the moment we carry out explicit acts of identification.[47] If that had been the case it would certainly have been preposterous to suggest that our experiences were already prereflectively given as inner temporal objects. But although Husserl might be right in claiming that the act-transcendent identity of the object is only *thematically* given when we perform syntheses of identification, i.e., syntheses in which the object of different acts is related and compared and identified as being the same, there is certainly also room for the notion of a passive type of identity-fusion on the prepredicative and precategorial level. The taking of several different appearances as being appearances of one and the same object is the result of an *aesthetic synthesis*, that is, it is an achievement of sensibility and the implicit "synthesis of recognition" of time-consciousness,[48] not an intellectual process of identification.[49]

When my intentional act is given as an identity across differences, when it is given as a clearly demarcated enduring unity in a manifold of temporal phases, and as something with a temporal *location* that one can return to again and again, it is given as a temporal object. We are, as Husserl puts it, dealing with a self-objectivation when our experiences are located in immanent time.[50] But to repeat the question: When does this self-objectivation occur? One possibility is to claim that the constitution of the act as a temporal object is an automatic outcome of the retentional modification. This interpretation can, for instance, find support in the manuscript C 5, where Husserl writes: "Im urphänomenalen Strömen der Urpräsenz transzendiert sich dieses Leben selbst, es konstituiert die immanente Zeit, den Erlebnisstrom mit seiner Vergangenheit und Zukunft."[51] In short, the *Zeitigung* should be regarded as a self-ontification. It is when the previous primal impression is retained in the retention that the act is constituted as a temporal entity, wherefore the entire *retentional sequence* must be regarded as existing in immanent, i.e., constituted time.[52]

However, this theory is also faced with difficulties. To claim that the retentional modification is in itself a constitution of the act as a temporal *object* is to interpret the relation between the actual and the retentionally backward sinking phase of the experience as a kind of objectifying, reflective self-awareness. For a number of already familiar reasons this is an unacceptable account. But it is also a theory that Husserl himself—despite the above-quoted passage—seems to reject. Not only does he point out that it is necessary to distinguish the functioning ego with its Living Present (*lebendige Gegenwart*), comprised of primal impression *and* retentional horizon, from the temporal system of objectified consciousness,[53] but he also states that the retention does *not* turn the elapsed phase of the experience into an object. He argues that that which is passively retained remains preontical; he denies that the sequence of primal impressions is a temporal sequence; and he writes that the unity of the flow is constituted in the flow itself as a *quasi*temporal order by virtue of the continuity of retentional modifications.[54]

But in this case, the question remains. When does consciousness appear to itself as a *temporal object*? My suggestion is quite simple. We only experience our acts as temporal *objects* when we reflect, be it in an ordinary act of reflection or in the particular reflection in recollection. When this happens, the identity of the act appears across the differences in givenness. If I remember my joy of yesterday, it is the very experience which I had yesterday that I now recall and re-present. The identity of the experience is established across a change in temporal givenness. If I reflect upon my present perception, the perception is given as that which remains identical across the differences in respectively prereflective and reflective givenness, i.e., it is given as the *same* as what was previously experienced unthematically. It is only in reflection, where we are confronted with a relation between two different acts, the reflecting and the reflected, that the latter can appear as transcendent vis-à-vis the first. On the prereflective level, where there is only one experience, it cannot appear as a temporal object, since it cannot appear as transcendent in relation to itself.

Our original prereflective awareness of the stream of consciousness is an experience of a unity, and it is only reflectively that we discriminate the different moments of the stream. Originally, consciousness does not appear to itself chopped up in bits. It is nothing jointed; it simply flows.[55] As Michalski puts it, to isolate one act is not like detaching one independent element from another, but rather like tearing off a fragment of material from a whole that is thereby left in tatters.[56] The relation between two acts must rather be likened to the relation between two waves in the same stream than to two wagons in the same train: "Bewußtsein ist eine Einheit. Ein Akt ist nichts für sich, er ist Welle im Bewußtseinsstrom."[57] It is only due to a special apprehension, namely, when we thematize the acts, that they are constituted as enduring objects in subjective time.[58] When we reflect, we impose a new temporal form upon our experiences, they are made into subjective objects and posited in or injected into sequential time. To quote Brand: "Indem die lebendig-strömende Gegenwart auf sich selbst zurückkommt, ontifiziert sie sich zum 'strömenden Bewußtsein' d.h. sie nimmt sich selbst zum Thema und sieht sich nun selbst strukturiert nach den möglichen Unterschieden des Jetzt, des Soebengewesen und des Kommend zugleich in ihrer Folge und Deckung."[59] We consequently end up with the following schema:

> Absolute flow — functioning subjectivity — prereflective self-awareness
> Subjective time — thematized subjectivity — reflective self-awareness

Fortunately, it is not difficult to find passages where Husserl himself seems to favor exactly such an account. In §37 of *Zur Phänomenologie des inneren Zeitbewußtseins*, Husserl writes that our perceptual act or perceptual consciousness is not in immanent time, is not a constituted temporal unity, but a moment of or a wave in the self-temporalizing, flowing experiencing itself.[60] In a later supplementary text in the same volume, he writes: "Therefore *sensation*—if by 'sensation' we understand *consciousness* (not the immanent enduring red, tone, and so forth, hence not that which is sensed)—and likewise *retention, recollection, perception*, etc. are *nontemporal*; that is to say, *nothing in immanent time.*"[61] But whereas Husserl claims that our acts (be they perceptions, recollections, anticipations, imaginations, judgments, etc.), qua absolute constituting consciousness, reveal themselves, but not as immanently given temporal objects, he also quite explicitly writes that the very same acts appear in subjective time with duration and temporal location qua *objects of reflection.*[62] In a manuscript from 1917, one finds the following formulation: "Das letzte Bewußtsein ist nichts anderes als der ursprüngliche Fluss, bevor sich ein reflektierendes Blick darauf richtet."[63] In a similar vein, Husserl writes that it is necessary to distinguish the reflected pole, which is in time, from the living, functioning pole, which is not in time.[64]

> We must therefore distinguish: the prephenomenal being of experiences, their being before we have turned toward them in reflection, and their being as phenomena. When we turn toward the experience attentively and grasp it, it takes on a new mode of being; it becomes "differentiated," "singled out." And this differentiating is precisely nothing other than the grasping [of the experience]; and the differentiatedness is nothing other than being-grasped, being the object of our turning-towards.[65]

> Aber meine thematische Erfahrung vom Ich und Bewußtsein ist in ihrer Art selbst Stiftung einer Fortgeltung—eines bleibenden Seins, des Seins des Immanenten.[66]

> Müssen wir nicht sagen, natürlich ist es das "apperzipierende" Ich, durch das der Strom gegenständlich wird. Aber das bloße Strömen wird eben erst durch das Betrachten etc. gegenständlich und durch die Vermöglichkeiten des "immer wieder." Das "Vor-Sein" des strömenden Seins ist eben "jederzeit" gegenständlich zu machen und ist nur so transzendental zu beschreiben.[67]

Obviously, this position raises several questions. One of them I will return to and attempt to answer in chapter 10: If reflection changes the givenness of our prereflective experiences, how then are we to achieve insight into their prereflective structure? As it will turn out, it is necessary to distinguish between different types of reflection. Reflection permits us to differentiate, discriminate, and demarcate, but this differentiation is not necessarily imposed from without, is not necessarily foreign to the experience in question.

A different question concerns the relation between the temporality of the thematized acts and the temporality of lived consciousness. So far, I have denied that our acts are prereflectively given as inner objects in subjective time, but this is not to say that their manifestation is strictly atemporal. On the contrary, even if it is acknowledged that the insertion of the experiences into sequential time is not merely an automatic outcome of the very streaming, but the result of a particular objectifying performance,[68] it is hard to deny that the very prereflective manifestation involves some kind of streaming unification: "This unity becomes constituted originally through the fact of the flow itself; that is to say, it is the flow's proper essence not only simply to exist but to be a unity of experience and to be given in internal consciousness, in which a ray of attention can extend toward it. (This ray is not itself an object of attention. It enriches but does not alter the stream to be considered; it rather 'fixes' it and makes it objective.)"[69]

Ultimately, reflection presupposes the constitution of a temporal horizon. It would be impossible without the ecstatic unity of the flow. When reflection sets in, it initially grasps something that has just elapsed, namely, the motivating prereflective phase of the flow. The reason why this phase can still be thematized by the subsequent reflection is that it does not disappear, i.e., it is not cut off from the Living Present but remains united with it through retention. But the unity in question is not the unity of a temporal object, is not the product of an identification or ontification, but a lived unity established through the passive synthesis of the streaming.[70] When an experience occurs, it automatically acquires an unchangeable location in the stream. I can only locate an act in recollection if it already has a position. As times goes by, it will naturally become more and more distant, but it will forever keep its temporal position. It will always remain after the acts that preceded it and prior to the acts that succeded it. I deny neither this nor the fact that the acts are intrinsically temporal. But I do deny that the acts are prereflectively given as distinct enduring objects, as objects that arise, endure, and perish. Thus one must distinguish between the passive self-constitution, self-temporalization, and self-unification of the lived stream and its subsequent reflective objectivation. As Husserl puts it: "The intuitional phases [*Anschauungsphasen*] blend into one another continuously, but this continuity is given only in a reflexive perception that objectivates the identifying flow."[71]

So far I have argued against the attempt to distinguish between two different types of prereflective self-awareness, between the constituted givenness of our acts and experiences and the self-manifestation of the absolute flow. The absolute flow of experiencing simply is the prereflective self-manifestation of our experiences. However, to make this point is not to deny that there are good reasons for insisting upon the *difference* between our singular and transitory acts and the abiding dimension of experiencing, between *die Erlebnisse* and *das Erleben*.[72] In fact there seems to be one excellent reason. After all, it makes perfect sense to say that I had an experience of joy which has now passed. I might even completely forget about it and only recall it much later. But whereas the act can become past and absent, the dimension of self-manifestation that allows for presence and absence cannot itself become past and absent. Whereas we live through a number of different experiences, our self-awareness remains as an unchanging dimension. To use a striking image by James, it stands permanent, like the rainbow on the waterfall, with its own quality unchanged by the events that stream through it.[73] In other words, the moment we adopt a diachronous perspective, it becomes not only legitimate but highly appropriate to distinguish the strict singularity of the *lebendige Gegenwart* from the plurality of changing experiences.[74] To use a nice formulation by Klawonn, the latter are exposed in it.[75] It is their exposure in this field of first-personal givenness which makes them mine. And of course this exposure is not something incidental to their being, but that which makes them conscious subjective experiences.

But once again, it would be fundamentally misleading to imagine an empty or pure field of self-manifestation on which different experiences subsequently make their entry. The absolute flow has no self-manifestation of its own, but *is* the very self-manifestation of the experiences. As already mentioned, Husserl calls the acts waves in the self-temporalizing flowing experiencing itself. Prior to reflection, there is no awareness of inner objects, and there is no distinction between the givenness of the act and the self-manifestation of the flow. The prereflective self-awareness of the experience is nothing but the perpetual self-manifestation of the flow. They are one and the same. Inner time-consciousness is simply the name for the prereflective self-awareness of our acts, and this flowing self-awareness is not itself an intentional act, a temporal unity or an immanent object,[76] but a pervasive dimension intrinsic to consciousness. As for the enduring intentional acts, they cannot be separated from the flow either, since they are nothing but its own *reflective* self-manifestation. That is, the absolute flow of experiencing and the constituted stream of reflectively thematized acts are not two separate flows, but simply two different manifestations of one and the same flow. Thus Husserl can write: "Wir sagen, ich bin, der ich bin in meinem Leben. Und dieses Leben ist Erleben, seine reflektiv als einzelne abzuhebenden Bestandstücke heißen rechtmäßig 'Erlebnisse', sofern in ihnen irgendetwas erlebt ist."[77] Through inner time-consciousness one is aware both of the stream of consciousness (prereflective self-awareness), of the acts as demarcated temporal objects in subjective time (reflective self-awareness), and of the transcendent objects in objective time (intentional consciousness).

Husserl alternately speaks of absolute time-constituting consciousness as an unchangeable form of presence (as a *nunc stans*) and as an absolute flux.[78] Regardless of which description one choses—and ultimately both are attempts to capture the unique givenness of this dimension—it should be obvious why one must not only avoid speaking of the absolute flow as if it were a temporal object, but also avoid interpreting the flow as a sequence of temporally distinct acts, phases, or elements.

> Diese strömend lebendige Gegenwart ist nicht das, was wir sonst auch schon transzendental-phänomenologisch als Bewußtseinsstrom oder Erlebnisstrom bezeichneten. Es ist überhaupt kein "Strom" gemäß dem Bild, als ein eigentlich zeitliches (oder gar zeiträumliches) Ganzes, das in der Einheit einer zeitlichen Extension ein kontinuierlich-sukzessives individuelles Dasein hat (in seinen unterscheidbaren Strecken und Phasen durch diese Zeitformen individuiert). Die strömend lebendige Gegenwart ist "kontinuierliches" Strömendsein und doch nicht in einem Auseinander-Sein, nicht in raumzeitlicher (welträumlicher), nicht in "immanent"-zeitlicher Extension Sein; also in keinem Außereinander, das Nacheinander heißt—Nacheinander in dem Sinne eines Stellen-Außereinander in einer eigentlich so zu nennenden Zeit.[79]

Inner time-consciousness cannot be temporal in the empirical sense of the word, it cannot be reduced to a succession of mental states. Not only would such a succession not enable us to become conscious of succession, it would also call for yet another consciousness which could be conscious of this succession, etc., and we would be unable to avoid an infinite regress.[80] As Husserl writes, it makes no sense to say of the time-constituting phenomena that they are present and that they have endured, that they succeed each other, or are copresent, etc. In short, they are not "present," "past," or "future" in the way empirical objects are.[81] Inner time-consciousness is a field of experiencing, a dimension of manifestation, which contains all three temporal dimensions. The structure of this field of experiencing (primal impression–retention–protention) is not temporally extended. The retentions and protentions are not past or future in regard to the primal impression, nor are they simultaneous, as long as "simultaneity" is used in its ordinary sense. They are "together" or "co-actual" with it.

Ultimately, the structure of constituting time-consciousness cannot be adequately grasped using temporal concepts derived from that which it constitutes. Thus, in a certain way inner time-consciousness is atemporal,[82] but only in the sense that it is not intratemporal. Time-constituting consciousness is not *in* time, but it is not merely a consciousness *of* time; it is itself a form of temporality.[83] Temporality constitutes the infrastructure of consciousness. Consciousness is inherently temporal, and it is as temporal that it is prereflectively aware of itself. Thus, although the field of experiencing neither has a temporal location nor a temporal extension, and although it does not last and never becomes past, it is not a static supratemporal principle, but a living pulse (*Lebenspuls*) with a certain temporal density and articulation and variable width, i.e., it might, as Larrabee has put it, stretch.[84] In fact, the metaphor of *stretching* might be appropriate not only as a characterization of the temporal ecstasis, but also as a description of the *Längsintentionalität*, since it avoids the potentially misleading and naturalizing talk of the flow as a sequence or succession of changing impressions, slices, or phases.

Inner time-consciousness, as the absolute dimension of manifestation, is an ecstatic unity of presencing (primal impression) and absencing (retention-protention).[85] This is what allows it to constitute objects with temporal duration, but this is also what allows it (in a quite different way) to reveal itself in its very stretching. The self-manifestation of consciousness has a temporal horizon. Only that type of ecstasis permits it to be what it is, a Living Present, a streaming self-awareness. Only that type of infrastructure allows for temporal self-awareness, for reflection and recollection.

Derrida on Retention

Husserl's analysis of inner time-consciousness certainly leaves a score of problems unsolved. Nevertheless, I hope it has become clear that (1) Husserl takes the elucidation of the nature of self-awareness to be of crucial significance for phenomenology; (2) he operates with the notion of a prereflective temporal self-awareness; and (3) he ascribes it a differentiated infrastructure.

One of the questions raised by Husserl's account concerns the notion of *Längsintentionalität*. If the self-manifestation of consciousness takes place through the retentional modification, are we then only self-aware of that which has just passed? Is consciousness initially unconscious, and does it only gain self-awareness the moment it is retained? Let me expand the focus a bit in order to throw light upon this problem.

To a certain extent, Derrida's contribution to a clarification of self-awareness can be located in his persistent attempt to problematize, if not to say undermine, the notion of *presence*. Traditional metaphysics defined Being as identity in presence. But although Husserlian phenomenology attempted to move beyond the conceptual framework of this metaphysics of presence, it never really succeeded, according to Derrida,[86] but remained convinced that identity is more basic than difference, proximity more original than distance, and presence prior to every kind of absence and negativity. This is not only clear from its use of the notion of evidence—the measure of truth and validity—which is defined as intuitive self-givenness, but also from its understanding of transcendental subjectivity, which is conceived as pure self-presence, as a self-sufficient immanence, purified from all types of exteriority.[87]

Derrida now attempts to demonstrate that all meaning, being, and manifestation, including the self-presence of subjectivity, far from being original and simple, are products of an irreducible process of differentiation, and therefore always already furnished with a reference to alterity. Should this demonstration prove to be convincing, Husserl's argumentation, and the entire foundation of a metaphysics of presence would be threatened.[88]

Derrida's claim that Husserl conceives of absolute subjectivity as a self-sufficient immanence purified from all types of exteriority and alterity is highly problematic, but it is interesting to notice that Derrida's subsequent criticism is decisively inspired by his reading of Husserl. It was Husserl's own analyses, especially his reflections on the structure of inner time-consciousness which, according to Derrida, made it clear that it is impossible to speak of the simple self-identity of the present.[89] It was Husserl's own investigation of the role played by the *retention* which raised serious doubts about the adequacy of the *principle of principles*.[90]

According to Derrida it would be impossible to understand the relation between retention and primal impression, and to comprehend the perpetual retentional modification, if the primal impression were a simple and completely self-sufficient ground and source. The primal impression is always already furnished with a temporal density, and the retentional modification is not a subsequent addendum to, but an integrated part of the primal impression. Rather than being a simple, undivided unity, self-awareness is characterized by an original complexity, by a historical heritage. The present can only appear to itself as present due to the retentional modification. Presence is differentiation; it *is* only in its intertwining with absence.[91] "One then sees quickly that the presence of the perceived present can appear as such only inasmuch as it is *continuously compounded* with a nonpresence and nonperception, with primary memory and expectation (retention and protention). Neither are these nonperceptions added to, nor do they *occasionally* accompany, the actually perceived now; they are essentially and indispensably involved in its possibility."[92]

It consequently proves necessary to distinguish the pure primal impression, which is an empty a priori possibility, a theoretical limit-case, and the phenomenological present, which only appears to itself as genetically complex. We might infer that there must be something like a primal impression, but it is never experienced as such. The primal impression will always be gone before it can be fixed by consciousness. To be punctual and to be experienceable are exclusive determinations. Thus, every self-aware experience contains retention, that is, the irreducible *alterity of the past*.[93] For this reason it is necessary to ascribe a transcendental, that is, a constitutive significance, to a nonpresence in self-awareness.[94]

To be more precise, self-presence must be conceived as an originary *difference* or *interlacing* between now and not-now, due to the intimate relation between primal impression and retention. Consciousness is never given in a full and instantaneous self-presence, but presents itself to itself across the difference between now and not-now. Self-awareness is possible thanks to the retentional trace. It emerges on the background of a nonidentity, and it is haunted by the alterity of the absent and always presupposes an *othering*.[95] In Lévinas's words, the self-manifestation of subjectivity implies a temporal dephasing; it is a self-presence across a primal fracture.[96]

> As soon as we admit this continuity of the now and the not-now, perception and nonperception, in the zone of primordiality common to primordial impression and primordial retention, we admit the other into the self-identity of the *Augenblick*; nonpresence and nonevidence are admitted into the *blink of the instant*. There is a duration to the blink, and it closes the eye. This alterity is in fact the condition for presence.[97]

> Dans l'identité absolue du sujet avec lui-même la dialectique temporelle constitue *a priori* l'altérité. Le sujet s'apparaît originairement comme tension du Même et de l'Autre. Le thème d'une intersubjectivité transcendantale instaurant la transcendance au cœur de l'immanence absolue de l' "ego" est déjà appelé. Le dernier fondement de l'objectivité de la conscience intentionnelle n'est pas l'intimité du "Je" à soi-même mais le Temps ou l'Autre, ces deux formes d'une existence irréductible à une essence, étrangère au sujet théorique, toujours constituées avant lui,

mais en même temps seules conditions de possibilité d'une constitution de soi et d'une apparition de soi à soi.[98]

These reflections certainly testify to the difficulty of reconciling a temporally articulate self-awareness with an absolute irrelational self-coincidence. But they also have some rather disturbing implications. Although the retentional self-manifestation of consciousness is prereflective and nonobjectifying, it is also *delayed*, since consciousness appears to itself not as it is, but as it has just been. There thus appears to be a blind spot in the core of subjectivity, i.e., the field of presencing is centered around a fundamental absence: Initially, consciousness is unconscious, and it only gains self-awareness *nachträglich* through the retentional modification.[99]

Insofar as Derrida's reflections are meant to account for the nature of self-awareness, they are faced with some problems that are easily detected on the basis of our discussion in chapters 1 and 2.

At first sight, Derrida's description of the relation between primal impression and retention appears somewhat misleading. Although one might characterize the relation between the primal impression and the retention as a question of internal differentiation, it is strictly speaking erroneous to characterize it with terms like "delay" and "absence." As was pointed out above, the retention and protention are not past or future in regard to the primal impression. They are "together" with it, and the self-manifestation of stretched consciousness consequently possesses the full structure primal impression–retention–protention. Thus, it is not the retention, but that which is given in it, namely, the retained, which is past and absent. Nevertheless, Derrida's characterization retains a certain pertinence the moment one turns to *Längsintentionalität*. It is in this context that one—albeit with an unfortunate and potentially misleading, but practically unavoidable, formulation—can speak of the actual phase of the stream retaining the backward sinking phase of the stream, and it is against that background that it can be claimed that temporal self-manifestation takes place across a primal fracture, and that it includes the alterity of the past.

However, if the self-manifestation of consciousness only takes place in and through the retentional modification, there will only be self-awareness of the just-past phase of the stream; the initial phase of consciousness will only become conscious when it is retained. But how does this agree with our conviction that we are in fact aware of our experiences the moment they occur? And how can we be at all aware of something *as* past, unless we are also aware of something present against which we can contrast it? If self-presence is only constituted in the difference between retention and primal impression, there will be nothing left to explain this difference or, more correctly, there will be nothing left to explain our experience of this difference. It will be a merely postulated difference with no experiential basis. Thus, self-awareness will ultimately become a product of an unconscious difference.[100]

Rather than leading to an expansion of the field of self-presence, Derrida's description of the role of the retention threatens to undermine the possibility of self-awareness from within. To claim that self-awareness is not a manifestation *sui generis*, but the product of a decentered play of unconscious structural differences, is basically to face all the problems of the reflection theory once again.

Husserl himself was well aware of these problems. He anticipated Derrida's line of thought, and although he occasionally seriously considered it,[101] he ultimately and quite explicitly rejected it:

> What about the beginning-phase of an experience that is in the process of becoming constituted? Does it also come to be given only on the basis of retention, and would it be "unconscious" if no retention were to follow it? We must say in response to this question: The beginning-phase can become an object only *after* it has elapsed in the indicated way, by means of retention and reflection (or reproduction). But if it were intended *only* by retention, then what confers on it the label "now" would remain incomprehensible. At most, it could be distinguished negatively from its modifications as that one phase that does not make us retentionally conscious of any preceding phase; but the beginning-phase is by all means characterized in consciousness in quite positive fashion. It is just nonsense to talk about an "unconscious" content that would only subsequently become conscious. Consciousness is necessarily *consciousness* in each of its phases. Just as the retentional phase is conscious of the preceding phase without making it into an object, so too the primal datum is already intended—specifically, in the original form of the "now"—without its being something objective.[102]

Thus, Husserl's analysis is not meant to imply that consciousness only becomes aware of itself through the retention. Husserl explicitly insists that the *retentional* modification presupposes an *impressional* (primary, original, and immediate) self-manifestation, not only because consciousness is as such self-given, but also because a retention of an unconscious content is impossible.[103] The retention retains that which has just appeared, and if nothing appears, there is nothing to retain.[104] Thus, retention presupposes self-awareness. It is this self-awareness which is retentionally modified when $P(t)$ is transformed into $Rp_{(t)}$. The tone is given not only as having-just-been, but as having-just-been *experienced*.[105]

This clarification allows for a final remark about the relationship between the *impressional* self-manifestation and the *Längsintentionalität*. We are not dealing with two independent and separate types of prereflective self-awareness, but with two different descriptions of the same basic phenomenon. As already mentioned, Husserl uses the term *Längsintentionalität* to designate the absolute self-manifestation of consciousness, but this self-givenness does not merely concern the elapsing phases, but takes its point of departure in an immediate impressional self-manifestation. Conversely, this impressional self-manifestation stretches to include the retentionally given. As Husserl writes, "Das impressionale Bewußtsein rechnen wir in dieser Hinsicht so weit, als die noch lebendige Retention reicht."[106]

Henry on Impressionality

Whereas Derrida argues that Husserl failed to draw the full implications of his discovery of the retentional modification, we find the exact opposite criticism in Henry, namely, that Husserl assigned a far too great significance to the work of the retention.

Whereas post-Husserlian phenomenology has generally tried to rectify what was believed to be an imbalance in Husserl's account of the relation between immanence and transcendence, namely his disregard of *exteriority*, Henry has accused Husserl of never having managed to disclose the true *interiority* of subjectivity in a sufficiently radical and pure manner. Thus, according to Henry, the basic problem in Husserl's phenomenology is not that it somehow remained unable to free itself from immanence, but on the contrary, that it kept introducing external elements into its analysis of this immanence. As Henry even puts it, it is downright absurd to accuse Husserl of having advocated a philosophy of pure presence, since Husserl never managed to conceive of a presence liberated from horizontality.[107]

Henry takes consciousness to be through and through impressional, not in the sense that it is always affected by impressions, but in the sense that its very being is constituted by its impressionality, that is, by its pure and immediate self-manifestation.[108] As we have already seen, Husserl advocates a similar position. He also operates with the notion of an *impressional* self-manifestation, and claims that our experiences are impressions in the sense that we are conscious of them as impressed.[109] But although Husserl did realize that impressionality is the basic mode of self-manifestation, Henry accuses him of taking this impressionality to be a type of manifestation which is constituted in the temporal flow.[110] That is, instead of conceiving of impressionality as a truly immanent, nonhorizontal, and nonecstatic self-manifestation, Husserl treats it as a givenness in inner time-consciousness, that is, as a givenness which is intrinsically caught up in the ecstatic-centered structure of primal impression–retention–protention. According to Henry, however, this conception is ruinous to a correct understanding of impressionality. It implies that the primary self-manifestation is retentionally mediated, and it consequently furnishes impressionality with a rupture and an exteriority which is completely foreign to its nature: "Dès ce moment, en effet, la donation extatique de l'impression dans la conscience interne du temps a remplacé son auto-donation dans l'impressionalité et la question de l'impression est perdue de vue."[111] Against this background it is hardly surprising that Henry also objects strongly to Derrida's interpretation of the relation between primal impression and retention. To claim that the self-manifestation of the first is due to the intervention of the latter and that subjectivity only gains self-presence in temporal adumbrations is in Henry's eyes tantamount to a complete nihilation of subjectivity. Henry certainly acknowledges that the double intentionality of the retention is an ecstatic happening in inner time-consciousness, but in contrast to other phenomenologists, he does not take inner time-consciousness to be the original self-manifestation of subjectivity; instead, he understands it as the primary self-objectivation.[112] In reality, the double intentionality of the retention presupposes the impressional self-manifestation, and the principal question pertaining to the self-constitution of subjectivity consequently concerns this impressionality. Thus, Henry can reproach classical phenomenology for having been so preoccupied with the analysis of the self-objectivation of transcendental life that it overlooked the truly fundamental level of self-manifestation.[113]

According to Henry, the dimension of primary self-manifestation is nonecstatic, nontemporal, and nonhorizontal.[114] It is nonhorizontal insofar as the manifestation does not presuppose or entail a reference to anything transcendent or absent. It is nonecstatic in the sense that the living ego never appears to itself across a recollection or oblivion, and it is immediate in the strict sense of being neither mediated nor delayed. We are ultimately dealing with a *self-affection* characterized by its complete unified self-adherence and self-coincidence,[115] and neither is this unity constituted (by anything else) nor is it extended in protentions and retentions.[116] Thus, in contrast to Heidegger and Merleau-Ponty, Henry does not conceive of self-affection as a temporal self-positing, but as something taking place prior to the self-temporalization. As Yamagata points out, the passivity of the impressional self-affection is by no means to be conflated with the passivity of the retentional modification. The latter deploys a horizon and a fracture which are absent in true immanence.[117] In fact, absolute subjectivity is not a stream of ever-changing impressions, and neither is it characterized by a self-manifestation which keeps disappearing and reappearing due to the fluid nature of the streaming. There is always one and the same Living Present without distance or difference: "Mais ce qui ne change jamais, ce qui ne se rompt jamais, c'est ce qui fait d'elle une impression, c'est en elle l'essence de la vie. Ainsi la vie est-elle variable, comme l'Euripe, de telle façon cependant qu'au travers de ses variations elle ne cesse d'être la Vie, et cela en un sens absolu: c'est la même Vie, la même épreuve de soi qui ne cesse de s'éprouver soi-même, d'être la même absolument, un seul et même Soi."[118] That which remains identical is not an empty and formal Kantian "I think," but the radical and concrete self-affection of life. When our experiences pass, there is something which neither changes nor disappears, namely, the everlasting self-affection.[119]

To complicate matters somewhat, Henry has recently deviated from his firm declaration that the self-manifestation of subjectivity is completely nontemporal. As he admits, the very notion of self-affection is not a static but a dynamic notion. Self-affection understood as the process of affecting and being affected is not the rigid self-identity of an object, but a subjective *movement*,[120] and this movement can best be described as the self-temporalization of subjectivity. But, as he then adds, we are still dealing with a unique form of temporalization, which is absolutely immanent, nonecstatic, and nonhorizontal.[121] We are dealing with an affective temporality, and even though it seems to involve a perpetual movement and change, nothing is changed. The living ego does not have a past, a future, or a present. It is always the same self affecting itself. Or, more precisely, the self is nothing but the unchanging movement of affective self-manifestation.[122]

Although both Derrida and Henry end up criticizing Husserl's theory of inner time-consciousness, they both remain deeply influenced by his account.[123] To a certain extent, both of them have succeded in articulating elements central to Husserl's position more clearly than Husserl himself. At the same time, however, both also seem to end up defending too radical positions themselves. The question is whether Husserl's own account might not provide us with a sound position that avoids the opposing excesses of both Henry and Derrida.

I have already mentioned some of the problems that Derrida's position seems to be confronted with. Ultimately, his argumentation contains a puzzling tension. On the one hand, he wants to stress the intimate connection and continuity between the primal impression and the retention. It is a falsifying abstraction to speak of them in isolation and separation. But, on the other hand, he also wants to describe the retention as being different from and foreign to the primal impression. Only this will allow him to speak of impressional self-awareness as being mediated and constituted by the alterity of the retention.

When it comes to Henry, I do not think that the difference between his view and Husserl's is quite as marked as Henry himself seems to believe. Husserl would certainly accept that the impressional self-manifestation is immediate in the sense of being neither mediated nor delayed.[124] He would probably also accept Henry's description of the abiding and unchanging character of the absolute dimension of experiencing. The remaining and decisive question is then whether this living field of manifestation has an ecstatic articulation or not. Husserl claims that it does, and he insists—rightly I believe—that it would be impossible to account for the possibility of reflection and recollection if it did not. But after Henry has acknowledged the dynamic and even temporal nature of self-affection, the disagreement has dwindled considerably.[125]

Taken in isolation, the primal impression is not unconscious, and to suggest that is to succumb to a variant of the reflection theory. But when this is said, it should immediately be added that the primal impression taken in isolation is an abstraction and theoretical limit-case. It is never given alone. The concrete and full structure of the Living Present is primal impression–retention–protention.[126] This is the structure of prereflective self-awareness. It is "immediately" given as an ecstatic unity, and is not a gradual, delayed, or mediated process of self-unfolding. Prereflective self-awareness has an internal differentiation and articulation, an original complexity, but to speak of it as being mediated or delayed is to remain determined by a conception which sees primal impression and retention as two different and separate elements. One has to avoid the idea of an instantaneous, nontemporal self-awareness, but one must also stay clear of the notion of a completely fractured time-consciousness which makes both consciousness of the present and of the unity of the stream unintelligible.[127]

6

The Lived Body

So far, the analysis of self-awareness has not included any reference to the body. But is this silence acceptable, or does it not rather express a falsifying abstraction? One of the questions that was raised earlier is how to reconcile the first-person and the third-person perspectives: What is the relation between myself as a subjective, elusive dimension, and myself as an intersubjectively accessible mundane object? I do not think this problem can be unraveled unless the body is taken into consideration, and unless the two following questions have been answered: When are we aware of our body and how are we aware of it?

We have already seen that the subject-use of "I" cannot be substituted by any physical description of myself, but does this imply that the self-awareness it articulates is the self-awareness of a disembodied, immaterial subject? Is our body a mere contingent and external appendage, or is our subjectivity necessarily embodied? The following analysis will reveal that our body can appear in quite different ways, and that the decisive differences between self-manifestation and hetero-manifestation, between self-awareness and object-awareness, between a first-person and a third-person perspective, do not coincide with the traditional difference between mind and body. The body itself can appear in a first-person perspective, and the investigation of this bodily self-appearance belongs as an integrated part to the elucidation of the structure and nature of self-awareness.[1] The analysis of the different forms of bodily appearance will not only match and corroborate our previous analysis of the relation between prereflective and reflective self-awareness. It will also allow for a further elucidation of this relationship and will present us with insights that are indispensable if we are to understand how we can eventually appear to ourselves as mundane objects and interact with Others in a common world.

The Perceiving Body

At the end of chapter 4, I briefly indicated that Husserl's attempt to disclose the nature of prereflective self-awareness led him not only to temporality but also to an examination of the body. Although it is well known that Husserl undertook a systematic and comprehensive analysis of the intentional structure of consciousness, and that he ascribed a privileged status to perception in his survey of the hierarchy of foundation existing between the different types of intentional acts, what is less known is that Husserl also addressed the problem of the constitutive function of the body as early as the lectures *Ding und Raum* from 1907, precisely in connection with an extensive analysis of perception.

A predominant feature in Husserl's analysis of perception is his reflections concerning the adumbrational givenness of the perceptual (spatiotemporal) object. The object is never given in its totality, but always appears from a certain perspective. A careful consideration of this apparently banal fact reveals several implications, which are of direct relevance for an understanding of the importance attributed by Husserl to the body.

Every perspectival appearance is always an appearance of something for someone; there is always a genitive and a dative of manifestation. Can an examination of this appearance provide us with any clues about the nature of the one for whom the object is given? That which appears perspectivally always appears *oriented*. Since it also presents itself from a certain angle and at a certain distance from the observer, the point should be obvious. There is no pure point of view and there is no view from nowhere, there is only an embodied point of view. A subject can only perceive objects and use utentils if it is embodied. A coffee mill is obviously not of much use to a disincarnated spirit, and to listen to a string quartet by Schubert is to enjoy it from a certain perspective and standpoint, be it from the street, in the gallery, or in the first row. Every perspectival appearance presupposes that the experiencing subject has itself a relation to space, and since the subject only possesses a spatial location due to its embodiment,[2] Husserl argues that spatial objects can only appear for and be constituted by embodied subjects. His thesis, however, is not merely that a perspectival appearance presupposes the *existence* of a body, but that it presupposes the *self-givenness* of the body. Let us assume that I am sitting in a restaurant. I wish to begin to eat, and so I pick up the fork. But how can I do that? In order to pick up the fork, I need to know its position in relation to myself.[3] That is, my perception of the object must contain some information about myself, otherwise I would not be able to act on it. On the dinner table, the perceived fork is to the left (of me), the perceived knife is to the right (of me), and the perceived plate and wineglass in front (of me). Every perspectival appearance implies that the embodied perceiver is itself cogiven as the zero point, the absolute indexical "here" in relation to which every appearing object is oriented. As an experiencing, embodied subject I am the point of reference in relation to which each and every of my perceptual objects are uniquely related. I am the center around which and in relation to which (egocentric) space unfolds itself.[4] Husserl consequently claims that bodily self-awareness is a condition of possibility for the constitution of spatial objects, and that every worldly experience is mediated and made possible by our embodiment.[5] This is a type of argumentation encountered in both Merleau-Ponty and Sartre as well (although they—just like Heidegger—tend to emphasize the *practical* nature of primordial spatiality to a larger extent than Husserl):

> the perceptive field refers to a center objectively defined by that reference
> and located *in the very field* which is oriented around it. Only we do not
> see this center as the structure of the perceptive field considered; *we are*
> *the center.* . . . Thus my being-in-the-world, by the sole fact that it *realizes* a
> world, causes itself to be indicated to itself as a being-in-the-midst-of-the-
> world by the world which it realizes. The case could not be otherwise,
> for my being has no other way of entering into contact with the world
> except to *be in the world.* It would be impossible for me to realize a world in
> which I was not and which would be for me a pure object of a surveying
> contemplation. But on the contrary it is necessary that I lose myself in the
> world in order for the world to exist and for me to be able to transcend
> it. Thus to say that I have entered into the world, "come to the world," or
> that there is a world, or that I have a body is one and the same thing.[6]

These reflections concerning the body's function as a condition of possibility for perceptual intentionality are radicalized the moment it is realized how intrinsically intertwined *perception* and *action* are. Not only does action presuppose perception, but our perception is not a matter of passive reception but of active exploration. The body does not merely function as a stable center of orientation. Its *mobility* also contributes decisively to the constitution of perceptual reality. It is not only our point of view, but also our point of departure.[7] As Gibson points out, we see with mobile eyes set in a head that can turn and is attached to a body that can move from place to place; a stationary point of view is only the limiting case of a mobile point of view.[8] In a similar manner, Husserl calls attention to the importance of bodily movements (the movement of the eyes, the touch of the hand, the step of the body, etc.) for the experience of space and spatial objects.[9] Ultimately, he claims that perception is correlated to and accompanied by the self-sensing or self-affection of the moving body. Every visual or tactile appearance is given in correlation to a *kinaesthesis* or *kinaesthetic experiencing*.[10] When I touch the surface of an apple, the apple is given in conjunction with a sensing of finger-movement. When I watch the flight of a bird, the moving bird is given in conjunction with the sensing of eye-movement:

> If we pay attention now purely to the bodily aspect of the things, this obviously exhibits itself perceptively only in seeing, in touching, in hearing, etc., i.e., in visual, tactual, acoustical, and other such aspects. Obviously and inevitably participating in this is our living body, which is never absent from the perceptual field, and specifically its corresponding "organs of perception" (eyes, hands, ears, etc.). In consciousness they play a constant role here; specifically they function in seeing, hearing, etc., together with the ego's motility belonging to them, i.e., what is called kinaesthesis. All kinaestheses, each being an "I move," "I do," [etc.] are bound together in a comprehensive unity—in which kinaesthetic holding-still is [also] a mode of the "I do." Clearly the aspect-exhibitions of whatever body is appearing in perception, and the kinaestheses, are not processes [simply running] alongside each other; rather, they work together in such a way that the aspects have the ontic meaning of, or the validity of, aspects of the body only through the fact that they are those aspects continually required by the kinaestheses—by the kinaesthetic-sensual total situation in each of its working variations of the total kinaesthesis by setting in motion this or that particular kinaesthesis—and that they correspondingly fulfill the requirement.[11]

Traditionally, one has distinguished the exteroceptors (eyes, ears, nose, mouth, skin), which provide us with sensations of external origin; proprioceptors which receive stimuli from muscles, joints, and tendons; and interoceptors (nerve endings in visceral organs), which provide us with sensations of internal organs. But it is important not to conflate Husserl's analysis of kinaesthesis with the discussion of *proprioception* found within sensory physiology or neurophysiology.[12] Husserl is not interested in the physiological makeup of the kinaesthetic experience, in whether or not it depends upon receptors located in muscles, tendons, and joints. The central point is that the kinaestheses contribute to our consciousness of perceptual reality in a radically different way than do our visual or tactile senses.[13]

Husserl's reflections, which in many ways anticipate Gibson's later work, were originally motivated by the following question: What is it that enables us to take several different appearances to be appearances of one and the same object? What is it that enables us to perceive one and the same object in a series of changing appearances? Needless to say, the appearances must share certain intrinsic qualities. The appearance of the underside of a dining table and the appearance of the front of a haystack are too diverse to be taken as appearances of one and the same object. But even a qualitative matching is merely a necessary and not a sufficient condition for their reference to one and the same object. After all, the appearance of the front of one piece of paper and the back of another match excellently, but we nevertheless conceive of them as being appearances of two similar but different objects.[14] A further necessary condition is that the appearances are experienced as belonging to the same continuum. Different appearances are only taken to present us with one and the same object if the appearances can be given in a continuous synthesis, that is, if there exists a sliding transition between them. According to Husserl, this continuity is kinaesthetically constituted. It is only through movement that an object can present itself in a synthetically unified series of appearances.

It is important not to misjudge Husserl's argumentation. He is not merely claiming that the kinaesthesis plays an important role when we are engaged in the exploration of an object, i.e., an exploration that seeks to gain more than one perspective on the object and to perceive several of its sides. Ultimately, Husserl is claiming that every perception of a perspectivally appearing object, including a single frozen perception of the front of an unmoving house, presupposes the contribution of the kinaestheses, and consequently of bodily self-awareness. This is so not only because the front of the house appears in front of me, i.e., refers to my indexical "here," but because of the intrinsic relation between the kinaesthetic system and our horizontal intentionality.

As I have already mentioned, one of the most basic elements in Husserl's theory of intentionality concerns the transcendence of the intentional object. Every object-manifestation allows us to distinguish be-tween the appearance and that which appears. Something only qualifies as an object if it is given as transcending its actual appearance. An object is exactly something that can appear in more than one way, and be given in more than one act. Strictly speaking, the transcendence of the object is only constituted the moment we are confronted with a manifold of different appearances of one and the same object. It is only then that the object appears as an identity across differences, as something that is irreducible to its actual manifestation.

However, even if it is granted that objects are act-transcendent, it might be objected that we in fact both can and do experience them at first glance. If I look at a house, I immediately experience it as a transcendent object, and do not first have to change my perspective on it or remember what it looked like a moment ago in order to establish its identity across visual and temporal adumbrations. This account is correct, but it overlooks the persistent contribution of our horizontal intentionality. Whenever we perceive an object, we are horizontally aware of its absent profiles. Already at first glance we intend the object as something that possesses a multitude of coexisting profiles. Naturally, we might subsequently realize that we were in error, and that what we took to be the front of a house was in reality a mirage, an optical illusion. But the possibility of error does not affect the central point, namely, that to intend something as an object is to intend it as transcendent.

But what has this to do with bodily self-awareness? When I look at something, I am not only in possession of an accompanying awareness of the present position of the body, I am also tacitly aware of the system of movements that I am capable of effectuating and which forms the horizon of the present position. The kinaesthetic experiencing is located in a systematic manifold of possible kinaesthetic situations; in short, it belongs to a kinaesthetic system. And as I have just pointed out, my ability to perceive an object from a certain perspective presupposes that I am simultaneously horizontally aware of the coexisting but absent profiles of the object. These absent profiles have a certain relationship to the present profile. They are all profiles which can become present if certain *movements* are executed. Whereas the present profile is correlated to my present bodily position, the absent profiles are all correlated to positions that I could adopt; that is, they are correlated to my kinaesthetic system. I would be unable to intend the absent profiles of the object, and consequently be unable to perceive objects altogether, if I were not in possession of a bodily self-awareness in the form of an "I can."

Let me turn toward a perceptual object in order to illustrate Husserl's line of thought. Whereas the actually appearing front of the armchair is correlated with a certain position of the body, the horizon of the cointended but momentarily absent aspects of the armchair (the backside and bottom, etc.) is correlated to my kinaesthetic horizon, that is, to my capacity for possible movements.[15] The absent aspects are linked to an intentional if-then connection. If I move in this or that way, then this or that aspect will become visually or tactually accessible. The backside of the armchair is only the backside of the same armchair that I am facing now because it can be brought into focus through the execution of a particular bodily movement: "Alle möglichen Abschattungen eines Objektes als Raumobjektes bilden ein System, das Zuordnung hat zu einem kinästhetischen System und zu dem kinästhetischen Gesamtsystem, derart, daß 'wenn' eine beliebige Kinästhese zum Ablauf kommt, 'notwendig' gewisse Abschattungen als zugehörige mitablaufen müssen."[16] Granted that we are faced with a motionless object, then if the kinaesthesis K_1 is constant during the time interval t_0-t_1, then the perceptual appearance A_1 is constant as well. And if K_1 changes into K_2 in the time interval t_1-t_2, the perceptual appearance A_1 changes into A_2 as well. One can consequently speak of a functional (but not an essential) dependency between K and A. A_1 is not always given in correlation with K_1, but A_1 is always given in correlation to some K.[17] Thus, Husserl takes perception to be a unified performance of two different but correlated functions. On the one hand, there is the kinaesthetic experiencing manifesting positions in a system of possible movements. On the other hand, there is the motivated sequence of perceptual appearances functionally correlated to these positions. Every series of perceptual appearances is correlated to a kinaesthetic system. Although the kinaesthetic experiencing is not interpreted as belonging to the perceived object, and although it does not itself bring objects to presence, it manifests bodily self-awareness, and thereby a unity and a framework which are indispensable if the object is to present itself horizontally or in a synthetically unified series of appearances.[18]

To summarize Husserl's position, perceptual intentionality is a movement that can only be effectuated by an embodied subject.[19] The central point is not that we can perceive moving objects in space, but that our very perception of these objects is itself a matter of movement.[20]

The Self-Manifestation of the Body

Husserl's analysis calls attention to the bodily side of perception, but so far two different issues have been presented more or less intertwined. On the one hand, we find transcendental arguments in support of the thesis that bodily self-awareness is a pervasive and necessary element in perceptual intentionality[21] and, on the other hand, we find an attempt to unravel the exact nature of this bodily self-awareness. Let me from this point on focus more explicitly on the latter issue. Let me turn from the question of *when* we are aware of the body to a discussion of *how* we are aware of it.

As Michel Henry points out, a phenomenological clarification of the body must take its departure in the original givenness of the body.[22] But how exactly is the body given when we perceive objects? Is it among the objects perceptually present? When I am watching an opera, I am normally not paying attention to the turn of my head when I follow the motions of the singers, nor to the narrowing of my eyes when I attempt to discern the features of the prima donna. When I give up and reach for my opera glasses, the movements of my hand remain outside the focus of my consciousness. When I am directed at and occupied with objects, my perceptual act and its bodily roots are generally passed over in favor of the perceived, i.e., my body tends to efface itself on its way to its intentional goal.[23] Fortunately, for had we been aware of our bodily movements in the same way in which we are attentively aware of objects, our body would have made such high demands on our consciousness that they would have interfered with our daily life. When I play Ping-Pong, my movements are not given as intentional objects. My limbs do not compete with the ball for my attention. If that were the case, I would be so inhibited that I would be unable to play efficiently. Habitual acts do not make high demands on our attention. They are to a certain extent automatic. It is almost as if the body lived a life of its own far from any supervision. But automatic acts are not necessarily unconscious.[24] If I execute movements without thinking about them, it is not because the movements are mechanical or involuntary, but because they are part of the functioning intentionality, because they are immediately and prereflectively self-given.[25] That is, although my movements might be absent as intentional objects, they are not absent in any absolute sense. In Henry's words, there is no distance or separation between the functioning body and the awareness of it, since it is given in and through itself. Our primary bodily awareness can consequently be described as a *self-sensitivity*, a *self-affection*, or an *impressional* self-manifestation: "*Movement is known by itself*; it is not known by something else, by the gaze of reflection, for example, or by some intentionality which would be directed to it."[26]

It has already been argued that the perspectival appearance of the fork provides me with an awareness of my own position. When I perceive the world, the body is simultaneously revealed as the unperceived term in the center of the world toward which all objects turn their face.[27] But, of course, there are other ways of being aware of one's own body than through visual perception—be it of other objects, or directly of the body itself. Under normal circumstances I do not need to observe my arm visually in order to be aware that it is moving. When I wish to move my body in order to pick up the fork, I can do so immediately. I do not first have to locate my hand, pinpoint its position in objective space, determine the location of the fork, and then steer the hand across the interval.

It is important to emphasize that the kinaesthesis is not merely an experiencing of *a* bodily position or movement. It is an experiencing of *my* bodily position and movement, and often an experiencing of a movement executed by me.[28] That is, the kinaesthesis often includes an awareness of oneself as agent. The presence of this component (of agency) is a further argument in support of the claim that it is legitimate to speak of bodily *self*-sensitivity or *self*-affection. I am not merely experiencing a certain body from within, so to speak. I am experiencing the movements of the body as my own actions. Of course, Husserl is not implying that I am explicitly initiating and willing every single movement. My awareness of my own movements can be divided into three subcategories: (1) I move, but involuntarily, be it because somebody pushes me or due to a convulsive twitching. (2) I am in attentive control of my bodily movements: I am standing on the diving board and decide to jump. (3) Finally, we have the vast majority of cases where my habitual movements occur without my supervision and explicit control. But for Husserl, this last group of movements should still be classified as free actions. They belong in the realm of the "I can." They are movements that I permit, and which I could prevent if I decided to.[29] We are certainly able to distinguish between 1 on the one hand, and 2 and 3 on the other. We can feel the difference between a free movement and a forced movement, but we would be unable to do so were it not for a sense of volition (or lack of the same) that accompanies the kinaesthesis. Ultimately it is the same conjunction that also permits us to distinguish between our own movement and the motion or transformation of the object.[30] If we lacked the ability to differentiate between changes in the perceptual field that occur as a result of our own activity (movement of eyes, head, or body), and changes in the perceptual field for which we are not responsible (motion of a bird, or consumation of a match by fire), if we lacked the ability to differentiate between change of object and change of place, our ability to constitute an objective reality would be seriously impeded.[31] But the components of kinaesthesis and volition enable us to distinguish voluntary self-movement, where both volition and kinaesthesis is experienced; involuntary self-movement, where there is a kinaesthetic experience, but no experience of volition; and other motion, where neither volition nor kinaesthesis is experienced.[32] Of course, this should not be misunderstood. Naturally, my experience of a moving object does entail a kinaesthetic component. But I am not kinaesthetically aware of the moving object; rather, I am kinaesthetically aware of my own body and am thereby able to perceive the motion of the object.

That even habitual movements such as typing or walking contain a component of volition becomes obvious in the cases where their execution is inhibited or in other ways fails to match our intentions. More generally speaking, we are normally prepared to describe our habitual or practiced movements as actions, as "I tried to hit the ball" or "I played one of Beethoven's sonatas," rather than as "the arm (or fingers) changed

position in space." But in this case the movements must to some extent
have been conscious. They are teleological *actions* which contain a reference to the objects at which they aim.[33] In order to comprehend these
actions, we cannot simply give a description of some objective changes in
geometrical space, we have to take account of the lived situation in which
they occur.[34] Thus, our movements display an original intentionality. It
is original, both in the sense that it is intrinsic to the movements (it
is not simply a question of interpreting the movements as if they were
intentional), but also in the sense that it is a form of intentionality, a
form of our being-in-the-world, which is more original and fundamental
than the one encountered in our theoretical attitude.[35]

At this point, my argumentation for the prereflective self-manifestation of my movements is faced with at least one obvious objection.
The body is certainly a condition of possibility for perceptual experience.
But to say that the body must exist in order for perception to occur
is not to say that the body is itself among the perceived objects. Quite
the contrary, it could be claimed that we become conscious of it only
when we look at it, or in other ways pay attention to it. This line of
reasoning could then appeal to the following consideration. The usual
indirect argument for the existence of prereflective self-awareness is the
possibility of reflection. If a thematical, reflective grasping of the experience is possible, the experience must already have been characterized
by a prior, unthematic prereflective self-awareness. However, when we
perform habitual acts (brushing our teeth, walking, typing, playing the
piano, etc.), we are usually unable to thematize the experience when
it happens without obstructing the operative performance in its very
flow, and afterward we are rarely if ever able to recall each of the single
movements. Thus, we lack the ability that normally allows us to conclude
that the movement was already given prereflectively. Should not this fact
make us pause, and eventually force us to acknowledge that although
proprioception does provide vital and essential information about the
body, it is an information which is processed unconsciously in the vast
majority of cases?

But is this observation really to the point? Although we might be
unable to distinguish and thematically isolate each and every one of our
movements, we are still aware of what we are doing. We can perform
habitual activities with minimal attention, but this does not make the
movements unconscious. When I am typing, I do not pay attention to the
movements of my fingers, but I am certainly aware that they are moving,
and I do not need to look down at my hands in order to find out. Were
my fingers suddenly to become anaesthetic, it would definitely make a
difference. Ultimately, one might ask if the objection does not confuse

two different levels of description. It takes it for granted that the body is already given prereflectively as an assemblage of organs. And it insists that we cannot speak of prereflective body-awareness unless we have the ability to discriminate between the movements of each of these organs. But is it not rather the case that our functioning body is given primarily as an undivided field, as a unity, and that the disintegration of the body into separate parts juxtaposed in space is a consequence of a subsequent objectification?[36] As Merleau-Ponty puts it, if I stand in front of my desk and lean on it with both hands, only my hands are stressed but the whole of my body trails behind them like the tail of a comet. It is not that I am unaware of the whereabouts of my shoulders or back, but they are simply swallowed up in the position of my hands.[37]

Our functioning body is present in such a fundamental and pervasive fashion that we only notice it explicitly when our smooth interaction with the world is disturbed, be it through voluntary reflections (philosophical or vain, e.g., when we gaze in the mirror), or in reflections forced upon us through limit-situations, such as sickness, pain, fatigue, etc.[38] In recent litterature on neurological afflictions there are several cases that can illustrate this point. Sacks, Cole, and Paillard have all described patients who had extensive damage or were almost totally deficit in muscular proprioception.[39] When these patients, shortly after the outbreak of their disorder, tried to move a limb or their entire body, they could initiate the movement, but had no control over where the moving part ended up. If they reached for something the hands would miss or overshoot wildly, and unless they kept an eye on their hands, they started "wandering" without their knowledge and might be "lost." That is, the hands would no longer be where the patient thought they were and could only be retrieved through vision. Subsequently these patients learned to control their movements, but only through intense mental concentration and constant visual vigilance. That is, they learned to rely on a combination of *visual proprioception* and *visual perception* of limb movements, and this enabled them to move around. Their awareness of their own body remained completely transformed, however. Every single movement had to be done attentively. Even to sit in a chair without falling out of it required constant attention. One of the patients could only stand if she looked at her feet, and she collapsed if she closed her eyes or if the light went out. If another patient sneezed while he was walking, his mental concentration would be disrupted, and he would fall over. Thus, the body had lost decisive parts of its self-sensitivity, and to some it felt dead or nonreal. In one of the patient's own words: "I can't feel my body. I feel weird—disembodied." "I feel my body is blind and deaf to itself . . . it has no sense of itself."[40] Obviously these patients almost completely lacked something that we take so much for granted in ordinary life that we are occasionally even prepared to deny its existence, namely, a pervasive, prereflective bodily self-affection or self-sensitivity. But to deny its existence is to claim that we all resemble the patients described by Sacks, Cole, and Paillard.

Let me add some brief comments in order to prevent the wrong conclusion from being derived from this example, namely, that the perception of spatial objects does after all not presuppose kinaesthetic experience. First of all, as Gibson has pointed out, proprioception (or kinaesthesis) is neither attached to a unique sense organ nor is it to be identified with a specific body sense. It is a general function common to all perceptual systems. All perception involves a kind of self-sensitivity, and all perception involves coperception of self and of environment. Gibson consequently distinguishes muscular, articular, vestibular, cutaneous, auditory, and visual kinaesthesis. As for the latter, Gibson argues that the very flow pattern of optical information provides us with awareness of our own movement and posture: "the world is revealed and concealed as the head moves, in ways that specify exactly how the head moves".[41] Although it is somewhat unfortunate to speak of coperception, since it implies that we perceive ourselves (rather than being merely prereflectively aware of ourselves), Gibson's theory has been confirmed through a number of experiments, for instance, through the so-called "moving room experiment." The subject is standing on a solid floor, but is surrounded by the walls of a small bottomless box hanging from the ceiling. If the walls are then moved slightly, the subject will sway or fall. The optical flow created by moving the walls forward gives him the impression that he is himself swaying backward. The muscular readjustments undertaken to compensate for this apparent sway cause him to fall.[42] A different example is provided by the Cinerama screen where, e.g., a ride in a roller coaster can be simulated. Second, although the patients lacked the vast part of their muscular proprioception, all of them apparently retained proprioceptive sensitivity in and voluntary control over their *eye movements*. Without this minimal control they would presumably have had no chance of supervising and controlling the movement of the rest of their body through visual feedback.[43] (Unfortunately Sacks's account is somewhat lacking in information. He writes that his patient had an *almost* total proprioceptive deficit,[44] but he does not specify which part remained in function). Third, it should be emphasized that the patients were not born in this way, and it is beyond doubt that their ability to regain control of their bodily movements as well as their persisting ability to perceive spatial objects profited decisively from conceptual schemes acquired while they were still in possession of full body awareness.[45] One can only speculate about their abilities if they had lacked muscular proprioception from birth, but a classical experiment by Held and Hein suggests one conclusion. Eight pairs of kittens were reared in darkness from birth until between the ages of eight and twelve weeks, when they attained the size and coordinational capacity to participate in the following experiment. Each pair of kittens was placed in an apparatus that allowed one kitten to move actively, whereas the other was restrained in holders and prevented from moving on its own. Both kittens were then exposed to the same kind of visual stimulation, but for the first it varied as a result of the kitten's own self-produced movements, whereas for the second it varied due to its being passively transported through an equivalent range of motion. When the kittens were subsequently tested, the restrained kittens showed gross deficiencies in spatial perception and coordination compared to their active companions.[46]

The Self-Objectivation of the Body

Insofar as the body functions as the zero-point that permits a perceptual view on the world, the body itself is not perceived. With a pregnant formulation, which we will later have reason to return to, Sartre even writes that the lived body is *invisibly* present, since it is exactly lived rather than known.[47] My body is my perspective on the world. It is not among the objects that I have a perspective on. To claim otherwise is to face an infinite regress.[48] When Husserl speaks of the position and movement of the functioning body, this should obviously not be taken to refer to the motion of a spatial object, nor to a position in objective space (just as time-consciousness is not itself a temporal object). If the latter had been the case, Husserl would have commited a *metábasis eis állo génos*. Originally, the body never changes position. It is always "here," namely, in the center of the situation. Other objects change their position relative to it. The "here" of the body is an absolute "here" which, in contrast to the place I am presently occupying, can never become a "there."[49] Ultimately, the distance between the subjective "here" and the objective "there" is not a question of spatial magnitude, since the "here" is not a point in objective space, but a dimension of manifestation. Originally, on the level of prereflective consciousness, the body is not given perspectivally, and I am not given to myself as existing in or as a spatial object (for which reason proprioception should not be misconceived as an introspective awareness of oneself as a physical object).[50] To assume otherwise is to miss the phenomenon of embodiment.

The problem of the body and its relations with consciousness is often obscured by the fact that while the body is from the start posited as a certain *thing* having its own laws and capable of being defined from outside, consciousness is then reached by the type of inner intuition which is peculiar to it. Actually if after grasping "*my*" consciousness in its absolute interiority and by a series of reflective acts, I then seek to unite it with a certain living object composed of a nervous system, a brain, glands, digestive, respiratory, and circulatory organs whose very matter is capable of being analyzed chemically into atoms of hydrogen, carbon, nitrogen, phosphorus, etc., then I am going to encounter insurmountable difficulties. But these difficulties all stem from the fact that I try to unite my consciousness not with *my* body but with the body of *others*. In fact the body which I have just described is not *my* body such as it is *for me*.[51]

As Sartre is quick to point out, we should be careful not to let our understanding of the lived body—be it our own body or the body of the Other—be guided by an external physiological perspective that ultimately has its origin in the anatomical study of the *corpse*.[52]

The lived body precedes the perceived body. Originally, I do not have any consciousness *of* my body. I am not perceiving it, I am it.[53] Obviously, this is not the only way the body can appear, however. Just as there are different types of self-awareness, there are different types of body-consciousness. All ultimately concern the way that I appear to myself.[54] Thus, Husserl emphasizes the importance of distinguishing between (1) the prereflective, unthematized lived body-awareness that accompanies and makes possible every spatial experience; and (2) the thematized consciousness *of* the body. It is necessary to distinguish the *functioning, subjective* body (*Leib*) and the *thematized, objective* body (*Leibkörper*), and to clarify their exact founding-founded relationship. My original body-awareness is not a type of object-consciousness, is not a perception of the body as a spatial object. Quite to the contrary, the latter is a subsequent move, which like every other perceptual experience is dependent upon and made possible by the prereflective functioning body-awareness: "Es ist hier auch zu beachten, dass bei aller dinglichen Erfahrung der Leib miterfahren ist als fungierender Leib (also nicht als bloßes Ding), und dass er, wo er selbst als Ding erfahren ist, eben doppelt und in eins als erfahrenes Ding und als fungierender Leib erfahren ist."[55]

Although one could have wished for a more precise formulation— the use of the term "erfahren" to denote both types of body-awareness is unfortunate, since it obscures their decisive difference—Husserl's point remains clear. The similarity between the description of the relation between the thematized and the functioning body, on the one hand,

and the standard characterization of the relation between reflective and prereflective self-awareness, on the other, clearly suggests the following conclusion: The constitution of the body as an object is not an activity exercised by a disincarnated subject that thereby acquires a proper vehicle of transportation. No, the constitution of the body as an object must be understood as the *self-objectivation* of the lived body. It is enacted by a subject already embodied. When, how, and why does this transformation occur?

According to Husserl, there is a close connection between the constitution of objective space and the self-objectivation of the lived body. Objective space is exactly a space which is *constituted* as being independent of my orientation and movement. We only experience space as objective when its coordinates are no longer dependent upon my indexical "here." But it is only by objectifying the body, only by viewing it as an object among objects, that its indexicality can be surmounted or suspended, something that has already happened when we have an experience of walking *through* space.[56] Basically, we are here confronted with a feature in Husserl's thinking which gradually became more and more prominent, namely, the thesis that the constitutive performance is characterized by a kind of reciprocity insofar as the constituting agent is itself constituted in the process of constitution. This is why Husserl occasionally speaks of the reciprocal codependency existing between the constitution of space and spatial objects, on the one hand, and the self-constitution of the ego and the body, on the other, and this is why he eventually claimed that the constitution of the world necessarily implies a mundanization and self-objectivation of the constituting subject.[57] In my later discussion of the relationship between self-affection and hetero-affection, I will return to some of these issues.

As mentioned earlier, my body is originally given as a unity. It is only subsequently that the kinaesthetic system and the sensing are split up and apprehended as belonging to specific parts of the body, only subsequently that the sensing is *localized* and that we are confronted with the experiencing subsystems of the fingers, eyes, hands, etc.[58]

If I touch a tabletop, I have a series of appearances that is experienced as belonging to the touched tabletop. When I slide over the top, I perceive the hardness, smoothness, and extension of the table. However, it is also possible to undertake a change of attention (a kind of reflection) so that instead of being preoccupied with the properties of the table, I thematize the touching hand, and I am then aware of a feeling of pressure and movement which are not apprehended as objective properties of the hand, but which are nevertheless localized in it and which manifests its function as an experienc*ing* organ.[59]

Originally, the kinaesthesis is given as the movement of our sensing —as our moving experiencing—and must consequently be distinguished from the perspectivally appearing motion of the body in space; and yet there is also a unity between the two.[60] As Husserl says, the kinaesthesis has an *exterior*.[61] When the sensing is localized in a part of the body, the kinaesthesis becomes localized as well. When the kinaesthetic experiencing is accompanied by and associatively united with the movements of the perceptually given body, it becomes possible to interpret one and the same movement as both a volitional activity and as a motion in space.[62] From then on, the kinaesthesis can be apprehended as the first-personal givenness of the spatial movement of a perceiving organ, for instance, as the movement of a feeling finger.[63]

It is important not to misunderstand this process of localization, especially since Husserl's formulations occasionally contain a dangerous ambiguity. Husserl often writes that one and the same sensation can be apprehended in two different ways, namely, as respectively an *Empfindung* and as an *Empfindnis*. When I touch the cold surface of a table, the sensation of coldness can be interpreted either as a sensuous property of the touched object or as a localized sensation in the touching hand.[64] But to speak in this way might suggest that the difference between the table and the hand is simply a difference between two objects; just as one and the same line in a well-known picture might be interpreted first as the side of a goblet and then as the outline of a face, one and the same sensation of coldness might be interpreted alternately as a property of the table and of the hand. However, as Husserl is well aware, the touched object and the touching hand do not at all appear in the same manner: the *Empfindnis* is not a material property of the hand, but the very embodied subjectivity itself. Whereas the properties of a material object are constituted adumbrationally, this is not the case for the localized sensations.[65] As Husserl quite aptly remarks, "Tastempfindungen sind nicht in der Haut als wie Stücke ihres organischen Gewebes."[66] Thus, rather than to say that the sensation is two-sided in the sense that it can be interpreted in two different ways, it is better to say that the sensation contains two radically different dimensions to it, namely, a distinction between the *sensing* and the *sensed*, and that we can focus upon either.[67]

When I realize that my hand is feeling or moving, that my ankle is throbbing or that my back hurts, I am localizing the sensing in different parts of my body. In itself this localization must first and foremost be seen as a *thematization* and not as a *reification* of the body. When my hand touches the table, and when I focus my attention upon the touching, I am aware of an experienc*ing* organ, and not of an object in space. Husserl writes: "If I do include them [the localized sensations], then it is not that the physical thing is now richer, but instead *it becomes body* [*Leib*], *it senses.*"[68] Thus, the localization does not suspend or negate the subjectivity of the body. Nevertheless, if the localization is to take place at all, if there is to be something in or on which the sensing is to be localized, these visually or tactually appearing body parts must be constituted as well. Thus, the localization of the sensing goes hand in hand with the tactual or visual constitution of a perspectivally appearing bodily exteriority, be it by one hand touching the other, or by the eye gazing on the foot. As Husserl puts it, the body is simultaneously constituted *perspectivally*, that is, as a *res extensa*, and with an *organization*, that is, as a complex of localized perceiving organs.[69]

Husserl explicitly emphasizes this peculiar two-sidedness of the body.[70] My body is given as an interiority, as a volitional structure, and as a dimension of sensing,[71] but it is also given as a visually and tactually appearing exteriority. What is the relation between that which Husserl calls the "*Innen-*" and the "*Aussenleiblichkeit*"?[72] In both cases I am confronted with my own body. But why is the visually and tactually appearing body at all experienced as the exteriority of *my* body? If we first examine the case of one hand touching the other, the touching hand (the experiencing organ) has a series of sensations which are objectified and interpreted as being properties of the touched hand (the perceived organ), and more specifically as being the surface of the touched hand. When I touch my hand, however, the touched hand is not given as a mere object, since it feels the touch itself, and this sensing does not belong to the touched hand as an objective property, but is localized in it as an *Empfindnis*.[73] The decisive difference between touching one's own body and everything else, be it inanimate objects or the bodies of Others, is that it implies a *double-sensation*. The relation between the touching and the touched is reversible, since the touching is touched, and the touched is touching.[74] It is this reversibility that testifies that the interiority and the exteriority are different manifestations of the same.[75]

> Nun ist aber jedes Organ einerseits durch Betasten taktuell konstituiert, und [durch] die dabei fungierenden Kinästhesen, andererseits aber selbst konstituiert als wirklich oder möglicherweise tastendes, so dass wir immer und notwendig in ursprünglichster Tasterfahrung, die den Leib als Körper und als Leib ergibt, ein funktionelles Beieinander von tastendem und getastetem Organ finden, und mit der jeweils vermöglichen Umkehrung, dass das getastete zum tastenden werden kann. Sowie diese Umkehrung statthat, kehrt sich auch die Funktion der dabei also stets sich deckenden Empfindungspaare um; was vorher auf der Oberfläche des getasteten Organs lokalisiert gegeben war, fungiert nun im Tasten für

das Gegenorgan, und was vorher in diesem fungierte, ist nun lokalisiert gegeben auf seinem Partner.[76]

Husserl justly emphasizes the importance of the *tactual* self-constitution of the body, but what about the *visual* self-constitution? To see a foot will not qualify as a bodily *self*-appearance or *self*-awareness unless I realize that it is my *own* foot. How do I realize that? Although the visual appearance of my own body is characterized by strange anomalies—as Husserl writes in a famous passage from *Ideen* II, the body is a "remarkably imperfectly constituted thing"[77]; I cannot perceive all of its aspects: I can neither move around it, nor can I approach or withdraw from it, and it systematically hides parts of itself from me.[78] It does not differ radically from the visual appearance of external objects. Whereas I cannot feel my hand and be in error about whose hand it is, I can see it and mistakenly attribute it to somebody else. That is, our visual self-appearance is not immune to the error of misidentification. But even if the seen foot is not factually moving and experiencing, it *can* move and feel and thereby unmistakenly reveal its subjectivity. My bodily parts, whether nose, eye, foot, or hand, are all given as parts of the same unity, not because of their material composition, but because all of them are felt and moved by the same self.[79] To put it differently, although *my* visually or tactually given bodily exteriority has properties in common with objects in the world, such as extension, weight, softness, smoothness, etc., it still differs radically from these objects.[80] It is experienced as *mine* because it is accompanied by and associated with a localized interiority.[81] If the touched hand or the seen foot lacked this dimension, it would also lack bodily self-awareness, and I would no longer *experience* it as *myself*, although habit might still convince me that it is mine. Anybody who has fallen asleep with her arm as a pillow knows how distressing and strange it is to wake up with a numb arm. When one touches the arm it does not respond, and feels alien.

Let me once more emphasize that the entire discussion concerning the self-appearance of the body is part of the elucidation of the structure and nature of self-awareness. We are by now in a position to distinguish several different types of bodily self-awareness. First of all, there is the immediate, nonarticulated, prereflective self-sensitivity. Second, there is the thematization and articulation of this experience, which localizes it in bodily organs, for instance, in the left hand. When the left hand then starts investigating the right hand (or foot or nose), I retain my prereflective body-awareness, but I also gain a new type of mediated, objectifying self-awareness. In this case we can speak of a *bodily reflection* taking place between the different parts of the body.[82] It is a thematic self-awareness characterized by difference and exteriority; the single parts of the body remain separated, and they gain contact through a surface which is exposed to the world.[83]

So far we have only discussed types of bodily self-appearance where the body reveals its subjectivity. This does not imply, however, that it is impossible to apprehend one's own body as a mere object. Not only can I be, live, feel, and move my body, I can also know and describe it theoretically as a complex of physiological organs. In this case we are confronted with a type of bodily self-appearance, in which I try to apprehend my body as if I were an Other in relation to it. Although organs like brain, kidney, etc. from a physiological point of view belong to the interiority of the body, they remain—from a phenomenological perspective—far more alien than the exterior surface of my body.

It is obvious that a more detailed clarification of this last type of bodily self-appearance is called for if one is to understand how one can appear to oneself as a mundane object, that is, if one is to understand the relation between one's awareness of oneself as an elusive subjective dimension, i.e., something which is neither a mental nor a worldly object, and one's awareness of oneself as an intersubjectively accessible entity in the world. However, at present the conceptual means necessary for such a clarification are not yet at our disposal. In chapter 9, however, I will return to the issue.

7

Self-Affection and Hetero-Affection

I n the preceding chapters, I have more than once spoken of prereflective self-awareness in terms of *self-affection*. It could be objected that there is nothing gained by replacing one term for another, but as I will attempt to show in the following, the notion of "self-affection" is in fact appropriate as a description of prereflective self-awareness since it not only captures a whole range of its defining features, but ultimately allows for new insights as well. At the same time, I will return to a question which was central to my discussion in part 1: Is it correct to describe primary self-manifestation as something that excludes all types of alterity, difference, and fracture? Let me present some different answers to this question—first Henry's, and then Husserl's, Sartre's, and Derrida's.

Henry and Pure Interiority

We have already encountered Henry's view concerning the unique and fundamental character of self-awareness. But his disclosure of absolute self-manifestation is by no means to be taken as a regressive deduction of a transcendental precondition, but as a description of an actual and incontestable dimension in lived subjectivity. This is clear from what might be one of Henry's most central claims, namely, that the self-manifestation of subjectivity is an immediate, nonobjectifying, and passive occurrence, and therefore best described as a *self-affection*.[1]

When speaking of affection it is paramount not to conflate the concepts of hetero-affection and self-affection. The first designates the (pre)givenness of a foreign (proto)object, the second a self-manifestation where there is no object, no exteriority, and no distinction between the givenness and that which is given. Thus, one should be careful not to follow Kant in conceiving of self-affection in terms of an "inner sense," for as Henry writes, this would ultimately disqualify it as a type of self-awareness. Outer affection is a relation between a sense organ and an external stimulus, and it implies a difference between the two. But if inner affection is to provide us with self-awareness, if it is to be a *self*-affection, it cannot entail a similar difference.

> This power of intuition, in the case of internal experience, is the internal sense. But this internal sense is truly a sense and, according to Kant himself, the sense always designates a-being-affected by a foreign content. That which is presented to the internal sense is therefore in principle something other, it is the very dimension of otherness, the non-ego as such. Therefore, how would ipseity be able to be born and take form in this dimension of radical otherness? How would an ego be able to present itself to us in the milieu of the non-ego as such? The structure of intuition excludes *a priori* the possibility of an intuition of the ego.[2]

To affect oneself and to be affected by oneself is what self-affection is all about. It is immediate and involves no difference, distance, or mediation between that which affects and that which is affected. Insofar as the self-manifestation of subjectivity is distinguished by this unified self-adherence and self-coincidence, insofar as it is given to itself directly and without having to pass through the world, Henry characterizes it as an *acosmic* and *monadic* interiority.[3]

One way to support Henry's description is to recall that experiences are essentially characterized by having a subjective "feel" to them, that is, a certain quality of "what it is like," or what it "feels" like to have them. When I am conscious, I "feel" my experience, i.e., I am aware of what it is like to have it. This way of "feeling" the experience does not presuppose the intervention or mediation of any sense organ or higher-order intentional act, but is simply a question of a direct and immediate *self-affection*.[4] To be in pain, embarrassed, happy, or stubborn is to be (self-)aware of it. It is, so to speak, both a way of being and a way of being aware. These experiences are given in, through, and for themselves.[5]

> Affectivity reveals the absolute in its totality because it is nothing other than *its* perfect adherence to self, nothing other than its coincidence with self, because it is the auto-affection of Being in the absolute unity of its radical immanence. *In the absolute unity of its radical immanence, Being affects itself and experiences itself in such a way that there is nothing in it which does not affect it and which is not experienced by it, no content transcendent to the interior*

experience of self which constitutes this content. Feeling presents itself as sensing itself at all points of its Being and this is precisely what a feeling is; herein also resides its transparency.[6]

According to Henrich, original self-acquaintance was not a performance but an irrelational occurrence. In Henry we encounter a very similar position, since he claims that self-affection is not a matter of self-spontaneity but of a fundamental and radical *passivity*. Self-affection is a given state, it is not something that one initiates or controls, but something that one cannot refuse, deny, or avoid. I am for myself, I am given to myself, but I am not the initiator of this donation. To phrase it differently, to be self-aware is to find oneself in a state that one cannot escape or surpass. It is to be *situated*.[7]

> [T]he relationship to self of the ego in its original ontological passivity with regard to self, his unity with self as an absolute unity in a sphere of radical immanence, as unity with self of life, permits itself neither to be surmounted nor broken.[8]

> *The structure upon which the impossibility of Being not to be entirely present to itself rests, the impossibility of its breaking the bond which attaches it to itself, of tearing itself away from itself and of existing outside itself, is non-freedom.*[9]

Some phenomenologists (and it will soon become clear who they are) have claimed that the self-manifestation of subjectivity necessarily entails a self-alienation or self-transcendence, and that subjectivity only manifests itself to itself when it becomes an Other to itself. Pure subjectivity has been taken to be so indeterminate that no self-awareness would be possible unless there were an object which subjectivity could be determined by. That is, the being of the subject has been taken to be so abstract in its purity that it needed a limit, a resistance, a radical alterity in order to be for itself. Thus, the essence of self-presence has been described as self-alienation, and interiority has been defined through radial exteriority. It has been claimed that division, separation, and opposition are structural elements in all kinds of manifestation, including self-manifestation. To phrase it differently, it has been claimed that the essence of subjectivity (its condition of possibility) is alterity.[10]

For Henry this entire approach is fundamentally mistaken. Subjectivity is absolute in the sense of being irrelative and completely self-sufficient in its radical interiority. It is immanent in the sense that it manifests itself without ever leaving itself, without producing or presupposing any kind of fracture or alterity.[11] Thus, Henry insists that the originary self-manifestation of subjectivity excludes all kinds of fracture, separation, alterity, difference, exteriority, and opposition: *"the suppression of otherness is merely the suppression of the foreign element, with respect to the essence, of that which covers it up and hides it from our eyes,"*[12] and with words very reminiscent of the position of the Heidelberg School, he adds that it cannot in any way be conceived of as a kind of relation.[13] The self-revelation of subjectivity does not imply any relation, for relationality has no place in radical immanence, an immanence so saturated with self-manifestation that it excludes the kind of lack which would necessarily accompany any kind of fracture or internal distance.[14] "A la structure intérieure de cette manifestation originelle n'appartient aucun Dehors, aucun Ecart, aucune Ek-stase: sa substantialité phénoménologique n'est pas la visibilité, aucune des catégories dont use la philosophie, depuis la Grèce en tout cas, ne lui convient."[15]

Although Henry is mainly preoccupied with the self-affection and self-manifestation of subjectivity, he does not deny the obvious existence of hetero-affection and hetero-manifestation. But he claims that it is absurd to conceive of hetero-affection as an unconscious relation between two ontic entities. A bed cannot be affected by a pillow. To speak of hetero-manifestation is to speak of something that manifests itself for someone. To speak of hetero-affection is to speak of something that affects someone. We are speaking of relations that presuppose a self as one of the relata. It is only a (self-affecting and self-manifesting) self that can be affected by something else. It is only because we are already given to ourselves that we can be affected by the world.[16] I can only encounter an appearing object if I am self-aware, if I am aware of the experience through which the object is made to appear. Thus Henry acknowledges the existence of hetero-affection, but it is a kind of affection that presupposes self-affection, not one that can explain or found it.[17]

In more general terms, Henry claims that intentionality presupposes self-awareness, and that the very act of transcendence presupposes the absolute self-coincidence of pure immanence:

> The act which appears as independent of its own forward movement, independently of the movement whereby it projects itself outside itself, reveals itself in itself, in such a way that this "in itself" means: without surpassing itself, without leaving itself. That which does not surpass itself, that which does not hurl itself outside itself but remains in itself without leaving or going out of itself is, in its essence, immanence. Immanence is the original mode according to which is accomplished the revelation of transcendence itself and hence the original essence of revelation.[18]

The intentional act can only relate to that which is other, if it is already acquainted with itself, and this self-manifestation is not itself a question of a perception or an intention or a movement of transcendence. Turning an argument by Sartre on its head (see page 129), Henry insists that the reason why an object cannot relate to that which is other is because it lacks a true immanence, not because it is too self-sufficient and self-identical. It is because ontic entities are not in possession of a self-manifesting immanence that they cannot transcend themselves.[19] It is against this background that Henry can claim: "*Self-manifestation is the essence of manifestation.*"[20]

The presentation so far could easily give the impression that Henry conceives of self-manifestation in a way that excludes every mediation, complexity, and alterity. To a certain extent this is true, but it is nevertheless possible to unearth certain passages which challenge or perhaps rather modify this interpretation.

First of all, Henry acknowledges that absolute subjectivity does transcend itself toward the world. Ultimately, absolute subjectivity is nothing but the immanent, nonecstatic, self-revelation of the very act of transcendence. To put it differently, Henry does acknowledge that an analysis of subjectivity confronts us with an ontological *dualism*: In every experience something is given to absolute subjectivity which is different from subjectivity itself. It is the Other, the nonego, which appears: "Certainly, subjectivity is always a life in the presence of a transcendent being."[21] To speak of an ontological dualism, to distinguish a pure interiority and a pure exteriority, is by no means to accept a classical Cartesian dualism. It is merely to insist on the existence of an absolute dimension of subjectivity, without which no hetero-manifestation would be possible.[22]

Second, and this was already pointed out in chapter 5, Henry is even prepared to ascribe a certain complexity and diversity to the life of the ego: "When we speak of the unity of the absolute life of the ego, we in no way wish to say that this life is monotonous; actually it is infinitely diverse, the ego is not a pure logical subject enclosed within its tautology; it is the very being of infinite life, which nevertheless remains one in this diversity."[23] In marked contrast to Heidegger and Merleau-Ponty, Henry does not conceive of self-affection as an ecstatic temporal self-positing, but he does admit that the very notion of self-affection is a dynamic and by no means a static notion. Self-affection understood as the process of affecting and being affected is not the rigid self-identity of an object, but a subjective movement best described as the immanent, nonhorizontal, and nonecstatic self-temporalization of subjectivity. We are dealing with an affective temporality, and even though it seems to involve a perpetual movement and change, nothing is changed. In fact, it would be wrong to characterize absolute subjectivity as a stream of consciousness. There is no streaming and no change, but always one and the same Living Present without distance and difference.[24]

Are these precisions—or perhaps rather modifications—sufficient? I have already mentioned some of the remarkable similarities between Henry and Henrich. Ultimately, Henry's position seems to share some of the strengths and weaknesses of the position of the Heidelberg School. Henry is undoubtedly the phenomenological thinker who has been most attentive to the problem of self-manifestation. His demonstration of its phenomenological significance is distinguished by its conceptual clarity. But his intense (almost monomaniacal) preoccupation with this topic also makes him vulnerable to the same kind of criticism that was directed against the Heidelberg School. Henry operates with the notion of an absolutely self-sufficient, nonecstatic, irrelational self-manifestation, but he never presents us with a convincing explanation of how a subjectivity essentially characterized by such a complete self-presence can simultaneously be in possession of an inner temporal articulation; how it can simultaneously be directed intentionally toward something different from itself; how it can be capable of recognizing other subjects (being acquainted with subjectivity as it is through a completely unique self-presence); how it can be in possession of a bodily exteriority; and finally how it can give rise to the self-division found in reflection. In short, his analyses remain deficient, since they never take the interplay between self-manifestation and hetero-manifestation into sufficient consideration.

Husserl on Self-Awareness and Affection

As I have argued in chapters 5 and 6, Husserl's discussion of self-affection is mainly to be found in his analysis of temporality and embodiment. But Husserl does not only take the notion of self-affection to be appropriate as a description of prereflective self-awareness, he also takes it to be illuminating when it comes to an understanding of the relationship between reflective and prereflective self-awareness.

Reflective self-awareness is often taken to be a thematic self-awareness and is normally initiated in order to bring the primary intentional act into focus. However, in order to explain the occurrence of reflection it is necessary that that which is to be disclosed and thematized is (unthematically) conscious. Otherwise there would be nothing to motivate and call forth the act of reflection. This argumentation affirms the founded status of reflection: it presupposes prereflective self-awareness. But it also calls for a proper analysis of the very process of motivation.

Husserl's general analysis of intentionality entails an important distinction between activity and passivity, a point which is also highly pertinent when it comes to an understanding of self-awareness. It is easy to find acts in which the subject is actively taking position, acts in which the subject is comparing, differentiating, judging, valuing, wishing, or willing something. But, as Husserl points out, whenever the subject is active, it is also passive, since to be active is to react on something.[25] Every kind of active position-taking presupposes a preceding *affection*: "Jedes Ich-tue ist Bezogensein des Ich auf ein Etwas, das ihm bewusst ist. Und bewusst muss schon dem Ich etwas sein, damit es sich ihm überhaupt zuwenden kann, und ohne Zuwendung ist keine Betätigung in Beziehung auf dieses Etwas. Die Zuwendung setzt voraus Affektion, aber affizieren kann wieder nur etwas, das bewusst ist, nur das kann auf das Ich einen grösseren oder geringeren 'Reiz' üben."[26]

If we follow Husserl a step further in his analysis, he distinguishes between *receptivity* and *affectivity*. Receptivity is taken to be the first, lowest, and most primitive type of intentional activity, and consists in responding to or paying attention to that which is affecting us passively. Thus, even receptivity understood as a mere "I notice" presupposes a prior affection. It presupposes that that which is now thematized was already affecting and stimulating the ego unheeded.[27] To be affected by something is not yet to be presented with an object, but to be invited to turn one's attention toward that which exerts the affection. If it succeeds in calling attention to itself, that which affects us is *given*, whereas it is only *pregiven* as long as it remains unheeded.[28]

The relevance of this analysis for our present problem is obvious. Reflection is not an act *sui generis*. It does not appear out of nowhere, but like all acts initiated by the subject and like all intentional activity it presupposes a motivation. To be motivated is to be affected by something and then to respond to it.[29] That which motivates reflection is a prior *self-affection*. I can thematize myself because I am already passively self-aware. I can grasp myself because I am already affected by myself.[30]

> Wenn immer ich reflektiere, finde ich mich "in bezug auf" ein Etwas, als affiziertes bzw. aktives. Das, worauf ich bezogen bin, ist erlebnismäßig bewußt—es ist für mich etwas schon als "Erlebnis," damit ich mich darauf beziehen kann.[31]

> [N]ur weil es [the ego] beständig passiv "vorgegeben" gewissermassen sich selbst Erscheinendes ist (obschon nicht in abschattender Darstellung

Dargestelltes), kann es aktiv erfasst, im eigentlichen Sinn gegeben, bedacht, erkannt und praktisch zum Thema eines reflektiven sich selbst so und so Wollens, sich ethisch Erneuerns usw. werden.[32]

When reflection sets in, it initially grasps something that has just elapsed, namely the motivating prereflective phase of the experience. I remain affected by that which is no longer present, and I therefore have the possibility to react on the affection and to thematize the backward sinking phase of the experience.

As I have mentioned earlier, when speaking of affection it is paramount not to conflate these two concepts of affection: self-affection and hetero-affection. I have spoken about the first, but what about the latter? Husserl has often made it clear that the concrete ego cannot be thought of independently of its relation to that which is foreign to it.[33] This was already spelled out in his theory of intentionality:

Nun gehört es eigentlich zum Wesen der intentionalen Beziehung (das ist eben die Beziehung zwischen Bewusstsein und Bewusstseinsobjekt), dass das Bewusstsein, d.i. die jeweilige *cogitatio*, Bewusstsein von etwas ist, was es nicht selbst ist.[34]

Das Ich ist nicht denkbar ohne ein Nicht-Ich, auf das es sich intentional bezieht.[35]

Contrary to what might be the immediate assumption, however, the primal affection is not exerted by objects. To be an object is precisely to be given (and not merely pregiven), and to be in possession of an act-transcendent identity. But prior to and founding the constitution of these fully fledged objects is the affection exerted by preontical unities, namely, the hyletic data that are presenced in the primal impression. These data are the most basic and primitive type of pregiven material which all egological activity presupposes.[36] Husserl writes:

[I]chliche Aktivität setzt Passivität voraus—ichliche Passivität—und beides setzt voraus Assoziation und Vorbewußtsein in Form des letztlich hyletischen Untergrundes.[37]

The word "impression" is appropriate only to original sensations; the word expresses well what is "there" of itself, and indeed originally: namely, what is pregiven to the Ego, presenting itself to the Ego in the manner of something affecting it as foreign [*ichfremd*].[38]

Husserl's realization that every constitution entails and presupposes a moment of facticity, the affection of the primal hyletic fact,[39] has far-reaching consequences, and it is of obvious relevance for an elucidation of the relationship between self-awareness and alterity, between self-affection and hetero-affection. This is especially so since Husserl often characterizes the hyle as a type of *alterity*:

> Innerhalb der Innerlichkeit das erste "Ichfremde," dem puren Ich vorgegeben, das Ich Affizierende (Reize Ausübende): das Hyletische.[40]

> Dann hätten wir zu sagen, das konkrete Ich hat in seinem Leben als Bewusstseinsleben beständig einen Kern von Hyle, von Nicht-Ich, aber wesentlich ichzugehörig. Ohne ein Reich der Vorgegebenheiten, ein Reich konstituierter Einheiten, konstituiert als Nicht-Ich, ist kein Ich möglich.[41]

Husserl is unequivocally stating that subjectivity is dependent on and penetrated by alterity. But how does this characterization of the hyle match with Husserl's better-known description of the hyle as an immanent content, as a real (*reell*) component of the experience itself which only gains intentional reference when subjected to an objectifying interpretation.[42] Husserl has often been criticized for operating with the notion of a formless, meaningless, and nonintentional sensual matter, and it has been claimed that this notion merely reveals Husserl's debt to the sensualism of British empiricism, rather than being the outcome of a proper phenomenological analysis. To a certain extent, this criticism is justified, but it does not tell the whole story. Husserl's concept of hyletic sensation is notoriously ambiguous, and it changed during the course of his life. Like the terms "adumbration" and "appearance," it can be interpreted both *noetically* and *noematically*. When speaking of a sensation, one can refer to the very process of sensing, but also to that which is sensed. And needless to say, it makes a difference whether one is speaking about an impressional episode in one's own sensibility or about the sensible presence of something transcendent.[43] In *Logische Untersuchungen*, Husserl claimed that there was no difference between the sensed and the sensing, but he later abandoned this position,[44] and thus a noematic interpretation of the hyle became viable. This is why Husserl can speak of the "Hyle im erweiterten Sinne des impressional oder wahrnehmungsmäßig weltlich Erscheinenden überhaupt."[45] A few references to his analysis of affection and kinaesthesis can corroborate this and can also show that Husserl eventually, particularly in his *genetical* phenomenology, came to view the hyle as being intrinsically meaningful.[46]

As already mentioned, Husserl speaks of a hyletic affection. However, this affection is not an affection exerted by an isolated, undifferentiated, senseless datum. If something is to affect us, impose itself on us, and arouse our attention, it must be sufficiently strong. It must be more conspicious than its surroundings, and it must stand out in some way through contrast, heterogeneity, and difference if it is to force us to heed it.[47] But as Husserl says, "Abhebung affiziert, und indem sie es tut, ist das Ich in gewisser Weise auf das ganze Feld bezogen; das Kontrastierende kontrastiert ja gegenüber seinem Hintergrund."[48] Ultimately, it is an abstraction to speak of an isolated hyletic affection. The affection is always exerted by something which is part of a configuration, it is always an affection from within a passively organized and structured field. To quote Mishara:

> It is not the stimulus itself which determines the magnitude of attractive force it exerts on the ego, but rather its "relative" height of contrast with respect to the other hyletic stimuli present in the field at any given moment. . . . "Affective" syntheses are those that reach consciousness, "penetrating" the topological surface as the highest peaks of the relief structure. "Preaffective" syntheses are those which, at any given moment, do not "penetrate" to egoic awareness. They form the valleys and the background relative to the "raised saliency" (*Abhebung*) of the more prominent figures.[49]

The letter "A" stands out if it is written on a white piece of paper, but not if it appears among other letters in a newspaper. Our attention will quickly be aroused if we are affected by something unusual and abnormal, such as the smell of gasoline in the ladies' room, to use an example by Husserl.[50] But, of course, if the affective force of the hyle depends in part upon the difference between the hyle and the surrounding field, the hyletic data cannot be undifferentiated, since no contrast can be established between a complex of senseless data.

As Bateson writes, information is a difference that makes a difference.[51] And whether something does make a difference is often a matter not simply of its own intrinsic properties, but of its relation to our current interests—interests which to a large extent are influenced by our former experiences. Thus, in *Zur Phänomenologie der Intersubjektivität* III, Husserl distinguishes between three different kinds of affection. (1) Something can attract my attention because it is of pertinence to my actual interest. If I am proofreading a text and looking for typographic errors, I will pay more attention to them than if I had merely glanced through the text.

(2) Something might attract my attention because of its relation to something I have experienced in the past. If I have once suffered from severe food poisoning after having eaten homemade sushi or if I am working as a cook in a Japanese restaurant, I might be more attentive to the quality of raw fish. (3) Finally, something—for instance, an explosion—might simply attract my attention due to its own overwhelming and intrusive qualities.[52]

Husserl's investigation of the body made it clear that one should distinguish between two very different types of sensations. On the one hand, we have the kinaestheses which should be interpreted noetically. They constitute bodily self-awareness and do not refer to objects. On the other hand, we have the hyletic sensations, which Husserl occasionally describes as *Merkmalsempfindungen* or *Aspektdaten*, and they can be interpreted noematically. They are not formless and senseless, but always imbued with meaning and configured in correlation to the kinaesthetic field.[53] This interpretation finds support in Husserl's classification of the hyletic sensations as being nonegological and the kinaestheses as being egological.[54] As *sensed*, the hyletic datum is not an immanent or worldless content or quality, nor is it a medium between subjectivity and world. Our *sensing* is already an openness toward the world, even if it is not yet a world of objects, and the hyletic datum is the primordial manifestation of worldly transcendence.[55] Since Husserl characterizes the hyle as a kind of alterity, it is obvious that he no longer takes it to be identical with or a part of consciousness.

However, these considerations do not warrant the conclusion that every differentiation between a hyletic affection and an object-manifestation should be abandoned. It remains possible to distinguish between hearing an increasing loudness and hearing an approaching object, feeling a local pain and feeling the prick of a needle. The hyle is underdetermined, and it is only by apprehending and interpreting it as something that a full-fledged object is constituted. To be affected by the hyle is to be affected by something which is not yet separated from subjectivity and therefore not yet constituted as an object. Thus Husserl speaks of the hyle as of an *interior* nonegological dimension which surrounds and affects the ego.[56] It is an *immanent* type of alterity which manifests itself directly in subjectivity, which belongs intrinsically to subjectivity and which subjectivity cannot do without.[57] Nevertheless, the hyle remains foreign. It is not produced by me, but is a domain which escapes my control. It is a facticity which is passively pregiven without any active participation or contribution by the ego.[58] Thus, the use of the terms "immanent" and "interior" does not indicate that the hyle is after all a real (*reell*) component of the experience itself. It simply designates that we are not yet confronted with the alterity of a constituted transcendent object, but merely with foreign components which are essential to the self-manifesting existence of subjectivity.[59] This idea is formulated in a passage from 1931:

> Konstitution von Seiendem verschiedener Stufen, von Welten, von Zeiten, hat zwei Urvoraussetzungen, zwei Urquellen, die zeitlich gesprochen (in jeder dieser Zeitlichkeiten) immerfort ihr "zugrundeliegen": 1) mein urtümliches Ich als fungierendes, als Ur-Ich in seinen Affektionen und Aktionen, mit allen Wesensgestalten an zugehörigen Modis; 2) mein urtümliches Nicht-Ich als urtümlicher Strom der Zeitigung und selbst als Urform der Zeitigung, ein Zeitfeld, das der Ur-Sachlichkeit, konstituierend. *Aber beide Urgründe sind einig, untrennbar und so für sich betrachtet abstrakt.*[60]

In the same manuscript, Husserl speaks of the original flowing nonego which constitutes the hyletic universe (the field of primordial pregivenness which all of our intentional interpretations presuppose) quite independently of any ego-contribution, although the ego is always present (*dabei*).[61] Both grounds are, as Husserl says, inseparable, both are irreducible structural moments in the process of constitution, in the process of bringing to appearance.

Since Husserl occasionally identifies the nonego with the world[62]—thereby operating with a more fundamental notion of the world than the concept of an objective reality which he attempted to nihilate in the (in)famous §49 of *Ideen* I—we are ultimately faced with the following interpretation: Subjectivity is a condition of possibility for appearance, but it is not the only condition, since Husserl also finds it necessary to speak of the world as a *transcendental nonego*.[63] Constitution is ultimately a process taking place and unfolding itself in the structure world/consciousness.[64] Consequently, constitution is neither to be understood as an arbitrary animation of senseless sensations, nor as an attempt to deduce or extract the world, the hyle, or the ontical *a priori* from a worldless subjectivity.

However, this overcoming of a type of absolute idealism that conceives a worldless ego to be the sole and supreme ground of constitution should not be interpreted as a reinstatement of a vanquished dualism. The separations between inside and outside, subject and object, ego and world are the result of a subsequent and founded distinction that merely articulates their phenomenological origin and common base, namely, the differentiated unity of functioning intentionality.[65]

All of the above testify to the intrinsic relation between subjectivity and alterity, but they do not per se say anything about the relation between

self-affection and hetero-affection. Another look at Husserl's analysis of
time and body should, however, make the connection apparent.

In *Analysen zur passiven Synthesis,* Husserl explicitly states that inner
time-consciousness taken on its own is a pure but *abstract* form. And he
further characterizes the phenomenology of inner time-consciousness as
an abstractive analysis which has to be complemented by a phenomenology of *association* dealing with the fundamental laws and forms governing the syntheses pertaining to the *content.*[66] *In concreto* there can be
no primal impression without hyletic data, and no self-temporalization
in separation from the hyletic affection. There can be no inner time-
consciousness, no prereflective self-awareness without a temporal content. Time-consciousness never appears in pure form, but always as a
pervasive *sensibility,* as the very sensing of the sensations: "We regard
sensing as the original consciousness of time."[67] Basically, this is the
reason why Husserl insists upon the *inseparability* between *Quer-* and
Längsintentionalität:[68] "Consequently, *two* inseparably united *intentionalities,* requiring one another like two sides of one and the same thing, are in-
terwoven with each other in the one, unique flow of consciousness."[69] My
consciousness of the tone as just past is dependent upon my awareness
of the phase of the flow correlated with the tone. There would be no
awareness of the just-past phase of the object *as past* apart from my present
(implicit) awareness that I had been aware of it. But to be aware of having
been aware of the object is precisely to be in possession of a temporally
stretched self-awareness.[70] The enduring tone and the streaming flow are
given conjointly and can only appear in this interdependent fashion.[71] (It
might not be completely inappropriate to compare Husserl's argumentation with Kant's refutation of idealism in *Kritik der reinen Vernunft.* Kant
argues that my consciousness of my own temporally determined existence
presupposes the existence of external objects.[72] Although Husserl would
not claim that self-awareness presupposes the existence of transcendent
objects, he does insist that it implies the simultaneous givenness of some
kind of alterity.)

We find a similar interdependence between self-affection and
hetero-affection when we turn to bodily self-awareness. As already mentioned, Husserl speaks of the reciprocal codependency existing between
the constitution of spatial objects, on one hand, and the constitution of
the body, on the other. The very exploration and constitution of objects
implies a simultaneous self-exploration and self-constitution. This is not
to say that original bodily self-awareness should be taken as an object-
intentionality, or that our self-sensitivity is merely a particular instance
of our hetero-sensitivity, but merely that it is a self-transcending consciousness which is self-aware. The body is not first given for us and

subsequently used to investigate the world. The world is given to us as bodily investigated, and the body is revealed to us in its exploration of the world.[73] It is when we perceive that we are aware of ourselves, and it is when we are affected that we appear to ourselves, i.e., it is exactly as exposed and self-transgressing subjects that we are given to ourselves.[74] To phrase it differently, we are aware of perceptual objects by being aware of our own body and how the two interact; that is, we cannot perceive physical objects without having an accompanying bodily self-awareness, be it thematic or unthematic.[75] But the reverse ultimately holds true as well: The body only appears to itself when it relates to something else—or to itself as Other.[76] As Husserl writes, "We perceive the lived body [*Leib*] but along with it also the things that are perceived 'by means of' it."[77] This reciprocity between self-affection and hetero-affection is probably nowhere as obvious as in the tactual sphere—the hand cannot touch without being touched and brought to givenness itself. In other words, the touching and the touched are constituted in the same process,[78] and according to Husserl this holds true for our sensibility in general. This is not only clear from his description of the inseparability of *Quer-* and *Längsintentionalität*, but also from his account of the relation between the kinaesthetic and the hyletic sensations: "Das System der Kinästhesen ist aber nicht im voraus konstituiert, sondern seine Konstitution erfolgt in eins mit der Konstitution hyletischer Objekte, auf die es jeweils hinauswill."[79]

More generally it might be asked whether self-affection does not always reveal more than itself. We are born and not self-generated, both in the sense that this is our given state, a state that we have not ourselves instigated or initiated, and which therefore refers beyond ourselves, but also in the sense that the subject appears to itself as affected—by something different than itself. To be affected is to live outside oneself, it is to be characterized by a principal openness. As Lévinas puts it, to be in possession of a receptivity or sensibility, in short to be exposed to affections, is an essential part of what it means to be a subject. But this incarnated sensibility is also a vulnerability, an exposure to the Other. Thus, insofar as consciousness is impressional, one can very well ask, as Lévinas does, whether it is not possessed by alterity and facticity, and characterized by a fundamental unrest and dissatisfaction.[80]

If the self-givenness of the touch is inseparable from the manifestation of the touched, if more generally self-affection is always penetrated by the affection of the world, and if inner time-consciousness presupposes a hyletic content, an affection by something not generated by consciousness,[81] it is untenable to introduce a founding-founded relation between self-affection and hetero-affection, since they are inseparable and interdependent.[82] Every affection reveals both that which affects as well as that which is affected (but not in the same way).

Against this background, it is obviously necessary to question any attempt to characterize self-awareness as a pure self-coinciding and self-sufficient irrelationality. This holds good for both reflective and prereflective self-awareness. In Husserl's words, reflective self-awareness presupposes a nonego, to which the ego is directed and from which it can then turn back on itself.[83] And as for prereflective self-awareness, Husserl explicitly writes that every experience possesses both an egoic and a nonegoic dimension.[84] These two sides can be distinguished, but not separated: "Das Ich ist nicht etwas für sich und das Ichfremde ein vom Ich Getrenntes und zwischen beiden ist kein Raum für ein Hinwenden. Sondern untrennbar ist Ich und sein Ichfremdes."[85]

I have earlier raised the question whether there might exist an incompatibility between intentionality and self-awareness due to their different directions, so to speak. But, as Ricoeur points out, the very suggestion that intentionality and self-awareness might be exclusive alternatives—that we are either so preoccupied with ourselves that every connection with the world is severed or so completely carried outside ourselves that the perception becomes unconscious—is based on a quasi-spatial and completely inadequate conception of consciousness: If I am directed toward the outside, I cannot at the same time be directed toward the inside.[86] Obviously, this does not exclude trivial exceptions, such as the difficulty of combining a reflective thematization of the structure of one's perception with the simultaneous attempt to watch a hockey game attentively. But it is only when I am paying attention to myself that a certain conflict might occur, not on the level of prereflective self-awareness.

Thus, self-awareness is not to be understood as a preoccupation with self that excludes or impedes the contact with transcendent being. On the contrary, subjectivity is essentially oriented and open toward that which it is not, be it worldly entities or the Other, and it is exactly in this openness that it reveals itself to itself. What is disclosed by the *cogito* is consequently not an enclosed immanence, a pure interior self-presence, but an openness toward alterity, a movement of exteriorization and perpetual self-transcendence. It is by being present to the world that we are present to ourselves, and it is by being given to ourselves that we can be conscious of the world.[87] This is not to say, however, that our consciousness of objects is mediated by self-awareness or that our self-awareness is mediated by our consciousness of objects. Self-manifestation and hetero-manifestation are strictly interdependent, inseparable, and co-original. They are after all two different dimensions of one and the same experience. In Straus's words, "In sensory experience I always experience myself *and* the world at the same time, not myself directly and the *Other* by inference, not myself before the *Other*, not myself without the *Other*, nor the *Other* without myself."[88]

Although it might be tempting to try to restrict the validity of this thesis with reference to either hallucinations or fantasies, which lack a really existing object, or experiences such as nausea, dizziness, and anxiety, which are very much self-aware although they are without intentional objects altogether, I think it would fail. One should be careful not to operate with a too narrow conception of the foreign and transcendent. Properly speaking it does not include only actually existing objects, but hallucinated and imagined objects as well, as any intentional analysis of hallucination and imagination will reveal. Even hyletic data can be characterized as a type of alterity, insofar as they have a nonegoic origin, being elements not generated by consciousness itself. As my subsequent analysis of reflection will disclose, the reflective relation of consciousness to itself might also be described in terms of a *self-othering*, i.e., even if consciousness could turn its attention so completely toward itself that everything else were excluded, it would not escape the confrontation with Otherness.[89] Finally, not only is it doubtful whether it is possible to be dizzy, anxious, and nauseous without at the same time perceiving some objects. Moreover, it might even be argued that we are by no means dealing with mere attendant phenomena, but rather with fundamental forms of disclosure. We are always in some kind of mood. Even a neutral and distanced observation has its own tone, and to quote Heidegger, *"Mood has always already disclosed being-in-the-world as a whole and first makes possible directing oneself toward something."*[90] Thus, although one must distinguish between intentional feelings, such as the desire for an apple or the admiration for a particular person, and more general and pervasive moods, such as the feeling of elation, sadness, boredom, nostalgia, or anxiety, etc., the latter are *not* without a reference to the world. They are not types of object-intentionality. They all lack an intentional object, and prereflectively they are not themselves given as psychic objects. But they do not enclose us within ourselves, but are lived through as pervasive atmospheres that lend their coloration to our intentional objects and deeply influence the way we meet the world.[91] Just think, for example, of moods like curiosity, nervousness, or happiness.

In the light of the preceding discussion, Husserl's view concerning the intrinsic connection between self-awareness, temporality, affection, and incarnation becomes apparent. It is impossible to separate prereflective self-awareness from inner time-consciousness, which is articulated in the tripartite ecstatic-centered structure primal impression–retention–protention. But there can be no primal impression without a hyletic content, and consequently no self-awareness without a hyletic affection. As was pointed out earlier, pure time-consciousness is an abstract form. *In concreto* it is a pervasive sensibility, the very sensing of the sensations. These sensations do not appear out of nowhere, however. They refer us to our bodily sensibility.[92] We consequently end up with something like a phenomenological counterpart to Castañeda's thesis. The transcendental foundation is an "I-am-here-now."

This outcome has made a number of phenomenologists stress the intrinsic relation between temporalization and spatialization—the exteriority of the world is involved in the movement of temporalization[93]—and made them insist on the inseparability of self-awareness, body-awareness, and world-consciousness:

> Ichbewußtsein . . . kann apriori nur Bewußtsein seiner selbst als eines denkenden sein, weil es ineins Bewußtsein des Spielraumes der Spontaneität eines Sichbewegens ist. Zum Ichbewußtsein gehört a priori Bewußtsein dieses Spielraumes als jeweils meines Spielraumes. Es ist der Spielraum der durch mein Bewegen zu erfüllenden Möglichkeiten, Dinge zur Erscheinung bringen zu können. Was ist aber dieser Spielraum? Er ist nichts anderes als die Welt unserer Erfahrung, zunächst die unmittelbare Umwelt. Wenn also zur Möglichkeit eines Ichbewußtseins als der "Vorstellung der Selbsttätigkeit eines denkenden Subjekts" unlösbar gehört das Bewußtsein der Spontaneität des "ich bewege mich," und wenn dieses das Bewußtsein eines Spielraumes der Bewegung in sich einschließt, der nichts anderes als die Welt ist, so ist damit erwiesen, daß Ichbewußtsein ineins Weltbewußtsein ist und daß es als solches der Grund der Möglichkeit einer Affektion der Sinne ist. . . . Damit dürfte geklärt sein, was es bedeutet, das Empfinden als Weise des In-der-Welt-Seins zu begreifen, und wie nur auf diesem Wege der legitime, phänomenologisch verifizierbare Begriff des Empfindens gewonnen und in das richtige Verhältnis zu den sogennanten höheren Erkenntnisleistungen gebracht werden kann.[94]

Thus, to revive a central thesis of Landgrebe, in the hyletic affection we are confronted neither with an objective world nor with a worldless subjectivity, but with their prior unity. We experience our being-in-the-world (as long as world is understood mainly as the nonegoic origin of meaning,[95] and as neither a cultural context nor an objective reality). Since there can be no primal impression without a hyletic content, and no hyletic content without a lived body, it must be concluded both that it would be a falsifying abstraction to overlook the latter in a discussion of the structure of self-awareness, and that the natures of temporality and embodiment cannot be exhaustively comprehended independently of each other.[96] We are dealing with an incarnated temporality, with an embodied, prereflective self-awareness, and it is exactly this prereflective *bodily* and *temporal* self-affection that makes reflective self-awareness possible.

To forestall misunderstandings, let me add that I am not arguing that Husserl would claim that every type of experience is a bodily experience, or that every type of self-awareness is a bodily self-appearance. I am only claiming that he takes the lived body to be indispensable for sense-experience and thereby of crucial (founding) significance for other types of experience. Husserl writes:

> Of course, from the standpoint of pure consciousness sensations are the indispensable material foundation for all basic sorts of noeses.[97]

> Hence in this way *a human being's total consciousness is in a certain sense, by means of its hyletic substrate, bound to the body* [*Leib*], though, to be sure, the intentional lived experiences themselves are *no longer* directly and properly *localized*; they no longer form a stratum on the body [*Leib*].[98]

This is why it can be claimed that every form of knowledge has its bodily roots, a thesis which was subsequently taken up by Merleau-Ponty.

Sartre on the Emptiness of Consciousness

Although Sartre certainly recognizes the existence of a prereflective self-awareness, he denies that it should be conceived along the lines suggested by the Heidelberg School, that is, as a strict irrelational self-coincidence, self-identity, or absolute self-presence. His most fundamental argument touches on the relation between intentionality and self-awareness. Not only does he believe both to be essential and defining features of consciousness, he also takes them to be interdependent, despite their crucial difference.[99] I have earlier mentioned Sartre's argument for the thesis that intentionality entails self-awareness, but he also argues for the reverse implication: consciousness can only be nonpositionally aware of itself if it is positionally aware *of* something; it acquires self-awareness exactly insofar as it is conscious of a transcendent object.[100] The easiest way to make this claim reasonable would be by arguing that if I were not conscious *of* something, I would be lacking that which is self-aware, namely, the intentional experience. But Sartre is purchasing an even more fundamental connection, since he claims that the self-*transparency* of consciousness is essentially dependent on its self-*transcendence.* Thus, Sartre is renowned for his very radical interpretation of intentionality. To affirm the intentionality of consciousness is to deny the existence of any kind of content in it.[101] There is nothing in consciousness, neither objects nor mental representations. It is completely empty and it is precisely because of this that it is self-aware and self-transparent through and through.[102] To deny the intentionality of consciousness would consequently be a denial of its self-awareness as well, since the introduction of any mental content into consciousness would burden it with a substantial opacity that would interfere with, block, and ultimately destroy its transparency.

However, to say that consciousness is characterized by intentionality is to affirm its fundamental emptiness and nonsubstantiality in more than one way. For Sartre, the being of intentional consciousness consists in its revelation of and presence to transcendent being.[103] To *be* conscious is to posit a transcendent object, that is, an object which is different from oneself. It is to be confronted with something which one is not, and it entails an awareness of this difference, i.e., a prereflective self-awareness of oneself as *not being* that of which one is conscious. In Sartre's words, "The structure at the basis of intentionality and of selfness is the negation, which is the *internal* relation of the For-itself to the thing. The For-itself constitutes itself outside in terms of the thing as the negation of that thing; thus its first relation with being-in-itself is negation. It 'is' in the mode of the For-itself; that is, as a separated existent inasmuch as it reveals itself as not being being."[104] Thus, consciousness is nothing apart from not being the transcendent object which it reveals. And it is precisely in this strong sense that consciousness needs intentionality, needs the confrontation with something different from itself in order to *be self-aware*; otherwise, it would lose every determination and dissipate as pure nothingness.[105]

> The negation then is explicit and constitutes the bond of being between the perceived object and the for-itself. The For-itself is nothing more than this translucent Nothing which is the negation of the thing perceived.[106]

> Thus the For-itself's Presence to being implies that the For-itself is a witness of itself in the presence of being as not being that being; presence to being is the presence of the For-itself in so far as the For-itself is not.[107]

> [F]or consciousness can appear to itself only as a nihilation of in-itself. . . . [108]

To use a striking formulation by Rosenberg, one might indeed say that, according to Sartre, consciousness only gives itself to itself through a sort of *via negativa*. Original self-awareness is a prereflective awareness of not being the object of which it at the same time is intentionally conscious.[109]

So far the criticism was aimed at the attempt to identify self-awareness with pure self-presence by insisting on the interdependence between self-awareness and self-transcendence. The self-awareness of subjectivity depends on its relation to something different from itself.[110] But Sartre is not only claiming that prereflective self-awareness cannot be understood as a self-sufficient preoccupation with self. He also claims that self-awareness is incompatible with strict self-identity, and that the self-awareness of subjectivity is dependent on its being different from itself! Let me attempt to clarify this enigmatic claim, since it ultimately concerns a fundamental issue: the internal differentiation of prereflective self-awareness.

We have just seen that Sartre takes the notion of *presence* to imply duality and therefore at least a virtual separation.[111] According to Sartre, this does not hold true only for our knowledge of transcendent objects, however, but even for our prereflective self-awareness:

> Presence to self . . . supposes that an impalpable fissure has slipped into being. If being is present to itself, it is because it is not wholly itself. Presence is an immediate deterioration of coincidence, for it supposes separation.[112]

> That is, one will never find nonthetic consciousness as a mode of being which is not, at the same time, in some way, absence from itself, precisely because it is presence to itself. Now presence to itself presupposes a slight distance from self, a slight absence from self. It is precisely this perpetual play of absence and presence, which it may seem hard to think of as existing, but which we engage in perpetually, and which represents the mode of being of consciousness.[113]

> Examination of nonthetic consciousness reveals a certain type of being which we will call *existence*. Existence is distance from itself, separation. The existent is what it is not and is not what it is. It "nihilates" itself. It is not coincidence with itself, but it is *for-itself*.[114]

Whereas the being of the object is characterized by solidity, positivity, self-sufficiency, and self-identity (a table is purely and simply a table, neither more nor less; it knows no alterity and cannot relate to that which is other),[115] this is not true for the being of subjectivity. My experience does not merely exist. It exists *for-itself*, that is, it is self-aware. But to be aware of one's perception, even prereflectively, is no longer simply and merely to perceive, but to withdraw, wrench away from, or transcend the perception. To be self-aware is to exist at a distance from oneself; it is to be engaged in an ontological self-interrogation. Self-awareness and self-identity are incompatible determinations, wherefore Sartre questions the validity of the law of identity when it comes to an understanding of subjectivity and writes that self-awareness presupposes a tiny fissure, separation, or even duality in the being of consciousness. It is this fracture that gives birth to the self.[116]

Already on the prereflective level we find what Sartre calls "a pattern of duality," "a game of reflections," or "a dyad" existing between *intentionality* and *self-awareness*. Both moments of consciousness are strictly interdependent and inseparable, but their functions are not identical and they do not coincide absolutely. Each of the two refers to the other as that which it is not, but upon which it depends. They coexist in a troubled unity, as a duality which is a unity, and the life of consciousness takes place in this perpetual cross-reference.[117]

When Sartre speaks of a fissure or separation in the being of consciousness, he is obviously not talking about consciousness being separated from itself by *some-thing*, since the introduction of any substantial opacity would split it in two, replacing its dyadic unity with the duality of two separated objects. No, for Sartre consciousness is separated from itself by *no-thing*; that is, the separation in question is, properly speaking, an internal differentiation or negation. But Sartre also claims that the nothing that separates consciousness from itself is at the root of time, and his description of the structure of consciousness gains credibility the moment we turn to *temporality*, that is, the moment we understand the perpetual self-differentiation, self-distanciation, and self-transcendence of subjectivity in temporal terms. Consciousness exists in the *diasporatic* form of temporality. Spread out in all three temporal dimensions, it is always existing at a distance from itself; its self-presence is always permeated by absence, and this unique mode of being cannot be grasped through the category of self-identity. On the contrary, temporality is a perpetual movement of self-transcendence which from the very beginning prevents absolute self-coincidence.[118]

Sartre's reflection can be interpreted as an attack on the Heidelberg School, since it criticizes the attempt to conceive of prereflective self-awareness as strictly irrelational. But at this point it becomes necessary to exhibit a certain caution. When Sartre speaks of a fissure in the core of consciousness or of a slight distance between the belief and its self-awareness, there is one objection that comes to mind immediately. Is he not contradicting himself? In his preliminary remarks on the difference between reflective and prereflective self-awareness, which I presented in chapter 4, Sartre claimed that reflection was characterized by a duality. He argued that it would have aporetical consequences if one were to introduce this duality into the core of consciousness, and concluded that it was impossible to distinguish the intention and its self-awareness on the prereflective level since they were one and the same. Now, however, he appears to reintroduce a dyad into the structure of prereflective self-awareness, a dyad that ultimately undermines the difference between reflective and prereflective self-awareness, and makes the latter vulnerable to the criticism that was successfully directed against the model of reflection, thereby endangering the very possibility of self-awareness. Thus, it has been argued that Sartre is unable to stick to his own insights concerning the nonpositional character of prereflective self-awareness, unable to tear himself away from the traditional subject-object model, and that he willy-nilly keeps introducing cognitive and epistemic elements into his description of self-awareness, thereby destroying its unity and translucency.[119]

That Sartre's account of the difference between prereflective and reflective self-awareness is ultimately somewhat unsatisfactory can also be seen from Sartre's description of reflection. Although he occasionally characterizes it as a type of *positional* consciousness, Sartre nevertheless insists that it differs radically from ordinary intentional acts. We have already seen that these entail a nihilation. To be conscious of a chair is to posit the chair as not being oneself. As Sartre says, *to know is to make oneself other*. But this specific element cannot pertain to reflection, at least not unmodified. A reflective self-awareness only counts as *self*-awareness if the reflecting *is* the reflected. Due to his view on the difference between the for-itself and the in-itself, reflective self-awareness cannot be described as an absolute identity, nor can it simply be the kind of troubled unity that is at play on the prereflective level, since this would efface the difference between reflective and prereflective self-awareness. Sartre is consequently faced with the difficulty of conceiving reflection in a manner that allows for both unity and separation, and his solution is to describe reflection as an infrastructural modification in consciousness that ultimately *deepens* or *increases* the fracture already existing in the prereflective dyad. As we have already seen, Sartre takes the prereflectively self-aware perception to possess a dyadic structure. This structure is doubled the moment we reflect, since we are then dealing with a prereflectively self-aware reflecting which is conscious of a prereflectively self-aware reflected. Although the two dyadic poles in reflective consciousness are inseparable (the reflecting only exists insofar as it reflects the reflected, and, as we shall soon see from Sartre's criticism of egological consciousness, the reflected is modified in the process), they nevertheless tend toward a higher degree of autonomy than the interdependent moments of the dyad. Sartre therefore claims that the nothingness separating the reflecting from the reflected is deeper than the nothingness separating the two interdependent moments of the dyad, i.e., that the reflective self-awareness involves a higher degree of nihilation.[120]

Sartre ends up claiming that the process of reflection entails a tripartite nihilation: There is the nothingness which divides the reflecting consciousness from itself there is the nothingness which divides the consciousness reflected upon from itself, and finally there is the nothingness which divides the reflecting consciousness from the consciousness upon which it reflects. Given all this, the following question does not seem completely unwarranted: Does my reflective self-awareness really exhibit this kind of convoluted structure? Has Sartre really given a faithful description of the phenomena, or has he rather been carried away by dialectical speculations?[121] At one stage, Sartre appears to have been aware of the problem, and he even admits that his description of the structure of the prereflective *cogito* does in fact utilize inappropriate terms.[122] But he never manages to give a more convincing account, and I do not think that he can avoid the criticism.

However, this critique does not entail that Sartre's reservations about describing the prereflective *cogito* as an irrelational self-coincidence are unfounded or irrelevant, but merely that his own conceptual framework and the specific tools used to conceive of the difference, fracture, and distance in prereflective self-awareness are somewhat inadequate. It is after all one thing to make an abstract distinction between intentionality and self-awareness, between the acts and their self-manifestation, between the experience and the experiencing, and something quite different to conceive of this distinction in terms of fracture and internal negation.

Derrida and the Fissure of Unfolding

Let me conclude with a brief look at Derrida, who has also conceived of self-awareness in terms of self-affection. One of the questions Derrida raises is whether self-affection is characterized by pure identity or rather by a dyadic structure. On the face of it, self-affection promises radical and self-sufficient immanence, purified from all references to exteriority and alterity. This purification and exclusion are essential if self-affection is in fact to provide us with immediate and undivided self-presence. But a closer look at its structure reveals that it necessarily entails a minimal division or fracture in order to function. Self-affection contains a structural difference between the affecting and the affected. This is obvious in different types of bodily self-affection: When I see a limited part of my body, or when I touch myself, I am confronted with a type of self-affection where a *contamination* has already taken place. The single parts of the body remain separated and gain contact through a surface which is exposed to the world.[123] But what about the most fundamental type of self-affection, the one to be found in temporality?[124] As we have already seen, Derrida claims that consciousness is never given in a full and instantaneous self-presence, but only presents itself to itself in its intertwining with absence. Since the retentional modification must be conceived as a self-alienation, even temporal self-affection breaks with pure interiority. Thus, Derrida argues that a subjectivity defined by self-affection cannot possibly be undifferentiated and self-enclosed since self-affection necessarily entails a minimal self-differentiation and self-division:[125]

> the possibility of auto-affection manifests itself as such: it leaves a trace of itself in the world. The worldly residence of a signifier becomes impregnable. That which is written remains, and the experience of touching-touched admits the world as a third party. The exteriority of space is irreducible there. Within the general structure of auto-affection, within the giving-oneself-a-presence or a pleasure, the operation of touching-touched receives the other within the narrow gulf that separates doing from suffering. And the outside, the exposed surface of the body, signifies and marks forever the division that shapes auto-affection.[126]

To construe prereflective self-awareness as self-affection is consequently to admit a minimal difference into presence as the very hinge upon which it turns in upon itself. Subjectivity can only be self-present when it folds back on itself, but this (un)folding introduces a fissure which forever prevents simple, immediate, or complete self-coincidence.[127] If something is to appear for itself, it must necessarily undergo a doubling or self-division. But this fracture of (un)folding makes that which appears be both inside and outside itself. Due to the (un)folding there is established a space in the interiority. It is furnished with both an exteriority and an alterity, and is thereby prevented from closing the gap and retrieving itself.[128] Thus, according to Derrida, the general structure of self-affection hinders it from closing in upon itself and from achieving a faultless self-presence. To admit that self-presence presupposes self-affection is to admit that self-presence can never be pure, since the very difference that allows self-presence to establish itself also makes it forever differ from itself. Since self-affection necessarily breaks the self-enclosed interiority and constitutes fractured self-awareness, self-affection is not only always accompanied by hetero-affection, it is itself a hetero-affection.[129]

For Derrida, self-affection is not effectuated by an already existing self; rather it is the process that gives rise to the self. But the self born out of self-affection is constituted as divided, as differing from itself. The difference or relation to oneself as Other is the angle that enables one to fold oneself upon oneself, but this constituting difference also forever prevents one from fully coinciding with oneself, from achieving complete self-identity. It makes the self be what it is only insofar as it simultaneously divides it.[130] "*Auto*-affection constitutes the same (*auto*) as it divides the same. Privation of presence is the condition of experience, that is to say of presence."[131] Since the self is the product of this movement of differentiation rather than its initiator, it would also be false to assume that that which (un)folds itself was simple and identical prior to its self-manifestation. There is no simple origin, but always already dissemination, division, spacing, and temporalization.[132]

The Differentiated Infrastructure of Self-Manifestation

Husserl, Sartre, and Derrida all oppose Henry insofar as they argue in support of some kind of interdependency between self-affection and hetero-affection. On closer examination, however, it is clear that their claims are not as similar as they might appear at first sight, and actually they seem to diverge at one crucial point and to argue in support of two different positions, one moderate and one far more radical. Either it is claimed that it is in our confrontation with that which we are not that we are self-aware, or it is claimed that it is by being confronted with that which we are not that we gain self-awareness. Needless to say, there is a subtle but decisive difference between claiming that my subjectivity is revealed to me in its exploration of the world and claiming that I am conscious of myself via the world. In the first, weaker case, it is claimed that self-awareness and self-affection never occur in isolation from hetero-affection. Self-manifestation is always accompanied by and inseparable from hetero-manifestation, i.e., it cannot take place on its own. Although this moderate thesis already presents a problem for any claim concerning the self-sufficiency of self-awareness, it does not justify the conclusion that the structure of self-awareness contains a fracture, but only that it is always accompanied by a fracture, namely, the fracture between self and Other, between immanence and transcendence.

At this point, however, the more radical thesis asserts itself. It might reasonably be asked whether self-awareness can really retain its purity, integrity, and autonomy if it never appears on its own. If auto-affection and hetero-affection are inseparable, is this not an indication of the fact that they are intertwined, interdependent, and perhaps ultimately even indistinguishable?[133] Thus it has been claimed that self-awareness is not only accompanied by alterity, but also mediated and contaminated by it. It might be tempting to opt for this latter radical position, but one should not overlook the problems that confront it. To claim that self-awareness is not a manifestation *sui generis*, but the result of a mediation, is basically to face all the problems of the reflection theory once again. To go further and claim that self-affection is always already a hetero-affection and that self-awareness is a product of a decentered play of unconscious structural differences is to advocate a position which, instead of contributing to a clarification of self-awareness, dissolves and eradicates the very phenomenon to be investigated.

But although Derrida's formulations are too excessive—it is not surprising that he has occasionally been accused of interpreting self-affection as a form of object-intentionality[134]—there is still something to be said for the radical thesis. After all, prereflective self-awareness is not only always accompanied by hetero-manifestation, it also has an inner articulation, a differentiated infrastructure. Thus, one should not forget the full ecstatic-centered structure of prereflective self-awareness: primal impression–retention–protention. The primal impression is an opening toward multiple otherness: It is open to the hyletic affection; it "geht der Zukunft entgegen, mit offenen Armen";[135] and it is accompanied by a retention, which provides us with "a direct and elementary intuition of otherness in its most primitive form."[136] Temporal self-manifestation is an ecstatic unity of presencing and absencing. Rather than confronting us with a motionless self-identity, self-affection qua self-temporalization can be said to confront us with a basic restlessness and noncoincidence.[137] It is a process of exposure and differentiation, not of closure and totalization.

Since prereflective self-awareness is characterized by this inner articulation, it is no wonder that a number of phenomenologists have chosen to speak of the existence of a pretemporal distance, absence, or even of a *protoreflection* in the core of the prereflective self-awareness. Brand, for instance, describes the perpetual self-affection in prereflective self-awareness as a "Reflexion-im-Ansatz."[138] In contrast to the solid self-identity of objects, the conscious self-presence of subjects already contains an incipient distance or absence. Ultimately this should come as no surprise. Even if it is granted that reflection cannot be the primary kind of self-awareness, it remains necessary to explain how it can rise out of prereflective self-awareness. As Sartre poignantly reminds us, the problem is not to find examples of the prereflective self-awareness, for they are everywhere, but to understand how one can pass from this self-awareness which constitutes the being of consciousness to the reflective knowledge of self, which is founded upon it.[139]

Sartre is by no means trying to deny the difference between a reflective and a prereflective self-awareness, but he nevertheless insists that the two modes of self-awareness must share a certain affinity, a certain structural similarity. Otherwise it would be impossible to explain how the prereflective *cogito* could ever give rise to reflection.[140] It is a significant determination of the originary lived experience that it allows for reflective apprehension, and needless to say, a theory of self-awareness which can *only* account for prereflective self-awareness is as deficient as its counterpart, the reflection theory. To phrase it differently, it is no coincidence that we do exactly speak of a pre*reflective* self-awareness. The choice of words indicates that there remains a connection. (It is interesting to notice that Henry takes the distinction between the reflective and the prereflective *cogito* to be equivocal, and he himself does not use the term "prereflective" as a designation of the originary self-manifestation.[141] Presumably, this is because the notion betrays a certain affiliation with the paradigm of reflection. To designate self-awareness as "prereflective" indicates that reflective self-awareness is still the yardstick.) The reason why reflection remains a permanent possibility is exactly that the reflexive scissiparity exists already *in nuce* in the structure of the prereflective *cogito*.[142] As Derrida puts it: "How can it be explained that the possibility of reflection and re-presentation belongs by essence to every experience, without this nonself-identity of the presence called primordial?"[143] In fact reflection merely articulates the differentiated unity of the Living Present,[144] a structure which Husserl himself occasionally calls the intrinsic *reflexivity* of consciousness.[145] As Held formulates it,

> In dieser Nachträglichkeit (Reflexion als "Nachgewahren") erweist sich dreierlei als immer schon vorausgesetzt: 1. die Unterschiedenheit des Vollziehers von sich selbst, durch die er sich selbst überhaupt thematisieren—oder wie Husserl sagt: "ontifizieren"—kann, 2. die Einheit seiner mit sich selbst, durch die er sich bei der Selbstthematisierung mit sich identifizieren kann, und 3. die Bewegtheit der Einheit-mit-sich-selbst im Sich-von-sich-selbst-Unterscheiden.[146]

> Es darf dann sowenig als gegenständliche Einheit und so wenig überhaupt primär als Einheit gedacht werden, daß der Gedanke innerer ichlicher

Pluralität für das ursprünglichste Verständnis des einzigen *nunc stans* dem Gedanken der Einheit zumindest gleichwesentlich ist.[147]

We consequently end up with the insight that prereflective self-awareness must be conceived not as a simple, static, and self-sufficient self-presence, but as a dynamic and differentiated openness to alterity. To acknowledge this is not in itself to furnish self-awareness with the kind of fracture that exists in reflective self-awareness, let alone in the so-called external types of reflexivity. Although one must avoid interpreting prereflective self-awareness as a self-relation, or as an instance where the act takes itself as its own object, one should not ignore the inner articulation in the dimension of experiencing.

8

Different Levels of Egocentricity

I will now change the focus slightly by turning to the issue of the ego. As was pointed out in chapter 3, a theory of self-awareness has to achieve clarity on a number of different issues. One of them concerns whether or not it makes any sense to speak of a subjectless or egoless self-awareness, i.e., whether one should opt for an egological or a nonegological theory of consciousness. Whereas an egological theory would claim that when I listen to a tune of Coltrane, I am at that time not only intentionally directed at the *tune*, nor merely aware of the tune being *heard*, but also aware that it is being heard by *me*, i.e., that *I* am *hearing* the *tune*, a nonegological theory would claim that self-awareness is merely the acquaintance of consciousness with itself, and that it is consequently more correct simply to say that there is an awareness of the hearing of the tune. This alternative between an egological and a nonegological account intersects with the alternative between a reflective and a prereflective theory of self-awareness, thus presenting us with four basic positions:

	Nonegological	Egological
Reflective	I	II
Prereflective	III	IV

Basically, it might be asked whether *self*-awareness is to be understood as an awareness of *a self*, or rather as the awareness which a specific experience has of *itself*. On closer examination, however, this way of putting the question is misleading. First of all, it presents us with a false alternative. Self-awareness is not *either* an awareness of a self *or* the awareness which an experience has of itself. On the contrary, it must be realized that there are different kinds of self-awareness. I can be prereflectively self-aware of my current perception, and I can reflect and thematize this perception. But I can also reflect upon myself as the intentional agent and subject of experience, that is, I can reflect upon myself as the one who thinks, deliberates, resolves, acts, and suffers. If I compare that which is given in two different acts of reflection, say, a perception of chirping birds and a recollection of a promenade, I can focus upon that which has changed, namely, the intentional acts, but I can also focus upon that which remains identical, namely, the subject of experience. Second, the formulation suggests that if self-awareness were a matter of the awareness which an experience had of itself, we would be dealing with a nonegological or subjectless type of self-awareness. But as will eventually become clear, this suggestion is mistaken.

These preliminary reflections demonstrate the need for a more thematic discussion of what it means to be an ego. Husserl's analysis of the egocentric structure of consciousness can provide us with insights, since he operates with several different *formal* concepts of the ego, or more correctly, with several different overlapping egological levels. In a moment I will attempt to distinguish and discuss the most important ones, but let me start somewhere else, namely, with a brief discussion of Sartre's well-known defense of the nonegological alternative.

Sartre and Nonegological Consciousness

Sartre's reasoning in *La transcendance de l'ego* basically employs three different arguments. First of all, Sartre takes issue with the tradition, and argues that the ego is *superfluous*. It has often been assumed that the mental life would dissipate into a chaos of unstructured and separate sensations if it were not supported by the unifying, synthesizing, and individuating function of a central and atemporal ego. But, as Sartre points out, this reasoning misjudges the character of the stream of consciousness. It does not need any transcendent principle of unification since it is as such an ecstatic flowing unity. It is exactly qua temporalizing that consciousness unifies itself. Nor is it in need of any exterior principle of individuation, since consciousness is per se individuated. Thus an adequate account of time-consciousness makes the intervention of the ego unnecessary, and it has consequently lost its *raison d'être.*[1]

Second, Sartre claims that the ego for essential reasons cannot possibly be a part of consciousness. As we have already seen, Sartre takes consciousness to be characterized by a fundamental transparency and emptiness. Its being consists in self-awareness, and there is consequently no part of it which at any time remains hidden or obscure. The ego, however, is quite different. It appears as something whose nature has to be unearthed gradually and which always possesses aspects yet to be disclosed. Since it is never given in its entirety and consequently never given adequately, it lacks the transparency of consciousness.

One could perhaps object that Sartre conflates the mundane and the transcendental ego. But his reply would be that each and every ego is mundane, and that the attempt to introduce the ego as a formal principle into the structure of transcendental consciousness will unfailingly introduce mundane and opaque elements as well, thereby ruining the purity and transparency of consciousness: "But, in addition, this superfluous *I* would be a hindrance. If it existed it would tear consciousness from itself; it would divide consciousness; it would slide into every consciousness like an opaque blade. The transcendental *I* is the death of consciousness."[2]

Sartre's third and final argument is to demonstrate that an adequate phenomenological description of lived consciousness will simply not find any ego, understood as an inhabitant in or possessor of consciousness. The ego is neither *necessary, possible,* nor *actual.* One occasionally says of a person who is absorbed in something that he has forgotten himself. This way of speaking contains a truth. When I am absorbed in reading a story, I have a consciousness of the narrative, and a nonpositional self-awareness, but according to Sartre, I do not have any awareness of an ego, nor of the reading being done by me. In a similar manner, if I am running after a streetcar, desperately trying to catch it, I will have a consciousness *of the streetcar-having-to-be-overtaken,* and a prereflective self-awareness, but that is all. Thus, Sartre seems to accept Lichtenberg's critique of Descartes. The traditional rendering of the *cogito* affirms too much. What is certain is not that "I am aware of this chair," but that "there is awareness of this chair."[3]

Prereflective consciousness has no egological structure. As long as we are absorbed in the experience, *living* it, no ego will appear. This only happens when we adopt a distancing and objectifying attitude to the experience in question, that is, when we reflect upon it. But even then we are not dealing with an I-consciousness, since the reflecting pole remains nonegological, but merely with a consciousness *of* I. The appearing ego is the object and not the subject of reflection: "the ego is an object which appears only to reflection."[4] As a transcendent entity (cf. the title of Sartre's book) the ego exists outside of consciousness, and it should consequently be left as a study-object for the objectifying sciences, such as psychology.[5] When I engage in a reflective exploration of this object, I will be examining it as if it were the ego of an Other. That is, I will assume the perspective of the Other on myself, and naturally this perspective will never reveal the original self-givenness of my own subjectivity.[6] Thus, Sartre can write: "The reflective attitude is correctly expressed in this famous sentence by Rimbaud (in the letter of the seer): "I is *an other.*"[7]

Let me try briefly to summarize Sartre's account of the way in which the ego appears. When we reflect, we thematize a till then prereflectively self-aware experience, say, a perception of a chair. During this thematization, the perception continues being conscious of its object, the chair, but it undergoes a certain modification. It is turned into a psychical (quasi)object, and is experienced as being owned or had by an ego. But what does it exactly mean that the thematized perception acquires an egological structure? It cannot be that the ego somehow appears as a real constituent part of the act, appearing and disappearing with the act itself. In this case there would be as many egos as there are acts, and "I" am obviously not confronted with a new ego each time "I" reflect. What happens is that the reflection situates the experience within an egological context. The experiences are interpreted as manifesting states, traits, and qualities which belong to an egological totality. Just as a number of separate experiences of loathing, disgust, and repugnancy might be taken to be manifestations of a more permanent attitude toward a given person, an attitude which then appears as a transcendent unity, as a matrix that organizes and relates the different experiences to each other, the ego can be seen as the overarching unity of all mental states, traits, dispositions, etc. That is, the ego is always experienced as transcending the particular act or state of mind in question, and not only because the ego is taken to persist when the act or disposition has disappeared, but also because it is apprehended as being related to other acts and mental states as well. It is one and the same ego that heard the cries of playing children, enjoyed a calvados or a tune by Coltrane, worried about the peace process in the Middle East, felt an enduring fascination for Japanese Zen gardens, decided to study philosophy, etc. Thus, the ego is not contained *in* any of the reflected experiences (psychical objects). It transcends each of them and is characterized by its peculiar elusive givenness since it, as Sartre says, only appears out of the corner of the eye. It is the horizon and ideal noematic unity of the reflected experiences, and it vanishes if one tries to scrutinize it too directly.[8]

Sartre's argumentation apparently supports the position of the Heidelberg School. But is it really convincing? Is it really legitimate to attribute *self*-awareness to an impersonal and nonegological stream of consciousness, or does one not rather reduce the experience to a third-person entity if one insists on speaking of it in strict nonegological terms? It is obviously possible to speak of the ego the way Sartre does, that is, to understand the ego as a personal self with habits, character traits, persisting convictions, etc.[9] But is that the only way? As I have already indicated, one does not have to conceive the ego as a transcendent owner of experiences; it is also possible to describe the very first-personal mode of givenness of an experience as its most basic form of egocentricity.

In this case the ego would not be something standing apart from or opposed to the stream of consciousness, but would be an essential part of its structure.

Thus, one has to question both Sartre's and Merleau-Ponty's revised paraphrases of the *cogito*. It seems inadequate to render the *cogito* as either "there is a perception of a chair" or as "somebody perceives a chair."[10] Both versions overlook one significant detail. When I and my alter ego simultaneously perceive a chair, both of these prereflective perceptions might be anonymous in the sense of lacking an explicit thematization of the ego.[11] But they are *not* anonymous in the sense of being undifferentiated, regardless of whether "undifferentiated" is taken to imply strict numerical identity (in which case the two streams of consciousness would have merged) or merely qualitative identity. On the contrary, there remains a vital difference between the two individuated perceptions. Only one of them is given in a first-personal mode of presentation for me, and I would be unable to perceive the chair if that were not the case. I take this to be a decisive and sufficient argument against the nonegological theory of consciousness.[12]

Consequently, the problem with Sartre's argumentation is that he operates with a too narrow concept of the ego. However, it might be argued that he eventually came to realize this deficit himself. For whereas in *La transcendance de l'ego* he characterizes the prereflective, nonegological field of consciousness as *impersonal*, he describes this view as mistaken in both *L'Être et le néant* and "Conscience de soi et connaissance de soi." It is not the ego which personalizes consciousness; it is consciousness which by means of its fundamental selfness (*ipséité*) allows the ego to appear: "if consciousness does not have an ego at the level of immediacy and nonreflexivity, it is nonetheless personal. It is personal because it is a return, in spite of everything, to itself."[13] At this point one might merely object to Sartre's terminology. It would be more reasonable to ascribe a fundamental egocentricity to consciousness as such and reserve the term "personal" for the higher egological levels. That a careful distinction between different concepts of ego is indispensable should, however, be obvious. Against this background, let me now proceed to Husserl.

The Egocentricity of First-Personal Givenness

In *Logische Untersuchungen*, Husserl initially advocated a nonegological conception of consciousness (a conception which resembles the one adopted by Sartre in *La transcendance de l'ego*), but he later abandoned this position. As Marbach has shown, one of Husserl's principal reasons for this change was the difficulties his theory encountered when it came to a phenomenological analysis of intersubjectivity![14] A condition of possibility for investigating intersubjectivity is that one operates with a conception of subjectivity that allows one to demarcate one consciousness from another, thereby allowing for plurality.[15] But as long as Husserl held on to a nonegological theory which operated with anonymous experiences belonging to nobody[16] and which took the unity of consciousness to be nothing but the sum total of all contiguous experiences, he was faced with the following difficulty: If I encounter a crying child, we would say that I experience not my own sorrow, but the sorrow of somebody else. But it is exactly this distinction which will evade me as long as I opt for a nonegological theory. As Marbach puts it: "Die Analyse phänomenologischer Erfahrung bringt einen kardinalen Unterschied zur Geltung: ich habe Bewußtseinserlebnisse, die ich als 'eigene' bezeichne, und ich habe Bewußtseinserlebnisse von Bewußtseinserlebnissen, welche nicht 'eigene,' vielmehr 'fremde' sind. Soll Klarheit herrschen, kann nicht mehr von 'niemandes' Erlebnissen gesprochen werden."[17] In my empathic appresentation of the child's sorrow, I am both self-aware and aware of somebody else. I am conscious of two different subjects. What is it that permits me to distinguish between my own experience (of empathy) and the Other's experience (of sorrow)? Whereas my own experience is given to me originarily in a first-personal mode of presentation, this is obviously not the case with the child's sorrow.[18] And it is clear why I never confuse my own experience with the Other's experience.[19] The first-personal givenness of the Other's experience is fundamentally inaccessible to me. This is why the Other is characterized by a fundamental alterity and transcendence. This is why the Other is given to me as an Other: "if what belongs to the Other's own essence were directly accessible, it would be merely a moment of my own essence, and ultimately he himself and I myself would be the same."[20]

When Husserl realized this, he abandoned his nonegological theory. Every conscious experience, even an anonymous one, belongs to a subject, i.e., either to me or to somebody else. It cannot belong to nobody. Whether a certain experience is experienced as mine or not does not depend on something apart from the experience, but on the givenness of the experience. If the experience is given originarily to me, in a first-personal mode of presentation, it is experienced as my experience, otherwise not. Obviously this form of egocentricity must be distinguished from the I-consciousness discussed by Castañeda. We are not (yet) confronted with a thematic awareness of the experience as being owned by or belonging to ourselves. It is the particular primary presence of the experience rather than some specific content which makes it mine, and distinguishes it from whatever experiences Others might have.[21] In short, all the experiences of which I am self-aware are necessarily *my* experiences. They are my experiences, and exclusively my experiences, since I am the only one who can be self-aware of them:[22]

> Einheit einer Seele, je einer, hinsichtlich alles ihr zugehörigen Psychischen, ist Einheit aus ihrer eigenen, nur ihr selbst zugänglichen originalen Erfahrung; nur in eigener selbsterlebter Erfahrung ist die Seele *originaliter* und nur ihr selbst zugänglich.[23]

> Das ursprünglichst Meine ist mein Leben, mein "Bewusstsein," mein "ich tue und leide," dessen Sein darin besteht, mir als fungierendem Ich ursprünglich vorgegeben, d.i. im Modus der Originalität, des Es-selbst zugänglich erfahrbar, erschaubar zu sein. All mein Leben ist original für mich erschaubar, es ist fungierendes und dann anonymes Leben oder aktuell erschautes und dann thematisches.[24]

Ultimately, Husserl tends to equate (1) the first-personal mode of givenness, (2) self-awareness, (3) a certain basic sense of egocentricity, and (4) the very life of consciousness.[25]

I have earlier presented Pothast's arguments against an egological theory of self-awareness: If the ego is conceived as something standing opposed to or above the experience, it is difficult to understand why the ego's awareness of the experience should count as a case of *self*-awareness. Husserl's discussion of the originary givenness of my own experiences has, however, disclosed a notion of the ego or self, in which it is not something standing apart from the stream of consciousness, but is a structural part of its givenness. It is the very first-personal mode of presentation of the experience, its very self-manifestation or self-affection, which constitutes the self in its most basic form.[26] For the very same reason, it is bizarre to argue against an egological theory of self-awareness by pointing out that prereflective self-awareness is a passive, given state which precedes all egological initiative.[27] The very same thing can be said about our selfhood. To be a self in the most basic sense is a gift, the result of a happening (*Ereignis*), and not something that we decide to become.[28]

Granted that it is the shared mode of givenness that makes two experiences belong to the same subject, i.e., granted that it is their exposure in the same field of primary presence which makes different experiences of one and the same self,[29] it is possible to answer one of the questions raised in chapter 3: How can self-awareness bridge the temporal distance between different experiences and what is it that allows me to remember a former experience as mine? To recall Husserl's distinction between two different types of reflection, when I remember a past conversation, I am thematically concerned with the conversation, and not with my earlier experience of it. But I always have the opportunity to reflect. I can reflect upon my present recollection of the past conversation, but I can also reflect upon my past experience of the conversation. In the latter case, the relationship between my present and my past experience cannot be compared to the one entertained by two different beads on one and the same string of pearls. Whereas it is possible to examine the beads without being aware of their relation to each other or to the string, and whereas we would need to assure ourselves that they were in fact joined by an uninterrupted string in order to be certain that they are connected, this is not the case for the two experiences. In order to determine whether a past experience is really mine, I do not first need to assure myself of the uninterrupted, temporal continuity between my present reflection and the past experience, but I can do so immediately. Or to be more exact, I do not have to do anything, since no criterial self-identification is involved.[30] If an experience is reflectively accessible to me in recollection, it is necessarily and automatically given as *my past* experience. To argue against the unity of mind by pointing to alleged interruptions in the stream of consciousness (such as dreamless sleep, coma, etc.) is consequently pointless, since one thereby makes the erroneous assumption that it is the *contiguity* between two experiences that makes them part of the same subjectivity, rather than their shared manner of givenness.

More generally, for me to *remember* an episode is not simply for me to think of something, nor simply for me to think of something that happened in the past. It is to re-present something that happened in my own past and which I experienced when it occurred. To remember something is to remember something past which has been present for me. As Brough puts it, "What is remembered was once present in the same unity of time in which the memory is now actual. To cast the matter in egological form, what is remembered is an elapsed position of my own life, recaptured through its actually present portion."[31] It consequently makes no sense to say that I remember *x* without remembering it as having been experienced by me (although I will not thematize this fact in an ordinary recollection), nor can I remember a past event and be in doubt about whether I am the one who originally experienced it.[32] That recollection is immune to the error of misidentification is not, however, to say that the experience in question is necessarily veridical, nor that recollection excludes all types of error. It is certainly possible to confuse and mix several different past experiences, just as it is possible to remember something that we have read, heard, or dreamed about as something that we have experienced in real life.[33] Consequently, if I remember an episode as having taken place ten years ago, I cannot infer that I existed ten years ago, but only that I have had experiences before.[34]

It could, of course, be objected that there are several different types of memory. I might remember not only the conversation I had yesterday, but also how to drive a car, the name of the Danish queen, or the year of the Punic Wars, and of course this does not imply that I necessarily recall the episode in which I learned about the fact for the first time, or even that I experienced the historic event myself. But first of all, one might simply point out that one is only referring to what is known as *episodic* memory (in contrast to what is known as respectively *semantic* and *procedural* memory) and, second, that it might in fact be more appropriate to say that one *knows* the name of the Danish queen or the year of the Punic Wars, or how to drive a car, than that one *remembers* it.[35]

I can only remember the past episode if I implicitly remember my past experience of the episode, and I can only do that if the experience was self-aware when it originally occurred.[36] As Frank formulates it:

> Um mich zu *erinnern*, daß *ich* es war, der soeben ganz in Gedanken verloren über der leeren Seite Papier brütete, ganz ins Niederschreiben vertieft, mußte ich damals schon ein Bewußtsein davon haben. Dieses Bewußtsein mußte ferner mit sich vertraut sein, sonst könnte ich nicht im nachhinein darauf zurückkommen als auf ein solches, das immer noch *meines* heißen darf.[37]

The Ego as a Principle of Focus

The argument for the egological nature of consciousness considered so far is not Husserl's only argument. There is after all more to the egological nature of consciousness than its first-personal givenness. One finds another kind of description that underlines the ego's function as a *structuring principle* in Husserl's repeated characterization of the ego as a *pole or center of action and affection.*[38] Thus the emphasis is changed from considering the ego as a *field* to viewing it as a principle of *focus*. This is obvious in experiences such as concentrating on a task, making a decision, suffering a slight, feeling ashamed, scolding somebody, expecting an event, or initiating a reflection. These acts entail only not a reference to an object, but also a reference to the subject as the *agent* or *patient* of the act, and their full intentional structure must therefore be named *ego-cogito-cogitatum*.[39]

> In solchen Wacherlebnissen des Erfahrens, Erkennens, Schließens, Wertens, Wollens finden wir als eigentümliches Zentrum des Erlebens, als das sich darin Betätigende oder das darin bewußt Erleidende das Ich, es ist der identische Pol, das Zentrum von Aktionen und Passionen, das letztere in Zuständen wie: ich bin traurig, ich bin vergnügt, ich genieße. . . . Das Ich ist hier überall dabei als in diesen Akten lebendes, als sie vollziehendes, als durch sie auf das Wahrgenommene, Geurteilte, Gewollte bezogenes. Das Ich ist kein Kasten, in dem ichlose Erlebnisse stecken, oder eine Bewußtseinstafel, auf der sie aufleuchten und wieder verschwinden, oder ein Erlebniskomplex, ein Bewußtseinsfluß oder etwas in ihm Zusammengebautes, sondern das Ich, von dem hier die Rede ist, ist aufweisbar an jedem Wachheits-oder Akterlebnis als Pol, als Ichzentrum, und damit als an der eigentümlichen Struktur dieser Erlebnisse beteiligt, an ihnen als ihrem Ausstrahlungspunkt oder Einstrahlungspunkt und doch nicht an ihnen als Teil oder Stück.[40]

In order to clarify this notion of the ego as a center or pole of action and affection, Husserl underlines the difference between (1) the intentional act in which we are attentively directed at an object, and (2) our horizontal awareness of the object's surroundings. Let us assume that I am studying a picture in an exhibition hall. Apart from being thematically directed at the picture, I am also conscious of the floor I am standing on, the clothes that I am wearing, the light, the smell and sound of the other visitors, etc. As Husserl puts it, "Gegenständlich aufgefasst ist sehr viel mehr als aufmerksam betrachtet und speziell gemeint. Vielerlei ist nebenbei bemerkt, oder eigentlich gar nicht beachtet, aber doch für uns da."[41] I am conscious of all the surrounding objects, and I can at will choose to change my attention and focus upon them, though at the moment it is only the picture to which I am attentively directed. According to Husserl, it is only the latter which constitutes an explicit *I-consciousness*. Thus, Husserl takes *attention* to be the specific *actionality mode* (*Aktualitätsmodus*) of our intentional acts. The ego lives in these *cogito-*acts, they are carried out by the ego, and Husserl therefore describes attention as an ego-ray (*Ichstrahl*).[42] The attentional modifications are interpreted as modifications of the "glance" of the ego when it shifts its attention from one theme to another.

Naturally, the life of consciousness does not consist only of wakeful *cogitos*, with an attentive, grasping, position-taking ego. There is an underground to the attentive ego-life. There are obviously also passive states, where the ego is deactivated, where it is out of function and has disappeared (not perished).[43] When it comes to habitual acts, for instance, they are both intentional and prereflectively self-aware, but they lack any explicit ego-reference.[44] The ego is not involved in these inattentive acts as a ruling principle. But they are still characterized by an implicit ego-reference, not only because of their self-givenness, but also because they constitute the ego's horizon. Through a change of attention, the ego can always send its gaze into its surroundings, and thereby appropriate the experiences.[45]

Ultimately, an adequate investigation of egological consciousness would have to undertake a much more detailed taxonomy, since the precise character of the ego-involvement differs from act-type to act-type. The ego is present in voluntary acts in a different way than in involuntary acts, just as one must distinguish the egological character of experiences where I am formally present, such as attentive perceptions or recollections; experiences where I am emotionally engaged and responding with feelings of joy, indignation, or hatred; and acts for which I am responsible and of which I am the author.[46] The ego is present in different ways when I scrutinize a menu written in French, when I am hit by a snowball, and when I decide to climb up a rock face.

The Act-Transcendence of the Ego

In *Ideen* II, Husserl at one point states that the way in which the ego functions as a pole of action and affection is analogous to the way in which our body functions as a center of orientation for all sensuous phenomena. And in *Zur Phänomenologie der Intersubjektivität* I he asks whether the metaphor of an I-center and an ego-ray would lose all content if one completely disregarded the bodily subject.[47] As illustration of this line of thought, one might refer to a passage in Pfänder's *Einführung in die Psychologie* (which can be found in Husserl's private library), where attention is described in a way that makes the reference to the body very tangible: Figuratively speaking, that which we are conscious of does not present itself to consciousness as a "flat surface" but in a relief. The highest point of this relief is the point nearest the "attentive subject" and its base is farthest away from him. There are objects that stand in the foreground and objects that stand in the background of consciousness, and that which is in the foreground is nearer the subject and is noticed by him, while that which stands in the background is farther away and not particularly noticed.[48]

Marbach has caught on to this and has argued that the attempt to introduce a pure ego as a center of attention has failed, since it is properly speaking *superfluous*. It is possible to find a center of attention in consciousness. But it is not formed by a pure and formal ego; rather, it is formed exactly by our bodily, kinaesthetic subjectivity.[49] However, this is not to say that there are not good reasons for operating with a pure and formal ego but that, according to both Marbach and Kern, they must be found elsewhere, more precisely in an analysis of the structure of *presentiating* (*vergegenwärtigende*) acts. In order to understand their argumentation, it is necessary to introduce yet another concept of the ego.

On several occasions, Kern has remarked that the ego qua center of attention is a structural moment in the intentional act, and *not* a principle of unity or of self-awareness:

> Dieses reine Ich, dieser "Ichpol" Husserls, hat eigentlich mit dem *Selbstbewußtsein* des intentionalen Erlebens nichts zu tun. Es ist nicht das Prinzip des Selbstbewußtseins eines intentionalen Erlebnisses und bezeichnet auch nicht die Struktur seines Selbstbewußtseins. Man kann nach dem bisher Ausgeführten nicht sagen, daß es das Ich sei, das sich des *cogito* bewußt ist, sondern man muß sagen: Das intentionale Erleben ist sich seiner selbst ungegenständlich "urbewußt," und *wenn* dieses intentionale Erleben die Form *cogito* hat, d.h. vom Ich vollzogenes ist, *dann* ist sich dieses Erlebnis auch dieser Ichstruktur "urbewußt."[50]

It is definitely one thing to claim that the singular act has an egological structure, and something different to claim that the ego functions as an act-transcendent unity in the stream of consciousness. Husserl, however, makes both claims. He speaks not only of the ego-pole as a structural moment in our attentive acts, but also of the ego as an act-transcendent identity-pole that is shared by all experiences belonging to the same stream of consciousness.[51] At this point, we encounter an ego which must be distinguished from the singular experiences, just as we earlier had to distinguish the changing acts or experiences from the abiding dimension of self-manifestation or experiencing. The ego is not contained immanently in the acts, since it preserves its identity, whereas the singular acts arise and perish in the stream of consciousness, replacing each other in a permanent flux.[52] Although the ego must be distinguished from the acts in which it lives and functions, it cannot in any way exist independently of them. It is a transcendence, but in Husserl's famous words, *a transcendence in the immanence*.[53]

The decisive question is now: How is this identical ego experienced; how is it given to consciousness? Or to phrase the question in a way that makes it quite clear that we are in fact dealing with a new aspect of the ego, and not simply returning to the one treated in our discussion of the first-personal mode of presentation: When does my self-awareness contain a reference to this *act-transcendent* identity? Acts of perception possess a prereflective self-awareness, but self-awareness is merely a necessary and not a sufficient condition for *I-consciousness*. According to Kern, the latter entails more than simple, immediate self-awareness (which he claims is egoless); it also entails a duality, difference, or distance which is bridged. The ego cannot be experienced as an act-transcendent identity in a simple act of presentation, be it attentive or not, but only in *presentiating* and *self-displacing* experiences, such as imagination, recollection, and reflection.[54] Presentiating acts entail a fission. The act of reflection entails a fission between the reflecting and the reflected ego; the recollection a fission between the present and the past ego; the act of fantasy a fission between the imagining and the imagined ego.[55] But we are dealing with a fission of a rather peculiar kind. It does not destroy the identity of the ego; quite the contrary, it reveals a hitherto concealed aspect of its being: its act-transcendence. As Husserl says with regard to recollection, the present ego is characterized by its remarkable ability to transfer itself to the past and to be conscious of its identity in this doubling:[56] "Ich bin nicht nur und lebe nicht nur, sondern ein zweites Ich und ein zweites ganzes Ichleben wird bewußt, spiegelt sich gleichsam in meinem Leben, nämlich vergegenwärtigt sich in meinen gegenwärtigen Erinnerungen. . . . Das jeweilige Ich ist aber kontinuierlich durch alle diese Reproduktionen hindurch identisch, identisch mein Ich, und in seiner vergangenen Wirklichkeit mir in der jetzigen Erinnerung bewußt in einer sicheren Gewißheit."[57] It is only when subjectivity displaces itself from its present situation to a presentiated situation, and when it is aware of its identity across this difference, that we are dealing with a truly egological self-awareness. *We can only speak of an experience as being owned by an ego if we operate with a difference between the experience and the ego, and we only need to do that when we realize that the ego retains its identity through different experiences. But in order for that realization to occur, it is necessary to relate and compare different experiences, and this is exactly what takes place in presentiating acts.*[58] Thus, as Bernet has pointed out, Husserl's notion of a pure ego cannot simply be taken as a manifestation and confirmation of his adherence to a metaphysics of presence, since Husserl only introduced the pure ego the moment he started taking intentional acts characterized by self-division, self-absence, and self-alienation seriously.[59]

It is essential not to misunderstand the argument. To claim that subjectivity only acquires an explicit I-consciousness in its *self-othering*[60] is not an argument in favor of a reflection theory of self-awareness, nor does it entail an acceptance of Sartre's thesis concerning the ego's being a product of reflection. It is true that reflection confronts us with a particular type of I-consciousness, but this is due to the identity across differences which it (as well as other acts of presentiation) reveals, and not to the self-objectivation peculiar to it. Moreover, whereas Sartre claimed that reflection presents us with a consciousness of "I" and not with an I-consciousness, since the appearing ego is the object and not the subject of reflection, it is in fact the entire process of reflection which is egological. When I reflect, I am not simply confronted with some indefinite individual who perceives something. If I were, I would not say, "I perceive a black billiard ball," but "Somebody perceives a black billiard ball." By saying "I," I am clearly affirming the identity between the reflecting and the reflected subject. Both of the experiences (the reflecting as well as the reflected) are part of the I-consciousness, since the act-transcendent identity of the ego is only revealed across this difference.[61] To a certain extent it might be said that the ego qua act-transcendent identity can only appear in the synthesis between the actual and the presentiated consciousness. It is constituted, i.e., brought to givenness, in this process. But it is by no means an arbitrary or falsifying constitution. It simply articulates something that already existed beforehand, namely, the abiding dimension of self-manifestation.[62]

So far I have distinguished three (partly overlapping) notions of an ego and three arguments for an egological theory of consciousness. Consciousness must be characterized as egological due to (1) its first-personal mode of presentation, (2) its frequent possession of a structural pole of action and affection, and (3) presentiating acts also manifest a more specific reference to the ego as a transcendent principle of identity.

I take all three to constitute different, irreducible levels of egocentricity, which moreover display a founding-founded relation in the sense that 2 presupposes 1, whereas 3 presupposes both 1 and 2. Although I can understand why Kern and Marbach wish to emphasize the third level, I do not see why one should accept their claim that only this level truly qualifies as egological. When it comes to the second level, Marbach's main argument appears to be that a *pure* ego is superfluous since bodily subjectivity, which Marbach assumes to be nontranscendental, is sufficient for an understanding of attention. However, this is a somewhat peculiar argument. If a number of experiences contain a reference to the bodily subject as the pole of orientation, this must be taken into account when engaged in an analysis of the egocentric structure of consciousness, regardless of whether or not the body has a transcendental status. Moreover, even if Husserl at the time of *Ideen* I (which is Marbach's reference) denied that transcendental subjectivity is embodied, he most certainly changed his mind later on.

As for the first level, I think it is simply a mistake to ignore the significance of the first-personal mode of presentation and consequently to describe the singular acts of presentation, be they attentive or not, as anonymous and egoless. However, in order to recognize the genuine difference between this first level, which lacks any reference to the ego as an attentive agent, patient, or act-transcendent principle, and the two subsequent levels, one might eventually utilize a distinction between *self* and *ego*. One could then reserve the term "ego" for levels 2 and 3, but continue to speak of the fundamental selfhood of the very givenness of the experiences.

Temporality and Depersonalization

When I originally introduced the first-personal mode of givenness as the most basic sense in which the experience could be said to be ego-centric (see page 12), I added that this did not preempt the question whether there might be types of awareness which either lacked the first-personal mode of givenness altogether, or types which possessed an act-transcendent ego as well. That the latter is in fact the case has been shown. But what about the first question? Let me look at a puzzling remark found in Husserl, and then turn to some observations from outside of phenomenology.

According to Husserl, the most fundamental constitutive synthesis of them all, the very process of temporalization, is a synthesis taking place in pure passivity.[63] It is regulated by strict and rigid laws, and it is by no means initiated, influenced, or controlled by the ego.[64] Thus Husserl occasionally suggests that the investigation of the *nunc stans* leads to a preegological level, i.e., to a level of egoless streaming: "Die Strukturanalyse der urtümlichen Gegenwart (das stehend lebendige Strömen) führt uns auf die Ichstruktur und die sie fundierende ständige Unterschichte des ichlosen Strömens, das durch eine konsequente Rückfrage auf das, was auch die sedimentierte Aktivität möglich macht und voraussetzt, auf das radikal Vor-ichliche zurückleitet."[65]

However, a closer examination of Husserl's analysis of the structure of inner time-consciousness reveals a recurrent emphasis on the fact that the ego-pole is present *everywhere* in the Living Present.[66] Thus, Husserl claims that even the anonymous stream of consciousness is unthinkable without an original ego-pole as the center of action and affection.[67] Husserl's simultaneous reference to the egoless and egological character of the stream of consciousness makes it evident that a conceptual equivocation is at play. (That Husserl can speak of an ego-*pole* at this level also illustrates that he was not always terribly concerned with respecting his own conceptual distinctions.) When Husserl speaks of an egoless streaming, the term "egoless" does not refer to the missing presence of the ego; above all, it does not designate an absolutely preindividuated ground. In fact, to conceive of the stream of consciousnes as preegological in the sense of being preindividuated would face the same severe problems as Husserl's original nonegological theory of consciousness. It would be impossible to speak of a plurality of streams, and consequently impossible to recognize the radical transcendence of the Other.[68] But as Husserl says: "Die Zeit meines strömenden Lebens und die meines Nachbarn ist also abgrundtief geschieden, und selbst dieses Wort sagt noch in seiner Bildlichkeit zu wenig. Sowie sie als diese Zeit (mit dem Sinn von Zeit, der eben in der Monade als solcher, eigenwesentlich gegründet ist) einig würde mit der nachbarlichen, wären wir beide ein Ich mit einem Leben, einem Erlebnisstrom, einem Vermögen usw."[69] The term "preegological" means that the ego is not participating or contributing to the (self-)constitution of the process in any *active* or *attentive* way. Thus, Husserl is mainly referring to the passivity of the streaming, which is beyond the influence of the ego.[70] It is not the ego which unifies the experiences. This is taken care of by the very process of temporalization. But although the passive syntheses are not initiated by me, they still happen to me, not to somebody else or to nobody. That the process is not initiated by the ego does not imply that the ego is absent, but merely that its manner of participation is a *being-affected-by*. Thus, it remains exactly possible to designate the I-reference of the passive experiences as an affective one.[71]

At this point, the phenomenological analysis is confronted with questions coming from a completely different direction. If it is the first-personal givenness of the experience which makes it *my* experience, and if I cannot be in doubt about this "ownership," what are we then to do with the cases known from psychopathology, where a person has experiences which he claims is somebody else's? Thus, among the so-called first-rank symptoms of schizophrenia, one finds what might broadly be defined as experiences of *depersonalization*. People not only feel that their experiences are controlled by Others, they may even believe that someone Other than themselves think their thoughts.[72] Not only does this seem to contradict Shoemaker's thesis about first-person experience ascriptions being immune to the error of misidentification,[73] it also seems to contradict the claim that it is the first-personal mode of presentation which constitutes the egocentricity of the experience in question. To be aware of a certain experience from a first-person perspective is apparently not sufficient for regarding the experience as one's own.

Some might be tempted to brush aside this objection with reference to the fact that the person suffering from depersonalization is after all insane, and by arguing that it would be absurd to suggest that a theory of self-awareness should be falsified by insane beliefs. However, the label "insane" is of little relevance in this context. Even if it must be granted that the understanding of pathological phenomena depends upon a prior comprehension of normal processes, i.e., even if it is conceded that we are faced with obvious limit cases, and although most normal spectators might be convinced that the claims of the depersonalized patient are false if not downright incomprehensible, it would be wrong simply to substitute the first-person perspective with a third-person perspective whenever it was convenient. A phenomenological analysis of self-awareness obviously has to take the way in which the subject experiences himself seriously. Although it would be too much to demand that an investigation of self-awareness should actually be able to explain the phenomenon of depersonalization, at least it has to remain compatible with it; i.e., it will not do to advocate a theory which implicitly denies the possibility of depersonalized experiences. It is, for instance, an open question whether Henry's conception of an absolutely unbroken and self-coinciding immanence allows for an understanding of how something like depersonalization and radical dissociation can occur.[74]

The first step toward a clarification of this problem is, however, to describe and interpret the phenomenon of depersonalization correctly.[75] Obviously there is nothing wrong in thinking that foreign thoughts occur in foreign minds. It is only the belief that foreign thoughts occur in one's *own* mind that is pathological and dreadful. Thus, although the experiences of a subject suffering from depersonalization have been described as experiences which lack the peculiar quality of *my-ness*, one might question the accuracy of this description, at least as long as the term "my-ness" is used to designate the first-personal mode of givenness of our experiences. Even if the depersonalized experiences might appear as intrusive or strange, they cannot lack this formal kind of my-ness, since the subject is aware that it is he himself rather than somebody else who experiences these foreign thoughts. Since the afflicted subject does not confuse thoughts occuring in foreign minds with foreign thoughts occuring in his own mind, it is also questionable whether any invalidating misidentification has taken place. Since one remains the subject of the alien thought, the foreignness of the experience cannot be due to a lack of ownership in the formal sense, but might rather be due to a lack of authorship, or because the experience is in other ways felt to be intrusive, compulsive, or unreal.[76] I have earlier mentioned the distinction between voluntary self-movement and involuntary self-movement. Graham and Stephens have suggested that a similar distinction might be used in order to make the claim of the schizophrenic comprehensible. I might experience voluntary self-movement, but I might also experience that I am moved by Others. To believe that a thought which occurs in my mind is somebody else's thought can be compared to a situation where I acknowledge that *my* arm went up while denying that I raised it.[77]

A person afflicted by depersonalization might complain that he is no longer himself. How can one make this complaint intelligible? When our self-expectations are disappointed or violated, we might feel that there is something wrong with ourselves, and finally feel that we are no longer ourselves. Thus, intense experiences of self-change (for instance, of the kind occuring in adolescence) might provoke momentary feelings of depersonalization. One assumes that one has certain characters and qualities, and when one discovers that this is not the case, one becomes unsure about whether one is really oneself, or not rather a stranger.[78]

As both Schilder and Sass have pointed out, the feeling of depersonalization might ultimately be due to an exacerbation of self-awareness, a kind of *ultrareflection*, rather than due to a lack or loss of self-awareness. As Schilder observes, "all depersonalised patients observe themselves continuously and with great zeal, they compare their present dividedness within themselves with their previous oneness-with-themselves. Self-observation is compulsive in these patients. The tendency to self-observation continuously negates the tendency to live, and we may say it represents the internal negation of experience."[79] The subject is so obsessively preoccupied with his experiences that they are gradually transformed and substantialized into objectlike entities, which are then experienced as alien, intrusive, involuntary, and independent.[80] Just as our movements might become inhibited if we pay too much attention to them, something similar can happen with our mental life. Due to the continual self-observation and compulsive self-analysis the normal integrated whole of our experiences is split apart. Although the experiences are continuously given "from the inside," they now appear as alienated fragments. Ultimately, an intense self-analysis might not only detach the experiences from each other, but also end up dissociating them from the analyzing subject as well.

A related interpretation can be found in Laing, who has attempted to make the phenomenon of depersonalization comprehensible through the notion of "ontological insecurity." According to Laing, an ontologically insecure subject might feel that its self-identity is so feeble, vulnerable, and precarious that it retreats from direct contact with the world and

Others in order to sustain its identity and protect itself from the persistent threat of being engulfed by reality. This retreat takes the form of a division between its inner, true self and its outer, false personality. Its public appearance and social bearing become a matter of role playing, a mask, an external hide. The perceptions, feelings, and thoughts of its social self are compulsively monitored with such a critical detachment that they lose spontaneity and become lifeless and unreal, and its interactions with Others are deemed to be so automatic and inauthentic that they finally converge with the actions of a stranger.[81] Detachment leads to reification and ultimately to depersonalization. The subject's relationship to itself is turned into an interpersonal relationship where the observing inner self treats the observed outer personality as if it were an alien presence or foreign person.[82] Since obsessive self-reflection might also come to be relied upon to help sustain the individual's precarious ontological security, it might be illustrative to quote one patient: "I forgot myself at the Ice Carnival the other night. I was so absorbed in looking at it that I forgot what time it was and who and where I was. When I suddenly realized I hadn't been thinking about myself I was frightened to death. The unreality feeling came. I must never forget myself for a single minute."[83]

These descriptions of depersonalization do not confront us with a phenomenon which contradicts our basic assumptions about the nature of self-awareness. On the contrary, they even anticipate our own analysis of reflection as an *alterating* or even *alienating* form of self-awareness. That is, a phenomenological analysis of reflection might exactly facilitate an understanding of this apparently so incomprehensible phenomenon.[84] Even normal reflection might be accompanied by a feeling of detachment and dissociation, and depersonalization can be viewed as an extreme form of self-objectivation that occurs when self-observation turns into self-reification. Of course, this is not to say that alteration and alienation are such integrated parts of the *conditio humana* that we all suffer from different degrees of depersonalization. We are dealing with a pathological phenomenon. But it is a pathological phenomenon which from a phenomenological perspective can be understood as a disorder of self-awareness, and which becomes more comprehensible the moment we have worked out a detailed account of the different modes of self-manifestation.

9

The Person, the Body,
and the Other

S o far nothing has been said about the way in which the structure of my self-awareness might be influenced by my interaction with Others.[1] That such a connection exists, however, has been pointed out by Lévinas and Ricoeur, for instance. As the latter writes, it is first and foremost when I am accused and feel *guilt* that I become aware of myself as the responsible agent of an act. He continues: "I form the consciousness of being the author of my acts in the world and, more generally, the author of my acts of thought, principally on the occasion of my contacts with an other, in a social context. Someone asks, who did that? I rise and reply, I did. Response—responsibility. To be responsible means to be ready to respond to such a question."[2]

My discussion of and distinction between the three different levels of formal egocentricity obviously do not exhaust the issue, and at least one additional type of self-awareness must also be accounted for, namely, the one Husserl calls *mundane* self-awareness. After all, not only can I be aware of myself as a subjective pole of attention or as an act-transcendent principle of subjective identity, but I can also be aware of myself as a worldly entity, be it in a *personalistic* attitude where I appear to myself as one subject among many, that is, as a person or human being, or in a *naturalistic* attitude where I appear to myself as a causally determined thing among things.[3]

Mundane Self-Awareness

Husserl takes the human being (which he occasionally also calls the real, empirical, or personal ego) to be a constituted, worldly transcendence.

157

In contrast to the pure ego, which in its empty formality can be grasped adequately in pure reflection, the human person is thematized in a mundane (empirical or personal) reflection.[4] It is never given adequately, but appears adumbrationally and must be investigated and unearthed gradually, step-by-step. Prompted by external circumstances it might suddenly reveal hitherto concealed aspects of itself, or acquire and develop quite new traits.[5]

> In order to know what a human being is or what I myself am as a human personality, I have to enter into an infinity of experience in which I come to know myself under ever new aspects, according to ever new properties, and in an ever more perfect way. Only this experience can exhibit (or perhaps repudiate) what I am and even that I am. . . . On the other hand, in order to know that the pure Ego is and what it is, no ever so great accumulation of self-experience can profit me more than the single experience of one sole and simple cogito.[6]

Not only can I be aware of myself as a perceiving or remembering subject, I can also be aware of myself as a hard-working Hawaiian physicist or as a tubercular middle-aged male. Despite these obvious and radical differences, it should not be forgotten, however, that we are dealing with different types of *self-awareness*, and not with different subjects. In each case, I am aware of *myself*.

For Husserl, the *person*, or personal ego, and the *psyche*, or psychological ego, are not two different subjects but two radically different *mundane* perspectives on the subject. The personal ego is how I appear to myself in the personalistic attitude. It is this subject which is studied by the human and social sciences. The psyche, on the other hand, is consciousness taken as a part of the psychophysical complex, and it belongs to the study field of the natural sciences. Whereas the person is the socialized subject, a member of the social world, the psyche is the naturalized subject, a part of the natural world.[7] When it comes to the relation between these two stances, Husserl claims that the personalistic attitude is far more natural than the naturalistic one. The naturalistic psychophysical attitude is secondary and founded. It presupposes the personalistic attitude and is won through a process of abstraction and self-oblivion.[8]

When speaking of personal self-awareness, it might be natural to assume that we are about to leave the sphere of self-awareness proper in order to commence an investigation of a related but nevertheless different nest of problems, namely, the ones pertaining to the issue of personal identity. What is it that secures personal identity over time? What is it that permits us to speak of the continued existence of a person? In fact, however, the problem I wish to clarify is quite different. I am interested in how the subject *acquires* mundane self-awareness, and in what it is that enables it to apprehend itself as a worldly entity. The reason this question is crucial is because any convincing theory of self-awareness has to be able to explain the connection and transition between the two dimensions of the subject, its private and its public face. As Castañeda puts it: "One serious problem for any theory of *self*-consciousness is to provide an account of *I*-hood that reconciles, assuages, or dissolves the deep-rooted tension between the nonworldliness and the worldliness of the *I*'s. Nonworldliness arises from the internality of *self**-reference; worldliness springs forth from the externality of SELFreference, which necessitates the embodiment of each I."[9] Obviously, it will not do to end up with a theory of self-awareness which conceives of the self-manifestation of subjectivity in such a way that it becomes incomprehensible how the subject could ever appear to itself as a mundane entity. It thus needs to be spelled out how I can assume this mundanizing perspective on myself.

Part of the answer has already been given. As I argued in chapter 6, if one wishes to understand the relation between the self as a subjective, elusive dimension, and the self as an intersubjectively accessible mundane object, one has to take the *body* into consideration. To acknowledge the embodied nature of subjectivity is only the first step, however. As we have already seen, there are several different forms of bodily self-appearance, and to be prereflectively aware of one's position and movement is not yet to appear to oneself as a mundane, transcendent object. But as Husserl says, it is when I become *alienated* from my body that I discover myself as a human being.[10]

How should one understand this enigmatic sentence? According to Husserl, I can appear as a mundane object for myself, but it is not a self-apprehension which is immediately accessible. It presupposes a fundamental change in attitude toward oneself, a change which is occasioned by the Other—and that is the essential point.

Although I can perceive my adumbrationally given bodily exteriority on my own, this perception does not present me with an ordinary worldly object. Under normal circumstances the visually or tactually given surface of, say, my left hand will be accompanied by a localized interiority. And even in borderline situations where this is not the case, I will at most be presented with bodily fragments, never with the entire body. As already mentioned, my body systematically hides parts of itself from me and consequently remains a "remarkably imperfectly constituted thing."[11] Furthermore, it has to be realized that there is more to being a worldly object than merely to appear adumbrationally. A worldly object is an object which is *intersubjectively* accessible, that is, it is constituted with an intersubjective validity, and it can be grasped from a third-person perspective. But to perceive one's own body in such a way is literally to apprehend it from the perspective of the Other, as the bearer of social, cultural, and scientific properties. And this perspective is not something I adopt on my own. The first body to be apprehended by me in such a fashion is the body of the Other, and it is only subsequently that I learn to grasp my own body in a similar way.[12] As Husserl says, I cannot experience my own intersubjective *"Realitätsform"* directly, but only mediated through empathy.[13]

Husserl elaborates this idea in his description of a special kind of experience of the Other, namely, the situation in which I experience the Other as experiencing myself. This "original reciprocal coexistence," where my indirect experience of an Other coincides with my self-experience, can be described as a situation where I see myself through the eyes of the Other.[14] When I realize that I can be given for the Other in the same way as the Other is given for me, that is, when I realize that I myself am an Other to the Other, my self-apprehension will be transformed correspondingly:

> Es verschwindet der Unterschied zwischen Selbst und fremdem Ich, der Andere fasst mich als Fremden auf, wie ich ihn als für mich Fremden auffasse, er ist sich selbst ein "Selbst" usw. So erfolgt Gleichordnung; eine Mannigfaltigkeit gleichartiger, in gleichem Sinn selbständiger, sich fühlender, wollender Ich. Weiter: Ich mit seinem festen Habitus, mit bestimmten Gewohnheiten des Sich-gehabens, Wirkens, des Denkens und Redens usw. Das wird an Anderen beobachtet, und die Anderen beobachten uns, und so erwächst teils durch Selbstbeobachtung unter dem Bild Anderer, teils durch die Beobachtung Anderer die Idee der Persönlichkeit überhaupt, der eigenen und fremden.[15]

It is in the light of this discussion that Husserl distinguishes the subject taken in its bare formality from the social ego or personalized subject and claims that the origin of personality must be located in the social acts. An awareness of oneself as an ego-pole is not sufficient for a personal self-awareness. It demands a social relation to other subjects as well. To exist as a person is to exist socialized in a communal horizon, where one's bearing to oneself is appropriated from the Others.

> Der im solipsistisch fingierten Subjekt notwendig vorhandene Pol aller Affektionen und Aktionen, das durch den Erlebnisstrom hindurchgehende Motivationssubjekt, das als solches beständiges

Subjekt eines Strebens in mannigfaltigen Modalitäten ist, wird zum
Ich und damit zum personalen Subjekt, gewinnt darin personales
"Selbstbewußtsein," in der Ich-Du-Beziehung, in der durch Mitteilung
ermöglichten Strebensgemeinschaft und Willensgemeinschaft.[16]

According to Husserl, personal self-awareness is a type of self-awareness
which is *a priori* inseparable from the Other. I cannot possibly perceive
myself as a human being directly, on my own, independently of the Other.
It is the Other who is first perceived as a person and as a human being, and
it is only subsequently that this mode of apprehension becomes available
to myself. It is only when I apprehend the Other as apprehending me,
and when I take myself as the Other to the Other, that I apprehend
myself in the same way that I apprehend them, and that I become aware
of the same entity that they are aware of, namely, myself as a person.[17] In
short, my personhood is intersubjectively constituted.[18] It is no wonder
that Husserl often asserts that the personal reflection, in contrast to the
pure reflection, is characterized by a complex and indirect intentional
structure.[19]

Since my encounter with the Other occasions a *mundanization*
of my self-apprehension, Husserl also argues that empathy leads to *self-
alienation*.[20] The pertinence of this characterization is particularly striking
the moment it is realized that it is also through the Other's perception of
my body (which in many ways is superior to my own, for instance, when
we are dealing with a visual presentation of my neck or my own eyes),[21]
and through my appropriation of his view on my body, that a *naturalistic*
self-apprehension is made possible. It is through the Other that I learn
to carry out an objectifying, ideative, and abstractive apprehension of my
own body[22] which conceives of it as a part of nature, as a mere complex
of physiological organs embedded within and determined by causal relations in the world.[23] "Das Subjekt, das für sich selbst nie Objekt werden
kann in der unmittelbaren Selbsterfahrung (in der blossen Reflexion),
wird für den Anderen Objekt und wird dann für sich selbst durch Identi-
fikation des Subjekts der Innenbetrachtung und des Subjekt-Objekts, das
der Andere in seiner Aussenbetrachtung meines Leibes diesem zumisst,
zum Objekt—zum Objekt in der mir und ihm gemeinsamen Natur."[24]

Ultimately, the personalistic and the naturalistic attitudes mentioned above are interconnected. My encounter with the Other typically
provokes two distinct changes in my self-apprehension. I become someone different (namely, socialized) as well as something different (an
empirical object). In Theunissen's words: "Terminologically, we bring this
becoming-*an*-Other and becoming-*something*-Other down to one common denominator, in that we characterize the alteration that I undergo

through the Other, in the here as in the there, as 'alter-ation' [*Veränderung*]. As reification, my becoming human is a substantializing alter-ation; as communalization, it is a personalizing alter-ation."[25]

The Alienating Gaze of the Other

Husserl's analysis of the intersubjectively mediated self-objectivation finds a remarkable echo in part 3 of *L'Être et le néant*, where Sartre argues that a sufficiently thorough examination of the structure of the *cogito* leads us to the Other. This is not only because there are experiences, such as sympathy, shame, shyness, or hatred, which unambiguously refer to the Other, but because the encounter with the transcendent being of the Other proves to be a condition of possibility for a certain type of self-awareness:[26]

> What the *cogito* reveals to us here is just factual necessity: it is found—and this is indisputable—that our being along with its being-for-itself is also for-others; the being which is revealed to the reflective consciousness is for-itself-for-others. The Cartesian *cogito* only makes an affirmation of the absolute truth of a *fact*—that of my existence. In the same way the *cogito* a little expanded as we are using it here, reveals to us as a fact the existence of the Other and my existence for the Other.[27]

Sartre's approach to the problem of intersubjectivity is characterized by an ingenious reversal of the traditional direction of inquiry. Usually the pertinent question has been: How can I experience (objectify) the Other in a way that preserves her subjectivity, transcendence, and alterity? Sartre, however, takes this approach to be misguided. What is truly peculiar and exceptional about the Other is not that I am experiencing a *cogitatum cogitans*, but that I am encountering somebody who is able to perceive and objectify me. The Other is the being for whom I appear as an object, and it is consequently through an awareness of myself qua being-an-object for an Other that foreign subjectivity is revealed to me.[28]

This line of thought is forcefully displayed in Sartre's renowned analysis of shame. According to Sartre, shame is not a feeling which I could elicit on my own. It presupposes the intervention of the Other, and not merely because the Other is the one before whom I feel ashamed, but also and more significantly because the Other is the one that constitutes that of which I am ashamed. I am ashamed not of myself qua being-for-itself, but of myself as I appear to the Other. I am existing not only for myself but also for Others, and this is what the shame undeniably reveals to me.[29]

To feel shame is to confess instantaneously. It is to accept the Other's judgment, and to acknowledge that I am what the Other takes me to be. But although the shame confronts me with a dimension of being that I must acknowledge as mine, this acknowledgment is of a rather peculiar and indirect nature. When I feel ashamed, a modification of my prereflective self-awareness has taken place since I am *prereflectively* aware of being an *object*. But it is not for myself that I am an object, it is for the Other. It is for the Other, and not for myself, that I appear in my being-for-Others, and although I experience the fact that I am taken as an object, the exact nature of this object will always elude my grasp: "Thus originally the bond between my unreflective consciousness and my *Ego*, which is being looked at, is a bond not of knowing but of being. Beyond any knowledge which I can have, I am this self which another knows."[30] This incapacity is not only due to the freedom of the Other (I can never determine exactly what the Other apprehends me as), but also because I am fundamentally incapable of sharing his view. Always remaining prereflectively self-aware, I cannot objectify myself as merciless as the Other does, since I lack the sufficient distance. I can *signitively* experience that the Other provides me with an outside, but I cannot face it, I cannot have an intuition of it. It is no wonder that Sartre claims that I experience the Other's gaze as an alienation, and that he calls my being-for-Others an *ecstatic* and *external* dimension of being.[31]

> This is because of the fact that by means of the upsurge of the Other there appear certain determinations which I *am* without having chosen them. Here I am—Jew, or Aryan, handsome or ugly, one-armed, etc. All this I am *for the Other* with no hope of apprehending this meaning which I have *outside* and, still more important, with no hope of changing it. Speech alone will inform me of what I am; again this will never be except as the object of an empty intention, any intuition of it is forever denied me.[32]

But precisely what kind of modification does my self-awareness undergo due to my encounter with the Other? Sartre writes that the gaze of the Other paralyzes my transcendence. The gaze of the Other reduces me to that which I am (I am what the Other takes me to be) and so it furnishes me with the self-identity of an object. To apprehend myself as seen is to apprehend myself as seen in the midst of the world, as a thing among things.[33] It is to find myself in a situation where I use *language* and adopt a third-person perspective on myself, apprehending myself as an Eskimo, an intellectual, an exploited miner, or a failed piano teacher.[34]

The petrifying gaze of the Other provokes a *mundanization* of my self-apprehension and throws me into worldly space and time.[35] I am no longer given to myself as the temporal and spatial center of the world. I am no longer simply "here," but next to the door, or on the couch. And I am no longer simply "now," but too late for the appointment.

Individuality and Intersubjectivity

For both Husserl and Sartre, mundane self-awareness entails a self-apprehension from the perspective of the Other, and it therefore has the encounter with the Other and the Other's intervention as its condition of possibility. It is, in other words, a type of self-awareness which does not have its origin in the self but depends upon *radical alterity*.[36] When I experience the Other as experiencing myself and when I take over the Other's objectifying and alienating apprehension of myself, my self-awareness is mediated by the Other. Through the Other a type of self-awareness is made possible wherein I apprehend myself as seen in the midst of the world, as a person among persons, and as an object among objects.[37] Whereas (pure) reflection never turns me into a true mundane (psychophysical) object to myself—it thematizes me, it does not mundanize me[38]—this can happen intersubjectively, when I use language to describe myself through concepts acquired from the Others, for instance, when I read, appropriate, and accept a psychological or psychiatric diagnosis concerning myself.

In marked contrast to Sartre, however, Husserl does not view the personalization as a falsification of subjectivity, but as a maturation and enrichment of it. I am the subject not only of actual experiences, but also of diverse developing personality structures, and although the latter process does entail a self-objectivation, we are by no means confronted with something sharing the same regional ontology as physical objects.[39] I am not only a pure ego, but also a person, with abilities, dispositions, habits, interests, character traits, and convictions, and to focus exclusively on the first is to engage in an abstraction, since this identity pole, far from being identical or coextensive with subjectivity, is merely a structural moment in the latter.[40] Given the right conditions and circumstances, the ego acquires a personalizing self-apprehension, i.e., it develops into a person and as a person.[41] And this development intrinsically depends upon the Other.

It is Husserl's analysis of the intersubjective nature of the person which is behind statements to the effect that the I needs a Thou, an alterity which is itself an ego, in order to be an I. As he says, if there were no Thou, there would be no I either, i.e., the I is only an I in contrast to a Thou.[42] These statements conceal a certain ambiguity, however. On the one hand, Husserl denies that the ego taken in separation from the alter ego remains an ego, since they are interdependent. On the other hand, he occasionally claims that the absolute ego is singular to an extent that rules out multiplication as meaningless, for which reason it cannot be *an* ego (among many).[43]

The solution to this seeming contradiction can be found if one examines the manuscript B I 14. Husserl writes that "I" does not admit of any plural as long as the word is used in its original sense. Others can experience themselves as I, but I can only experience myself as I. Besides myself there is no other I about whom I can say, "This is me." Precisely for that reason it is impossible to speak about *an* I, as long as "I" really means I. For myself, I am the only I.[44] When Husserl mentions the absolute singularity of the ego, and denies that it can be put into the plural, he is obviously referring to the unique egocentric givenness of my own consciousness. I am only self-aware of myself and can never ever be self-aware of anybody else. This kind of uniqueness does not exclude Others, however: "Das einzige Ich—das transzendentale. In seiner Einzigkeit setzt es 'andere' einzige transzendentale Ich—als 'andere,' die selbst wieder in Einzigkeit Andere setzen."[45] Husserl obviously considers this egocentricity to be of paramount importance. As he says, the "I am" is the intentional ground for the ego that thinks it. It is the primal fact that a philosopher must never overlook.[46]

If we combine these reflections with our discussion of the irreducible first-personal mode of presentation, it becomes clear that Husserl takes subjectivity to possess an intrinsic and absolute individuality and uniqueness.[47] As an absolute feature this individuality is original and fundamental; it is not something which the subject only acquires subsequently through a confrontation and interaction with Others,[48] although the peculiarity of this mode might only become apparent through the contrast: "Für den Menschen, der keine Einfühlung erlebt hätte, oder vom Standpunkt der Abstraktion von jeder Einfühlung gibt es keine Innerlichkeit einer Äusserlichkeit, der Mensch hätte alle die Erlebnisse und alle die Gegenständlichkeiten überhaupt, die der Titel Innerlichkeit befasst, aber der Begriff der Innerlichkeit wäre verloren."[49]

As long as we focus on the first-personal mode of givenness of the stream of consciousness, we are dealing with a kind of pure, formal, and empty individuality which the subject shares with all other subjects. They are, so to speak, unique in exactly the same way. This is hardly surprising given our discussion in chapters 1 and 2. My direct self-acquaintance is not mediated by knowledge of any identifying properties. It is so pure and formal that it does not provide us with an insight into any of our distinctive features. When it comes to the true individuality of the subject, it only manifests itself on the personal level, in its individual history, in its moral and intellectual convictions and decisions.[50] It is through these acts that I define myself; they have a character-shaping effect. I remain the same as long as I adhere to my convictions. When they change, *I* change.[51] Since these convictions and endorsed values are intrinsically social, we are once more confronted with the idea that the ego in its full scope and concretion cannot be thought or understood in isolation from the Other. The ego is only fully individualized when personalized, and this only happens intersubjectively. I only become a personal ego through my life with Others in our communal world: "According to our presentation, the concepts I and we are relative: the I requires the thou, the we, and the 'other.' And furthermore, the Ego (the Ego as person) requires a relation to a world which engages it. Therefore, I, we and world belong together."[52]

To apprehend oneself as a social and worldly entity is quite different from the self-awareness which is directly accessible in pure reflection, but as I have already pointed out, we are not dealing with distinct and separate subjects, but with different manifestations of one and the same subject.[53] Ultimately, mundane self-awareness is a founded objectifying self-interpretation.[54] And to return to the question raised above, the possibility of mundane self-appearance becomes comprehensible the moment one considers the embodied nature and intersubjective openness of subjectivity.

The Exteriority of the Body

At this stage, however, we are confronted with a number of interrelated questions. It is one thing to claim that our encounter and interaction with the Other can occasion decisive changes in the mode of our self-givenness. But how do we experience the Other in the first place? Is the encounter with the Other something that I am absolutely unprepared for? Is the alterity of the Other so radical and overwhelming that I have no chance of anticipating it? Or is my encounter with the Other, rather, preempted by and made possible through the very structure of temporal and bodily self-givenness? Is it because I am always already an Other to myself that I can encounter Others? Is it the alterity of my own subjectivity that guides me in my apprehension of the alterity of the Other?

According to Sartre, it is a decisive mistake to claim that the relation to the Other is an essential, intrinsic, and *a priori* feature of subjectivity.[55] As he rightly points out, any theory of intersubjectivity which attempts to bridge the gap between the self and the Other by emphasizing their similarity, indistinguishability, and *a priori* interconnectedness is in danger of relapsing into a solipsistic monism and hence of losing sight of the real issue: our concrete encounter with this or that *transcendent* Other. Sartre thus insists that if the *being-with* (*Mitsein*) did in fact belong essentially to the structure of the for-itself, it would forever make an encounter with the radical Other impossible. If solipsism is to be defeated, the relation to the Other cannot belong to the ontological structure of the for-itself, the possibility of the Other cannot be deduced from the for-itself. The existence of the Other must be regarded as a contingent fact, and the being-for-Others as a mode of being which only establishes itself through the concrete encounter with the Other.[56]

Sartre consequently denies that my bodily self-awareness contains a dimension of exteriority and alterity from the very start. On the contrary, it is only when the Other's apprehension of my body influences the way in which I live it that it becomes alien. It is the Other that teaches me to adopt an alienating attitude toward my own body. Thus, Sartre claims that the appearance of the body as an object is a relatively late occurrence. It presupposes a prior consciousness of the lived body, a consciousness of the world as a complex of instrumentality, and most significantly a perception of the body of the Other. The child has used her body to explore the world and examine the Other before she starts looking at her body and discovers its exteriority.[57] Though, it should be stressed that Sartre believes it to be a decisive mistake to think that my original encounter with the body of the Other is an encounter with the kind of body described by physiology. Even when the body of the Other is given as an object it remains radically unlike other objects. This is so not only because the foreign body always appears in a *situation*, that is, in a meaningful context supported by that very body, but also because the body is perceived first as a unity, and only subsequently as a complex of externally juxtaposed bodily parts.[58] For Sartre as well the *personalistic* attitude is prior to the *naturalistic* one.

Against this background, one can understand why Sartre attempts to belittle the significance of the double-sensation. As he writes, it is a matter of empirical contingency that I can perceive myself and thereby adopt the Other's point of view on my own body, i.e., make my own body appear to me as the body of an Other. It is an anatomical peculiarity, and neither something that can be deduced from the fact that consciousness is necessarily embodied, nor something that can serve as the basis for a general theory of the body.[59] The body's being-for-itself and the body's being-for-Others are two radically distinct and incommunicable ontological dimensions of the body.

Prior to my encounter with the Other my body is not given explicitly and thematically to me. However, even when I do start examining my perceptual organs I will not be able to grasp them as *experiencing*. I cannot apprehend my hand or my eye in its process of revealing an aspect of the world to me. The moment I perceive or touch my body I establish a distance between me and it. The body is present, but as a complex of objects, and not as myself. When I perceive my hand, the hand is by no means indicated as the invisible center of reference, as the indexical "here," but as a worldly object in space. That which is touched belongs to the sphere of objects, that which touches does not. I cannot see the seeing eye, I cannot touch the touching hand:

> Either it is a thing among other things, or else it is that by which things are revealed to me. But it can not be both at the same time.[60]

> To touch and to be touched, to feel that one is touching and to feel that one is touched—these are two species of phenomena which it is useless to try to reunite by the term "double sensation." In fact they are radically distinct, and they exist on two incommunicable levels.[61]

This claim must be questioned, however, because it seems to replace the unbridgeable dualism between mind and body with an equally unbridgeable dualism between lived body and perceived body. Rather than dealing with different dimensions or manifestations of the same body, we seem to be left with different bodies. And this conclusion is unacceptable, not the least because Sartre's position also makes it incomprehensible how we should be able to recognize other embodied subjects in the first place.

What has Husserl to say on this issue? Husserl has often underlined the structural similarity between empathy and recollection.[62] Recollection entails a self-displacement or self-distanciation, qualities that are needed if I am to be capable of empathy, if I am to meet the Other as a self. This line of thought is continued when Husserl speaks of the affinity between the depresentation effectuated by original temporalization and the self-alienation taking place in empathy: "Self-temporalization through depresentation [*Ent-Gegenwärtigung*], so to speak (through recollection), has its analogue in my self-alienation [*Ent-Fremdung*] (empathy as a depresentation of a higher level—depresentation of my primal presence [*Urpräsenz*] into a merely presentified [*vergegenwärtigte*] primal presence).[63] Husserl appears to regard the step from depresentation to self-alienation as an intensification of alterity, and more generally he seems to consider the ecstatic-centered self-differentiation which is due to the process of temporalization to be a condition of possibility for empathy, for an openness toward the Other.[64]

An analogous reasoning that relates our ability to encounter an Other with an internal manifestation of alterity can also be found in Husserl's analysis of bodily self-awareness. Although I cannot naturalize my body on my own, I do perceive it visually and tactually. As Claesges writes, "Dadurch hat den Leib im Sinne des Begriffes der 'Doppelrealität' zugleich ichlichen und ichfremden Charakter."[65] Even if it were granted that the phenomenon of double-sensation does not confront us with an experience where one and the same hand is simultaneously experienced as both touching and touched, it still presents us with an ambiguous setting in which the hand alternates between two roles, that of touching and that of being touched. That is, although the very touching cannot be touched, the touching can be experienced, and the phenomenon of double-sensation does provide us with an experience of the dual nature of the body. It is the very same hand which can appear in two different fashions, as alternately touched and touching. In contrast to the self-manifestation of, say, an act of judging, my bodily self-givenness consequently permits me to confront my own exteriority. This experience is crucial for empathy,[66] and it serves as the springboard for diverse alienating forms of self-apprehension. It is exactly the unique subject-object status of the body, the remarkable interplay between *ipseity* and *alterity* characterizing the double-sensation which permits me to recognize and experience other embodied subjects.[67] When my left hand touches my right, I am experiencing myself in a manner that anticipates both the way in which an Other would experience me and the way in which I would experience an Other. This might be what Husserl is referring to when he writes that the possibility of sociality presupposes a certain intersubjectivity of the body.[68]

Husserl's reflections anticipate Merleau-Ponty's, whose own position is quite unequivocal: The self-manifestation of subjectivity *must* be contaminated by alterity. Otherwise intersubjectivity would be impossible. Thus, Merleau-Ponty takes self-coincidence and the relation with an Other to be mutually incompatible determinations. If the self-manifestation of subjectivity were in fact characterized by a pure and unbroken self-presence, if I were given to myself in an absolutely unique way, I would not only lack the means of ever recognizing the embodied Other as another subjectivity. I would also lack the ability to recognize myself in the mirror, and more generally be unable to grasp a certain intersubjectively describable embodied person as myself.

> If the sole experience of the subject is the one which I gain by coinciding with it, if the mind, by definition, eludes "the outside spectator" and can be recognized only from within, my *cogito* is necessarily unique, and cannot be "shared in" by another. Perhaps we can say that it is "transferable" to others. But then how could such a transfer ever be brought about? What spectacle can ever validly induce me to posit outside myself that mode of existence the whole significance of which demands that it be grasped from within? Unless I learn within myself to recognize the junction of the *for itself* and the *in itself*, none of those mechanisms called other bodies will ever be able to come to life; unless I have an exterior others have no interior. The plurality of consciousness is impossible if I have an absolute consciousness of myself.[69]

For Merleau-Ponty, subjectivity is essentially incarnated. To exist embodied is, however, to exist neither as pure subject nor as pure object, but to exist in a way that transcends the opposition between *pour-soi* and *en-soi*. It does not entail losing self-awareness; on the contrary, self-awareness is intrinsically embodied self-awareness, but it does entail a loss or perhaps rather a release from transparency and purity, thereby permitting intersubjectivity: "The other can be evident to me because I am not transparent for myself, and because my subjectivity draws its body in its wake."[70]

Since intersubjectivity is in fact possible, there must exist a bridge between my self-awareness and my awareness of Others; my experience of my own subjectivity must contain an anticipation of the Other, must contain the seeds of alterity.[71] If I am to recognize other embodied subjects as foreign subjects, I have to be in possession of something that will allow me to do so. When I experience myself and when I experience an Other, there is in fact a common denominator. In both cases I am dealing with *incarnation,* and one of the features of my embodied self-awareness is that it per definition comprises an *exteriority.* When my left hand touches my right, or when I gaze at my left foot, I am experiencing myself, but in a way that anticipates the manner in which I would experience an Other, and an Other would experience me. Thus, Merleau-Ponty can describe embodied self-awareness as a presentiment of the Other—the Other appears on the horizon of this self-experience—and the experience of the Other as an echo of one's own bodily constitution. The reason why I can experience Others is because I am never so close to myself that the Other is completely and radically foreign and inaccessible. I am always already a stranger to myself and therefore open to Others. The secret of the Other is in reality the secret of my own being, and the being-for-Others a dimension which belongs intrinsically and essentially to the for-itself.[72] My bodily existence in the world is from the very beginning intersubjective and social, and my concrete encounter with the Other is not first and foremost a question of radical alienation, but merely a revelation of my basic openness. Instead of accepting Sartre's claim that the Other is the foundation of my own objectivation, Merleau-Ponty consequently emphasizes that the gaze of the Other can only objectify me, if I notice it, for which reason my objectification cannot take place in complete passivity. Second, he points to the fact that I can only perceive that the Other perceives me, if both of us are visible, that is, if both of us belong in the same world. It is this shared background that makes every conflict and struggle possible.[73] The Other as object and myself as object for the Other are merely inauthentic modes of intersubjectivity, and Sartre's account of the being-for-Others is therefore insufficient. According to Merleau-Ponty, Sartre failed to uncover the primordial intersubjectivity which is a permanent dimension in our existence and which makes alienation, conflict, and objectivation possible in the first place.[74]

In *Phénoménologie de la perception*, Merleau-Ponty calls attention to the fact that an infant will open its mouth if I take one of its fingers between my teeth and pretend to bite it. But why does it do that? It might never have seen its own face in the mirror, and there is no immediate resemblance between its own felt, but unseen mouth, and the seen but unfelt mouth of the adult. But Merleau-Ponty suggests that the infant is able to cross the gap between the visual appearance of the Other's body and the proprioceptive appearance of its own body exactly because its lived body has an outside and contains an anticipation of the Other. The infant does not need to carry out any process of inference. Its body schema is characterized by a transmodal openness that immediately allows it to understand and imitate Others.[75]

Merleau-Ponty's observation has recently been substantiated by a number of empirical studies concerned with infant imitation. A series of experiments conducted by Meltzoff and Moore demonstrated successful facial imitation in newborn babies (the youngest being forty-two minutes, the oldest seventy-two hours).[76] It would have been natural to assume that this imitation should be classified as an automatic, reflexlike, stimulus-driven behavior, but a number of findings suggested differently. Using slightly older babies (twelve to twenty-one days), it was shown that the facial imitations of these babies were highly differentiated. They were able to imitate a number of different types of actions (tongue protrusion, mouth opening, and lip protrusion), and the range and specificity of these imitative acts indicated that we were dealing with more complex behavior than mere reflexlike mechanisms. This interpretation was supported by additional studies. One experiment showed that the infants were able to imitate across temporal gaps, something that mere reflexes cannot do. Another experiment showed that when six-week-old babies were shown an unusual gesture of large tongue protrusion to the side, they were at first unable to imitate it, but the babies gradually corrected and improved their imitative attempts until success was obtained. That is, the imitation involved effort and progressive approximation. Babies that were unable to imitate the gesture became frustrated and cried. All of these findings suggest that the facial imitation in young infants is a goal-directed, intentional activity, and not merely an automatic reflex.

As Stern points out, one of the crucial questions about facial imitation is, how "do babies 'know' that they have a face or facial features? How do they 'know' that the face they see is anything like the face they have? How do they 'know' that specific configurations of that other face, as only seen, correspond to the same specific configurations in their own face as only felt, proprioceptively, and never seen?"[77] Meltzoff and Moore suggest that the infant has a primitive body schema that allows it to unify the visual and proprioceptive information into one common "supramodal," "cross-modal," or "amodal" framework, i.e., that babies have an innate capacity to translate information received in one sensory modality into another sensory modality,[78] and against this background they reach a conclusion very similar to Merleau-Ponty's:

> One interesting consequence of this notion of supramodality is that there is a primordial connection between self and other. The actions of other humans are seen as like the acts that can be done at birth. This innate capacity has implications for understanding people, since it suggests an intrinsic relatedness between the seen bodily acts of others and the internal states of oneself (the sensing and representation of one's own movements). A second implication of young infants' possessing a representation of their own bodies is that it provides a starting point for developing objectivity about themselves. This primitive self-representation of the body may be the earliest progenitor of being able to take perspective on oneself, to treat oneself as an object of thought.[79]

In short, if the infant is to experience an Other it has to be in possession of a type of bodily self-awareness that permits it to bridge the gap between interiority and exteriority.

To introduce the notion of incarnation into a discussion of self-awareness is of course to contest its self-sufficiency in more than one way, since it also entails taking *birth* seriously. To be born is not to be one's own foundation, but to be situated in both *nature* and *culture*. It is to possess a physiology that one did not choose oneself. It is to find oneself in a historical and sociological context that one did not establish oneself. It is to be given to oneself as something to be comprehended, and to have the task of self-comprehension in front of one.[80] Birth is essentially an intersubjective phenomenon, not only in the obvious sense, because I was born by somebody, but because this very event only has meaning for me through the Others. My awareness of my birth, of my commencement, and of my mortality is intersubjectively mediated; it is not something I can intuit or remember on my own. I do not witness my coming into being, but I do always already find myself alive.[81]

To phrase it differently, to introduce the notion of incarnation into a discussion of self-awareness is to transform the very concept of subjectivity under discussion:

> There is therefore no occasion to ask ourselves why the thinking subject or consciousness perceives itself as a man, or an incarnate or historical subject, nor must we treat this apperception as a second order operation which it somehow performs starting from its absolute existence: the absolute flow takes shape beneath its own gaze as "*a* consciousness," or a man, or an incarnate subject, because it is a field of presence—to itself, to others and to the world—and because this presence throws it into the natural and cultural world from which it arrives at an understanding of itself. We must not envisage this flux as absolute contact with oneself, as an absolute density with no internal fault, but on the contrary as a being which is in pursuit of itself outside.[82]

When Merleau-Ponty insists that the only way to comprehend the relation between self-awareness, world-experience, and empathy is to seek the common ground behind their fixed difference, and to conceive of the subject as an intersubjective field,[83] he is, however, treading a very narrow line. To deny any alterity in the self might be to deny the possibility of intersubjectivity. But to exaggerate the moment of alterity, and to overlook the difference between intra- and intersubjective alterity, is to deny not only self-awareness, but ultimately intersubjectivity as well, since the difference between self and Other, between the first-person and third-person perspectives, would disappear.[84] Merleau-Ponty was aware of this danger himself, and he occasionally admits that there is in fact an experiential dimension which remains unique for each and every individual. There exists an *experienced solipsism*, which will forever remain unsurpassable: I can never experience the Other's pain in the same way as he, nor can he experience mine.[85] More generally, I can never be aware of the Other's experiences in the same way as he himself, nor can he be aware of mine. Thus, it seems necessary to modify the radical thesis. Not every self-awareness is already an experience of oneself as Other. But there are forms of self-awareness which contain a dimension of alterity and exteriority, for instance, the phenomenon of double-sensation, i.e., our bodily reflection.

Infantile Self-Awareness

It hardly needs emphasizing that there is a difference between claiming that certain types of self-awareness presuppose the presence and intervention of the Other and claiming that self-awareness is per se a social phenomenon. But it might prove useful to take a brief look at the latter claim. Among its most well-known advocates is Mead, who insists that the constitution of the self is a social process, and that self-awareness is intersubjectively mediated. To be self-aware is to become an object to oneself in virtue of one's social relations to Others:[86]

> The individual experiences himself as such, not directly, but only indirectly, from the particular standpoints of other individual members of the same social group, or from the generalized standpoint of the social group as a whole to which he belongs. For he enters his own experience as a self or individual, not directly or immediately, not by becoming a subject to himself, but only in so far as he first becomes an object to himself just as other individuals are objects to him or in his experience; and he becomes an object to himself only by taking the attitudes of other individuals toward himself within a social environment or context of experience and behavior in which both he and they are involved.[87]

Although Mead acknowledges that it is possible to speak of a singular and isolated self if one equates it with the mere existence of consciousness,[88] he insists upon distinguishing sharply between consciousness and self-awareness:

> Consciousness, as frequently used, simply has reference to the field of experience, but self-consciousness refers to the ability to call out in ourselves a set of definite responses which belong to the others of the group. Consciousness and self-consciousness are not on the same level. A

man alone has, fortunately or unfortunately, access to his own toothache, but that is not what we mean by self-consciousness.[89]

> The taking or feeling of the attitude of the other toward yourself is what constitutes self-consciousness, and not mere organic sensations of which the individual is aware and which he experiences.[90]

The claim that self-awareness only comes about on an intersubjective level in the interaction with other subjects is often connected to a thesis concerning the intrinsic relation between language-use and self-awareness. To become self-aware is something that is achieved in and through the intersubjective medium of language. A child is only in possession of self-awareness when it has acquired a sufficient mastery of language to be able to refer to itself with "I."[91]

But to suggest that the child only becomes self-aware when it masters the use of the first-person pronoun, or when it is able—as has also been suggested—to recognize itself in the mirror, is not only to operate with a concept of self-awareness very different from the one I have been using in the previous discussion. It is also to operate with an unacceptably narrow conception of self-awareness. One way to illustrate this is to ask how one should characterize the infant's experience of self, world, and Other prior to this watershed. According to one traditional view, the infant initially lives in a kind of *adualism* where there is exactly no distinction between self, world, and Other. Thus "adualism," "primary narcissism," or "symbiosis" are terms used to describe the first period of the infant's life, a life where there is not yet any boundary between experience and reality, not yet any differentiation between ego and nonego.[92] Thus, it has been assumed that the infant is originally incapable of distinguishing itself from the caregiver, not only in the obvious sense that it is unable to *conceptualize* the difference between self and Other, but in the sense that the infant exists in a "state of undifferentiation, of fusion with mother, in which the 'I' is not yet differentiated from the 'not-I' and in which inside and outside are only gradually coming to be sensed as different."[93] This state of symbiosis has then been assumed to be the milieu from which the infant gradually separates itself in order to reach a sense of the difference between self and Other, only thereby acquiring self-awareness.

This traditional hypothesis has been rejected by dominant positions in contemporary developmental psychology. It is now taken for granted that the infant already from birth begins to experience itself, and that it never passes through a period of total self/Other indifferentiation. As both Stern and Neisser have argued, there is no symbiotic-like phase, and there exists no systematic and pervasive confusion between the child's experience of self and Other, nor between the child's experience of the Other and the world.[94]

According to Stern, language *transforms* and *articulates* the infant's experience of self and Other, but it does not constitute it. Already from birth onward, the infant gains possession of different prereflective and prelinguistic "senses of self." Stern disguishes between the *emergent self*, the *core self*, and the *subjective self*, and he argues that the infant already prelinguistically experiences itself as a distinct and coherent body, with control over its own actions, ownership of its own affections, a sense of continuity, and a sense of other people as distinct and separate interactants.[95]

In fact, the period between two and six months might be classified as the most social period in one's life. It is a period where the infant is preoccupied with social interaction. The social smile is already in place, and the child has a clear preference for perceiving other subjects rather than inanimate objects.[96] (This is a fact that also indicates that the infant is able to distinguish between foreign subjects and mere objects very early.) Although the infant still has very little command over its own locomotion, it has an almost fully developed control over its eye movements, and it is particularly through its gaze that the infant can function as a social partner. By controlling its own direction of gaze, it can regulate the level and amount of social stimulation. And through such gaze behaviors as averting its gaze, shutting its eyes, staring past, becoming glassy-eyed, etc., it can to a large extent initiate, maintain, terminate, and avoid social contact.[97]

It is also in the first year of life that the infant is most in need of social contact. The infant learns to grasp by nursing at the mother's breast. It becomes acquainted with its surroundings through the mother's carrying it around, and it "is the security provided by the mother in the field of locomotion, the emotional bait offered by the mother calling her child, that 'teaches' him to walk."[98] More generally, it is the (m)other who tempts the infant to explore itself and the world, and who provides it with sufficient emotional security to dare undertake such a venture. Without the Other's presence and intervention the full range of experience does simply not develop.[99] As Spitz's investigation of *hospitalism* showed, if the child is prevented from forming a secure attachment to another person in the first year of life, a gross maturational deficiency is the result. It is the interaction, dialogue, and reciprocity between infant and Other that provides the infant with an indispensable encouragement to commence and continue its self-development and world exploration. To be deprived of a close relationship with an Other leads to severe disorders in the infant.[100]

Around the age of seven to nine months a change occurs, insofar as the child realizes that itself and Others have subjective experiences or mental states which are potentially shareable. "Only when infants can sense that others distinct from themselves can hold or entertain a mental state that is similar to one they sense themselves to be holding is the sharing of subjective experience or intersubjectivity possible."[101] This change in the infant's experience of self and Other is evinced from the infant's attempt to share joint attention, intentions, and affective states, i.e., in the phenomena of *interattentionality, interintentionality,* and *interaffectivity.*[102] When infants of nine months follow the direction of the mother's gaze or pointing finger, they often look back at the mother and appear to use the feedback from her face to confirm that they have in fact reached the right target. They seek to validate whether joint *attention* has been achieved. As for the sharing of *intentions,* it is most obvious in protolinguistic forms of requesting. If the father is holding an item which the infant desires, it might reach out a hand, make grasping movements, and while looking back and forth between the hand and its father's face intone "Eh! Eh!" This request implies that the infant (prereflectively) apprehends the father as someone who can comprehend and satisfy its own intentions. Intentions have become shareable experiences.[103] Finally, the sharing of *affections,* or interaffectivity, which is presumably the first and most basic form of subjective sharing, can also be witnessed. If the infant is placed in a situation that is bound to generate uncertainty, for instance, by being approached by a new, unusual, and highly stimulating object, such as a bleeping and flashing toy, it will look toward the mother for her emotional reaction, essentially to see what it should feel in order to help resolve its own uncertainty. If the mother shows pleasure by smiling, the infant will continue its exploration; if she shows fear, the infant will turn back from the object and perhaps become upset.[104]

Stern argues that the infant's life is so thoroughly social that most of the things it does, feels, and perceives occur in different kinds of relationships, regardless of whether it is alone or not. It engages with real partners some of the time and with "evoked companions" almost all of the time. Its maturation requires this constant dialogue. But even when it comes to the thoroughly social types of self-experience, i.e., self-experiences which cannot take place alone, but which only occur when elicited and maintained by an Other, i.e., experiences which presuppose a complementary experience of a (real or imagined) Other, these experiences remain the child's own experiences. Even those of its experiences which depend upon the presence and action of the Other still belong entirely to itself. There is a *relation* but no *fusion* and no *distortion* between self and Other.[105] Even if the infant is affected and infected by its mother's frustration, it does not feel its mother's frustration nor does it ever identify its own pain or frustration as its mother's.

Around the age of fifteen to eighteen months, the child finally starts to reflect and objectify itself. It becomes able to perform symbolic actions, and it acquires some linguistic competence. That the child becomes able to assume a detached perspective on itself can be seen from its use of names and pronouns to designate itself and from its behavior before a mirror. Prior to this age, the infant presumably does not realize that it sees itself in the mirror. If one marks the face of the infant with rouge without its knowledge and it subsequently looks in a mirror, a younger child will point to the mirror and not to itself. But after the age of eighteen months, the child will touch the rouge on its own face. Since the confrontation with the mirror motivates a *self-directed* behavior, it is assumed that the child now recognizes what it sees in the mirror as its own reflection.[106]

But although this recognition testifies to the existence of self-awareness, its absence does obviously not imply the lack of self-awareness. Not only is the recognition of one's own reflection by no means the first or most basic type of self-awareness. We are after all dealing with a sophisticated type of self-identification, where a certain image is recognized as a *representation* of one's own body. That is, the self-awareness in question takes place across distance and separation. We identify "that other" as ourselves. But the child would not be able to perform this identification, which is assumed to take place through the perfect match between its *own* bodily movements and the movements of the image in the mirror, if it were not already in possession of a kinaesthetic self-awareness, if it were not already aware of its own bodily movements. In order to recognize oneself in the mirror, one must already be in possession of self-awareness. This is not to say, however, that the encounter with the mirror image might not occasion highly significant insights. Hitherto the child has never seen its own face or the visual gestalt of its entire body, but only perceived fragments of its bodily exteriority. But the mirror permits it to see itself as it is seen by Others, and might exactly bring it to the explicit realization that it is given to Others with the same visual appearance that it is being confronted with in the mirror.[107] A separate question is whether the confrontation with the mirror image is essential for the acquisition of a mundane self-awareness. This is hardly the case, and ultimately the interaction with (real) Others is of far greater significance. Not only do blind people not lack this type of self-awareness, but experiments have even indicated that social experience might be a precondition for the recognition of one's own mirror image. Apart from humans, chimpanzees and orangutans are also able to recognize their mirror image, and as Lewis and Brooks-Gunn narrate (accounting for research done by Gallup): "Chimpanzees reared in social isolation were unable to exhibit self-directed behavior in a mirror situation even after extensive exposure. As a further test of the importance of social experience, two of the original chimpanzees were given three months of group experience, after which time self recognitory responses began to appear."[108]

According to Stern, the different types of prereflective self-experience should not be taken as cognitive constructs, but as the lived, existential counterparts of the objectifiable, self-reflective, verbalizable self. However, even Stern's careful analysis of the infant's self-experience is not completely free from a certain objectivistic strain. To start with, Stern occasionally clouds the issue by claiming that we are dealing with self-experiences which occur outside of awareness. Since he seems to identify awareness with attention, and self-awareness with self-reflection, this is presumably only meant to imply that we are dealing with a non-conceptual and nonthematic kind of self-experience.[109] But Stern also makes it sound as if the infant's self-awareness is a result of its ability to discriminate itself from Others, and that this is merely an instance of its general ability to discriminate between different entities. He claims that the infant, far from being a *tabula rasa*, is predesigned to perceive the world in a highly structured fashion, and just as it very early is able to perceive and organize different stimuli into different natural categories, it has inborn capabilities that enable it to discriminate different gestalt constellations of stimuli in such a way that it can keep self and Other separate. When the infant feels the caress of the mother, hears the voice of the father, and sees its own hand, it is not overwhelmed by a surge of unstructured sensations, but is able to distinguish between itself, the father, and the mother as three distinct entities. It recognizes that the behavior of different persons is differently structured, it distinguishes one agent from another,[110] and it is ultimately able to discriminate the invariant structure that characterizes its own self-generated actions and experiences from the patterns belonging to the movement and actions of particular Others. Thus the infant's self-experience is exactly defined as the experiences of an *invariant pattern* or constellation that only arises on the occasion of its own actions or mental processes.[111]

This way of describing self-experience is, however, beset with a major problem. Even if an infant is able to distinguish between different entities in such a way that no confusion takes place, this does not answer the key question: How does the infant "know" that one of these experiential configurations is itself? But, of course, if one is forced to ask this question, thereby implying that self-awareness is the result of a successful criterial self-identication, something is fundamentally wrong. The problem of self-awareness is not primarily a question of a specific "what," but of a unique "how." It does not concern the specific content of an experience, but its unique mode of givenness. This is a fact that Stern eventually seems to realize himself, since he acknowledges that the infant's (direct and immediate) experience of proprioception and volition is of crucial importance.[112]

Stern also argues that the self-experience of the infant has four components: the experiences of *self-agency*, *self-coherence* (unity of locus, coherence of motion, coherence of temporal structure, coherence of form), *self-affectivity*, and *self-history*.[113] But these four components are not on the same level. The self-affectivity is by far the most fundamental. When the newborn feels hunger, pain, or frustration, it has conscious, that is, self-manifesting experiences. As Klawonn rightly points out, an infant does not have to be able to use the words "pain" and "mine" in order for it to feel the pain as its own. There is never a risk of its confusing its own pain with the pain of other infants.[114] Even prelinguistically an infant can be aware of itself qua itself, for this self-acquaintance does not require any thematic or conceptual identificaiton, but merely that the acquaintance has the requisite first-person form. Even prior to any conceptual discrimination between self and world or self and Other, the child is self-aware due to the unique first-personal mode of givenness of its experiences, that is, due to the intrinsic self-manifesting character of its consciousness. To claim that the child only gains self-awareness the moment it can discriminate between its own subjective experiences and objective reality is to remain spellbound by the paradigm of reflection. For in order to make such a thematic discrimination the infant must take itself as an object. Although self-manifestation goes hand in hand with hetero-manifestation, it is not a contrastive phenomenon. Self-awareness does not arise thanks to any discrimination between self and world, but is the condition of possibility for any such discrimination.

Although Stern's empirical investigations of infantile self-experience might be faulted for having certain conceptual flaws, they remain of obvious significance. They demonstrate that infants are in possession of very sophisticated types of self-experience far earlier than previously assumed, and they thereby deliver empirical evidence against any attempt to conceive exclusively of self-awareness as a product of a successful linguistic rule-following.

10

Self-Manifestation and Self-Comprehension

One of the questions raised in chapter 3 was whether subjectivity is accessible for direct theoretical examination and phenomenological description or only approachable *ex negativo*. As it has turned out, this question was in fact rather ambiguous and even partially misleading. The central question cannot be whether it is possible to examine and describe subjectivity, since this is obviously the case. For instance, Husserl's analysis of the noetic structure of perception can serve as an example of such a *reflective* investigation. The question is not whether subjectivity can be examined, since this is exactly what reflection permits us to do, but whether subjectivity can be grasped and thematized in its very functioning, that is, whether an adequate phenomenological description of the anonymous, functioning life is at all possible: "Was es als 'Leben' aber gerade zu verstehen gilt, ist dieses 'Erlebnis' im Augenblick des *Vollziehens*—und nicht des Schauens, das das Er-lebte bereits in eine Distanz hineinstellt und sich somit vom Erlebten als *gewesenem* Ge-lebten trennt."[1] However, if it turns out to be necessary to eliminate every distance in order to grasp subjectivity in its very functioning, one might very well ask whether the light necessary for vision will not disappear as well.[2]

Pure and Impure Reflection

In chapter 8, I briefly touched upon Sartre's analysis of reflection. According to Sartre, the process of reflection falsifies its subject matter. When reflected upon, the original nonegological experience is submitted to an egological interpretation and thereby provided with opaque and transcendent elements. On closer examination, Sartre's conclusion is somewhat astonishing. Does he not as a consequence exclude the possibility of a phenomenological description of lived consciousness? However, Sartre does in fact distinguish between two very different types of reflection, the *pure* and the *impure*, and I have so far only described the latter. Impure reflection is the kind of reflection which we encounter daily. It operates with an epistemic duality, and must be classified as a type of knowledge. It is called impure because it transcends the given and interprets the reflected in an objectifying manner, thus giving rise to the psychic unity that we know under the name *ego*.[3]

In contrast, pure reflection presents us with a pure (unfalsifying) thematization of the reflected. It is the ideal form of reflection, but it is much harder to attain since it never emerges by itself, but must be won by a sort of purifying *catharsis*. In pure reflection, reflected consciousness does not appear as an object and is not given perspectivally as a transcendent entity existing *outside* reflecting consciousness. Reflecting consciousness "does not then detach itself completely from the reflected-on, and it can not grasp the reflected-on 'from a point of view.' Its knowledge is a totality; it is a lightning intuition without relief, without point of departure, and without point of arrival. Everything is given at once in a sort of absolute proximity."[4] Quite in keeping with this, Sartre claims that pure reflection never learns or discovers anything new, but always discloses and thematizes that which it was already familiar with beforehand, namely, the original nonsubstantial streaming of prereflective consciousness. One should consequently avoid calling it knowledge and instead use the term *"recognition."*[5]

Sartre's distinction between these two types of reflection is important. As we have repeatedly seen, it is one thing to be self-aware, and something quite different to reach a philosophical comprehension of subjectivity, especially since the theoretical attitude seems to entail an objectivation and consequently a falsification of its subject matter. One solution is to argue that subjectivity can only be approached *ex negativo*. A different alternative is to claim that there must exist something like pure reflection. Unfortunately, Sartre's alternative is faced with one difficulty, its obvious *ad hoc* character. Sartre admits at one point that his entire ontology is based upon the work of (pure) reflection, and that only this type of reflection can disclose consciousness as it really is,[6] but he never explains how this reflection might be possible, or how we can achieve it.[7] That such an explanation is required should, however, be obvious. Not only can the very possibility of such a reflection not be taken for granted, Sartre is also faced with the problem of reconciling it with the rest of his theory, especially with his more general account of reflection.

Nevertheless, the notion of a pure reflection remains of obvious relevance, since it appears to be a condition of possibility for a *phenomeno-logical* investigation of functioning subjectivity. At this point it is natural to inquire whether Husserl might provide us with the lacking analyses and conceptual tools, particularly since Husserl himself distinguishes between a *natural* reflection and a *transcendental* reflection.[8] When I grasp myself as a mundane object (be it in the personalistic or naturalistic attitude), I am given to myself as a constituted, objectified, and transcendent entity. When asked whether this provides me with adequate knowledge of myself, Husserl's answer is of course no, since it prevents me from attaining an understanding of my own constituting, transcendental subjectivity.[9] It is at this point that the transcendental reflection makes its entry, since its specific aim is to thematize a subjectivity purified and detached from all contingent, extrinsic, and transcendent contexts.[10] From the very start, Husserl emphasizes that this is a type of reflection which is not immediately available, and a central part of his writings is precisely dedicated to the task of developing a procedure that can make it accessible. (Obviously, the claim that transcendental or pure *reflection* is harder to attain than the natural reflection does not contradict the thesis previously presented, that natural or mundane self-awareness is a constitutively founded self-apprehension. That which founds mundane self-awareness is not pure reflection, but pure prereflective self-manifestation).

> Wie komme ich dazu, mich über dieses Mich-verlieren in die Welt und Mich-einkleiden in ein weltliches Gewand zu erheben und meiner in meiner transzendentalen Reinheit und Eigenheit innezuwerden: als das Subjekt, in dessen apperzipierendem Erleben (sofern es mundanes Erfahren in sich ausbildet und aktiv betätigt) sich dieses "Es ist diese Welt da" und dieses "Ich bin Mensch in dieser Welt" als eine subjektive Leistung macht? Oder: Wie komme ich dazu, das Subjekt und Subjektleben rein in sich zu sehen, in dem und durch das für es selbst alles objektiv erfahrungsmäßig Seiende ist, und in weiterer Folge Bewußtseiendes jeder Art und Form ist?[11]

As is well known, Husserl's answer is: through the *epoché*. As he says, anyone can reflect and thereby focus his attention on his own consciousness, but no matter how carefully and attentively he does it, it will remain a mundane experience unless it is supported by the epoché.[12] In contrast to the positive sciences, phenomenology does not have immediate access to its own field of research. Prior to any concrete investigation it needs a certain method in order to escape the natural and mundane attitude.

Only through a methodical suspension of the validity of the *"general thesis"* can the analysis of transcendental subjectivity be commenced.[13]

To give a more detailed account of Husserl's notion of the epoché, and to distinguish and analyze his different ways to the transcendental reduction (i.e., the Cartesian, the psychological, and the ontological ways) would, however, lead too far.[14] Ultimately, it is doubtful whether Husserl's distinction between the natural and the transcendental reflections is really relevant to the present discussion. Husserl is certainly occupied with the problem of how we are to purge our self-apprehension from naturalizing and mundanizing elements. And to thematize the formal structures of my perception or to think of myself as a retired mountain guide are obviously two very different endeavors, despite the fact that both of them are reflections. Although Husserl examines this process of purification or catharsis in much greater detail than Sartre, and although he does in fact make it comprehensible how something like a transcendental reflection is both possible and feasible, he does not appear to be concerned with the really central issue. Husserl's discussion of the transcendental reduction and his analysis of the relation and difference between the natural and the transcendental reflections provide us with a method to liberate ourselves from a leveling self-interpretation and achieve an insight into our transcendental significance, but his reflections still present us with a subjectivity reflected upon, that is, with a thematized and objectified transcendental subjectivity. The more decisive question about whether subjectivity can be grasped and thematized in its very self-manifesting functioning is apparently neither raised nor answered.

But perhaps this silence is simply a direct consequence of Husserl's original *credo*: Reflection is the method for investigating consciousness, and it is consequently only through reflection that we can acquire adequate knowledge about consciousness.[15]

Obviously, this assumption demands an answer to the following questions: Are there any reasons to question the work of the reflection? Is there any reason to suspect that the prereflective experience might be changed radically when reflected upon? Is reflection, as Derrida seems to argue, a kind of falsifying mirror that transforms whatever it makes appear?[16] According to Husserl, however, these skeptical reservations must be rejected. As he points out, to have doubts about the work of reflection is itself a form of reflection. It presupposes the validity of that which it questions, and it is consequently inconsistent.[17] To claim that reflection falsifies lived experiences and that they elude it completely is ultimately absurd, since the very claim presupposes knowledge of those very same lived experiences, and the only way to gain that is through reflection.[18]

At this point, however, a certain caution seems appropriate. So far it has simply been taken for granted that reflection—in contrast to prereflective self-awareness—is a type of object-intentionality, namely, a higher-order intentional act which takes the primary act as its object. Husserl himself imprudently speaks of a "reflective perception." But is this really appropriate? It is certainly not difficult to find reasons for insisting upon the difference between reflection and perception.

1. In contrast to perception, reflection does not involve any sense organ, no inner eyeball. In order to acquire reflective self-awareness, there is no need to move the appropriate organ into an appropriate relation with its object.[19]

2. There is a radical difference between the givenness of, respectively, (a) our perceptual objects, and (b) the perceptual acts we reflect upon. Whereas our perceptual objects are essentially characterized by their adumbrational appearance—the object is never given in its totality, but always in a certain restricted profile—this is not the case for our perceptual acts.

3. The perceptual object is act-transcendent, not a part or moment of the stream of consciousness. On the contrary, there is no such transcendence between the reflecting act and the act reflected upon. Both belong to the same stream of consciousness.

4. Object-intentionality is characterized by its existence-independence, i.e., the intentional directedness does not presuppose the existence of that which is intended. Reflection, however, necessarily entails the existence of that which it intends. There can be no reflection if the reflected act does not exist. In this sense, reflection is a founded act, a nonindependent moment of a whole.[20]

Henrich criticized the attempt to understand self-awareness on the basis of the subject-object model. But the question is whether this criticism was sufficiently thorough. Although it was pointed out that prereflective self-awareness cannot be understood in this way, Henrich had a tendency to continue interpreting reflective self-awareness in subject-object terms, as an objectifying thematization, and it was against that background that he concluded that the original subjective dimension evades our theoretical gaze and remains inaccessible for direct description and investigation.[21]

Whether or not Henrich's skepticism is justified might depend upon how one interprets the notion of an "objectifying thematization." If it is necessarily taken to imply reification and mundanization, then it is one thing, but if it simply means the constitution of identity, the case is different. I am certainly not denying that there are forms of reflection which are alienating and even reifying, but it also has to be realized that "reflection" is exactly a polysemical term. Ultimately, the question is whether it might not also be appropriate to acknowledge the existence of a form of reflection which is nothing but a higher form of *wakefulness*, nothing but a simple "*schauendes Hinnehmen.*" It is tempting to follow Pothast when he suggests that reflection, rather than being an *intentionalization*, might be an *intensification* of the primary experience,[22] or Fink, when he claims that reflection, rather than being an explicit self-reification, is simply a more articulate and intense form of self-awareness.[23]

Reflection and Self-Alteration

Although pure reflection, rather than being a reification or mundanization, might be nothing but an intensification or accentuation of the primary experience, it nevertheless cannot be denied that it changes the givenness of the experience reflected upon—*otherwise there would be no need for reflection.* Reflection does not merely copy or repeat the original experience. As Husserl explicitly admits, it *alters* it. It is now given thematically and no longer just lived prereflectively.[24] I have earlier mentioned that our original prereflective awareness of the stream of consciousness is an awareness of a unity, and that it is only subsequently that we discriminate the different moments of the stream, only subsequently that we posit or inject the experiences into sequential time. Similarly, our functioning body is primarily given as an undivided unity and is only disintegrated into different parts and organs the moment we pay attention to it. It is reflection that permits us to make this differentiation and demarcation. But it is not necessarily a differentiation which is imposed from without, i.e., it is not necessarily foreign to the experience in question. In a passage from *Zur Phänomenologie des inneren Zeitbewußtseins,* quoted earlier, Husserl writes that the experience to which we turn attentively in reflection acquires a new mode of being. It becomes "differentiated," and he claims that this differentiatedness is nothing other than its being grasped.[25] Husserl also speaks of reflection (and recollection) as a process that discloses, disentangles, explicates, and articulates all those components and structures of meaning which were contained implicitly in the prereflective experience.[26] Thus, one should not confuse the fluctuating unity of our lived experiences with a formlessness or lack of structure. On the contrary, our lived experiences possess an organic or morphological structure and internal differentiation, and it is ultimately this that makes them accessible to reflection and conceptual articulation,[27] an articulation which might not represent a falsification but rather a consummation of the experience.[28] As Husserl puts it, in the beginning we are confronted with the so to speak dumb experience which must then be made to articulate its own sense.[29]

To claim that pure reflection is simply to be understood as an accentuation or thematization of the primary experience is not to say, however, that it should be classified as a mere *attentional modification*.[30] Already in *Logische Untersuchungen*, Husserl made it clear that attention is a particular feature or mode of our primary act, but it is not a new act.[31] Reflection, however, is a new (founded) act, and reflective self-awareness is a *relation* between two different experiences.[32] An attentional modification will allow objects in the background to become themes. The subject itself, however, is not a marginal object, and it will not be thematized through a mere attentional modification. A more decisive change of attitude is called for.[33] Perhaps one can say that the attentional modification is a *horizontal variation*, whereas the reflection implies a *vertical alteration*. Whereas the attentional modification thematizes something that for accidental reasons has remained unthematic, reflection thematizes something that for essential reasons has been unthematic— that is, something which could only become a theme through reflection. This is exactly the case for our experiences. They cannot be directed toward themselves, for they cannot become their own themes. This can only happen through a new act.[34]

Even if it is conceded that reflection can disclose the structures of lived experience (and not merely the structures of reflected consciousness),[35] it might still be objected that there remains something which it cannot thematize, namely, the structures of prereflective *givenness*. Whatever transformation the prereflectively lived experience undergoes when it is reflectively thematized, it is a transformation that pertains to its givenness, and more specifically a change from a nonthematic to a thematic givenness. Reflection alters the mode in which the primary act is experienced, it does not change the content of the act. That which is grasped in reflection is consequently not the particular prereflective givenness, but that which is given, that which remains identical throughout the change of givenness, namely, the basic structures of perceiving, imagining, recollecting, etc.[36] That is, although we can thematize the noetic structures of the act (for instance, the components of quality and matter), we will never be able to thematize the structures of its prereflective givenness, since this mode of givenness will always escape our reflective gaze. But this objection appears to overlook the fact that reflection supervenes on prereflective self-awareness. The reflective disclosure of the intentional structures of a perception passes through the primary givenness of this perception. And that which is thematized in reflection is not the perception in isolation from its self-manifestation, but exactly the prereflectively self-given perception. Obviously we will only be able to grasp these structures as they are reflectively articulated, and not as they are lived through, but this is hardly a problem. The aim of reflection is to remove the anonymity and naïveté of prereflective experience, not to relive or reproduce it.

To reflect upon something is not necessarily to turn it into a foreign object, for it might be nothing more than to thematize the experience in question, and by doing that, by fixating the experience attentively, it is obviously possible to notice new features.[37] At best a reflection is simply an accentuation of the structures inherent in the lived experience rather than a process which adds new components and structures to it. But in this case, the persistent fear that reflection is somehow prevented from attaining true subjectivity seems unfounded. Pure reflection deserves to be called a *disclosing modification* rather than a *concealing falsification*. The main difference between prereflective self-awareness and pure reflection consequently turns out to be a question of articulation. Thus, the slightly surprising conclusion is that the difference between pure and impure reflections might be greater than the difference between prereflective self-awareness and pure reflection.

I think it is decisive not to exaggerate the difficulties connected to a description of subjectivity, but one should not underestimate them either.

As I mentioned above, reflection might not entail a self-reification, but it does entail a kind of doubling or fracture or, as Fink puts it, a kind of *self-fission*, since it confronts me with another aspect of myself. It presents us with the coexistence of a double(d) subject: a reflected and a reflecting. Following Husserl, Fink even speaks of reflection as a *self-multiplication*, where I exist together or in communion with myself.[38] Of course, this should not be taken too literally. Reflection does not split me into two different egos; it does not turn me into a true Other to myself.[39] Reflection is neither a kind of empathy, nor a case of schizophrenia or multiple personality disorder.[40] It is a kind of self-awareness. But it is a kind of self-awareness which is essentially characterized by an internal division, difference, and distance.[41] To some extent it is even distinguished by a certain detachment and withdrawal, since it deprives the original experience of its naïveté and spontaneity. To put it differently, even if reflective self-awareness does not confront us with ourselves as transcendent objects, it does not merely differ from prereflective self-awareness by its intensity, articulation, and differentiation, but also by its quality of *othering*. Reflective self-awareness is characterized by a type of *self-fragmentation* which we do not encounter on the level of prereflective self-awareness.

One of the significant consequences of this is that there will always remain an unthematic spot in the life of the subject. It is, as Husserl says, evident that the very process of thematization does not itself belong to the thematized content, just as a perception or description does not belong to that which is perceived or described.[42] Even a universal reflection will contain a moment of naïveté, since reflection is necessarily prevented from grasping itself. Whereas the originary self-manifestation is total and in this sense, nonhorizontal, reflective self-thematization to a certain extent remains horizontal—not in the sense of presenting us with a transcendent adumbrational object, but in the sense of presenting us with an aspect or fragment of the full subjective life. Thus, reflection never provides us with adequate self-awareness. It only gives us partial and fragmented insights, and will forever miss something important, namely, itself qua anonymously functioning subject-pole.[43] I cannot grasp my own functioning subjectivity because I am it: That which I am cannot be my *Gegen-stand*, cannot stand opposed to me.[44]

The Invisibility of Subjectivity

As I mentioned above, Husserl's distinction between the natural and the transcendental reflections, and his standard account of the different ways to the reduction, do not explicitly deal with the difficulties involved in a description and an analysis of functioning subjectivity. Fortunately, however, this is not to say that Husserl does not treat this topic at all, but simply that his treatment must be sought elsewhere. Particularly as Husserl started investigating the depth-dimension of subjectivity, it became clear to him how evasive a theme subjectivity really is, especially the nature of its own self-manifestation. As Brough observes, the description of the absolute flow puts a fundamental strain upon language, since that which is to be described is unlike any object, unlike all other phenomena.[45] This is repeatedly brought to the fore in Husserl's descriptions, since he keeps stressing their fundamental shortcomings: We speak of absolute subjectivity in conformity with what is constituted (if anything a strong affirmation of the thesis that it is impossible—and fundamentally misleading—to analyze absolute subjectivity in strict separation from that which it constitutes), and we describe it with predicates appropriate for temporal unities. For example, we call it streaming, standing, present, although properly speaking it neither exists in the now nor as extended in time. But we lack more adequate names.[46] Is it at all possible to speak about the ultimate condition of manifestation without treating it as a constituted transcendent object? Husserl's realization of the difficulties connected to an investigation of lived subjectivity was perhaps never expressed more acutely than in the following passage from the Bernauer Manuscripts:

> In diesem Sinn ist es also nicht "Seiendes," sondern Gegenstück
> für alles Seiende, nicht ein Gegenstand, sondern Urstand für alle
> Gegenständlichkeit. Das Ich sollte eigentlich nicht das Ich heissen, und
> überhaupt nicht heissen, da es dann schon gegenständlich geworden ist,
> es ist das Namenlose über allem Fassbaren, über allem nicht Stehende,
> nicht Schwebende, nicht Seiende, sondern "Fungierende," als fassend, als
> wertend usw.—Das alles muß noch vielfach überdacht werden. Es liegt fast
> an der Grenze möglicher Beschreibung.[47]

Already in a lecture from 1906–7, Husserl asked how we are to grasp the prephenomenal being of consciousness, i.e., its being prior to reflective thematization.[48] If the absolute flow can only be described through a thematization, if every thematization entails an ontification, and if that which is taken to be the *"urphänomenale Gegenwart"* cannot be the ultimate exactly because it is a constituted phenomenon, then the prospects do indeed look poor.[49] When I reflect, I encounter myself as a thematized and temporalized ego, whereas the Living Present of the thematizing ego eludes my thematization and remains anonymous. And it is a fundamental anonymity which can be lifted but never grasped. As Merleau-Ponty was later to point out, our temporal existence is both a condition for and an obstacle to our self-comprehension. Temporality contains an internal fracture that permits us to return to our past experiences in order to investigate them reflectively, but this very fracture also prevents us from fully coinciding with ourselves. There will always remain a difference between the lived and the understood.[50]

The remaining question is whether or not this outcome constitutes a major problem for phenomenology. Have we reached a dead end, so to speak, or are we rather faced with an unavoidable but quite harmless impasse? As I have already argued, I take the latter to be the case. Reflection cannot apprehend the anonymous life in its very functioning, but neither is it supposed to. Its aim is to lift the naïveté of prereflective experience, and not to reproduce it. Nevertheless, it might still be maintained that especially phenomenology remains confronted with a basic problem. According to Husserl's *principle of principles*, phenomenology is supposed to base its considerations exclusively on that which is given intuitively in the phenomenological reflection. But since reflection never manages to capture or fixate the prereflective functioning life, any investigation of the latter, that is, any claim concerning the existence or nature of the most fundamental dimension of subjectivity, of the very source of the intentional life, should be regarded as unphenomenological.

However, as Held has pointed out, a phenomenological analysis of the anonymous functioning life must avoid two pitfalls: It must withstand the recurrent temptation to substantialize and reify its subject matter, but neither can it satisfy itself with a disclosure based merely on a regressive deduction.[51] The decisive question remains whether phenomenology can offer any alternative ways to illuminate this field. Let me briefly try to show that this is in fact the case.

Phenomenology has often been criticized for its seeming inability to tackle the problem of intersubjectivity. If the task of phenomenology is to investigate the conditions of manifestation, and if this investigation is to proceed by way of focusing exclusively upon the relation between the subject and that which is given for it, i.e., upon the relation between the constituting subject and the constituted phenomenon, one might indeed wonder whether phenomenology will not always be prevented from giving an adequate analysis of the Other. To speak of a foreign subject, of an Other, is to speak of something that for essential reasons will always transcend its givenness for me. Qua foreign subject it will be in possession of a self-manifestation which is principally inaccessible to me. For the very same reason, phenomenology will be unable to account for it, and must consequently remain stuck in solipsism.

There is no need, at this point, for a refutation of this persistent and misleading criticism.[52] What is significant is that it has occasioned a very intensive discussion within phenomenology concerning the problem and status of the Other. A discussion which somewhat paradoxically can also provide us with resources for describing functioning subjectivity.

An absolutely central aspect of the phenomenological approach to the problem of the Other is that it makes no sense to speak of an Other, unless it is in some way given and experienceable. It is impossible to encounter, let alone respect the irreducible alterity of the Other, unless it appears or manifests itself in some way.[53]

That it is possible to *experience* the Otherness of the Other does not imply, however, that I experience the Other in the same way as the Other experiences herself, nor that the subjectivity of the Other is accessible to me in the same way that my own subjectivity is. But this is not a problem. Quite to the contrary. It is only because foreign subjectivity evades my direct experience that it is given as Other. As Husserl says, "if what belongs to the Other's own essence were directly accessible, it would be merely a moment of my own essence, and ultimately he himself and I myself would be the same."[54] The self-awareness of the Other is inaccessible and transcendent for me, but it is exactly this inaccessibility, this limit, which I can experience.[55] And when I do have an authentic experience of another subject, I am exactly experiencing that the Other evades me. Thus, the givenness of the Other is of a most peculiar kind. As Lévinas remarks, the absence of the Other is exactly his presence as Other.[56] To demand more, to claim that I would only have a real experience of the Other if the originary self-givenness of the Other were given to me, is nonsensical. It would imply that I would only experience an Other if I experienced him in the same way that I experience myself, i.e., it would lead to an abolition of the difference between self and Other, to a negation of the alterity of the Other, of that which makes the Other Other.[57]

At this point, it is natural to use the insights obtained through the investigation of the givenness of the Other in an attempt to understand functioning subjectivity. There seems to be a profound analogy between reflection (understood as a thematic experience of myself) and empathy (understood as a thematic experience of the Other). In both cases we are dealing with a thematic experience of something which is already pregiven and functioning prior to the thematization, and which can never be exhaustibly grasped since it remains nonobjectifiable in its core.[58]

As an illustration of this coincidence, one might make a brief comparison between Lévinas's description of the Other and Henry's characterization of the self. Lévinas argues that the Other cannot appear for me as a theme without losing its radical alterity. I cannot presentify it without compromising its Otherness. When I perceive objects, I am their condition of manifestation, and they consequently appear as my creations. In contrast, my encounter with the Other is not conditioned by anything in my power, but can only offer itself from without, as an epiphanic visitation: "*The absolute experience is not disclosure but revelation.*"[59] For Lévinas, to encounter the Other is to be affected in radical passivity by something "invisible" in the sense of not being representable, objectifiable, thematizable, etc.[60] Henry describes the absolute passivity of self-affection in very similar terms. And whereas Henry emphasizes the absolute difference between any worldly, horizontal object-manifestation, and the nonhorizontal, immediate character of self-manifestation, Lévinas says the same of the Other: It offers itself immediately, i.e., independently of all systems, contexts, and horizons.[61] Although the radical immanence of the self and the radical transcendence of the Other cannot be thematized, this does not testify to their insignificance, nor does it represent a deficiency that must be remedied. It is due to the fact that functioning subjectivity and radical alterity both belong to a totally different ontological dimension than the one dominated by vision.[62] To phrase it differently (and here it is of course Henry who is speaking), it is not because the Other is an Other, but because it is a self that I cannot perceive it directly. It it because transcendental life is characterized by its absolute immanence that intentionality can never grasp it. And this concerns my own ego as well as the ego of the Other.[63]

The major insight to be gained by this comparison is the following. We have seen that the Other is characterized by a very peculiar mode of givenness: the Other persistently evades objectivation, but this does not prevent us from experiencing her. Quite to the contrary, the Otherness of the Other is exactly manifest in her elusiveness and inaccessibility. Something similar is the case with the subjectivity of the subject. It cannot be thematized, but this does not prevent it from being given. Not only is it characterized by its radical self-manifestation, but we even encounter its *anonymity* and *evasiveness* every time we try (and fail) to catch it in reflection, i.e., the reflection points toward that which both founds it and eludes it, and these features are not deficiencies to overcome, but rather the defining traits of its prereflective givenness. Thus, although there might be fundamental limits to the power of reflection and self-comprehension, there is no blind spot in the core of subjectivity. To claim that is, once again, to remain spellbound by the reflection theory.

Ultimately, it must be realized that one cannot approach functioning subjectivity as if it were merely yet another object. As Henry rightly emphasizes again and again, the primary self-manifestation of subjectivity is a unique type of manifestation. It can neither reveal itself in the world, nor be grasped by any category pertaining to the world. He consequently argues that it is a type of manifestation which will remain concealed for a type of thinking which adheres to the principle of ontological monism, and which only conceives of manifestation in terms of horizon, transcendence, and ecstasis.[64] The manifestation of subjectivity is not only utterly different from the visibility of worldly objects, it is also characterized by a certain elusiveness, not in the sense that it does not manifest itself, but in the sense that there will always remain something which eludes reflective thematization. Since absolute subjectivity cannot appear in the visibility of exteriority, since it evades every gaze and remains hidden from view, it is called obscure and invisible,[65] and Henry is consequently led to his radical conclusion: The unique manifestation of absolute subjectivity can be called an *invisible revelation.* "The foundation is not something obscure, neither is it light which becomes perceivable only when it shines upon the thing which bathes in its light, nor is it the thing itself as a 'transcendent phenomenon,' but it is an *immanent* revelation which is a presence to itself, even though such a presence remains 'invisible.' "[66]

One might perhaps criticize Henry for making use of an unnecessarily paradoxical terminology, but his point is quite clear. The fundamental invisibility should not be interpreted as a mode of nonmanifestation. It is invisible, it does not reveal itself in the light of the world, but it is not unconscious, nor the negation of all phenomenality, but simply the primary and most fundamental kind of manifestation.[67] Since Henry's entire oeuvre is devoted to a study of exactly this kind of manifestation, it might be described as the ambitious attempt to develop a *phenomenology of the invisible*.[68]

It is in this move that we can locate one of the important differences between Henry's and Henrich's positions. The investigation of the self-givenness of absolute subjectivity, and of the condition of possibility for manifestation, does not carry us beyond phenomenology, but only beyond a certain narrow conception of phenomenology which identifies it with the investigation of act-intentionality and object-manifestation.[69] As long as one only operates with the latter kind of manifestation, functioning subjectivity cannot be approached phenomenologically. Instead we have to make do with regressive inferences, or base our theory on insights gained *ex negativo* through a criticism of the reflection theory.

The situation changes if it is acknowledged that there are in fact two completely different types of manifestation. Absolute subjectivity is characterized by its evasiveness and unthematizability. This is not a deficiency to be overcome, but rather the defining feature of the manifestation of functioning subjectivity. *Pace* Tugendhat, it should consequently be realized that the inevitable anonymity and evasiveness of functioning subjectivity cannot simply be dismissed as an exposure of the aporetic point of departure, nor taken as a mere symptom of the insufficiency of our present investigation or method of analysis. It is a serious misunderstanding to assume that functioning subjectivity is some substantial entity, and then claim that our analysis of its self-manifestation is a failure, since it fails to disclose such an entity.[70]

11

Self-Awareness and Alterity: A Conclusion

One of the objectives of this book was to throw light upon the relationship between self-awareness and alterity. But whereas in the preceding I have distinguished and analyzed several different types of self-awareness, the concept of alterity has so far been employed rather unsystematically. There are different kinds of alterity, and if one wishes to investigate to what extent self-awareness might be influenced or conditioned by it, it is essential to specify exactly what kind of alterity one is referring to.

As should have become clear from my presentation, however, I think it is possible to distinguish three fundamentally different types of alterity: alterity in the form of (1) nonself (world), (2) oneself as Other, and (3) Other self. But the suggestion that there are other types of alterity than the alterity of the Other has been challenged by Lévinas (mainly in writings prior to *Autrement qu'être ou au-dela de l'essence*).

According to Lévinas, the world I am living in is a world filled with objects which all differ from me, and which are therefore all characterized by a certain alterity. I encounter and handle these objects with different attitudes, practical as well as theoretical. But when I study them or consume them or utilize them in work, I am constantly transforming the foreign and different into the familiar and same, and thereby making them lose their strangeness.[1] Although intentionality does relate me to that which is foreign, it is a nonreciprocal relationship. It never makes me leave home. As Lévinas puts it, the knowing subject acts like the famous stone of the alchemists: It transmutes everything it touches. It absorbs the foreign, annuls its alterity, and transforms it into the same.[2]

According to Lévinas, the alterity of the world and worldly entities, as well as the alterity that can be found internally in the self, are all purely formal types of alterity. They are all differences that can be thought, assimilated, and absorbed by the subject, and they therefore remain differences inherent in and interior to a totality dominated, controlled, and constituted by the subject.[3]

Lévinas certainly makes it clear that one has to stress the difference between negativity and difference, on the one hand, and real alterity, on the other. In traditional metaphysics (Spinoza and Hegel), negativity is essential for (self-)determination, but whereas negativity can be *aufgehoben* and thereby assimilated into a totalitarian system, this is not the case for true alterity: "If one could possess, grasp, and know the other, it would not be other."[4] As long as the Other is conceived as being related to, or correlated with, or dependent upon subjectivity, as long as it is something that can be absorbed by or integrated into the subject, we are not dealing with true alterity, but merely with a game of internal difference.[5]

According to Lévinas, Western philosophy has been characterized by this attitude toward alterity. It has been inflicted with an insurmountable allergy, with a horror for the Other that remains Other, and has consequently and persistently tried to reduce alterity to sameness.[6] Thus, for Lévinas as well, Western philosophy might be criticized for its *ontological monism*. In other words, difference has been reduced to identity, transcendence to immanence, the Other to the same.

For Lévinas, true and radical alterity can only be found in the Other: "The absolutely other [*Autre*] is the Other [*Autrui*]."[7] The alterity of the Other does not consist in possessing a quality which distinguishes it from me. A distinction of this nature would imply a kind of underlying similarity and comparability which would annul the alterity.[8] It should thus come as no surprise when Lévinas insists that the distinction between the Same and Other is not simply a provisional rupture of a totality, or when he denies that they are in any way intertwined.[9]

According to Lévinas, a true encounter with the Other is an experience of something that cannot be conceptualized or categorized. It is a relation with a total and absolute alterity, which is irreducible to interiority.[10] It is an encounter with something that is not merely absorbed by the subject, and which does not simply leave it untouched, unmoved, and unchanged. On the contrary, a true encounter with radical alterity is an encounter that overwhelms me and shakes me in my very foundation.[11] Lévinas's originality is that he takes the problem of justice and injustice to provide us with an original, nonreductionistic approach to the Other. The authentic encounter with the Other is not perceptual or epistemic, but ethical in nature. It is in the ethical situation where the Other questions me and makes ethical demands of me, i.e., when I have to assume responsibility for the Other, that he is present in a nonallergic manner.[12] The true encounter with the Other is not a thematization of the Other, but a nonindifference toward the Other.[13]

I think that Lévinas is right insofar as he wishes to underline the radical alterity of the Other. In our confrontation with the Other we do encounter an irreducible type of alterity. Thus, one should definitely distinguish the alterity in myself and the alterity of worldly objects from the alterity of the Other, and it is important to counter the suggestion that we are simply dealing with three different variations of one and the same alterity. Whereas I can disclose and determine the object, the Other evades my comprehension, and can never become truly present for me. The Other is not only different, it is alien, and possesses a far more radical kind of transcendence than any object. But one can acknowledge this and still insist that the alterity of the world and the alterity in the self are genuine types of alterity, and not merely games of internal differences controlled by the subject. On the contrary, they are exactly types of alterity essential for the self-constitution of subjectivity.

As I pointed out in the preface, my aim was threefold. I wished to present a systematic and comprehensive reconstruction of Husserl's theory of self-awareness; I wished to discuss and clarify some central topics in phenomenology; and finally, I wished to make a more general contribution to the current philosophical discussion of self-awareness.

The first part of my investigation basically argued that first-personal self-reference differs from diverse forms of object-reference, and it was suggested that the reason is that we are acquainted with our own subjectivity in a way that is radically different from the way in which we are acquainted with objects. Next, I attempted to substantiate this suggestion through a series of arguments in defense of a prereflective form of self-awareness. The main argument (1) consisted in a criticism of the reflection theory and demonstrated that this model cannot explain what it sets out to explain. Reflective self-awareness presupposes a more basic kind of self-awareness, and since our experiences are reflectively accessible they must already be prereflectively self-aware. Two additional arguments corroborated this claim by arguing that (2) if our experiences are essentially characterized by their first-personal givenness, this implies that there is something it is like for the subject to have an experience, even prior to reflection; and (3) indexical reference, even the kind found in ordinary perception, entails a minimal and tacit form of self-awareness.

In short, it was argued that self-awareness is not merely something that comes about the moment we direct our attention at our conscious life. In its most basic form, it is not the result of a relational, mediated, conceptual, or objectifying process; rather, it is an immediate, internal, and pervasive feature of our consciousness. To phrase it differently, an analysis of self-awareness is not merely an analysis of an exclusive problem about how we manage to pay attention to ourselves, or about how we are able to discriminate between ourselves, the world, and other subjects. It is rather an analysis of what it means to be conscious. To be conscious is to be immediately and noninferentially aware of whatever experience one is undergoing, and to be aware of that is to be acquainted not simply with transcendent objects, but with one's own subjectivity.

At this stage a number of urgent questions emerged. Not only was a more detailed investigation of the primary self-manifestation called for, but it was also argued that a convincing account of self-awareness could not itself afford to proceed in a purely formal and regressive manner. Self-awareness is a feature of subjectivity, but so are temporality, intentionality, reflexivity, corporeality, and intersubjectivity, and it was suggested that a simultaneous consideration of these different aspects would not only considerably increase our understanding of self-awareness, but also call into question the attempt to conceive of it in terms of a pure, independent, and self-sufficient self-presence.

To a large extent, my analyses in part 2 provided answers to the questions raised at the end of part 1. I have discussed to what extent subjectivity can be described phenomenologically and to what extent it evades theoretical examination. I have accounted for the egocentric nature of consciousness. I have described the internal structure of prereflective self-awareness, I have distinguished and analyzed a variety of different forms of reflection, and through an extensive analysis of temporal and bodily self-affection, I have attempted to show how the self-division, self-alteration, and self-alienation that we encounter in reflective self-awareness could emerge. I have discussed to what extent self-awareness might depend upon the intervention of the Other, and to what extent our ability to recognize Others presupposes an experience of our own exteriority. I have examined the relationship between self-awareness and intentionality, and argued for an interdependency between self-manifestation and hetero-manifestation. So far the only question with which I have not dealt explicitly concerns the relationship between self-awareness and the unconscious, but I have decided to save that discussion for the appendix.

One of my goals was to avoid both of the following pitfalls. The first persistently ignores the difference between self-manifestation and object-manifestation, and conceives of self-awareness in terms of reflection, inner perception, or introspection. The second acknowledges the unique nature of self-manifestation, but in its attempt to liberate and rescue subjectivity from a leveling and reifying reductionism, it reinstates a kind of Cartesian dualism, and conceives of subjectivity as an independent, autonomous, and self-sufficient substance.

One does not escape the reflection model as long as one persists in taking prereflective self-awareness as a kind of marginal object-consciousness. Prereflective self-awareness does not share the ordinary dyadic structure of appearance, for it is not at all a particular act but a dimension of pervasive self-manifestation. It is a self-manifestation intrinsic to our experiences and characterized by its unthematic, implicit, immediate, and passive nature. But although prereflective self-awareness is neither relational nor mediated, it is not as undifferentiated, simple, pure, and self-sufficient as one might think at first.

I have argued that it is appropriate to conceive of prereflective self-awareness in terms of *self-affection*, since it not only captures a whole range of its defining features, but ultimately allows for new insights as well. As Husserl argued with regard to reflection, qua intentional activity it presupposes a motivation, namely, a prior self-affection. Subjectivity is affected by itself, and it can choose to respond to this affection. With its connotations pointing to the sphere of both sensibility and emotion,[14] to speak of self-affection indicates that we are faced with an immediate, direct, nonobjectifying, and nonconceptual self-acquaintance, a self-acquaintance characterized by exposure and radical passivity. To be a subject is a given state and not something that one initiates, regulates, or controls. At the same time, the notion of self-affection suggests that we are dealing not with a static self-identity, but with a dynamic restlessness. Even though we are obviously not confronted with a subject-object dichotomy, there is still a certain articulation or differentiation involved. Thus, to conceive of prereflective self-awareness in terms of self-affection permits one to establish the necessary connections to both bodily self-appearance, temporality, and reflection.

Due to its intrinsic temporal articulation and differentiated infrastructure, prereflective self-awareness cannot be conceived as a pure and simple self-presence. The primal impression is not an independent source of presencing, but is always already furnished with a temporal density, always already accompanied by a horizon of protentional and retentional absencing. Only this temporal ecstasis explains the possibility of temporal self-awareness, of reflection and recollection.

To speak of a pure self-manifestation is a falsifying abstraction. Self-manifestation always occurs in the form of an impressional sensibility; that is, it cannot occur in separation from hetero-manifestation, not because it is itself a form of object-manifestation, nor because it needs the confrontation with alterity in order to gain self-awareness, nor because the self-awareness in question is in any way mediated, but exactly because it is our self-transcending subjectivity which is self-aware. Self-awareness is not to be understood as a preoccupation with self that excludes or impedes the contact with transcendent being. On the contrary, subjectivity is essentially oriented and open toward that which it is not, and it is exactly in this openness, exposure, and vulnerability that it reveals itself. What is disclosed by the *cogito* is not an enclosed immanence, a pure interior self-presence, but an openness toward alterity, a movement of perpetual self-transcendence.

A further striking manifestation of the interrelation between self-awareness and alterity can be found in the different forms of reflection, since they are all characterized by a certain degree of *self-othering*. And again, it is not enough simply to acknowledge the existence of these *alterating* and *alienating* forms of self-awareness. (It is called "alterating" because reflective self-awareness is established across an internal difference and distance—a self-displacement which is essential for the acquisition of an explicit I-consciousness—and because it does not merely copy or repeat the original experience but alters its givenness. It is called "alienating" because there are mundane forms of reflective self-awareness which are mediated by the Other.) One of the central tasks was exactly to understand how our primary self-manifestation could give rise to these transmutations. If it had in fact been characterized by a radical self-coincidence, and distinguished by the solidity of its simple, tight, and closed self-presence, it would have been very difficult to comprehend how we could ever have attained the necessary self-detachment and self-distance that permits us to reflect, and eventually even to adopt, a mundane perspective on ourselves.

In order to understand how mundane self-awareness is made possible, the analysis of bodily self-manifestation proved of decisive importance. It enabled us to reach a better understanding of the relation between prereflective and reflective self-awareness, a better understanding of the relation between intentionality and self-awareness, a better understanding of the relation between self-affection and hetero-affection, and finally, through an analysis of the double-sensation and the process of localization, a better understanding of how we experience our own exteriority, an experience which is crucial for empathy, and thereby for the whole range of alienating self-apprehensions.

I hope I have succeeded in making it clear why the topic of self-awareness is by no means of mere incidental interest to phenomenology, but rather of absolute crucial importance to it. Not only would its own preferred reflective methodology remain unaccounted for and obscure, but without an adequate understanding of self-awareness, its detailed analysis of act-intentionality and object-manifestation would also lack a proper foundation. That is, without an elucidation of the unique givenness of subjectivity, it would be impossible to account convincingly for the appearance of objects, and ultimately phenomenology would be incapable of realizing its own proper task, namely, a clarification of the condition of possibility for manifestation.

At the same time, I believe that my reconstruction of Husserl's theory of self-awareness contributes yet another piece to the gradually emerging reappraisal of Husserl as a thinker who in many ways anticipated and contributed to the central post-Husserlian discussions in phenomenology.[15] Not only has it turned out that Husserl was by no means so taken up by his "discovery" of object-intentionality that he never escaped the reflection model, never managed to raise the more fundamental question concerning the Being of consciousness, and never stopped operating a model of self-manifestation based on the subject-object dichotomy.[16] On closer examination, Husserl also reveals himself as a thinker of alterity, facticity, and passivity, and by no means is he, as Derrida occasionally maintains, a thinker who remained stuck in the metaphysics of presence, stubbornly conceiving of absolute subjectivity in terms of a self-sufficient immanence purified from all types of exteriority and difference.[17] In this regard, Henry's estimation is really more to the point, since he claims that it is downright absurd to accuse Husserl of having advocated a philosophy of pure presence. Of course, for Henry this is intended as a criticism, but as I have already pointed out, I think Husserl offers us a theory that avoids the excesses of both Derrida and Henry. He does not advocate a philosophy of pure presence. But this is not because the question concerning the unique nature of self-manifestation has eluded him, but because he, in contrast to Henry, believes it to be intrinsically ecstatic.

Ultimately, the problem of self-awareness is intertwined with a remarkable number of other issues, including temporality, egocentricity, alterity, intentionality, affection, and attention. Obviously, I do not claim to have dealt exhaustively with all of these issues, nor to have provided definitive answers to the questions raised in chapter 3. But I do claim to have shown that there are substantial insights to be gained from phenomenology when it comes to the problem of self-awareness, insights which allow for a more substantial and detailed understanding of the nature of self-awareness than the one offered by the theories examined in chapters 1 and 2. At the same time, however, I think it is undeniable that contemporary phenomenology can profit from the conceptual clarity and problem-oriented approach found in the discussion of the Heidelberg School as well as in analytical philosophy. I hope that my own contribution can in some modest way further the dialogue between these diverse philosophical traditions, which despite decisive methodological differences, each in its own way struggles with a number of common problems.

Appendix: Self-Awareness and the Unconscious

In the preceding chapters we have repeatedly come across formulations like the following: Every intentional consciousness is necessarily self-aware; our subjectivity is characterized by a fundamental self-manifestation; if I see, remember, know, think, hope, feel, or will something I am *eo ipso* aware of it. But where do these assertions leave us with respect to the *unconscious?* Are all experiences self-aware per se, and is the notion of an unconscious consciousness a contradiction in terms? Or to phrase the question in a more direct and polemic way: How can anyone who is familiar with Freud's "discovery" of the unconscious possibly maintain that consciousness is intrinsically self-aware?

Both Freud and the unconscious are such vast topics that it is out of the question to commence an in-depth investigation at this point. Nevertheless some brief remarks might not only clarify some of the issues discussed already, but also be sufficient in order to show that only a particular (mis)interpretation of, respectively, self-awareness and the unconscious leads to the view that we are dealing with incompatible determinations.

Freud

The easiest way to avoid a head-on collision is to point out that Freud himself, perhaps through Brentano's influence, accepted the thesis that all conscious acts are self-aware! We are immediately and noninferentially aware of any conscious process that occurs. It is exactly because we are aware of it that we call the psychical process in question *conscious.*[1] Thus, we find the following slightly surprising statements in Freud:

> Now let us call "conscious" the conception [*Vorstellung*] which is present to our consciousness and of which we are aware, and let this be the only meaning of the term "conscious."[2]

We have no right to extend the meaning of this word [*bewußt*] so far as to make it include a consciousness of which its owner himself is not aware. If philosophers find difficulty in accepting the existence of unconscious ideas, the existence of an unconscious consciousness seems to me even more objectionable.[3]

And after all, a consciousness of which one knows nothing seems to me a good deal more absurd than something mental that is unconscious.[4]

For all his preoccupation with the unconscious, self-aware consciousness remains of central significance to Freud. After all, as he states in *Das Unbewusste*, it is the point of departure for his investigation.[5] It is exactly when we wish to comprehend various conscious phenomena that we are forced to assume the existence of the unconscious as their cause and sole explanation.[6] It is in consciousness and for consciousness that the unconscious reveals itself (in the form of lacunas, ruptures, obsessive thoughts, etc.),[7] and the quality of being conscious consequently remains the one light which can illuminate the path and leads us through the darkness of mental life.[8]

Although Freud acknowledges the central significance of self-awareness, it is striking how little he has to say about it. One gets the impression that he believes it to be of such self-evident and unproblematic nature that no further reflections are necessary: "There is no need to discuss what is to be called conscious; it is removed from all doubt."[9] However, a closer examination reveals that Freud's nonchalant attitude conceals a rather naive understanding of self-awareness: "In psychoanalysis there is no choice for us but to assert that mental processes are in themselves unconscious, and to liken the perception of them by means of consciousness to the perception of the external world by means of the sense-organs."[10] Freud thus subscribes to a version of the reflection theory. A psychical process becomes conscious when it is made the object of a reflection or introspection.

At this stage, the possibility of a reconciliation between psychoanalysis and a phenomenological theory of self-awareness presents itself. The latter does not contradict, but rather complements the findings of psychoanalysis, not only because psychoanalysis operates with a problematic concept of self-awareness which should be amended, but also because the notion and understanding of the un*conscious* is parasitic upon one's understanding of and acquintance with the conscious. As a rather well-known remark by Fink has it: "One thinks one is already acquainted with what the 'conscious,' or consciousness, is and dismisses the task of first making into a prior subject matter the concept against which any science of the unconscious must demarcate its subject matter, i.e., precisely that of consciousness. But because one does not know what consciousness is, one misses in principle the point of departure of a science of the 'unconscious.' "[11]

To repeat, the existence of the unconscious does not constitute a problem for a theory of self-awareness, as long as the latter merely insists upon the intrinsic connection between consciousness and self-awareness. Even Freud acknowledges that it is the self-awareness of a psychical process that makes it conscious.

Unfortunately, this way of avoiding a skirmish might be a bit too easy. Although the existence of the unconscious does not constitute any danger to the central theses concerning the nature of self-manifestation defended above, it might, however, question the range and pervasiveness of self-awareness. Although psychoanalysis might concede that there is an intrinsic and essential relation between consciousness and self-awareness, it certainly denies any intrinsic and essential relation between the mental and the conscious, and will presumably deny both that subjectivity is essentially characterized by self-manifestation and that any hetero-manifestation, any intentional reference to the world, is necessarily self-aware. As Freud puts it:

> The physician can only shrug his shoulders when he is assured that "consciousness is an indispensable characteristic of what is psychical," and perhaps, if he still feels enough respect for the utterances of philosophers, he may presume that they have not been dealing with the same thing or working at the same science. For even a single understanding observation of a neurotic's mental life or a single analysis of a dream must leave him with an unshakeable conviction that the most complicated and most rational thought-processes, which can surely not be denied the name of psychical processes, can occur without exciting the subject's consciousness.[12]

At this point, it is necessary to take the bull by the horns and ask exactly what the unconscious is. Although the concept has by now entered everyday language to an extent where it is taken for granted that there exists unconscious experiences, unconscious feelings, thoughts, and perceptions, it would be an exaggeration to claim that we are dealing with a particularly clear and well-defined concept.

Following Searle, one might illustrate a prevalent and rather popular conception of the unconscious—a conception which Freud himself occasionally subscribes to—through the following image. Our mental states and psychic processes are like fish in the sea. No matter how deep the fish swim, they keep their shapes. The fish at the bottom which we cannot see has exactly the same shape as it has when it surfaces. When the mental state is at the bottom it is unconscious. When it surfaces it becomes conscious.[13] Basically, all psychic processes are unconscious and to bring them to consciousness is like fishing a perch up in the daylight. Thus, if the mind is compared to the sea, my conscious experiences only compose a minimal fraction of the totality of mental states which I have at any given moment. That is, at any given moment I (or something else in me) perceives, believes, wishes, remembers, imagines, wills, etc., a variety of things, but I am simply not aware of it.

According to this interpretation, the unconscious mental state has everything the conscious mental state has, including intentionality and egocentricity; it just lacks the conscious quality. It is exactly like the conscious state except that it is unconscious. Thus, consciousness is taken to be a completely extrinsic, nonessential feature of the emotion or intention. It does not contribute in any significant way to the constitution of the state in question, but is a simple varnish.[14]

This reifying interpretation has on all days been criticized by phenomenologists. Thus, it has been claimed that Freud's description of the unconscious is marred by a number of misleading metaphors, which ultimately miss the true significance of both the conscious and the unconscious. One cannot simply subtract the conscious "quality" from a feeling or intention and expect it to remain a feeling or intention. And the unconscious in the proper sense is not at all to be identified with an ordinary intentional act devoid of self-awareness, but rather with a quite different depth-structure in subjectivity.[15]

Let me emphasize that the phenomenological criticism is not directed against the very concept of the unconscious, but against a special objectifying misinterpretation of it. But how then is the unconscious conceived of by phenomenologists?

Phenomenology and the Unconscious

To start with, it cannot be emphasized too often that prereflective self-awareness is not an intentional, thetic, objectifying, or epistemic act. This implies that the self-awareness in question might very well be accompanied by a fundamental *ignorance*.[16] Although I cannot be unconscious of my present experience, I might very well ignore it in favor of its object, and this is of course the natural attitude. In my daily life I am absorbed by and preoccupied with projects and objects in the world. Thus, pervasive prereflective self-awareness is definitely not identical with total self-comprehension, but can instead be likened to a precomprehension that allows for subsequent reflection and thematization.

Some might think it more appropriate to call a subjectivity which we have no knowledge of and persistently ignore an unconscious or preconscious subjectivity. But whether or not we should equate the consciously given with the attentively and thematically given, and consequently deny that subjectivity is conscious prior to reflection, is more than a mere terminological dispute. If one chooses to identify the conscious with the thematically known, one has adopted a terminology that reflects a far too narrow conception of both consciousness and manifestation. This has been persistently pointed out by both Husserl and Henry. But as the latter also writes: "Once the concept of the unconscious appears, it is the sign that we are approaching an original region, because the unconscious is often only a name attributed to absolute subjectivity by philosophies incapable of grasping the essence of the foundation other than by projecting it into the night of a hinter world which we have psychoanalyzed."[17]

At this point it is hardly necessary to point out that any argument to the effect that the unconscious must per definition be inaccessible for a thinking devoted to *manifestation*, and that anything that cannot be accessed through direct reflection is off limits for phenomenology, is based upon a superficial conception of phenomenology. It is quite appropriate to distinguish between a surface phenomenology and a depth phenomenology. The moment phenomenology moves beyond an investigation of object-manifestation and act-intentionality, it enters a realm that has traditionally been called the unconscious.

I will not go into a detailed discussion of this aspect of Husserl's thinking, but let me give a few examples as illustration.

The theme of the persisting influence of the past is particularly brought to the fore in Husserl's *genetical phenomenology*. As Husserl points out, our apperceptions do not arise out of nothing. They have a genesis and are formed by previous experiences. Through a process of *sedimentation*, our experiences leave their trace on us and thereby contribute to the formation of cognitive schemas and diverse forms of apprehension and expectations which guide, motivate, and influence subsequent experiences: "The Ego always lives in the medium of its 'history'; all its earlier lived experiences have sunk down, but they have aftereffects in tendencies, sudden ideas, transformations or assimilations of earlier lived experiences, and from such assimilations new formations are merged together, etc."[18] This influence can hardly be called conscious. Nor do we have any awareness of the very formation of concepts and habitualities. Thus, my intentional life is affected by an obscure underground. We are dealing with constitutive processes which remain inaccessible for

direct appropriation.[19] Particularly so, since many of the most fundamental habitualities were established in the first years of life. And as
Husserl readily acknowledges, the early childhood constitutes a dark limit
which cannot be crossed. It cannot be reappropriated from a first-person
perspective.[20]

More generally, Husserl concedes that the intentional activity
of the subject is founded upon and conditioned by an obscure and
blind passivity, by drives and associations, and that there are constitutive
processes of an anonymous and involuntary nature taking place in the
underground or depth-dimension of subjectivity that cannot be seized
by direct reflection.[21] Once again, the supremacy of reflection (and the
validity of the *principle of principles*) is called into question. Reflection is not
the primary mode of consciousness, and it cannot uncover the deepest
layers of subjectivity. But although it must be acknowledged that there are
depth-dimensions in the constitutive process which do not lie open to the
view of reflection, this does not imply that they remain forever completely
ineffable. They can be disclosed, not through a direct thematization,
but through an indirect operation of dismantling and deconstruction
(*Abbau*). We are dealing with feeble processes of preaffective passive
syntheses which are only accessible to consciousness through an elaborate
"archaeological effort,"[22] an effort, however, which has its obvious point
of departure in that which is *conscious*. Husserl is thus quite clear in saying
that the riddle of the unconscious can only be solved through an elaborate
analysis of the Living Present,[23] and as he declares in *Analysen zur passiven
Synthesis*, his investigation of the problems of passivity and affectivity could
well carry the title "a phenomenology of the unconscious."[24]

Occasionally, Husserl speaks of the unconscious as if it includes all
that which we are not currently paying attention to, but which could be
thematized through a mere change of attention. As illustration Husserl
mentions a situation where, in the course of a philosophical reflection,
he suddenly feels an urge to smoke. He automatically picks up a cigar and
lights it, without paying attention to the process, and without interrupting
his reflections. This urge is then called an *unconscious* affection.[25] This
notion of the unconscious, which more or less coincides with Freud's
notion of the preconscious, is by no means used consistently by Husserl.
As has already been pointed out, it is far more usual (and I believe,
more appropriate) for him to employ a notion of the conscious which is
sufficiently broad to include all those phenomena which this particular
concept of the unconscious is meant to capture.

According to Husserl, all affections can be graded according to
their strength on a scale from 1 to 0, where zero equals the absolute
unconscious.[26] This grading is particularly pertinent when it comes to the

problems of *forgetting* and *sleeping*. As the retentional sequence becomes more and more complex, the initial affection grows weaker and weaker. It loses its differentiation and distinctive qualities, it recedes into the background, becomes vague, and is finally lost in the "night of the unconscious."[27] "Alle Sonderaffektionen sind im Nullstadium in eine ungeschiedene Gesamtaffektion übergegangen; alles Sonderbewußtsein ist übergegangen in das eine, immerfort vorhandene Hintergrundbewußtsein unserer Vergangenheit überhaupt, das Bewußtsein des völlig ungegliederten, völlig undeutlichen Vergangenheitshorizontes, der die lebendige, bewegliche retentionale Vergangenheit abschließt."[28] At this point, the retained has become unconscious.[29] Why do we say that it has become unconscious, however, and not simply that it has ceased to exist? Because even at this stage, the retained has not disappeared completely. It lies dormant, but can be reawakened in an act of recollection: "Weckung ist möglich, weil der konstituierte Sinn im Hintergrundbewußtsein in der unlebendigen Form, die da Unbewußtsein heißt, wirklich impliziert ist."[30] And for Husserl this unconscious is not a mere privation or a phenomenological nought, but a marginal mode (*Grenzmodus*) or fundamentally altered form of consciousness.[31]

When it comes to the problem of sleeping, Husserl suggests that the gradual decrease of interest in the world which occurs as we fall asleep affects the way in which we are aware of ourselves as well, thereby confirming the interdependency between auto- and hetero-affection. When I am no longer "pursuing any affections," when I am no longer paying attention to the weaker and weaker "call of the world," and when that which reaches my consciousness becomes more and more undifferentiated, I drift into sleep. Thus, only a subjectivity affected by differentiated unities can remain conscious, whereas a gradual diminishing of this differentiation would eventually make it fall asleep.[32] To sleep means that there is nothing which gains relief, there is no discrimination, but a complete fusion, a sameness without difference.[33] This state of complete nondifferentiation (the state of dreamless sleep) is not nothing, however, is not the negation or suspension of subjectivity, but merely the zero limit of conscious vitality (*Bewußtseinslebendigkeit*).[34] It is a state of absolute ego-passivity where no intentional action can take place,[35] and consequently a state that excludes the possibility of thematic self-awareness. In Husserl's words,

> Nur wo Erlebnisse abgehoben sind, nur wo hyletische Daten z.B. "für sich" bereit liegen, Vorstellungen für sich, auch Leervorstellungen, da kann Affektion statthaben und da findet sie notwendig statt. Das Abgehobene ist auf das Ich bezogen, und das Ich als Pol ist in Funktion und ist für

sich da. Nur dann kann eine Reflexion statthaben. . . . Offenbar ist all das auch wichtig für die Lehre vom innersten Bewußtsein. Ist überhaupt ein mannigfaltiger Bewußtseinsstrom da mit Abgehobenheiten, so ist auch sein Ich wach, d.i., es ist mit da als Abgehobenheit in beständiger Funktion als Identitätspol der Affektionen und Aktionen, für sich selbst vorgegeben und in jederzeit möglicher Reflexion gegeben.[36]

Vielmehr ist sehr wohl denkbar ein stummes und leeres Leben, ein traumloser, leerer Schlaf sozusagen als ein Leben, das zwar auch diese notwendige Struktur hatte und innerlich passiv-wahrnehmungsmäßig erschien, aber ohne jede Abhebung, daher ohne jede Icherfassung, ohne jedes Spiel von Einzelaffektionen und Akten, so daß das Ich sozusagen keinen Auftritt hatte und schlafendes Ich, bloße Potentialität für die Ego cogitos war. Die Möglichkeit eintretender Abhebungen durch Modifikation des Lebens besteht immerfort, und damit die Möglichkeit des Erwachens.[37]

Und wäre das Leben ein "eintöniges" Dasein, etwa ein Ton in immer gleichförmigem, unterschiedslosem Verlauf, so könnte ich nicht zurück. Das ist sogar sehr bedeutsam. Wäre der "Anfang" des Lebens, die Anfangsperiode eine endlose Eintönigkeit, so wäre es eine Periode undurchbrechbaren Vergessens.[38]

Thus, Husserl occasionally suggests that dreamless sleep is in fact a period of undifferentiated experiencing. We are not confronted with ruptures in the self-given stream of consciousness, but since the very lack of differentiated affections allows of neither reflection nor recollection, the periods of dreamless sleep will always in retrospect appear as anonymous and empty gaps, as if nothing took place.[39]

Self-Luminosity and Self-Transparency

For Husserl the unconscious is not located on the same level as our object-intentionality. It is not merely an ordinary intentional act devoid of self-awareness. It is a dimension of opaque passivity which makes up the foundation of our self-aware experience. It is exactly *in* and not *behind* or *outside* or *independently* of our conscious experiences that we find these impenetrable elements. Thus, one can argue in favor of a pervasive self-awareness, deny the separate existence of unconscious *acts*, and still accept the existence of the unconscious in the sense of subjective components, which remain ambiguous, obscure, and resist comprehension. That is, one should distinguish between the claim that our consciousness is characterized by an immediate self-awareness and self-luminosity and the claim that consciousness is characterized by total self-transparency. One can easily accept the first and reject the latter, i.e., one can argue in favor of the existence of a pervasive self-awareness and still take self-comprehension to be an infinite task.[40]

On closer examination, I think it is at least necessary to distinguish between the six following claims: (1) There is much going on in our mental life that we pay no attention to; (2) our self-comprehension is neither instantaneous nor infallible, but a matter of gradual disclosure; (3) our present experiences are in part motivated and influenced by the sedimentations of previous experiences, which are no longer conscious; (4) our present experiences contain aspects and depth-structures that resist reflective appropriation and direct comprehension; (5) our experiences are to some extent conditioned by neurophysiological processes, which are absolutely inaccessible for reflection and first-person appropriation; and (6) we are currently having experiences such as perceptions, thoughts, feelings, etc., of which we have no consciousness.

As I see it, the claim that subjectivity is essentially characterized by its self-manifestation is a claim that can be reconciled with theses 1–5. It is only the last thesis that constitutes a problem. But is this last thesis really sound? Does it really make sense to speak about unconscious intentions and feelings? Can somebody think, feel, or wish something without being aware of it?

Let us imagine that Peter says to Mary, "Paul believes that mountain climbing improves his health." Peter might be justified in ascribing this belief and countless others (such as, "Watermelons do not play football" or "3+3=6") to Paul, even if Paul is presently thinking about other matters, even if he is sound asleep. But is the reason why Peter is justified in ascribing these "unconscious" beliefs to Paul really that the beliefs exist actually in Paul's unconscious, as if they were like fish in the sea which only occasionally surface? Or is it not rather absurd to assume that Paul's mind should literally be crowded with countless unconscious beliefs, i.e., that Paul should incessantly (awake and asleep) be thinking, "Mountain climbing improves my health," "Watermelons do not play football," "3+3=6," etc., without being aware of it?

Certainly there is more to subjectivity than meets the eye and more than can be grasped by a single reflection. Our mental life does not consist only of actual experiences, but also of enduring habits, interests, character traits, and convictions. As Sartre points out, to hate and to perceive somebody are two quite different things. To perceive somebody is an actual experience, and obviously the perception only lasts as long as the experience; they are after all one and the same. Thus, if I at two separate occasions perceive the same person, I am dealing with two different perceptions. If, however, I am repulsed by a certain person, I might reflectively say, "I hate this man." By doing that I am not merely articulating a particular experience, but expressing a more permanent attitude toward the person. Contrary to the perception, my hatred transcends its concrete manifestation. Its being and its appearance do not coincide. It cannot only remain part of my personality when I am preoccupied with quite different matters, but it is able to manifest itself as identically the same at a number of different occasions. If during a period I regularly encounter the man and feel loathing, disgust, repugnancy, etc., it might be different appearances of the same hatred. The hatred thus appears as a transcendent unity, as a matrix that organizes and relates a number of actual experiences to each other.[41] One might describe Paul's passion for mountain climbing in a similar manner. We are dealing with a certain latent *disposition* which can manifest itself in conscious experience if certain conditions obtain, and not with an actual occurent feeling of passion which persists regardless of whether Paul is aware of it or not. In short, I think it is more plausible to give a dispositional account of our habits, interests, convictions, etc., than to accept a reifying interpretation of the unconscious. And, as Klawonn rightly points out, every mental disposition retains an essential relation to self-awareness. They are only *my* mental dispositions because they occasionally manifest themselves in my actual self-aware experience.[42]

Let me repeat that I am not trying to deny the existence of the unconscious, but simply to criticize a special reifying interpretation of it. It is in particular the attempt to locate the unconscious on the surface level, i.e., to insist that there are fully fledged intentional acts (perceptions, wishes, beliefs) or feelings (like pain or happiness) which are unconscious, that I find problematic. One argument often presented in favor of a strong thesis about the unconscious is that if one can be in a certain mental state and not only fail to realize it but even sincerely deny it, the state must be unconscious. But it is by no means evident that this argument really holds. For instance, one might very well be in love or depressed and deny it. (1) Prior to reflection a depression is not an intentional object. It is prereflectively given as a mode that pervades our conscious experiences, and it colors everything which we encounter. At an early stage this might happen rather subversively, and it can be hard to determine whether or not we are dealing with a depression. We might even sincerely deny it, since we think we are just stressed or tired. But this is not to say that the depression is unconscious in any significant sense. (2) From the way in which Peter acts toward Mary, we might say that Peter is in love with Mary. Peter might not be aware of this. He does not know that the way he feels about Mary is in reality love. He does not realize the real motives for his actions toward Mary. But this is not to say that apart from the conscious and ambiguous feelings which Peter has toward Mary, he has a separate unambiguous and unconscious love for her.[43] Peter's experiences are conscious, but their real meaning might often be hidden to him, but visible to Others.[44] Perhaps one can compare the "unconscious" love in Peter to a puzzle picture. The hidden gnome was there right in front of us all the time (and by no means behind the picture), but only now did we discover him. And now that we have discovered him, the picture makes far more sense. Pieces that before had no connection are suddenly seen as integrated parts.[45] (3) Even pain, to use a well-known example by Sartre, might serve as an illustration. Let us assume that I am sitting late at night trying to finish a book. I have been reading most of the day and my eyes are hurting. How does this pain originally manifest itself? Not yet as a thematic object of reflection, but by influencing the way in which I perceive the world. I might become restless, irritated, have difficulties in focusing and concentrating. The words on the page may tremble or quiver. Even though the pain is not yet apprehended as a psychical object, it is not absent or unconscious. It is not yet thematized, but given as a vision-in-pain, as a pervasive affective atmosphere that influences and colors my intentional interaction with the world.[46] Or consider the following example. I am sitting in a restaurant, enjoying the food and the animated conversation. Initially, I was annoyed by a pain, but I have become absorbed by other matters, and am no longer paying attention to it. During a break in the conversation I again notice the pain, and I am even inclined to say that it is the same pain as before. Does this imply that the pain continued while I was not aware of it, and that it can consequently exist unconsciously? Just as I do not stop being prereflectively aware of my body when I converse with a friend, the pain does not necessarily cease to exist as felt just because the conversation distracts my attention from it; it simply becomes a part of the lived intentionality. As Sartre writes, "I exist the pain in such a way that it disappears in the ground of corporeality as a structure subordinated to the corporal totality. The pain is neither absent nor unconscious; it simply forms a part of that distance-less existence of positional consciousness for itself."[47] So far the pain has only been given prereflectively, but of course this can change. I can halt my conversation and focus my attention on the pain. In this case, as Sartre argues, I transcend the lived pain and posit the pain as a transcendent psychic object. Different isolated twinges of *pain* are apprehended as manifestations of one and the same *suffering*. Qua psychic object, this suffering is revealed through a series of aches as their overarching unity.[48] But we still have not exhausted the different forms of pain manifestation. I might not only apprehend the concrete pains as the manifestation of a suffering. I can also classify and characterize the suffering through concepts acquired from Others: It is a case of glaucoma. At this stage, the pain has become accessible to Others. They can describe it and diagnose it as a *disease*. And when I conceive of it in a similar manner, I adopt an objectifying and alienating third-person perspective on my pain.[49]

Sartre's analysis is illuminating since it cautions us not to conflate different levels of description. When I take a drug against the pain in my eyes, what happens? Does the drug make the pain disappear, or does it simply remove my awareness of it? The usual arguments presented in favor of the thesis that pain can exist unconsciously are based upon either a too narrow concept of the conscious—only the attentively given is conscious—or upon a confusion between pain as sensation and pain as disease.

Granted that pain is painful, and that it consequently makes no sense to speak of an unfelt and unconscious pain, one might ask if a similar argument can be used with other types of experiences.[50] Does it make sense to speak of an unconscious tasting of coffee? An unconscious hearing and appreciation of Miles Davis? An unconscious desiring for chocolate? If an unconscious *experience* is to deserve its name, and not merely be an objective, physical process, it must presumably be subjective. After all, we do not call a stone, a table, or the blood in our veins unconscious. But where is this subjectivity to manifest itself? Supposedly in the particular first-personal givenness of the experience. But it is difficult to imagine how an unconscious experience should possess such a feature. Unconscious experiences are per definition without a first-personal givenness; there is nothing it is like for the subject to have them. But can one really abstract the peculiar subjective givenness of the experience from the experience and still retain an experience, or is the ontology of experiencing not rather a first-person ontology?[51] If it is a defining feature of an experience that there is necessarily something it is like for the subject to have it, it will be just as nonsensical to speak of an unconscious experience as to speak of an unconscious consciousness. And to make use of a related argument, if every reference with an indexical component presupposes a self-reference or self-presentation, i.e., if it is only by being tacitly aware of our own subjective perspective that we can refer indexically, it will hardly make sense to speak of unconscious perceptions or unconscious identifying references to particulars either.

A more radical and ambitious strategy would be to argue for the intrinsic connection between *experience, meaning,* and *intentionality,* and for the claim that there is no meaning, and therefore no intentionality, in a world without conscious experience. As Strawson has recently put it:

> [M]eaning is always a matter of something meaning something *to* something. In this sense, nothing means anything in an experienceless world. There is no possible meaning, hence no possible intention, hence no possible intentionality, on an experienceless planet. . . . There is no entity that means anything in this universe. There is no entity that is about anything. There is no semantic evaluability, no truth, no falsity. None of these properties are possessed by anything until experience begins. There is a clear and fundamental sense in which *meaning, and hence intentionality, exists only in the conscious moment.*[52]

Strawson consequently claims that experience is a necessary condition for genuine aboutness, and he suggests that there is an analogy between the sense in which a sleeping person might be said to be in possession of beliefs, preferences, etc., and the sense in which a CD might be said to contain music when it is not being played by a CD player. Considered merely as physical systems neither of them is intrinsically about one thing rather than another, neither of them has any intrinsic (musical or mental) content. Strictly speaking, "it is no more true to say that there are states of the brain, or of Louis, that have intrinsic mental content, when Louis is in a dreamless and experienceless sleep, than it is true to say that there are states of a CD that have intrinsic musical content as it sits in its box."[53]

Of course, this does not exclude that there might be different nonconscious states and processes which play a causal role in our experience, but to speak of such nonconscious processes is not per se to speak of unconscious experiences.[54] Some have been tempted to describe the unconscious as an objective occurrence, and have even identified it with neurophysiological processes.[55] In the latter case we would definitely be dealing with something that forever remained inaccessible for reflection and first-person appropriation. Nor would it any longer make sense to speak in an emphatic sense of *my* unconscious. We would be dealing with objective, physical, and natural processes, purified from everything subjective and personal. But obviously this particular interpretation of the unconscious poses no threat to a theory about the intrinsic self-manifestation of subjectivity.

Forms of Dissociation: Sleepwalking and Hypnosis

In chapter 2, I briefly referred to Armstrong's position in *A Materialist Theory of the Mind*. According to Armstrong, mental states such as perceptions or feelings are not necessarily self-aware. Whether or not a given mental state is conscious (i.e., self-aware) depends upon whether or not a further mental state is directed toward it. Armstrong thus compares introspection to an inner mental eye and writes that a mental state is conscious insofar as it is the object of an introspection. Just as there are many features of our physical environment which we do not perceive, there are many mental states of which we are unaware, namely, all those which we do not currently introspect.[56] I do not think it is necessary to provide further arguments against this conception of self-awareness, but in his discussion Armstrong refers to a number of psychological phenomena, such as sleepwalking and hypnosis. And I think it is worthwhile to take a closer look at these intriguing phenomena, particularly since they seem to constitute exceptions to the claim that all surface phenomena (such as perceptions, beliefs, intentions) are characterized by their first-personal givenness.[57]

Episodes of sleepwalking normally last from a few seconds to a few minutes, but they can last up to half an hour or longer. Examples of sleepwalking might be briefly standing up, then going back to bed, partially dressing, or going to the bathroom. But more unusual cases are known as well, as in the case of a college student who formed the habit of getting up in his sleep, dressing, walking down to the river almost a mile away, undressing, taking a swim, dressing, walking back to his room, undressing, and retiring, only to wake up in the morning without any awareness of what had happened during the night.

In order to prevent the sleepwalker from engaging in his nocturnal activities, several remedies have been tried. One has been to place pots of cold water next to the bed, and another to tie the person to the bedpost, but they all usually fail, since the sleepwalker often "learns" to avoid the pots or even to untie the cord.

How should the state of the sleepwalker be described? Although it was previously assumed that sleepwalking was the acting out of a dream, this is no longer taken to be the case, since the sleepwalker does not recall any dreams if awakened. In one sense his behavior meets the criteria of wakefulness: His eyes are open, he is able to stand and walk, to avoid obstacles, to find his way about in familiar surroundings. He can even answer questions correctly, giving monosyllabic replies. On the other hand, his facial expression is rigid, and he performs habitual acts characterized by automaticity and rigidity, thus giving him the appearance of a robot, or of somebody in a trance. And, most important, the sleepwalker appears to be quite unaware of what he is doing. He is not only unable to remember any of his actions, he also seems to lack any consciousness of his actions at the time of their performance. Thus, if you awaken a sleepwalker during the episode, he will generally be very confused and will not know where he is or what he has been doing.[58]

Sleepwalkers are generally able to perform actions that seem to require both intelligence and consciousness, but since they have no awareness of these actions, Armstrong suggests that sleepwalking presents us with a case where we have mental activity without self-awareness. The sleepwalker must perceive his surroundings in order to perform the actions he does, but his perceptions are unconscious.[59] To substantiate this interpretation Armstrong also refers to the case of the long-distance driver who suddenly "wakes up," realizing that he has just driven many miles without any consciousness of the driving.[60] The driver must obviously have been perceiving the road, otherwise the truck would have ended up in the ditch, but since he has no recollection of these perceptions, they must have occurred unconsciously. However, this example is less striking, since there are several alternative explanations at hand. Habitual acts are exactly defined by not demanding any attentive surveillance on our part. They are characterized by a certain automatism, and the absentmindedness of the truck driver might exactly reflect the lack of attention required, rather than any actual gap in self-aware consciousness. Attention does not define consciousness, but it might influence our powers of recollection. And if these fail, it will in retrospect be as if nothing transpired (cf. p. 210).

Needless to say, the central question is whether Armstrong's interpretation is the only possible and plausible one. It is reasonable to assume that sleepwalking is not merely a sequence of automatic reflexes. But are we really confronted with examples of unconscious intentionality? We take ordinary dreaming to be a self-aware experience because we can often recall it when we are awake. But it is precisely this ability that we lack when confronted with sleepwalking. And if we are not able to recollect the experiences, what kind of proof do we have that they were self-aware when they occurred? So far none. This does not prove, of course, that the experiences were unconscious, since we might merely have forgotten them, owing to profound amnesia. But so far this hypothesis is unsubstantiated and merely postulatory.

To try to shed some light upon the problem, a brief digression is in order at this point. In French, hypnotism is known as a *somnambulisme provoqué*. And the state of the hypnotized subject can in fact resemble that of the sleepwalker. If the hypnotic state is sufficiently deep, it may be accompanied by spontaneous amnesia, and the subject will have no awareness of what has passed when he returns to normal consciousness.[61] It is, however, also possible for the hypnotist to provoke such amnesia in the subject artificially, just as during the hypnosis he might instruct the hypnotized to be capable of remembering everything afterward, in which case the subject will do so.[62] Finally, it is also possible in a subsequent hypnotic session to lift the amnesia and make the subject recall everything that transpired in a former session. Now, what is particularly remarkable is that the same holds true of the sleepwalker. If the individual is later hypnotized, he might recall everything that occurred during the episode of sleepwalking. This procedure has been used in the case of people who have committed crimes while sleepwalking. They were unaware of them, but they were able to recall their criminal acts under hypnosis.[63]

Since it is in fact possible to recall experiences one has had during sleepwalking, these experiences cannot have been unconscious—only that which is originally self-aware can subsequently be recollected as one's own past experience—and the phenomenon of sleepwalking consequently fails to constitute a refutation of the thesis that asserts an intrinsic relation between perceptions and self-awareness. This is not to say, however, that it is not a very paradoxical phenomenon, and it might in fact pose a difficulty, not for the thesis concerning self-awareness, but for that concerning the *unity* of the stream of consciousness.

In his *Principles of Psychology,* James gives a long and very interesting account of hypnosis, reporting on research done by Janet and Binet. Both originally argued that consciousness might be split into parts which coexist but ignore each other. Let me give some examples. A common symptom in persons suffering from hysterics was anesthesia. Sight, hearing, smell, taste, or feeling might fail. But Janet and Binet showed that in the case of such types of anesthesia there remained a sensibility in the "anesthetic" part in the form of a secondary consciousness, which was cut off from the primary or normal one. If the subject was pricked or burned in the "anesthetic" region, he would not feel it, of course. But if subsequently hypnotized, he would often complain about the pain. Thus, the pain was felt, not by the normal subjects, but by a secondary self which could be evoked under hypnosis. The latter might have experiences or even act without the normal subject's being aware of it. On one occasion Janet whispered suggestions to a man in alcoholic delirium, who was being questioned by a doctor, and thus led him to walk, sit, kneel, and even lie facedown on the floor while he remained firm in the belief that he was standing beside his bed.[64]

Recently this line of research has been continued by Hilgard, the foremost representative of the so-called *neodissociation theory* of hypnosis.

According to Hilgard numerous experiments have shown that hypnosis can present us with the phenomenon of *coconsciousness*: the existence of two separate, dissociated but concurrent *conscious* experiences. Of one the normal hypnotized subject is aware, of the other he is unaware,[65] and it is only by using special techniques that responses may be elicited from this secondary consciousness, which Hilgard has dubbed the *hidden observer*:

> He [E. A. Kaplan] gave a deeply hypnotized subject the suggestions that his left arm was analgesic and insensitive and that his right arm would write automatically; the subject would not be aware of what he was writing. When the experimenter pricked the left (anesthetic) arm several times with a hypodermic needle, the other hand wrote: "Ouch, damn it, you're hurting me." After a few minutes had passed, the subject, oblivious to what had transpired, asked Kaplan when he was going to begin the experiment.[66]

If one interprets the hypnotic state in terms of dissociation, whereby dissociation is defined as the process of creating and maintaining amnesic barriers or vertical splits between the various sectors of conscious experience,[67] hypnosis obviously does not confront us with unconscious experiences in any absolute sense. The hypnotized subject might be unable to smell household ammonia, or only see two out of three colored boxes in front of him, or become incapable of hearing certain words, and may even perform actions, such as automatic writing, without being aware of it. These behavioral features notwithstanding, what we are confronted with is best described not as instances of unconscious experience, i.e., experiences lacking self-awareness, but rather as ordinary self-aware experiences which have been rendered inaccessible due to a particular kind of hypnosis-induced dissociation.[68] Thus the various objects and actions are still experienced consciously, as is clear from the response from the "hidden observer," but what we have are experiences which are momentarily hidden behind an amnesialike barrier. As James puts it:

> It is therefore to no "automatism" in the mechanical sense that such acts are due: a self presides over them, a split-off, limited and buried, but yet a fully conscious, self.[69]

> [W]e must never take a person's testimony, however sincere, that he has felt nothing, as proof positive that no feeling has been there. It may have been there as part of the consciousness of a "secondary personage," of whose experiences the primary one whom we are consulting can naturally give no account.[70]

Thus, to return to the issue at stake, Armstrong's interpretation is by no means the only one possible. Neither hypnosis nor sleepwalking seems to confront us with unconscious perceptions, but rather with situations where self-aware subjectivity is split into two parts, a normal and an abnormal stream of consciousness. In itself, this is very puzzling and I do not pretend to be able to explain the phenomenon. It should be emphasized, however, that the separation or doubling is not absolute. Through hypnosis or therapy the amnesic barrier can be raised and the two streams of experiencing integrated, so that the normal subject gains awareness of both.[71]

Notes

When quoting from a text, I have used the English translations when available. The first reference given is always to the original version, followed by a reference to the translation in parentheses.

When referring to those of Husserl's works that have been published in *Husserliana,* the reference is indicated by the abbreviation *Hua* followed by the volume and the page numbers. When referring to Husserl's unpublished manuscripts, the reference employs the abbreviation "ms." and the standard numbering system as used by the Husserl-Archieves in Leuven, Belgium (see "Works Cited," page 271). I follow the original pagination where available, and, when it is not available, I refer to the pagination given on the manuscript transcriptions.

Preface

1. Ricoeur 1950, 59 (1966, 60–61). As Mohanty has shown, it is possible to find positions within Indian thought that exactly deny the compatibility between intentionality and self-awareness. Thus, Samkara held that consciousness, being essentially self-revealing and self-sufficient, was unable to entertain an intentional reference to something different from itself, whereas the Naiyayika took the exact opposite stance: Being in essence directed toward something different from itself, consciousness could not simultaneously be occupied with itself (Mohanty 1972, 37, 165–167).

2. This perspective is not foreign to phenomenology. For instance, Merleau-Ponty, who taught child psychology at the Sorbonne from 1949 to 1952, advocated the thesis that an understanding of infantile self-awareness is paramount if one wishes to understand the connection between self, world, and Other (Merleau-Ponty 1945, 407).

3. Nagel 1974, 437.

4. For a discussion of these (and other) different types of self-awareness see Tugendhat 1979, 27–33.

5. Taylor has recently advocated such a view (1989, 49–50). Cf. Ricoeur 1990, 18.

6. The difference is particularly striking if one considers the so-called "brain criterion" of personal identity. According to this, a person P_2 at t_2 will be the same person as P_1 at t_1 just in case P_2 at t_2 has the same brain as P_1 at t_1 (cf.

Noonan 1991, 5). But even a defender of this view would have to admit that a given person's first-personal experiential evidence of his own continued existence is not mediated by or inferred from any knowledge he may have concerning the identity of his own brain.

7. Cf. Henrich 1966, 231; 1970, 261; 1982a, 131; Frank 1984, 300; 1986, 44–45, 50; 1991b, 530, 536, 557, 562; Cramer 1974, 584, 590, 592; Castañeda 1979, 10; 1989a, 137.

8. My rather selective use of arguments taken from analytical philosophy of mind and language might occasion a certain criticism which I would like to forestall from the very start. It might be objected that I have only taken those arguments into consideration which support, clarify, or improve my own basic position, rather than to confront the whole range of more skeptical and reductionistic (naturalistic) arguments, which also abound. There is a certain truth in this, and obviously I am not denying that such a confrontation could be worthwhile and fruitful. However, to engage in such a confrontation would be to commence a different enterprise than the one I am pursuing. I am not particularly interested in defending the existence of self-awareness, but in reaching a clarification of its more specific composition. The problems that occupy me are problems very much debated in current phenomenology (cf. the essays in Zahavi 1998a), and I do not think that the very attempt to contribute to this discussion is in need of any explicit justification. Furthermore, I do believe that sufficient arguments for both the existence and the significance of self-awareness will be given in the following to avoid the accusation of having simply committed a *petitio principii*.

Chapter 1

1. It is consequently somewhat surprising to read that any attempt to reach an understanding of self-awareness through an indexical analysis of "I" is reductionistic, since the very purpose of indexical analysis is to reduce the first-person perspective to a third-person perspective (Klawonn 1991, 26, 31). In fact, I think Klawonn could have found additional arguments for his own position in the indexical analyses of Shoemaker, Castañeda, and Perry.

2. Castañeda 1966, 144.

3. Anscombe 1981, 33.

4. Anscombe 1981, 27.

5. Shoemaker 1968, 559; Anscombe 1981, 28; Castañeda 1968, 261.

6. Wittgenstein 1958, 66–67.

7. It has also been claimed that it is impossible that I should feel pain and be mistaken about its being pain, but it is not this kind of incorrigibility which is of relevance for the moment.

8. Shoemaker 1968, 557; 1984, 103. As McGinn points out, it is in fact possible to imagine a situation where the assertion "I am seeing a canary" implies a misidentification of the subject (1983, 51). If for instance Jill and Jack are viewing a video, and both of them erroneously believe Jack to be figuring in it, Jill might at a certain moment ask Jack, "What are you doing now?" and referring to the video

he might answer, "I am looking at a canary," thus misidentifying as himself the person that sees a canary. As should be obvious, however, this derived counter-example does not in any way affect the validity of Shoemaker's argument that the error of misidentification is excluded in genuine cases of *self-awareness*.

9. In contrast to Shoemaker, McGinn does not take it to be a contradiction in terms to speak of an *incorrigible identification,* and he consequently argues that it is better to distinguish between criterial and noncriterial forms of identification and categorize the subject-use of "I" among the latter than to deny altogether that something is identified (McGinn 1983, 55; cf. Evans 1982, 218). A similar conclusion might be reached if one believes that there is more to reference than a mere description or classification of a certain kind of object, namely, an *identification* of a particular object, and at the same time wishes to avoid claiming that the subject-use of "I" does in fact not refer at all.

10. Shoemaker 1984, 102.

11. Shoemaker 1968, 561.

12. Shoemaker 1968, 562–63.

13. Shoemaker 1984, 105.

14. Shoemaker 1968, 567.

15. Castañeda 1989a, 127.

16. It should be noticed that I am not claiming that a person who is only in possession of an identifying third-person description of himself *must* fail to realize that he himself is the person in question. I am merely saying that nothing would force him to draw that conclusion.

17. Evans 1982, 255–56; Castañeda 1967, 12.

18. Castañeda 1967, 12.

19. Castañeda 1966, 131.

20. Castañeda 1966, 138; 1987b, 414. Cf. Chisholm 1981, 18–19.

21. Castañeda 1966, 138–39.

22. For those having reservations about this example since the demonstrative reference is effected indirectly (via a mirror), Castañeda has constructed more fantastic thought-experiments yielding the same result (cf. Castañeda 1966, 141–42).

23. Anscombe 1981, 22. This problem could be avoided if one formulated the definition in first-person terms: "'I' is the word I use to speak of myself," but this definition is obviously circular (Pothast 1971, 24).

24. Nozick 1981, 72–73.

25. Perry 1979, 3.

26. Perry 1979, 12.

27. Cf. Nagel 1965, 355; Lewis 1979, 520–21.

28. Anscombe 1981, 32–33. A similar conclusion can be found in Malcolm 1988, 160.

29. Wittgenstein 1958, 67.

30. Shoemaker 1968, 555.

31. Cf. Anscombe 1981, 31–32.

32. McGinn 1983, 54.

33. Strawson 1959, 95.

34. Hume 1888, 252.

35. One example given is the following: "In a dream, I can seem to see myself from a point of view *outside* my own body. I might seem to see myself running towards this point of view. Since it is *myself* that I seem to see running in this direction, this direction cannot be towards *myself*. I might say that I seem to see myself running towards *the seer's point of view*" (Parfit 1987, 221). In this case my dream-perception would not entail a reference to myself as the subject of experience, but merely as the object of experience. As Klawonn has pointed out, however, this example is problematic, since Parfit is using the words "I" and "myself" to refer to two quite different things:

> Take for example the sentence, "*I* might seem to see *myself* running towards this point of view," or the sentence, "it is *myself* that *I* seem to see running in this direction." Here the use of the word "I" (in "*I* seem to see. . . .") is linked up with the first-person perspective of the seer, whereas "myself" is used to refer to a body—or somebody—that is present in the visual field of the seer. And when Parfit talks about "running towards *the seer's point of view*," it is certainly not any seer's point of view which is relevant in this context. What he is talking about is the point of view of the seer who is myself—seen from the point of view of the person who is having the dream. The uses of the word "I" and "myself" which are linked up with the first-person perspective are—as far as I can see—the fundamental ones, whereas the possibility of referring to my body as seen from the outside as "myself" is a secondary one which is created by my tendency to identify with the body that I am normally associated with. If my body were to become "an external object" more permanently, I would not continue using the word "myself" about it; and if this body also had its own subjective field of experience—so that it was not just a body, but somebody—I would not consider this individual as being myself. It would be somebody else. (Klawonn 1990, 47)

36. Parfit 1987, 517. Cf. 1987, 252.

37. Klawonn 1991, 28–29.

38. Klawonn 1991, 5, 141–42; James 1890 I, 226–27; Smith 1989, 93. In fact Smith employs a distinction between the *mode* and the *modality* of presentation (1989, 16–17), but although this is a highly pertinent *Husserlian* distinction, I do not find it linguistically felicitous, and will therefore continue to speak of the first-personal mode of presentation, rather than of the first-personal modality of presentation.

Chapter 2

1. Although the object-use of "I" makes use of third-person evidence, it still has to be distinguished from a mere external self-reference, since any correct use of "I" implies that the user believes that he himself is the person referred to, i.e., even the object-use of "I" is an *emphatic* kind of self-reference.

2. To quote Fichte:

> While you were thinking of your table or your wall, you were, for yourself, the
> *thinking subject* engaged in this act of thinking, since you, as an intelligent reader,
> are of course aware of the activity involved in your own act of thinking. On the
> other hand, what *was thought of* in this act of thinking was, for you, not you
> yourself, but rather something that has to be distinguished from you. In short,
> in every concept of this type [i.e., in every concept of an object], the thinking
> subject and what is thought of are two distinct things, as you will certainly
> discover within your own consciousness. In contrast, when you think of *yourself,*
> then you are, for yourself, not only the thinking subject; you are also at the same
> time that of which you are thinking. In this case the subject and the object of
> thinking are supposed to be one and the same. The sort of acting in which you
> are engaged when you are thinking of yourself is supposed to turn back upon
> or "revert into" yourself, the thinking subject. (Fichte 1797, 522 [1994, 107])

3. Locke 1975, 107, 127.

4. Armstrong 1993, 323–26. For further examples of the claim that conscious mental activity (in distinction from unconscious mental activity) is the result of an *internal monitoring,* cf. Lycan 1997.

5. Kant 1923, 248–49 (1983, 73).

6. Natorp 1912, 30; Kant 1971, A 402.

7. Shoemaker 1968, 563–64; Frank 1991b, 445; Henrich 1966, 197.

8. The first use of the term *"Heidelberg School"* is found in Tugendhat 1979, 10, 53. Cf. Frank 1986, 35. When one witnesses the embittered discussion about who was the first to point out the difficulties facing the reflection theory (cf. Schmitz 1982, 132), it is interesting to notice that much of the German criticism was anticipated by the Danish philosopher K. Grue-Sørensen in his discussion of the theories of Fichte, Herbart, Fries, Brentano, Natorp, Rickert, Rehmke, etc., in a book dating from 1950.

9. This chain of thought is brought to its (paradoxical) culmination by Rickert, who argues that the ego is incapable of being both the subject and the object of consciousness simultaneously, since this would imply a transgression of the principle of identity. Consequently, if self-awareness is to be possible, a self-division has to take place in the ego, so that the epistemic relation can be established between *different parts* of the ego (cf. Rickert 1915, 42).

10. Whether there is a difference between the two will be discussed in part 2.

11. Cramer 1974, 563.

12. This is basically the same argument which Shoemaker put forth. See also Henrich 1970, 268; 1982b, 64; Frank 1991b, 498, 529; Schmitz 1991, 152.

13. Cf. Jones 1956, 131.

14. Frank 1984, 303; 1991b, 440; Pothast 1971, 38.

15. Henrich 1970, 265. As Sartre writes about reflection: "It implies as the original motivation of the recovery a prereflective comprehension of what it wishes to recover" (Sartre 1943, 195 [1956, 156]).

16. Rosenthal 1993, 157.
17. Rosenthal 1993, 165; 1997, 735–37, 743, 745.
18. Rosenthal 1993, 160.
19. Rosenthal 1997, 750; cf. Rosenthal 1997, 741.
20. Cf. Frank 1991a.
21. Nagel 1986, 15–16; Jackson 1982; James 1890 I, 478.
22. Nagel 1974, 436; Searle 1992, 131–32.
23. Smith 1989, 82, 95; Flanagan 1992, 61–68; Goldman 1997, 122; Van Gulick 1997, 559; Strawson 1994, 12, 194.
24. As James writes (quoting Lotze): "Even the trodden worm . . . contrasts his own suffering self with the whole remaining universe, though he have no clear conception either of himself or of what the universe may be" (James 1890 I, 289).
25. Occasionally it has been argued that insofar as the secondary sense-qualities are to some extent subject- or mind-dependent, we are in fact experiencing ourselves when we perceive objects with color, taste, or smell. But I think this is an obvious fallacy. Even if the secondary sense-qualities were subjective, ontologically speaking, they are not subjective, phenomenologically speaking, and it is only the latter perspective which is of relevance in this context.
26. In the appendix, I will discuss whether it ultimately makes sense to speak of such an experience, i.e., whether it is appropriate to call such an unconscious process an *experience.*
27. McGinn 1997, 298.
28. Henrich 1970, 260 (1971, 6). Cf. Hart 1998.
29. Fichte 1797, 526 (1994, 111–12).
30. Shoemaker 1968, 567; Chisholm 1981, 36–37; Tugendhat 1979, 77–78. This epistemic importance of self-awareness is also stressed by Castañeda, who speaks of the epistemological priority of "I" over all the demonstratively used pronouns. Having thought about an object by means of a demonstrative, it is necessary to restructure the thought if one is to rethink it. Having once thought "this is dangerous" in the presence of a loaded gun, I will not refer to the same object later on if I simply think "this was dangerous," or "the loaded gun was dangerous." In the first case, the object originally referred to may not any longer be present, and will thus no longer be reachable by means of a "this." In the second case, one might ask, "Which loaded gun?" That is, the description might fail to refer univocally because there are many objects having the property mentioned. To ensure the reference, it is necessary to think, "The loaded gun, which *I* saw then, was dangerous." Castañeda emphasizes that he is not claiming that the thinker has to perform a physical or psychological act of translation. The point he wishes to make is a *logical point,* and might merely entail an implicit use of "I" (Castañeda 1966, 145–46).
31. Kapitan 1997.
32. McGinn 1983, 17; Henrich 1982a, 152.
33. Smith 1983, 100.
34. Strawson 1959, 21. Cf. 1959, 15–30, 119.
35. Cf. Kapitan 1997.

36. Castañeda 1987b, 440–41.
37. Hart 1998. See also note 30 above.
38. Castañeda 1989a, 120, 136.
39. Castañeda 1989b, 30; Castañeda 1989a, 121, 132.
40. Castañeda 1989a, 137.
41. Castañeda 1989a, 132.
42. For a compact analysis of Brentano's theory of intentionality, and for arguments against taking Brentano's position to be phenomenological, see for instance Zahavi 1992 or 1995.
43. Brentano 1874, 142–43.
44. Brentano 1874, 171. We are consequently presented with an additional argument against the reflection theory. If self-awareness is really a higher-order intentional act, where one perceives one's primary intentional act, and if the primary intentional act is characterized by its consciousness of an intentional object, the structure of self-awareness would be: A *perception of (a perception of a blooming tree)*. This would imply, however, that self-awareness entails a *double* awareness of the intentional object, and this is not the case. However, as we shall soon see, a related criticism can be directed against Brentano's own proposal.
45. Brentano 1874, 171. This type of reasoning can be found in Ryle, who writes as follows:

> [E]ven though the self-intimation supposed to be inherent in any mental state or process is not described as requiring a separate act of attention, or as constituting a separate cognitive operation, still what I am conscious of in a process of inferring, say, is different from what the inferring is an apprehension of. My consciousness is of a process of inferring, but my inferring is, perhaps, of a geometrical conclusion from geometrical premises. The verbal expression of my inference might be, "because this is an equilateral triangle, therefore each angle is 60 degrees," but the verbal expression of what I am conscious of might be "Here I am deducing such and such from so and so." But, if so, then it would seem to make sense to ask whether, according to the doctrine, I am not also conscious of being conscious of inferring, that is, in a position to say "Here I am spotting the fact that here I am deducing such and such from so and so." And then there would be no stopping-place; there would have to be an infinite number of onion-skins of consciousness embedding any mental state to process whatsoever. If this conclusion is rejected, then it will have to be allowed that some elements in mental processes are not themselves things we can be conscious of, namely those elements which constitute the supposed outermost self-intimations of mental processes; and then "conscious" could no longer be retained as part of the definition of "mental." (Ryle 1949, 162–63)

46. Brentano 1874, 199.
47. Brentano 1874, 179–80 (1973, 127–28).
48. This account gets somewhat more complicated the moment Brentano starts applying his distinction between perception, judgment, and feeling to self-awareness, ultimately claiming that we have a threefold awareness of the act itself:

"Consequently, every mental act, even the simplest has four different aspects under which it may be considered. It may be considered as a presentation of its primary object, as when the act in which we perceive a sound is considered as an act of hearing; however, it may also be considered as a presentation of itself, as a cognition of itself, and as a feeling toward itself" (Brentano 1874, 218–19 [1973, 154]). This aspect of his theory is, however, of no immediate relevance to us.

49. Brentano 1874, 41, 181; Brentano 1928, 15, 20.

50. Brentano 1874, 182–83.

51. Cf. Pothast 1971, 75; and Cramer 1974, 581, who moreover claims that later phenomenological attempts to understand self-awareness remain beset with similar problems (Cramer 1974, 583–84, 592–93). See also Henrich 1970, 261.

52. We find a similar problem in Fichte, who, in his early writings at least, seems unable to abandon the subject-object model completely when it comes to self-awareness:

> [T]here is a type of consciousness in which what is subjective and what is objective cannot be separated from each other at all, but are absolutely one and the same. . . . The consciousness in question is our consciousness of our own thinking.—Hence you are immediately conscious of your own thinking. But how do you represent this to yourself? Evidently, you can do this only in the following way: Your inner activity, which is directed at something outside of you (viz., at the object you are thinking about), is, at the same time, directed within and at itself. . . . Self-consciousness is therefore immediate; what is subjective and what is objective are inseparably united within self-consciousness and are absolutely one and the same. (Fichte 1797, 527–28 [1994, 112–13])

> The I should not be considered as a mere subject, which is how it has nearly always been considered until now; instead, it should be considered as a subject-object in the sense indicated. (Fichte 1797, 529 [1994, 114])

53. Henrich 1970, 267–68.

54. Henrich 1970, 274.

55. Henrich 1982a, 152. Cf. Schmalenbach 1929, 318, 324.

56. Henrich 1970, 275, 277, 280, 284.

57. Frank 1986, 34, 61; 1991a, 71, 405; 1991b, 597; Pothast 1971, 76–78; Henrich 1970, 266, 273; 1982a, 142. Actually, Frank explicitly denies that self-awareness is a "*présence à soi*," since he takes this expression to designate a kind of self-presentification which is completely indebted to the reflection model (Frank 1989, 488; 1991a, 24). It is, however, difficult to find a more perfect candidate for a pure immediate self-presence than the completely irrelational self-acquaintance, which is so close to itself that every kind of mediation is excluded.

58. Frank 1991b, 438. Cf. Frank 1991a, 7, 161.

59. Kern 1989, 51–53.

60. Cf. Shoemaker 1968, 563–64.

61. Henrich 1970, 276.

62. Frank 1991a, 252; Cramer 1974, 573.

63. Pothast 1971, 64.

64. Pothast 1971, 76, 81.
65. Henrich 1970, 276, 279.
66. Henrich 1970, 280; 1982a, 145–46. Cf. Frank 1991a, 16–17; 1990, 113. These reflections are developed by Henrich in an unpublished manuscript, which Frank summarizes in Frank 1991b, 590–99.
67. Frank 1986, 50.
68. Frank 1986, 53.
69. Frank 1990, 73.
70. Frank 1990, 10, 83; 1991b, 589, 591.
71. Frank 1991b, 591.
72. Frank 1991b, 595.
73. Henrich 1982a, 150. Cf. 1982a, 152, 157; 1982b, 102.
74. Henrich 1982a, 169. Cf. 1982a, 155, 162–63.
75. Henrich 1966, 220. Thus it is no coincidence that Henrich holds Fichte's theory of self-awareness to be unsurpassed (1966, 231).
76. Frank 1991b, 599; 1990, 125, 135. Cf. Cramer 1974, 591.

Chapter 3

1. Cf. Henrich 1970.
2. Castañeda 1970, 191.
3. Although Frank reaches a similar conclusion, he does not offer any solution himself (Frank 1986, 55; 1991a, 26–27; 1991b, 574, 587–88).
4. Henrich 1970, 279.
5. Pothast 1971, 66.
6. As Smith has argued, the self-reference entailed in immediate epistemic self-awareness is so formal that the further nature of this self is left undetermined, for which reason it might *as well* be embodied, social, etc. (Smith 1989, 106; cf. Nagel 1986, 42).
7. Heckmann 1991, 72; Nagel 1986, 33, 56; Frank 1991a, 405.
8. In *Fluchtlinien* Henrich in fact makes a distinction between the awareness of oneself as a subject and the awareness of oneself as a person:

> Ein Wesen, das Selbstbewußtsein hat, muß sich aber von der Struktur dieses Bewußtseins her immer in einer doppelten Relation verstehen: als einer unter vielen und als einer gegenüber allem. Insofern der selbstbewußte Mensch einer unter anderen ist, ist er "Person." Er weiß sich zu unterscheiden von allen anderen, weiß aber auch, daß er wie sie in die gemeinsame Welt gehört, —daß er als Person ein Lebewesen ist und einen Platz unter allen Weltdingen hat. In einer anderen Hinsicht ist aber jedes selbstbewußte Wesen radikaler und von allem unterschieden, von dem es weiß. Es greift über die Welt als ganze aus und findet, was immer es in ihr denkt oder antrifft, in derselben Korrelation zu dem Einen, das es ist, insofern es von sich weiß. Die Welt ist ihm der Inbegriff dessen, was es überhaupt denken und antreffen kann. In diesem Sinn ist jeder Mensch nicht nur Person, sondern ebenso "Subjekt." (Henrich 1982a, 20–21; cf. 1982a, 137–38, 154)

Although Henrich acknowledges this duality, it does not make him reconsider or elaborate his characterization of the primary self-acquaintance.

9. Henrich 1982a, 149.

10. Merleau-Ponty 1945, 417 (1962, 363).

11. Cf. Frank 1991b, 585; Henrich 1982a, 144.

12. Mohr 1988, 72–73.

13. Tugendhat 1979, 21 (1986, 12–13).

14. Tugendhat 1979, 22.

15. Tugendhat 1979, 10–11, 45, 50–51, 54, 57, 66–67.

16. Tugendhat 1979, 55–61, 68–70, 83; Mohr 1988, 71–75. That Tugendhat can accuse Henrich of having conceived of self-awareness in terms of an informative self-identification can only strike one as somewhat bizarre.

17. Various convincing critiques have already been given. Cf. Henrich 1989; Soldati 1988; Frank 1986, 70–92; 1991a, 415–46.

18. Tugendhat 1979, 87–90.

19. Tugendhat 1979, 73.

20. Tugendhat 1979, 21, 26.

Chapter 4

1. A discussion which the Heidelberg School virtually ignores in their derogatory treatment of Husserl's theory of self-awareness.

2. Henry 1963, 14, 32, 64, 67; 1966, 5. Cf. *Hua* 16, 141–42.

3. Henry 1963, 36, 50.

4. Henry 1963, 44, 279, 329, 352; 1966, 22–23.

5. Henry 1963, 47, 52.

6. Henry 1963, 183, 186.

7. Sartre 1943, 18, 20, 28; 1948, 62.

8. Cf. Armstrong and Malcolm 1984, 194.

9. Sartre 1948, 64–65; 1943, 20–21. Armstrong holds a somewhat different view: "[C]onsciousness is simply a further mental state, a state 'directed' towards the original inner states," (1993, 94). Thus, there is no intrinsic connection between the mental states and our consciousness of them, and mental states like the feeling of pain might consequently exist without being conscious. That is, unconscious pain is possible (1993, 107, 312). I will briefly return to Armstrong's position and the topic of pain in my discussion of the unconscious in the appendix.

10. Sartre 1943, 20 (1956, liv).

11. Sartre 1943, 19.

12. Sartre 1943, 19–20 (1956, liii). Whereas the early Sartre speaks of an irreflective or nonreflective self-awareness, he later increasingly opts for the term "prereflective self-awareness."

13. Cf. Henrich 1966, 231; Tugendhat 1979, 52–53; and especially Frank 1984, 300; 1986, 43–45; 1990, 53–57; 1991b, 530–31, 536.

14. Cf. Frank 1991b, 532; 1990, 53–57.

15. *Hua* 19, 382.

16. Frank 1990, 52–53.
17. Cf. Sartre 1948, 88.
18. *Hua* 15, 78; 8, 57.
19. *Hua* 3, 162, 168, 251, 349; 10, 291; 9, 29.
20. *Hua* 14, 45.
21. *Hua* 10, 291 (1991, 301, translation slightly altered).
22. *Hua* 10, 126–27 (1991, 130, translation slightly altered).
23. *Hua* 3, 550; 10, 119.
24. *Hua* 8, 88; 9, 306–7.
25. *Hua* 8, 471; 10, 126.
26. *Hua* 8, 188; cf. 3, 549.
27. Cf. Bernet 1983, 42.
28. Cf. *Hua* 11, 320.
29. In *Ideen* II, Husserl distinguishes between "*die immanente Wahrnehmung*," which he equates with reflection, and "*das innere Bewußtsein*," which he claims is a nonthematic kind of self-awareness that precedes reflection (*Hua* 4, 118).
30. *Hua* 4, 248.
31. *Hua* 15, 492–93.
32. Henry 1965, 76, 153.
33. *Hua* 14, 316; 8, 89; 6, 458.
34. *Hua* 8, 90.
35. *Hua* 14, 431; cf. 14, 29; 29, 183–84; Ms. C 2 3a.
36. *Hua* 3, 95, 162–64.
37. *Hua* 10, 119.
38. Cf. Brand 1955, 68–69; Landgrebe 1963, 197.
39. *Hua* 8, 89.
40. *Hua* 11, 367; 8, 85, 93–94, 131; 9, 205; 13, 85–86, 164.
41. *Hua* 7, 264.
42. *Hua* 8, 88–89; 10, 118.
43. *Hua* 3, 77, 95; 4, 118; 8, 411; 11, 292.
44. Bernet 1994, 320.
45. Cf. Ms. L I 15 37b.
46. *Hua* 16, 49–50.
47. *Hua* 6, 161.
48. *Hua* 16, 55 (1997, 46).
49. *Hua* 9, 183.
50. Cf. *Erfahrung und Urteil*, §§8, 22, 33; *Hua* 11, 8; 9, 433; 6, 165. Obviously one should not identify and limit the horizon to the spatiotemporal surrounding. A piece of chalk might also refer to its aesthetic, practical, and scientific aspects (cf. Ms. A VII 2 9a). It should be emphasized that since the "horizon" is a concept used to describe components in the field of consciousness, and not the objective relationship that might pertain between *x* and *y*, everything that is part of the horizon or background is conscious.
51. Gurwitsch 1974, 258–59, 274–78.
52. Gurwitsch 1966, 267–68.
53. Fink 1966, 51; cf. Sartre 1943, 382–83.

54. Gurwitsch 1985, 4; cf. 1974, 339–40.

55. *Hua* 24, 252.

56. One can find numerous statements to this effect. See for instance *Hua* 1, 81; 4, 318; 8, 189, 412, 450; 13, 252, 462; 14, 151, 292, 353, 380; Ms. C 16 81b. This view is echoed in the following passage by Fink:

> [K]eineswegs leben wir in völliger Selbstvergessenheit zunächst einmal nur nach "außen" gerichtet und finden plötzlich eine ganz neue Richtung möglichen Blickens und entdecken so uns selbst. Alles menschliche Vorstellen, Erkennen, Wollen, alles Wachbewußtsein überhaupt ist immer schon ein gewisses Offensein des Ich für sich selbst; es ist mit sich vertraut, ist sich bekannt, lebt in einem Mitwissen seiner selbst. Alles gegenständliche Wissen ist immer zugleich auch ein Umsichselberwissen des Ich. Und dies ist nicht bloß eine psychische Tatsache, es ist vielmehr eine Wesensstruktur des Bewußtseins. Ein isoliertes Gegenstandsbewußtsein aber gibt es nie. "Gegenstand" kann es nur geben, wo Etwas sich aus einer Gegend heraushebt und einem Ich entgegensteht; d.h. Gegenstandsbewußtsein ist notwendig strukturell verbunden mit Weltbewußtsein und Ichbewußtsein. (Fink 1992, 115–16)

57. *Hua* 17, 279–80 (1969, 273).

58. Cf. Bernet 1994, 318–25.

59. Castañeda 1987a, 133.

Chapter 5

1. *Hua* 10, 276, 334.

2. *Hua* 10, 10–19.

3. In James one finds a related account (cf. James 1890 I, 609–10). For a comparison of Husserl's and James's philosophy of time, see Cobb-Stevens 1998.

4. The exact width of the perception depends upon our interest. If we are listening to a (short) melody, we might say that we perceive the entire melody in its temporal extension. If we focus upon the single notes, a perceived note becomes past the moment it is succeeded by a new (*Hua* 10, 38).

5. Ms. L I 15 37b. Thus, Husserl claims that we always and unthematically anticipate that which will occur a moment later. That this anticipation is a concrete part of our experience can be seen from the fact that we would be surprised if the figure which we took to be a mannequin suddenly moved and spoke, or if the door we opened concealed a stone wall. Our surprise can only occur against the background of an anticipation, and since we can always be surprised, we always have a horizon of anticipation (*Hua* 11, 7).

6. *Hua* 9, 202 (1977, 154, translation slightly altered).

7. *Hua* 10, 372; Ms. C 2 11a.

8. Ms. C 3 8a.

9. As Brough has persistently pointed out, it is also important not to conflate the object's temporal phases or modes of givenness with concrete parts of the object. The object might appear now, but it is not identical with the now (Brough 1993, 512–16; 1991, xxvii).

10. *Hua* 11, 324–25; 13, 162.

11. *Hua* 10, 41, 118, 333. Duval has argued that it is in fact only in the dialectic between oblivion and recollection that the past is constituted, whereas retention only furnishes us with a consciousness of *duration* (Duval 1990, 62, 67). A more radical suggestion can be found in Lévinas. Lévinas argues that it is possible to unearth a form of time more original and more temporal than ecstatic time, and he claims that Husserl's analyses overlook the true diachronous character of time, insofar as temporality is persistently taken as a form of intentionality. The future is taken to be something that will eventually become present for me. It is that which is protended, anticipated, and expected. But thereby the radical novelty of the future is annulled. In a similar manner the past is conceived as that which is retained in the retention, that is, as something which has been present for me. But thereby the true passing of time is overlooked as well (Lévinas 1991b, 77; 1982, 161, 169, 238). According to Lévinas, true time is *dispersed* and cannot be held together in the present by the subject. The temporality of time is passive and irrecoverable, the contrary of intentionality (Lévinas 1974, 90). The diachronous past cannot be recovered or represented by memory, but is *immemorial*. It has never been present. And true future is that which cannot be known but overwhelms us unexpectedly (Lévinas 1974, 30, 66; 1979, 64). Diachronous time presents us with a manifestation of a noncoincidence, which is not merely a lack, but a relation to something which is absolutely different. Thus, true diachronous time is a relation to the absolute Other, an Other which can be neither assimilated nor absorbed by experience and comprehension. Lévinas consequently characterizes time as the relation between the subject and the Other (Lévinas 1979, 9–10, 13, 17). The relation to both past and future, and the givenness of the past and the future in the present, are due to the encounter with the Other. It is the encounter with the Other that fractures my self-coincidence and stops the process of totalization. The temporal continuity of consciousness is overwhelmed every time it is exposed to the face of the Other. It is the encounter with the Other which conditions time-consciousness (Lévinas 1961, 314). It is this overwhelming meeting which is the origin of time, and it consequently makes no sense to speak of true time in an isolated subject (Lévinas 1979, 64, 68–69). When I encounter the Other, I assume responsibility for a past independently of any concrete guilt that I could ever acquire through my own deeds, and for any future unintended and unexpected consequences of my acts. This is the ethical significance of true time. I have a past and a future because of my responsibility for the Other. Thus, Lévinas understands true diachronous time to be a question of responsibility and devotion (Lévinas 1991b, 45; 1991a, 186, 192–93). Although Lévinas might be right in claiming that ethics opens a new temporal dimension, I cannot follow him when he claims that ethical time is the truly fundamental form of time, the one that conditions ecstatic time. To claim that it is the encounter with the

Other that fractures the self-coincidence of subjectivity also seems to presuppose a questionable assumption, namely that subjectivity is originally characterized by self-coincidence (see page 197).

12. *Hua* 10, 182.

13. *Hua* 10, 81, 100.

14. This is a slightly modified version of a diagram found in Ms. L I 15 22b—a diagram that incidentally makes it comprehensible why Merleau-Ponty in *Phénomenologie de la perception* could write that time, rather than being a line, is an entire web of intentionalities (1945, 477).

15. Cf. Held 1966, 48.

16. *Hua* 11, 233, 293; 4, 102; *Erfahrung und Urteil*, 205.

17. *Hua* 10, 80.

18. *Hua* 10, 22; cf. Ms. L I 13 3a.

19. *Hua* 10, 333 (1991, 345).

20. *Hua* 10, 73, 76, 358; Ms. C 17 63b.

21. Ms. C 2 8a; Ms. C 7 14b; Ms. L I 17 9a.

22. *Hua* 3, 182.

23. Ms. L I 12 3b.

24. Cf. Brough 1972, 308–9; Sokolowski 1974, 156–57.

25. *Hua* 11, 292.

26. *Erfahrung und Urteil*, 304 (1973, 204); cf. *Hua* 4, 102.

27. *Hua* 11, 293.

28. Sokolowski 1974, 154, 156–57; Brough 1972, 318. Let me stress that I am obviously not accusing either Sokolowski or Brough of having overlooked the existence of the notion of prereflective self-awareness in Husserl, i.e., of having made the same mistake as Frank, Tugendhat, and Henrich. To a certain extent, but only to a certain extent, the difference between my interpretations and Brough's and Sokolowski's interpretations might simply be a question of different accentuation and terminology.

29. Brough 1972, 304, 316.

30. Prufer 1988, 201.

31. *Hua* 4, 118–19; 10, 83, 89–90, 119, 126–27; 23, 321. Cf. Ms. L I 15 35a–36b.

32. *Hua* 17, 279–80; 4, 118.

33. Husserl's phenomenological analysis of self-affection has often been over-shadowed by the better-known analyses of Heidegger and Merleau-Ponty. In Heidegger's reading of Kant, the essence of time is taken to be pure self-affection (Heidegger 1991, 194). To speak of self-affection, however, is to speak not merely of a process in which something affects itself, but of a process that involves a self—not in the sense that self-affection is effectuated by an already existing self, but in the sense that it is the process in and through which selfhood and subjectivity are established: "As pure self-affection, it forms in an original way the finite selfhood, so that the self can be something like self-consciousness" (Heidegger 1991, 190 [1990, 130]; cf. 1991, 189). Thus, qua pure self-affection, time turns out to be the essence of subjectivity. This line of thought is continued by Merleau-Ponty, who claims that it is the analysis of time which gives us access

to the concrete structures of subjectivity, and which permits us to understand the nature of the subject's self-affection (Merleau-Ponty 1945, 469). Ultimately self-temporalization and self-affection are one and the same: "the explosion or dehiscence of the present towards a future is the archetype of the *relationship of self to self,* and it traces out an interiority or ipseity" (Merleau-Ponty 1945, 487 [1962, 426]). Temporality is an *"affection de soi par soi"*: That which affects is time as a thrust and a passage toward a future, that which is affected is time as an unfolded series of presents (Merleau-Ponty 1945, 487; cf. Heidegger 1991, 194). But at this stage, an intriguing ambiguity is revealed. At first Merleau-Ponty states that the affecting and the affected are one, since the thrust of time is nothing but the transition from one present to another. But then one page later, he characterizes self-affection as a *"dualité"* (Merleau-Ponty 1945, 487–88; cf. Depraz 1998). Thus, one is left with a question concerning the exact nature of self-affection, which I will take up later. Is it a strict unity or does it rather display a dyadic structure?

34. Ms. C 10 3b, 5a, 7a, 9b–10a; Ms. C 16 82a. Cf. Ms. C 16 78a; Ms. A V 5 8a; Ms. C 5 6a; *Hua* 15, 78.

35. Sokolowski 1974, 166; Hart 1998.

36. Brough 1972, 319.

37. *Hua* 10, 80–81 (1991, 85).

38. *Hua* 10, 80–81, 379. At one point Husserl speaks of the *Längs-* and *Querintentionalität* as the noetic and noematic-ontical temporalization (Ms. B III 9 23a). He also calls them respectively the inner and outer retention (*Hua* 10, 118).

39. Cf. *Hua* 10, 333.

40. *Hua* 10, 83 (1991, 88).

41. Cf. Cramer 1974.

42. Cramer 1974, 587.

43. Brough 1991, liii; Prufer 1988, 201.

44. An indirect confirmation of this interpretation can be found in the following passage from *Ideen* II, where Husserl discusses the nature of the reduced tone-sensation:

> Let us consider, as the most convenient example, a tone played on a violin. It can be apprehended as a real violin-tone and hence as a real occurrence in space. It then remains the same no matter whether I move away from it or approach it, or whether the door of the adjacent room, in which it is being played, is open or closed. By abstracting from material reality, I can still be left with a tonal spatial phantom, appearing with a determinate orientation, proceeding from a certain position in space, resounding through the space, etc. Finally, the spatial apprehension can also be suspended, and then it becomes a mere "sense datum" instead of a spatially sounding tone. In place of that consciousness of the tone which, out there in space, remains unchanged regardless of whether it moves closer or further away, the tone now appears, in the shifting of the focus onto the sense datum, as something which is changing continuously. (*Hua* 4, 22 [1989, 24])

I believe the point is clear. When Husserl speaks of the *Empfindungdatum* tone, he is speaking of the sensed and not of the sensing. (Cf. *Hua* 10, 333–34.)

45. It should be noted, however, that act-transcendence (which also characterizes hallucinated or imagined objects) is not identical with *objectivity*, and that object-identification is not a sufficient but merely a necessary precondition for objectivity. Following Husserl, one can speak of a primordial or subjective transcendence the moment the object is experienced as an intentional unity that transcends my *actual* experience (*Hua* 14, 344). But as long as it is still understood in correlation to *my* possible experience, it does not possess objectivity in any radical sense, but is merely a unity that *I* can intend in various acts. To perceive a truly transcendent object is to perceive an object which is not merely perceivable by *me*, but also perceiveable by Others (*Hua* 14, 8, 442; 1, 80, 136; 6, 370–71; 8, 180, 186–87).

46. *Hua* 11, 16; 10, 275.

47. *Hua* 11, 327; *Erfahrung und Urteil*, 64, 75.

48. *Hua* 11, 10, 110–11, 125, 128; 1, 96, 155; 17, 291.

49. *Hua* 4, 19; 24, 280; cf. Hart 1996a.

50. *Hua* 10, 84; 11, 210.

51. Ms. C 5 7a.

52. For another passage that can be read in favor of such an interpretation, cf. Ms. L I 21 34b.

53. *Hua* 11, 209.

54. *Hua* 10, 82, 118, 333, 371, 376; Ms. B III 9 14a–b.

55. James 1890 I, 239. To quote Bergson: "the deep-seated self which ponders and decides, which heats and blazes up, is a self whose states and changes permeate one another and undergo a deep alteration as soon as we separate them from one another in order to set them out in space" (Bergson 1927, 93 [1971, 125]). "Considered in themselves, the deep-seated conscious states have no relation to quantity, they are pure quality; they intermingle in such a way that we cannot tell whether they are one or several, nor even examine them from this point of view without at once altering their nature. The duration which they thus create is a duration whose moments do not constitute a numerical multiplicity: to characterize these moments by saying that they encroach on one another would still be to distinguish them" (Bergson 1927, 102 [1971, 137]).

56. Michalski 1997, 120.

57. Ms. L I 15 2b.

58. For further passages that might support this interpretation, see *Hua* 4, 104; 10, 36, 51, 112; Ms. C 10 17a; Ms. L I 19 3a–b, 10a.

59. Brand 1955, 78.

60. *Hua* 10, 75–76; cf. *Hua* 29, 194; Ms. L I 15 2b.

61. *Hua* 10, 333–34 (1991, 346); cf. *Hua* 10, 371–72; Ms. C 17 63a; L I 21 5b.

62. *Hua* 10, 112, 285, 293; 14, 29. Obviously our acts can also be constituted so as to appear in objective time, but this self-objectivation is of an even more founded kind since it is intersubjectively mediated. Cf. "Konstitution der einheitlichen Zeit und einheitlich-objektiven Welt durch Einfühlung," in *Hua* 15, 331–36.

63. Ms. L I 2 16a.
64. Ms. A V 5 4b–5a.
65. *Hua* 10, 129 (1991, 132).
66. Ms. C 12 3b.
67. Ms. C 16 59a.
68. Cf. Ms. C 16 49a.
69. *Hua* 10, 116 (1991, 121).
70. *Hua* 10, 116, 290.
71. *Hua* 10, 228–29 (1991, 236); cf. Sartre 1943, 197.
72. *Hua* 23, 326; cf. 14, 46; Ms. L I 1 3a.
73. James 1890 I, 630.
74. Klawonn 1994, 143; Brough 1972, 316.
75. Klawonn 1991, 77; cf. 1991, 128.
76. *Hua* 10, 127.
77. Ms. C 3 26a.
78. *Hua* 16, 65; cf. 10, 74, 113.
79. Ms. C 3 4a. For further distinctions between "*das Strömen*" and "*der Strom*," cf. Ms. B III 9 8a; Ms. C 15 3b; Ms. C 17 63b. As Merleau-Ponty writes, the justification of the river metaphor is not that time flows, but that it is one with itself (Merleau-Ponty 1945, 482).
80. Merleau-Ponty 1945, 483.
81. *Hua* 10, 75, 333, 375–76.
82. *Hua* 10, 112.
83. Cf. Kern 1975, 40–41; Bernet 1994, 197; Merleau-Ponty 1945, 483; Heidegger 1991, 192.
84. *Hua* 10, 376, 78, 112, 371; 11, 392; 15, 28; Ms. C 2 11a; Ms. C 7 14a. Cf. Held 1966, 116–17; Larrabee 1994, 196.
85. Fink speaks of retention and protention in terms of an "*Entgegenwärtigung*" (Fink 1966, 22).
86. Derrida 1972a, 187; 1967a, 9.
87. Derrida 1972a, 37, 61, 207.
88. Derrida 1967a, 68, 70.
89. Derrida 1967a, 71; cf. Costa 1994.
90. Derrida 1967b, 178, 244, 302
91. Derrida 1990, 120, 123, 127.
92. Derrida 1967a, 72 (1973, 64).
93. Derrida 1990, 127–28, 168, 240.
94. Derrida 1990, 166; 1967a, 5. In *La voix et le phénomène* Derrida also presents a slightly different argument in support of this claim. Derrida argues that the self-presence of subjectivity is an ideal form of presence (1967a, 5, 60), and since ideality is linguistically constituted, self-awareness cannot be isolated from language: "Since self-consciousness appears only in its relation to an object, whose presence it can keep and repeat, it is never perfectly foreign or anterior to the possibility of language" (Derrida 1967a, 14 [1973, 15]). And in this case, a nonpresence or difference (a sign, mediation, or signitive reference) is introduced into the heart of self-awareness (1967a, 15). I find it difficult to

follow this line of thought. Although one might be willing to accept that there is a nonpresence in self-awareness which has implications for the possibility and understanding of temporality and intersubjectivity (1967a, 40), Derrida's claim that self-awareness is a kind of ideality, and that the nonpresence and complexity involved in temporality is of an indicative, signitive character seems unfounded (1967a, 67). There can certainly be complexity of a nonsignitive kind.

95. Cf. Bernet 1994, 216, 235, 283.

96. Lévinas 1949, 162; 1974, 51.

97. Derrida 1967a, 73 (1973, 65).

98. Derrida 1990, 126–27.

99. Cf. Bernet 1994, 287–88; Bernet 1983, 50, 52.

100. Frank 1984, 307, 314, 321–22, 335.

101. Cf. *Hua* 10, 83. As Bernet has often pointed out, Husserl's description of the relation between primal impression and retention is by no means unequivocal. It contains both a confirmation of and an overcoming of the metaphysics of presence (Bernet 1983, 18). On the one hand, the retention is interpreted as a derived modification of the primal impression. But on the other hand, Husserl also states that no consciousness is possible which does not entail retentional and protentional horizons, that no now is possible without retentions (*Hua* 11, 337–38), and that the primal impression is only what it is when it is retained (Ms. L I 15 4a; cf. Ms. L I 16 12a; Ms. L I 15 22a; *Hua* 11, 315). Husserl was clearly wrestling with these issues, and it is undeniable (and perhaps also unavoidable) that he occasionally opted for some highly problematic accounts. Let me mention a few further examples. In *Ideen* II, Husserl characterized the retention as an objectifying immanent perception (*Hua* 4, 14); in *Vorlesungen zur Phänomenologie des inneren Zeitbewußtseins*, he designated the *Längsintentionalität* as a *Deckungseinheit* (*Hua* 10, 81); and in the manuscript L I 15 22a, he claimed that the *Längsintentionalität* is characterized by its *indirect* nature.

102. *Hua* 10, 119 (1991, 123).

103. *Hua* 10, 119.

104. *Hua* 10, 110–11, 119; 11, 337.

105. *Hua* 10, 117.

106. *Hua* 11, 138.

107. Henry 1989, 50.

108. Henry 1990, 33–34.

109. Cf. *Hua* 10, 89, 110–11, 119; 11, 337; 13, 25.

110. Henry 1990, 32.

111. Henry 1990, 49–50.

112. Henry 1990, 107.

113. Henry 1990, 130.

114. Henry 1963, 576, 349.

115. Henry 1963, 858.

116. Henry 1965, 139.

117. Yamagata 1991, 183.

118. Henry 1990, 54.

119. Henry 1990, 54.
120. Cf. Sebbah 1994, 252.
121. Henry 1994, 303–4, 310; 1996, 201–2.
122. Henry 1994, 311.
123. It is no coincidence that Henry, in *Phénoménologie matérielle,* describes *Vorlesungen zur Phänomenologie des inneren Zeitbewußtseins* as the most beautiful philosophical work in our century (Henry 1990, 31).
124. Cf. *Hua* 10, 111.
125. In chapter 7, I will return to an issue that constitutes a real cause for disagreement, namely Husserl's and Henry's conflicting views concerning the relationship between auto- and hetero-manifestation.
126. *Hua* 11, 317, 378; Ms. C 3 8b, 76a.
127. Frank 1990, 62–63.

Chapter 6

1. *Hua* 13, 253.
2. *Hua* 3, 116; 4, 33; 13, 239.
3. Cf. Perry 1993, 205.
4. *Hua* 11, 298; 4, 159; 9, 392.
5. *Hua* 14, 540; 6, 220; 4, 56; 5, 124. It is true that the horizontal appearance of my perceptual object (and the implied differentiation between present and absent profiles) is correlated with my being situated in a central "here" (*Hua* 4, 158); and it is also true that the object is only given horizontally because it is in principle impossible for any perceiving subject to be situated "here" and "there" simultaneously. This observation does not warrant the conclusion, however, that the horizontal givenness of the object merely manifests the finiteness of the observer—and Husserl is known for his rejection of any anthropological interpretation of the horizontal structure (cf. Sartre 1943, 354). Ultimately, it is the ontological structure of the object (its transcendence and worldliness) which necessitates that it can only be given for a subject situated in a "here." As Husserl declares in *Ideen* I, even God would have to perceive the object through its adumbrations (*Hua* 3, 351).
6. Sartre 1943, 365–66 (1956, 317–18). Cf. Merleau-Ponty 1945, 97; 1964, 177. For an illuminating discussion of Sartre's analysis of the body, cf. Cabestan 1996.
7. Sartre 1943, 374.
8. Gibson 1979, 53, 205.
9. *Hua* 11, 299.
10. *Hua* 11, 14–15; Ms. D 13 I 4a.
11. *Hua* 6, 108–9 (1970, 106, translation slightly altered).
12. For a discussion of such different terms as "reafference," "muscle sense," "vestibular sense," "proprioception," and "kinaesthesis," cf. Gibson 1982, 164–70.
13. *Hua* 16, 161.

14. *Hua* 16, 155.
15. *Hua* 11, 15.
16. *Hua* 9, 390; cf. 6, 164; 13, 386.
17. *Hua* 16, 179–80; 16, 269.
18. *Hua* 16, 159, 187–89; 11, 14–15; 4, 58, 66; 6, 109. Husserl's description of this correlation is marked by a certain vacillation, since he speaks interchangeably of a correlation between the kinaestheses and the hyletic sensations (in this connection often referred to as *Merkmalsempfindungen* or *Aspektdaten*) and of a correlation between the kinaestheses and the perceptual appearances. I have adopted the latter way of speaking, since it more clearly allows for a noematic interpretation of the hyle (see page 118).
19. *Hua* 16, 176.
20. Ultimately, Husserl's analysis of the constitution of space is rich in detail but also highly technical. So far I have only accounted for some elements pertaining to the constitution of the subject-relative *phantom space*, and have not touched upon the constitution of *objective space*. For a concise discussion of some additional aspects in Husserl's theory, see Drummond 1979–80.
21. *Hua* 4, 144; 11, 13.
22. Henry 1965, 79.
23. Cf. Behnke 1984.
24. They would only be unconscious if we operated with an unacceptable narrow conception of consciousness which equates it with thematic object-consciousness. Much depends upon terminology. In his article "Body Image and Body Schema: A Conceptual Clarification," Gallagher argues that the living, functioning body operates in a silent, nonconscious, prereflective fashion. But his main reason for calling this performance *nonconscious* is that "it is not an intentional object present to my consciousness," and "it does not have to be made the object of consciousness in order to do its work" (Gallagher 1986, 548–51). In a number of articles, Gallagher has stressed the decisive difference between *body schema* (which is the unthematic and preconscious system of motor capacities, abilities, and habits that enables movement and the maintenance of posture) and *body image* (which is the thematic and intentional consciousness of one's own body), and has faulted a number of earlier authors for mixing and confusing the two. However, his own concept of body schema seems itself to contain an ambiguity. It encompasses both the unthematic control and coordination of movement which occurs outside of conscious *attention*, that is, a kind of prereflective body-awareness, and the unconscious, or rather nonconscious, physiological processes which take place completely outside of consciousness (cf. Gallagher and Cole 1995, 371, 377). I think it would have been better to distinguish the two rather than to combine them under the concept of body schema.
25. Henry 1965, 128; Merleau-Ponty 1945, 168.
26. Henry 1965, 80 (1975, 58).
27. Merleau-Ponty 1945, 97.
28. *Hua* 16, 158.
29. *Hua* 14, 447; cf. *Hua* 4, 58, 152; Merleau-Ponty 1945, 160.

30. However, one should not underestimate the differences in the optical flow of information occasioned by motion of object, locomotion of observer, movement of head, or movement of eyes. As Gibson writes: "A pure transposition of total pattern, with gain of new detail on one side and loss of old detail on the other *specifies* an eye-movement, and this information is normally registered as such" (1982, 168). Whereas the motion of the object typically only causes a partial change in the visual field (the background remains stable), the movement of the observer normally transforms the entire field (cf. Gibson 1982, 180–93).

31. It has been argued that it is impossible to conceive of transcendent objects, that is, objects that transcend their present givenness or objects that can endure without being experienced by me, unless we are able to reidentify objects. But it is hardly possible to distinguish the case of one object being reidentified from the case of two qualitatively identical objects being perceived on two different occasions unless we can make sense of the notion of an absent object. To speak of an absent object, however, is to speak of an object that could become present through a change of position in space, and in order to conceive of such a thing we need the notion of an objective space (cf. Strawson 1959, 36–37). To speak of an objective space, however, presupposes an ability to discriminate and reidentify locations in space, and according to Husserl this ability is rooted in the kinaestheses. Two locations in space are distinguishable by being situated differently in respect to my own position (*Hua* 16, 275–76; 11, 14–15).

32. *Hua* 16, 176. Cf. Stern 1985, 80. Let me mention in passing that recent infant research indicates that the movements of the infant are accompanied by both a sense of volition and proprioception, and that the infant thanks to these components has an experience of self-agency that enables it to distinguish its own self-generated actions from the actions and movements of others. Stern reports on an experiment conducted on a pair of four-month-old conjoined twins just prior to their surgical separation. The twins shared no organs and had separate nervous systems, but were connected in a way that made them face each other. The twins often ended up sucking on each other's fingers, and Stern compared the resistance of each twin, when sucking on her own or on the twin's fingers, to having the fingers pulled out of her mouth. When Alice was sucking on her own fingers, her arm showed resistance to being pulled out, whereas her head did not strain forward after the retreating arm. When Alice was sucking on Betty's fingers, and Betty's arm was gently pulled away, there was no resistance in either Alice's own arms or in Betty's arm, but Alice's head did strain forward. Thus, when Alice's own arm was pulled away, Alice attempted to maintain sucking by bringing the arm back into her mouth. When Betty's arm was removed, Alice attempted to maintain sucking by following the arm with her head. Thus, Alice did not seem to have any confusion about whose fingers belonged to whom, and about what part of the body she had volitional control over. On several occasions, Alice happened to suck on Betty's fingers while Betty was sucking on Alice's fingers. The same experiment was carried out, with the same result. Although each twin had experiences of both sucking on a finger and having a finger sucked they still had no difficulty distinguishing self from Other, and Stern suggests that one of the

reasons the twins were able to make this distinction was due to their experience of volition and proprioceptive feedback (Stern 1985, 78–79).

33. Merleau-Ponty 1945, 161.

34. Straus 1966, 44.

35. Merleau-Ponty 1945, 444.

36. Merleau-Ponty 1945, 114.

37. Merleau-Ponty 1945, 116; cf. 1945, 168.

38. Cf. Gallagher 1986.

39. Sacks 1970, 43–54; Cole 1991; Cole and Paillard 1995.

40. Sacks 1970, 45, 51.

41. Gibson 1979, 118. Cf. Gibson 1979, 115, 126; 1966, 36–37, 200–1.

42. Neisser 1988, 37–38.

43. Cole 1991, 127–28.

44. Sacks 1970, 46.

45. Cole 1991, 123, 149.

46. Held and Hein 1963.

47. Sartre 1943, 372.

48. Sartre 1943, 378; Merleau-Ponty 1945, 107.

49. *Hua* 4, 158–59; 15, 265; Merleau-Ponty 1945, 162, 164, 173.

50. *Hua* 13, 240.

51. Sartre 1943, 350 (1956, 303).

52. Sartre 1943, 398; cf. Merleau-Ponty 1945, 403.

53. Sartre 1943, 355, 370–71, 376.

54. Sartre 1943, 388.

55. *Hua* 14, 57; cf. 457; 15, 326; 9, 392.

56. *Hua* 14, 62.

57. *Hua* 1, 130; 5, 128; 15, 546. For a further discussion of this aspect of Husserl's thinking, see Zahavi 1996.

58. *Hua* 4, 56, 155; 5, 118; 15, 296; Ms. D 12 III 37a; Ms. D 12 III 15. In *Philosophie et phénoménologie du corps*, Henry criticizes the notion of kinaesthetic sensitivity and claims that it is crucial not to conflate this *constituted* level with the truly original bodily subjectivity (1965, 124–25). But as far as I can see, it is Henry himself who fails to distinguish between the original unity of kinaesthetic experiencing and its subsequent localization.

59. *Hua* 4, 146; Ms. D 12 III 24.

60. *Hua* 6, 164; 15, 268.

61. *Hua* 15, 279.

62. As a tentative illustration of the difference between these two types of movements, or more correctly between these two different apprehensions of the same movement, one can compare the experience of a gesture as seen and as felt. While the visual experience in its objectivation of the hand presents space as something existing independently of the gesture, as something which the hand moves through, the kinaesthesis does not furnish us with an experience of space independently of the experience of the gesture. Space is experienced precisely as the hand's field of mobility.

63. *Hua* 15, 279; 4, 151, 56. In *The Varieties of Reference,* Evans is struggling with some related problems, and he briefly refers to the relation between our capacity to locate ourselves in objective space, that is, our capacity to think of ourselves as one object among others, and our ability to interpret our kinaestheses as movements in space (Evans 1982, 163).

64. *Hua* 15, 302; 13, 273; 5, 12, 118–19, 123; 4, 146–47.

65. *Hua* 4, 149–50.

66. *Hua* 13, 115.

67. As Claesges points out:

> Empfindung, so wie sie im kinästhetischen Bewußtsein möglich ist und notwendig ihm zugehört, ist, wie wir gesehen haben, in sich gedoppelt als Empfindung und Empfindnis und gehört dem Moment des Leibbewußtseins zu, ist von ihm untrennbar. Nun hat das Leibbewußtsein aber in sich selbst eine noetisch-noematische Doppelstruktur. Von daher ergibt sich, daß Empfindung nicht mehr der einen oder anderen Seite der Alternative Noesis—Noema zugeordnet werden kann. Man kann vielmehr sagen, daß Empfindung als Empfindung (Merkmalsempfindung) auf die noematische Seite, als Empfindnis aber auf die noetische Seite des (kinästhetischen) Bewußtseins zu setzen ist. (Claesges 1964, 134–35)

68. *Hua* 4, 145 (1989, 152, translation slightly altered). For some related observations, see Henry 1965, 170.

69. *Hua* 15, 302; 14, 282.

70. *Hua* 9, 197; 14, 414, 462; 4, 145.

71. *Hua* 14, 540; 9, 391.

72. *Hua* 14, 337.

73. *Hua* 4, 145.

74. *Hua* 14, 75; Ms. D 12 III 14.

75. *Hua* 14, 75; 13, 263.

76. *Hua* 15, 298.

77. *Hua* 4, 159.

78. *Hua* 14, 77.

79. Henry 1965, 171–72.

80. *Hua* 4, 151–52; 16, 162.

81. Cf. *Hua* 14, 4; 14, 328–29.

82. *Hua* 1, 128; cf. 15, 302.

83. Derrida 1967a, 88; Bernet 1994, 173.

Chapter 7

1. Henry 1963, 288–92, 301. In order to stress the radical difference between the appearance of constituted objects and the self-manifestation of constituting subjectivity, Henry usually avoids speaking of self-appearance or self-constitution. Instead he uses a number of different terms such as "self-affection,"

"self-manifestation," or even *"revelation"* (cf. Henry 1965, 98). The latter term has subsequently been employed by Marion who, in his article "The Saturated Phenomenon," argues that one can describe the self-sufficient, unconditioned, and nonhorizontal type of manifestation as a revelation (Marion 1996, 120).

2. Henry 1966, 12 (1969, 99). In *Kritik der reinen Vernunft,* Kant argues that every empirical knowledge presupposes intuition, and every intuition presupposes affection. If we are to acquire empirical self-knowledge, we have to stand in passive relation to ourselves and be innerly affected, so Kant consequently speaks of an *inner sense,* and claims that we affect ourselves when our mental states are given to this inner sense. However, this self-affection is not so much a question of providing new sensuous matter as it is a question of ordering or positing our mental states in *time.* Thus, Kant can deny that the self-knowledge obtained through self-affection provides us with knowledge of how we are in ourselves. It only gives us knowledge of how we appear to ourselves in time (Kant 1971, B 68–69, B 153–56).

3. Henry 1990, 166; 1966, 33; 1963, 858.

4. Henry 1963, 578, 580, 590.

5. Henry 1990, 22.

6. Henry 1963, 858–59 (1973, 682).

7. Henry 1963, 299–300, 422, 585; 1994, 305. As Lévinas points out, my individuality is not a matter of my own choice and doing. It is not the product of a *free* self-reflection, self-manifestation, or self-affection. It is something that is given as an undeserved and unjustified privilege (1974, 95, 147, 168, 180, 201; 1991b, 37–39).

8. Henry 1963, 854 (1973, 679).

9. Henry 1963, 363 (1973, 291–92); cf. 1963, 371.

10. Henry 1963, 86–87, 95–96, 138, 143, 262.

11. Henry 1990, 72. There are some striking similarities between Henry's position and some of Klawonn's claims in *Jeg'ets ontologi.* To mention but a few, Klawonn speaks of the ego-dimension's first-personal *autonomy.* The ego-dimension is given in and through itself; it is in this sense self-sufficient, and consequently not relative to or dependent upon anything else (1991, 79, 154). Its self-givenness must be understood in the light of its own simple nature, and is free from any kind of duality and relation (1991, 117–18). In a similar vein, Klawonn also argues that the field of primary presence is free from any temporal declination (1991, 256).

12. Henry 1963, 351 (1973, 282); cf. 352, 377, 419.

13. Henry 1963, 58, 396; 1990, 111.

14. Kühn 1994, 46.

15. Henry 1990, 7.

16. Henry 1963, 584, 598–99, 613.

17. Henry 1963, 576; cf. Heidegger 1991, 189–90.

18. Henry 1963, 279–80 (1973, 227).

19. Henry 1963, 195, 259, 319, 323, 328.

20. Henry 1963, 173 (1973, 143); cf. 1963, 168–69.

21. Henry 1965, 259 (1975, 187); cf. 1965, 99.

22. Henry 1965, 162. Since the ego cannot be conceived as an ontic entity, the difference between ego and nonego is not an ontical, but an ontological difference (Henry 1965, 51, 163). It is exactly for this reason that intentionality and self-awareness (transcendence and immanence) are compatible, rather than excluding alternatives: "Precisely because the self-knowledge of the original body is not a thematic knowledge, *because the 'self' and the ipseity of the body are not the terminus but the condition for this knowledge,* the latter is not enclosed within itself, it is not the knowledge *of* self, but the knowledge of transcendent being in general" (Henry 1965, 129 [1975, 93]).

23. Henry 1965, 127 (1975, 92).

24. Henry 1990, 54; 1994, 311.

25. *Hua* 4, 213, 337; Ms. E III 2 12b.

26. *Hua* 14, 44.

27. *Hua* 11, 84, 64; *Erfahrung und Urteil*, 81–83; Holenstein 1971, 196.

28. *Hua* 11, 162.

29. *Hua* 4, 217.

30. *Hua* 6, 111; 15, 120, 78.

31. Ms. C 10 13a.

32. *Hua* 14, 275. Thus, Husserl also calls attention to the particular kind of reflection found in conscience (*Hua* 8, 105).

33. *Hua* 14, 14.

34. *Hua* 13, 170; cf. 14, 51; 13, 92.

35. *Hua* 14, 244.

36. *Hua* 11, 150; 4, 214; 11, 168; Ms. E III 3 3a; Ms. E III 2 22b.

37. Ms. C 3 41b–42a.

38. *Hua* 4, 336 (1989, 348). However, as Husserl also points out, although all intentional activity requires an affection, it does not have to be a *sensuous* affection. It might also be an affection from the so-called "*sekundäre Sinnlichkeit*," i.e., from the entire complex of habits, inclinations, associations, etc., acquired through the process of sedimentation (*Hua* 4, 337).

39. *Hua* 15, 385; cf. 11, 164.

40. Ms. E III 2 22a; cf. Ms. C 6 4b.

41. *Hua* 14, 379. The reason why Husserl can speak of the hyle as being a *constituted* unity (rather than the material presupposed by all constitution) is because the term is occasionally expanded to include whatever might provide us with material for interpretation, ranging from sensations to the world itself. It is in this context that Husserl differentiates between the primal hyle (*Urhyle*) and subsequent forms of hyle, just as he also differentiates between the primal affection (*Uraffektion*) and subsequent forms of affection (Ms. C 3 62a; Ms. C 6 4b–5a; Ms. C 16 46b).

42. Cf. *Hua* 3, 192.

43. Sokolowski 1974, 91; cf. *Hua* 5, 10–11; 16, 148.

44. *Hua* 19, 362; 10, 127, 333–34.

45. Ms. C 3 62a.

46. Cf. Holenstein 1972, 86–117; Franck 1984, 138; Depraz 1995, 255; Soko-lowski 1970, 210–11.

47. *Hua* 11, 149–51; *Erfahrung und Urteil,* 80; Ms. B III 9 18a.

48. Ms. D 10 IV 11; cf. *Hua* 11, 138.

49. Mishara 1990, 38–39; cf. Schües 1998.

50. Ms. C 16 42a.

51. Bateson 1972, 453.

52. *Hua* 15, 54–55.

53. Thus, Husserl can write that it is an abstraction to speak of a purely passive world of sensations. They can only be understood in correlation with the active kinaestheses (*Hua* 11, 185). Cf. Claesges 1964, 71, 123, 131, 134–35; Landgrebe 1963, 120.

54. Ms. C 3 41b.

55. *Hua* 14, 379; 4, 130; 15, 287; 23, 266. For passages where Husserl opts for a noematic interpretation of the appearances, see *Hua* 13, 117, 377, 412–13; 14, 250; 4, 168, 201; *Erfahrung und Urtiel,* 88. I find some striking similarities between Husserl's mature view and the theory of sensation developed by Gibson in the article "The Useful Dimensions of Sensitivity" (see Gibson 1982, 350–73).

56. Ms. E III 2 22b.

57. *Hua* 15, 128, 375; 13, 406, 459; 14, 51–52, 337; 4, 356; Ms. E III 2 5a; Ms. E III 2 23a.

58. *Hua* 13, 427; 11, 386. For reflections concerning the connection between passivity and alterity, see Ricoeur 1990, 368.

59. However, it would be an exaggeration to claim that Husserl is particularly clear and consistent in his description of the hyle. To give but a single example, in *Hua* 14, 46, Husserl writes that the hyle belongs to life as its essential *correlate.* Six pages later, in a text from the same year (1921), he writes that the hyle "sich als reell einig mit dem Ichlichen gibt" (*Hua* 14, 52).

60. Ms. C 10 15b (my emphasis); cf. Ms. E III 2 24b.

61. Ms. C 10 16a.

62. *Hua* 15, 131, 287; Ms. C 2 3a.

63. Ms. C 7 6b.

64. Actually, this account is still too abstract, since it overlooks the third constitutive principle. For Husserl, constitution ultimately unfolds itself in the *tripartite* structure of *subjectivity, intersubjectivity,* and *world* (cf. Zahavi 1996).

65. Cf. Brand 1955, 28; Hart 1992, 12. Since subjectivity entails both self and alterity, it becomes understandable why transcendental phenomenology has occasionally been characterized as being beyond the opposition between idealism and realism (cf. Seebohm 1962, 153).

66. *Hua* 11, 118, 128; 1, 28; *Erfahrung und Urteil,* 76; Ms. L I 15 3a.

67. *Hua* 10, 107 (1991, 112); cf. *Erfahrung und Urteil,* 191; Lévinas 1949, 154.

68. *Hua* 11, 138; Ms. A V 5 7a; Ms. L I 17 9b; Ms. C 3 42a.

69. *Hua* 10, 83 (1991, 87).

70. Cf. Brough 1972, 321–22.

71. *Hua* 10, 118.

72. Kant 1971, B xl–xli, B 275–76.
73. *Hua* 5, 128; 15, 287. As Landgrebe writes:

> [B]ekanntlich ist die Fähigkeit, die motorischen Bewegungen zu beherrschen, das, was das kleine Kind am frühesten lernt. Es macht damit Erfahrungen in einer doppelten Richtung, eine Erfahrung von sich selbst und seinen leiblichen Funktionen und davon untrennbar eine sich immer mehr erweiternde Erfahrung von seiner umgebenden Welt. Jede neu erlernte Bewegung erweitert zugleich den Horizont des Erfahrbaren. Jede neue Erfahrung, die wir von unserer Welt gewinnen, ist zugleich eine neue Erfahrung von uns selbst in unseren Vermögen. (Landgrebe 1982, 67)

74. Benoist 1994, 57, 61; Bernet 1994, 321; Ricoeur 1990, 380.
75. *Hua* 4, 147.
76. *Hua* 13, 386; 16, 178; 15, 300.
77. *Hua* 5, 10 (1980, 9, translation slightly altered).
78. *Hua* 14, 75; 15, 297, 301.
79. Ms. D 10 11a. In Claesges's words: "Jedes Empfinden im taktuellen Bereich, das ein Phantom zur Gegebenheit bringt, bringt zugleich auch den empfindenden Leib mit zur Gegebenheit, weil die Stellungsdaten, durch die das Phantom gegeben ist, als Aspektdaten dem Leibe zugehören. Somit ist im taktuellen Bereich jedes Empfinden ein 'Sich-selbst-empfinden,' wodurch Empfindungen dann den Charakter von Empfindnissen annehmen. Damit ergibt sich eine gleichursprüngliche Gegebenheit von Leib und Außenwelt" (Claesges 1964, 112).
80. Lévinas 1949, 162; 1974, 30, 85, 92, 120–21; 1991b, 41. If affection is interpreted in terms of *desire*, it can also be described as a longing for alterity. Cf. Yamagata 1991, 189; Barbaras 1991, 108.
81. *Hua* 10, 100.
82. Barbaras 1991, 97–98, 104. Barbaras, however, goes too far when he infers their identity and indiscernability from their inseparability, and then adds that the self of self-affection is merely the crease of the world on itself (Barbaras 1991, 107), a suggestion which overlooks the singularity and irreducible first-person perspective of each and every self-awareness.
83. Ms. B III 9 105b.
84. Ms. C 10 2b.
85. Ms. C 16 68a.
86. Ricoeur 1950, 363.
87. Merleau-Ponty 1945, 344, 431–32, 467, 485, 487, 492; 1966, 164–65.
88. Straus 1958, 148.
89. Cf. chapter 10 and appendix.
90. Heidegger 1986a, 137 (1996, 129); cf. Sartre 1943, 387.
91. As Husserl puts it: "sind wir heiter gestimmt, so sieht sich dies oder jenes, worauf unser Blick fällt, freundlich, rosig, lieblich an" (Ms. M III 3 II 95; cf. Ms. M III 3 II 29–30; Ms. C 16 30b, 33b). More generally, Husserl claims that the affection exerted by the hyle is of an emotional nature: "Zu jedem Hyletischen

als für das Ich daseienden gehört es, daß es das Ich im Gefühl berührt, das ist seine ursprüngliche Weise, für das Ich in der lebendigen Gegenwart zu sein. Das Fühlen, fühlend bestimmt zu sein, ist nichts anderes, als was von Seiten der Hyle Affektion heißt." (Ms. E III 9 16a). "Die Gefühle sind es doch, die, oder als welche hyletische Daten bzw. die sinnlichen Objekte das aktive Ich motivieren (affizieren), es 'anziehen' oder 'abstossen'; dem Anziehen entspricht oder ist Hin-Wollen, dem Abstossen Wider-Wollen" (Ms. C 16 28a; cf. Ms. B III 9 79a–b; Lee 1998; Landgrebe 1963, 118, 121).

92. *Hua* 15, 324, 293; 13, 292; 4, 153; Ms. D 10 IV 15. Cf. Landgrebe 1963, 116–17.

93. Derrida 1972a, 14, 65; 1967a, 96. Derrida further argues that the ultimate condition of appearance, which he sees as a process of self-differentiation, is characterized by its double nature. On the one hand by separation, distinction, and fracture, and on the other by detour and delay. Whereas the first type of simultaneous, coexisting, difference can be understood as spatialization, the latter type of synchronous difference can be classified as temporalization (Derrida 1972a, 8, 19). It is in this intertwining between temporalization and spatialization that presence is constituted. Thus, the condition of manifestation is not simple and undifferentiated, but characterized by a minimal division, by its dyadic structure.

94. Landgrebe 1963, 120; cf. Landgrebe 1982, 81; *Hua* 6, 255; Straus 1956, 241–43, 254–55, 372; Claesges 1964, 100, 123, 131, 143; Brand 1955, 47; Rohr-Dietschi 1974, 87; Richir 1989.

95. *Hua* 15, 131, 287.

96. Franck 1984, 141.

97. *Hua* 5, 11 (1980, 10).

98. *Hua* 4, 153 (1989, 161, translation slightly altered).

99. Sartre 1936, 23–24; 1943, 17, 19, 28.

100. Sartre 1943, 212; 1936, 23–24.

101. This is of course why Sartre so strongly opposes the Husserlian notion of hyle (Sartre 1943, 26, 363). Whether Sartre's criticism is based upon a correct interpretation of Husserl is, however, a different question (see page 118).

102. Sartre 1943, 18, 20, 23; 1948, 63. Somewhat surprisingly, this formulation discloses a certain affinity between Sartre's theory and Aristotle's position in *De Anima*. This affinity becomes even more striking when Sartre, in *La transcendance de l'ego*, writes that consciousness is nothing (because no objects are contained in it) and everything (because it can be conscious *of* everything). Cf. Sartre 1936, 74; Aristotle 1984, 424a17, 429a18, 429b30.

103. Sartre 1943, 28.

104. Sartre 1943, 162 (1956, 123). If Sartre is right in this, it constitutes an additional argument for the thesis that every intentional consciousness must imply self-awareness. Otherwise it would not be able to be aware of the difference between the object and itself, and consequently unable to be aware of the object as ob-ject (cf. Sartre 1943, 214).

105. Sartre 1943, 27, 214–15.

106. Sartre 1943, 179 (1956, 140); cf. 1943, 213, 258; 1936, 28.

107. Sartre 1943, 161 (1956, 122).

108. Sartre 1943, 178 (1956, 139).

109. Rosenberg 1981, 257.

110. Sartre 1943, 28–29. It is in this connection that Sartre claims to have provided an ontological proof for the existence of a mind-independent reality. Needless to say, this "proof" is somewhat doubtful, since being different from and being independent of are two different issues.

111. Sartre 1943, 115.

112. Sartre 1943, 115–16 (1956, 77).

113. Sartre 1948, 69 (1967, 127); cf. 1948, 68; 1943, 112, 115–16.

114. Sartre 1948, 50 (1967, 114).

115. Sartre 1943, 33.

116. Sartre 1943, 115–16; 1948, 66, 69; cf. Merleau-Ponty 1964, 246.

117. Sartre 1943, 114, 117; 1948, 67. On the prereflective level, consciousness is characterized by the dyad *reflet-reflétant*, on the reflective level by the duality *réflexif-réfléchif.*

118. Sartre 1943, 116, 141, 144, 175–77, 182, 197, 245; 1948, 76. Despite his emphasis on time, and despite taking the dyadic structure of prereflective self-awareness to constitute the origin of temporality, Sartre nevertheless conceives of the structure itself as being atemporal (cf. Seel 1995, 141–42).

119. Cf. Wider 1989 and 1993a; Klawonn 1991, 116; Frank 1990, 83.

120. Sartre 1936, 28–29; 1943, 143, 176–77, 191–92; 1948, 78.

121. Wider 1993a, 741.

122. Sartre 1943, 106.

123. As to whether there might exist types of self-affection in the body itself which are not in need of this mundane mediation, such as stomach pains, Derrida classifies these as empirical oddities, with no universal significance (1967a, 88).

124. Derrida 1967c, 33; 1967a, 77, 93.

125. Derrida 1967a, 89, 92.

126. Derrida 1967c, 235 (1976, 165).

127. Derrida 1967a, 73, 76; 1972b, 299, 336.

128. Derrida 1972b, 219, 259, 264.

129. Derrida 1967a, 92; 1967c, 221, 237.

130. Derrida 1967c, 235; cf. Gasché 1986, 194, 232–33.

131. Derrida 1967c, 237 (1976, 166).

132. Derrida 1972b, 259, 299–300, 303.

133. Cf. Barbaras 1991, 107.

134. Yamagata 1991, 179.

135. *Hua* 15, 349.

136. Sokolowski 1976, 699; Brough 1972, 526.

137. Lévinas 1949, 223.

138. Brand 1955, 74; cf. Seebohm 1962, 126–27; Hart 1989, 58.

139. Sartre 1948, 63.

140. Cf. *Hua* 10, 115.

141. Henry 1965, 76.
142. Sartre 1943, 113, 194.
143. Derrida 1967a, 76 (1973, 67–68).
144. Ms. C 3 69a.
145. *Hua* 15, 543–44. One occasionally encounters a terminological distinction between *reflection* and *reflexivity*. One finds this distinction in Grue-Sørensen (1950, 133, 138), but also in Mohanty, who defines reflexivity as the prereflective transparency of consciousness and distinguishes it from reflection, which is a higher-order intentional act (Mohanty 1972, 159, 164, 168). Klawonn has argued that the term "reflexivity" should be avoided, since it suggests that the primary self-givenness is to be understood as a self-relation or self-differentiation (Klawonn 1991, 114).
146. Held 1981, 192.
147. Held 1966, 169; cf. 65, 170, 172. In Fink one finds the claim that reflection rather than producing merely exposes and articulates a plurality inherent in prereflective subjectivity:

> Das Selbstbewußtsein ist, wenn man den Satz nur richtig auffaßt, immer schon *reflektierend*. Das besagt auch: es gibt nicht zunächst ein schlichtes, einfaches Ich—und nachträglich in der Ausbildung einander überhöhender Reflexionsstufen mehrere, aber geeinte und einige Iche; das Ich ist vielmehr ursprünglich schon zersplittert und doch eins; es ist eine in sich multiple Einsheit, welche nicht die Vielfalt einfach in sich vorfindet, sondern immer erzeugt, solange es überhaupt "ist." Das Sein des Ich liegt gerade in seiner Mannigfaltigung *und* Einsheit. (Fink 1992, 128)

Chapter 8

1. Sartre 1936, 21–23; cf. Merleau-Ponty 1945, 466, 481. Referring to Husserl's investigations in *Zur Phänomenologie des inneren Zeitbewußtseins*, Sartre mentions in passing that the *Längsintentionalität* unites the chain of retentions, but he does not elaborate on this (Sartre 1936, 22).
2. Sartre 1936, 23 (1957, 40); cf. 1936, 25, 37, 74.
3. Sartre 1936, 31–32, 37. Employing Husserl's distinction between an ordinary reflection and a reflection in the recollection, Sartre points out that when we remember a past event, we also remember in a nonpositional manner our former experience of the said event. This experience can be thematized in reflection, but prior to that, i.e., as long as we focus upon the past event, the experience is cogiven in a nonpositional prereflective manner, and it can consequently furnish us with insights into the nature of prereflective consciousness, for instance, that it is egoless (Sartre 1936, 30–31).
4. Sartre 1936, 65 (1957, 83); cf. 1936, 37.
5. Sartre 1936, 35, 43–44, 54–55; 1943, 142.
6. Sartre 1936, 69.

7. Sartre 1936, 78 (1957, 97).

8. Sartre 1936, 58, 70.

9. Cf. *Hua* 14, 419.

10. Merleau-Ponty 1945, 249, 277.

11. Needless to say, there is also a difference between the absence of a thematic experience of the ego and a thematic experience of the ego's absence. On the prereflective level, there might be no explicit awareness of the experiences being mine, but there is certainly no awareness (not even prereflective) of the experiences not being mine. This argumentation is, however, still restricted to the level of ordinary perception. Whether there are deeper or abnormal (psychotic) types of consciousness lacking this egocentric feature will be discussed shortly.

12. As Scanlon puts it in his criticism of Sartre's account of recollection (cf. note 3, above):

> If I express what I recall in a reflective memory by the statement, "I saw a landscape from the train yesterday," I am not referring by "I" merely to some indefinite individual who saw a landscape yesterday. If I did, I should say, "Someone saw a landscape from the train yesterday." And I might not call upon reflective memory to substantiate that statement. By "I," I am referring to a definite individual, the same one who both saw a landscape from the train yesterday and who am now recalling reflectively that I did so. The "I" is posited, in other words, as belonging not only to the reflected experience but also to the reflective act. (Scanlon 1971, 339)

13. Sartre 1948, 63 (1967, 123); cf. 1943, 114, 142–43, 284; 1936, 19, 78–79.

14. Marbach 1974, 77, 90.

15. A recurrent problem in Merleau-Ponty's theory of intersubjectivity is that he comes very close to offending against this principle. He writes that our perceptual acts have a prepersonal structure, and that they are characterized by a fundamental anonymity. Thus, each and every perception takes place in an atmosphere of universality, they happen in the mode of "*das man*" (1945, 249, 277). Merleau-Ponty even speaks of a depersonalization at the core of our perceptions (1945, 159), and claims that there is no problem of an Other since it is neither I nor it that perceives, but an anonymous vision (*visibilité*) that lives in us (1964, 187). Merleau-Ponty reaches a similar conclusion in his studies of developmental psychology for, as he puts it, the problem of intersubjectivity is only a problem for adults. In the beginning of life one can speak neither of self-awareness nor of an experience of an Other. On this stage of shared and anonymous life there is no differentiation (1945, 407; 1960b, 32–33). Occasionally, however, Merleau-Ponty seems to realize that this model, rather than solving the problem of intersubjectivity, threatens to dissolve it by annulling every plurality (cf. 1945, 408–9; 1947, 125; 1988, 42–44).

16. *Hua* 16, 40.

17. Marbach 1974, 100. The decisive breakthrough occurred when Husserl discovered that it was possible to thematize foreign experiences through the

double reflection. Just as I in recollection can thematize my present recollecting ego and my past perceiving ego (see page 57), empathy allows me to reflect upon myself as empathizing ego and upon the Other as empathized ego. Thus, it is not only myself which can be made accessible for phenomenological description through reflection, but also the Other (*Hua* 13, 456).

18. In *Wesen und Formen der Sympathie*, Scheler argues that an analysis of our emotions corroborates the existence of a plurality of subjects. If one examines love or sympathy one is dealing with a true grasping of someone beyond oneself. A real intentional transcending is manifest, and our experience of sympathy can therefore, according to Scheler, serve as a direct argument against solipsism (1922, 57, 69, 81). Insofar as several kinds of emotions indicate a plurality of subjects, Scheler criticizes every theory arguing for the existence of a supra-individual unity of consciousness. From a phenomenological point of view, we are dealing with intentions whose structure is incompatible with the elimination of a real difference between the subjects (1922, 75):

> Hence fellow-feeling [*Mitgefühl*] does not proclaim the essential identity of persons, as Schopenhauer and von Hartmann allege, but actually presupposes a pure essential *difference* between them (this being also the ultimate basis of their difference in actual fact). The occurrence of a feeling in some sort of supra-individual spirit or universal consciousness, in which the two persons merely participate together, coalescing therein, as it were, would not be fellow-feeling at all. And if, as we saw, it is the very office of true fellow-feeling to dissipate the solipsistic illusion by apprehending the equivalent status of the other person *as* such, it cannot be at the same time a dim perception of the fact that neither of us really exists, but only some third party, of whom we are merely the functions. (Scheler 1922, 76 [1954, 65–66])

19. *Hua* 9, 416. To quote James:

> No thought even comes into direct *sight* of a thought in another personal consciousness than its own. Absolute insulation, irreducible pluralism, is the law. It seems as if the elementary psychic fact were not *thought* or *this thought* or *that thought*, but *my thought*, every thought being *owned*. Neither contemporaneity, nor proximity in space, nor similarity of quality and content are able to fuse thoughts together which are sundered by this barrier of belonging to different personal minds. The breaches between such thoughts are the most absolute breaches in nature. (James 1890 I, 226)

20. *Hua* 1, 139 (1960, 109); cf. 15, 12. This notion of a transcendent Other is of paramount importance to Husserl. As I have shown elsewhere, Husserl ultimately claims that my experience of objective validity is made possible by my experience of the transcendence (and inaccessibility) of foreign subjectivity. It is this transcendence, which Husserl designates as the first real alterity and as the source of all kinds of real transcendence, that endows the world with

objective validity: "Hier ist die allein eigentlich so zu nennende Transzendenz, und alles, was sonst noch Transzendenz heißt, wie die objektive Welt, beruht auf der Transzendenz fremder Subjektivität" (*Hua* 8, 495; cf. 17, 248; 14, 277; 15, 560; 1, 137, 173; Zahavi 1996).

21. Although Klawonn was not the first to point this out, he has still delivered a remarkably thorough and explicit defense for it (cf. Klawonn 1991).

22. *Hua* 8, 175; 13, 307, 443, 28, 56.

23. *Hua* 9, 415.

24. *Hua* 14, 429.

25. *Erfahrung und Urteil* 193; *Hua* 13, 184; 4, 252, 350; 14, 151; Ms. C 3 32a. For a profound investigation of Husserl's notion of *life,* see Montavont 1999.

26. Cf. Henry 1963, 580–81; 1965, 53; 1989, 55.

27. Henrich 1970, 276.

28. Henry 1966, 31.

29. Klawonn 1991, 5, 136.

30. Cf. Strawson 1966, 164.

31. Ms. C 10 13a.

32. *Hua* 14, 275. Thus, Husserl also calls attention to the particular kind of reflection found in conscience (*Hua* 8, 105).

33. Cf. *Hua* 10, 34.

34. It has recently been claimed that given the future possibility of certain advanced brain transplantations, one might in principle have veridical memories which, even though they are presented in the first-person mode, are not necessarily memories of one's own experiences. In this case one might quite reasonably say, "I do vividly seem to remember hearing that tune, but I do not know whether it was I or my brother who heard it" (Parfit 1987, 221). This example appears to violate the very notion of *remembering,* however. Even if something like these *quasimemories* were possible they would neither undermine our assumptions about the particular infallibility of ordinary memories, nor present us with something like impersonal experiences. As Evans has pointed out, for a subject to have apparent memories of, say, a burning tree, is for it to seem to him that a tree burned, that is, for it to seem to him that he himself saw a burning tree. Thus, an apparent memory of seeing a burning tree is necessarily an apparent memory of oneself seeing a burning tree (Evans 1982, 246–48). Finally, Parfit's claim seems to presuppose a highly questionable assumption, that memories are imbedded in the brain in a way that makes it possible to transfer them through brain transplantation. As Wilkes puts it: "What is really wrong with this whole approach is that it treats memories (and beliefs, thoughts, etc.) as if they were marbles in a bag: one can just 'take' one out of a brain, they are discrete and isolable" (Wilkes 1988, 40). For further arguments against this type of thought experiment, see Wilkes 1988, 1–48.

35. Cf. Ayer 1956, 136–37.

36. Assuming that it is possible to speak of unconscious perceptions, if such a perception were then later suddenly brought to consciousness, it would not appear as past, nor would its object.

37. Frank 1986, 90; Cf. Frank 1986, 51; Schmalenbach 1929, 316.
38. *Hua* 4, 310; 9, 315.
39. *Hua* 4, 107; 3, 179.
40. *Hua* 17, 362–63; cf. 4, 105.
41. *Hua* 23, 200.
42. *Hua* 3, 211–15; 4, 97–98.
43. *Hua* 3, 73; 14, 156; 4, 103; 15, 305.
44. *Hua* 3, 189.
45. *Hua* 4, 108.
46. Cf. Hart 1992, 68–69.
47. *Hua* 4, 105; 13, 248.
48. Pfänder 1904, 352–58.
49. Marbach 1974, 163, 172.
50. Kern 1989, 57.
51. *Hua* 13, 248; 9, 207; 4, 277.
52. *Hua* 4, 98; 17, 363.
53. *Hua* 3, 123–24, 179; 4, 99–100; 14, 43; 13, 246.
54. Kern 1989, 60–62; 1975, 66.
55. Thus, as Husserl points out, if I imagine a countryside, for instance, then my imagination must entail an imagined subject as well (a fantasy-modification of myself), since there must be a subject to whom the countryside is given in perspectival adumbrations (*Hua* 8, 131, 116). In imagination subjectivity can be Other than itself and thereby anticipate intersubjectivity (*Hua* 15, 335). For an analysis of this particular *othering*, see Depraz 1995, 259–68.
56. *Hua* 13, 318; 9, 208; 11, 309; cf. Fink 1992, 114, 117.
57. *Hua* 11, 309–10.
58. Kern 1975, 58, 62, 65.
59. Bernet 1994, 303–4.
60. Cf. Marbach 1974, 117–19; Bernet 1985, xliv.
61. Kern 1975, 65–66.
62. *Hua* 9, 208.
63. Ms. C 16 10a.
64. *Hua* 11, 235, 323, 72; 1, 125; Ms. C 17 63a–b.
65. *Hua* 15, 598.
66. Ms. C 16 7b; Ms. C 16 69b.
67. *Hua* 15, 350; Ms. C 16 68b; C 10 2a; C 10 15a–b.
68. Cf. Zahavi 1994a.
69. *Hua* 15, 339.
70. Ms. C 10 16a; *Hua* 17, 293; *Erfahrung und Urteil* 122.
71. Holenstein 1971, 140–41; Montavont 1993, 135. I will return to some of these issues in my discussion of the unconscious in the appendix.
72. Sass 1994, 22; Jaspers 1961, 101–3.
73. Natsoulas 1991–92.
74. Cf. Kimura 1997, 342.
75. It might also be crucial not to interpret the claims of the schizophrenic

too literally, but rather metaphorically. When somebody tells us that he is dead, it might be more promising to assume that he is seeking to convey an existential rather than a biological truth to us (Laing 1960, 37, 149; cf. Sass 1994, 30).

76. Perhaps this explanation might also be of value when it comes to an understanding of multiple personality disorder. One of the common phenomena in MPD is the type of asymmetrical awareness known as a one-way amnesic barrier. Personality A is aware of personality B's thoughts and actions, but B is not even aware of A's existence. But if A has a direct access to B's thoughts, why does A experience these thoughts as the thoughts of another person?

77. Graham and Stephens 1994, 100.

78. Rosenberg 1987; Schilder 1951, 40.

79. Quoted from Cutting 1997, 296.

80. Sass 1994, 12, 38, 91, 95; cf. Laing 1960, 74.

81. Laing 1960, 69, 72, 112, 137–38, 140.

82. Laing 1960, 74, 82, 168.

83. Laing 1960, 109.

84. Blankenburg has decribed schizophrenia as a loss of natural evidence (cf. Blankenburg 1979). This formulation rightly evokes a certain similarity between schizophrenia and the phenomenological attitude—as Fink once claimed, the epoché is a kind of methodical schizophrenia (Fink 1957, 329). In a similar vein, Husserl himself acknowledges that the phenomenological attitude involves a self-fission. We disengage ourselves from the ego directed naively at worldly objects in order to scrutinize its very functioning (*Hua* 8, 422, 427). Ultimately it is necessary to distinguish not merely the transcendental from the mundane ego, but also the phenomenologizing ego from the thematized phenomenological ego. One has to differentiate the ego which effectuates the reduction from the ego which is recognized as transcendental due to the reduction (*Hua* 8, 440). For some further reflections on this topic, see Bernet 1994, 9–18.

Chapter 9

1. Perhaps it could be argued that the third form of egocentric self-awareness, that is, the awareness of the ego as a transcendent principle of identity, as well as all kinds of reflective self-awareness are such advanced cognitive performances that they could only evolve intersubjectively. But one has to distinguish such a claim, which merely argues for a general dependency between a certain level of cognitive complexity and intersubjectivity, from a claim concerning the specific and intrinsic intersubjective nature of reflective self-awareness. In Hart, however, one encounters the latter, since he takes the constitution of the ego-pole to depend upon the Other (Hart 1992, 166). It is only through the encounter with the Other, and through his "originating gracious presence" where the subject becomes an Other to the Other, that it becomes capable of effectuating self-displacing acts, and thus comes to acquire both an egological as well as a reflective self-awareness (Hart 1992, 198, 202, 207). Even if this were true, I am, however,

somewhat reluctant to accept it as a tenable Husserl interpretation. On the contrary, it has a distinct Lévinasian tone to it.

2. Ricoeur 1950, 55 (1966, 56–57). Cf. Ricoeur 1990, 380. In *Autrement qu'être ou au-dela de l'essence*, Lévinas raises the following question: What is it that constitutes the irreplaceable and unsubstitutable individuality of the subject? Needless to say, the subject is not unique, like the Eiffel Tower. It is not unique by possessing qualities and traits which nobody else has. Nor is it a unique individual due to its particular position in space and time. But neither is my unique subjectivity a matter of my own choice or doing. For Lévinas, to be a unique subject is ultimately to be addressed by the Other (1974, 26, 91). The Other makes an irrefutable appeal to my responsibility, and my identity and uniqueness stem from the fact that I cannot escape this responsibility, which nobody can assume for me (Lévinas 1991a, 186; 1991b, 64; 1974, 29, 141, 215–17). To phrase it differently, it is the accusation of the Other which singularizes me. It is in the ethical relation that I receive my true individuality, since it is the responsibility that makes me unsubstitutable and irreplaceable. Thus, subjectivity is strictly speaking the sub-jection to responsibility (Lévinas 1974, 183), and insofar as my selfhood depends upon the Other, it is not characterized by self-sufficiency, but rather by a fundamental self-deficiency and lack (Lévinas 1974, 176; cf. Ricoeur 1990, 30). Lévinas is certainly pointing to important issues. Objects cannot be held responsible. This is an exclusive feature of subjectivity. But I find it hard to follow him when he seems to insist that responsibility is also the defining feature of subjectivity.

3. *Hua* 8, 71; 5, 146; 4, 174–75.

4. *Hua* 4, 249, 105; 1, 62. To complicate matters, Husserl also operates with a *transcendental* concept of the person. This is particularly clear in *Cartesianische Meditationen* (§32), where Husserl emphasizes that the ego-pole is by no means an empty and static pole. It is a developing structure, it has a history, and it is influenced and determined by its own previous experiences. Our acts leave behind sedimentations, and in this way the *transcendental* ego acquires enduring habits, convictions, an abiding style, a personal character (*Hua* 1, 100–101; 9, 210–12; 4, 214). For the very same reason, Husserl does not follow Sartre in claiming that the personal ego is a product of reflection (*Hua* 4, 251). It is on the contrary a product of sedimentation.

5. *Hua* 14, 204; 4, 252.

6. *Hua* 4, 104 (1989, 111).

7. *Hua* 4, 142–43, 175.

8. *Hua* 4, 183–84, 423, 443. Originally, we do not interact with each other as objects in space, but with each other as cosubjects (*Hua* 4, 183, 194). Originally, our subjectivity is not given to us as a causally conditioned appendix to the body (*Hua* 4, 190). Originally, our body is besouled through and through (*Hua* 4, 240). Or as it is formulated in *Zur Phänomenologie der Intersubjektivität II*: "Der lebendige Leib ist in seinem beständigen Funktionieren sich beständig äussernde Innerlichkeit" (*Hua* 14, 491).

9. Castañeda 1989b, 46.

10. *Hua* 13, 443.

11. *Hua* 4, 159; 14, 77.

12. *Hua* 13, 252; 14, 110, 485.

13. *Hua* 4, 200.

14. *Hua* 8, 136–37.

15. *Hua* 13, 243–44; cf. 15, 635.

16. *Hua* 14, 170–71.

17. *Hua* 6, 256; 14, 78, 418. In a manuscript from 1912, Husserl specifies this claim and asserts that although a solipsistic subject might in principle be capable of forming a personalistic self-apprehension on its own, it would lack the motive and occasion (*Hua* 13, 245).

18. *Hua* 14, 175; 6, 315; 4, 204–5; 15, 177; 15, 603; cf. Hart 1992, 71; Taylor 1989, 34–36.

19. *Hua* 4, 242, 250.

20. *Hua* 13, 342, 462; 4, 90, 111, 200; 15, 19, 589, 634; 14, 418.

21. *Hua* 5, 112.

22. *Hua* 14, 62–63.

23. *Hua* 14, 63; 4, 90, 138, 161, 167.

24. *Hua* 14, 86; cf. *Hua* 14, 85; 15, 289; 4, 90.

25. Theunissen 1977, 84 (1984, 89).

26. Sartre 1943, 260, 267, 289. One finds a comparable position in the writings of Scheler, who also claims that an intentional analysis of our emotions will reveal a reference to the Other. However, a decisive difference between Sartre and Scheler is that whereas the latter argues that there exists an a priori "*logique du cœur,*" and that certain of our experiences, such as guilt, responsibility, and love, refer to the Other even prior to and independently of every concrete encounter with the Other (Scheler 1922, 71–72, 225; 1916, 59, 557), Sartre resolutely rejects any a priorism when it comes to the issue of intersubjectivity. The emotions in question (guilt, love, shame, etc.) are only possible through the concrete encounter with the Other. An adequate analysis of these experiences will not reveal an a priori structure in my being which refers me to an equally a priori Other. It will reveal the presence of this or that concrete transcendent Other (Sartre 1943, 297). As I have shown elsewhere, it is, however, doubtful whether Sartre's own acccount of intersubjectivity is able to avoid every kind of a priorism. For a more detailed examination and estimation of Sartre's theory of intersubjectivity, see Zahavi 1996, 112–20.

27. Sartre 1943, 329 (1956, 282).

28. Sartre 1943, 302, 317.

29. Sartre 1943, 266.

30. Sartre 1943, 307 (1956, 261).

31. Sartre 1943, 287, 314, 334, 582.

32. Sartre 1943, 581 (1956, 524).

33. Sartre 1943, 309, 313, 317, 481.

34. Sartre 1943, 404, 422–23.

35. Sartre 1943, 313, 317; cf. *Hua* 4, 168, 177–78, 181, 202.

36. As I pointed out in chapter 3, this issue has been either completely ignored or too quickly settled by the Heidelberg School. As a single example, one can mention Frank, who claims that any theory that takes self-awareness to depend upon intersubjectivity is vulnerable to the same kind of criticism as the reflection theory of self-awareness (Frank 1986, 65; cf. Henrich 1970, 281). Although Frank's remark might be apt when it comes to the Mead- and Wittgenstein-influenced position of Habermas, this is certainly not the only way to relate subjectivity and intersubjectivity. For an extended discussion, see Zahavi 1996.

37. It has to be emphasized that we are still confronted with a type of *self-awareness*, that is, with an emphatic and intrinsic self-reference typically articulated through the use of "I," and not simply with a type of external self-reference discussed earlier, as when I am thinking of the tallest man in town, and that person happens to be me. In depersonalization, however, the self-alienation involved may be so radical that the emphatic nature of the self-reference is lost.

38. *Hua* 14, 85; 15, 289; 4, 90.

39. *Hua* 4, 345.

40. *Hua* 9, 210.

41. *Hua* 4, 265. Whereas Husserl is ready to ascribe an egological structure to the animal, he is ambiguous about whether it is also a person. He alternately denies and affirms it (cf. *Hua* 15, 177; 3, 73; 1, 101).

42. *Hua* 13, 6; 13, 247. Ultimately, it is not only the personality which is intersubjectively constituted. Husserl also argues that transcendental subjectivity exists as a member of transcendental intersubjectivity, and that the ego in its transcendental-constitutive functioning only is what it is within intersubjectivity (*Hua* 6, 175; cf. Ms. C 17 88b). Thus, one of Husserl's recurrent points is that a sufficiently radical carrying out of the transcendental reduction leads not only to subjectivity, but also to intersubjectivity (9, 344); just as he claims that a radical *self-*reflection necessarily leads to the discovery of absolute intersubjectivity and that the transcendental subjectivity in its full universality is exactly *inter*subjectivity (8, 480; 6, 275, 472): "Die konkret volle transzendentale Subjektivität ist das von innen her, rein transzendental einige und nur so konkrete All der offenen Ichgemeinschaft. Die transzendentale Intersubjektivität ist der absolute, der allein eigenständige Seinsboden, aus dem alles Objektive, das All des objektiv real Seienden, aber auch jede objektive Idealwelt, seinen Sinn und seine Geltung schöpft" (9, 344). The disclosing agent, the performer of the reduction, is the phenomenologizing ego, whereas the disclosed constituting subjectivity proves to be transcendental intersubjectivity (15, 73–75). For an extensive account, see Zahavi 1996.

43. *Hua* 6, 188; 15, 589–90.

44. Ms. B I 14 138a.

45. Ms. B I 14 138b; cf. *Hua* 14, 212.

46. *Hua* 17, 243–44; 14, 307; 29, 165.

47. Ms. C 17 15b; *Hua* 4, 299, 301.

48. *Hua* 15, 351.

49. *Hua* 13, 420.

50. *Hua* 14, 20–23, 196; 4, 299–300.

51. *Hua* 4, 111–12; 9, 214; cf. Hart 1992, 52–54. But Husserl would still insist that no matter how decisive a change in my personality I might undergo, and no matter how much my personality might be fractured, it would still be a break and a fracture occurring within the framework of an identical ego (*Hua* 15, 254).

52. *Hua* 4, 288 (1989, 301–2); cf. 4, 326, 242, 251; 15, 137.

53. *Hua* 4, 242; 8, 72.

54. *Hua* 9, 294.

55. Sartre's criticism is mainly directed against Heidegger's position in *Sein und Zeit* (cf. Heidegger 1986a, 114, 120). For a more detailed account of Heidegger's theory of intersubjectivity, see Zahavi 1996, 102–11.

56. Sartre 1943, 293–95, 412.

57. Sartre 1943, 385–86, 408–9.

58. Sartre 1943, 395.

59. Sartre 1943, 351, 408.

60. Sartre 1943, 351 (1956, 304); cf. *Hua* 4, 148; 13, 283.

61. Sartre 1943, 351 (1956, 304).

62. Cf. *Hua* 1, 144; 3, 325; 8, 175; 6, 189; 13, 188; 15, 447, 641, 416.

63. *Hua* 6, 189 (1970, 185); cf. 15, 642, 634.

64. For similar and related observations, cf. Derrida 1967a, 40; 1967b, 195; Bernet 1994, 303–4; Depraz 1995, 239–59; Benoist 1994, 28–40; and Hart 1992, 225, who even characterizes the retention and protention as "feeble forms of empathy."

65. Claesges 1964, 110.

66. *Hua* 15, 652; cf. Merleau-Ponty 1964, 176, 194.

67. *Hua* 8, 62; 15, 300; 14, 457, 462; 9, 197; 13, 263.

68. *Hua* 4, 297.

69. Merleau-Ponty 1945, 427–28 (1962, 373).

70. Merleau-Ponty 1945, 405 (1962, 352); cf. 1945, 402.

71. Merleau-Ponty 1945, 400–401, 405, 511. In *Jeget's Ontologi,* Klawonn claims that there is something like an automatically functioning *emphatic identification,* which serves as a transcendental precondition for the experience of Others (Klawonn 1991, 77). Klawonn might be right in this, but his observation can hardly count as a sufficiently thorough analysis of the relation between self-awareness and intersubjectivity. As Husserl once remarked with regard to Scheler's theory of empathy: "In dieser Hinsicht ist Schelers Theorie der Einfühlung das Widerspiel einer wirklich phänomenologischen Theorie. Es ist der Grundfehler des schlechten Nativismus, dass er . . . angeborene 'Vorstellungen,' wenn auch sehr unbestimmt allgemeine, voraussetzt und aller Entwicklung nur die Funktion zumisst, diese unbestimmte Allgemeinheit näher zu bestimmen" (*Hua* 14, 335). Obviously, the task must be to clarify what it is in the subject's self-acquaintance that enables it to recognize foreign subjectivity.

72. Merleau-Ponty 1945, 406; 1960a, 213, 215, 221; 1960b, 35; 1964, 74, 278; 1969, 186, 188.

73. Merleau-Ponty 1945, 408; 1964, 114–15, 298.

74. Merleau-Ponty 1945, 415.

75. Merleau-Ponty 1945, 165, 404–5; 1960a, 213, 221.

76. Meltzoff and Moore 1995. However, the timetable has changed drastically. Merleau-Ponty was referring to a fifteen-month-old child, and following Wallon he believed that the child lacked the neurological capacity to perceive external objects until after the process of myelinization had occurred between the third and sixth months of life (Merleau-Ponty 1988, 313).

77. Stern 1985, 51.

78. For a series of examples of amodal perception in children, see Stern 1985, 47–53. As Merleau-Ponty was to point out, the connection between the visual and tactile experiences of the body is not forged gradually. I do not translate the "data of touch" into the language of "seeing," or vice versa. There is an immediate awareness of the correspondence. Originally there is a basic stratum of experience which is anterior to the division of the senses (1945, 175–77, 262, 265). As Straus puts it, "the manyness of the modalities is controlled by the oneness of sensory experiencing" (Straus 1958, 155).

79. Meltzoff and Moore 1995, 53–54.

80. Merleau-Ponty 1945, 399.

81. Ricoeur 1950, 407, 412, 415; Merleau-Ponty 1945, 249; Husserl Ms. A VI 14a, Ms. A VI 45a.

82. Merleau-Ponty 1945, 515 (1962, 451); cf. 1945, 403–4, 413, 427, 467; 1960a, 140; 1969, 192.

83. Merleau-Ponty 1945, 415, 495, 515.

84. Cf. note 15, chapter 8, above.

85. Merleau-Ponty 1945, 408–12, 418, 514.

86. Mead 1962, 164, 172.

87. Mead 1962, 138.

88. Mead 1962, 164, 169.

89. Mead 1962, 163.

90. Mead 1962, 171–72.

91. Cf. Habermas 1991, 401–2; 1988 II, 93, 95, 138; 1989, 33–34.

92. Piaget and Inhelder 1969, 22.

93. Mahler, Pine, and Bergman 1975, 44; cf. Spitz 1983, 217, 249.

94. Neisser 1988, 40; Stern 1983, 51; 1985, 10; Butterworth 1995, 90. For a description of the revolution having taken place in infant research during the 1970s, see Stern 1985, who also accounts for the concrete research strategies employed, particularly the so-called *paired comparison preference* paradigm and the *habituation/dishabituation* paradigm.

95. Stern 1985, 6, 11, 69.

96. Stern 1985, 63, 72; Spitz 1983, 98–124.

97. Stern 1985, 21.

98. Spitz 1983, 19.

99. Stern 1985, 193, 197–98.

100. Spitz 1983, 19, 43.

101. Stern 1985, 124.

102. Stern 1985, 128.
103. Stern 1985, 129–31.
104. Stern 1985, 132.
105. Stern 1985, 105, 118.
106. Lewis and Brooks-Gunn 1979, 33–46; Stern 1985, 165.
107. Cf. *Hua* 14, 509; Ey 1973, 271.
108. Lewis and Brooks-Gunn 1979, 220.
109. Stern 1985, 6–7, 71.
110. Stern 1983, 56–62.
111. Stern 1985, 7, 65, 67.
112. Stern 1983, 65.
113. Stern 1985, 71.
114. Klawonn 1991, 45.

Chapter 10

1. Kühn 1994, 214.
2. Yamagata 1991, 174–75.
3. Sartre 1943, 194, 199, 201.
4. Sartre 1943, 195 (1956, 155).
5. Sartre 1943, 197; 1936, 48.
6. Sartre 1943, 190, 203.
7. He even admits this quite explicitly (cf. Sartre 1971).
8. *Hua* 7, 262; 1, 72.
9. *Hua* 17, 290; 8, 71; 7, 269; 6, 255, 264.
10. *Hua* 3, 117; 7, 267.
11. *Hua* 8, 77.
12. *Hua* 8, 79; 3, 107.
13. *Hua* 3, 136; 8, 427; 6, 265.
14. For a discussion of the difference between the Cartesian and the ontological ways to the reduction, see Zahavi 1997a, 56–67.
15. *Hua* 3, 165, 168, 175.
16. Derrida 1972b, 349, 359.
17. *Hua* 3, 174–75.
18. *Hua* 3, 174; Merleau-Ponty 1945, 412.
19. Cf. Smith 1989, 77.
20. *Hua* 3, 78; Sokolowski 1974, 187.
21. Henrich 1982a, 152.
22. Pothast 1971, 108.
23. Fink 1992, 116–17, 128.
24. *Hua* 1, 72.
25. *Hua* 10, 129.
26. *Hua* 10, 128; 11, 205, 236; 24, 244.
27. Linschoten 1961, 96–97.
28. Merleau-Ponty 1945, 207; Klawonn 1991, 100–101.

29. *Hua* 1, 77. Ultimately, the problem facing an investigation of consciousness might not be that different from the problem facing an investigation and description of the lifeworld. In both cases we are faced with a question concerning the relationship between the description and that which is described. And in both cases we are dealing with regions that evade exact conceptual fixation. But that it is impossible to develop a mathematics of experience, that we are forced to describe it with morphological concepts, is not a deficit. These concepts are indispensable for the task at hand, and are therefore the proper ones.

30. If reflection were to be accounted for in strict analogy with other types of attentive consciousness, that which motivated the reflection would have had to be particularly conspicuous, would have had to stand out in some way if it were to rouse my interest (*Hua* 17, 279; Ms. C 16 49a–b). But is such a conspicuousness really to be found in the perceptions that are subsequently reflected upon when compared to all the acts that remain unthematized? Husserl is rather silent when it comes to this problem, but in one text he points out that the present act, exactly by being present, stands out in comparison with all past acts (Ms. C 10 7a). Although this might explain why reflection is first and foremost a reflection upon an experience still existing, it does not, however, explain why we reflect upon certain acts and not upon others. But perhaps it is a mistake to seek a further explanation? Husserl has occasionally, in an almost Fichtean vein, described (philosophical) reflection as an expression of our basic freedom (see *Hua* 8, 19; 3, 62; 4, 213), and in this perspective the attempt to seek the sufficient reason for the act of reflection appears misguided. Lévinas has argued that it is the encounter with the Other which conditions and makes possible the unnatural movement of reflection. Reflection is a suspension of the natural spontaneity. It makes my thought detach from itself and join itself as if it were Other to itself. But this movement cannot arise out of nothing. It needs an impulse from without. This impulse comes from the Other, who interrupts and disrupts my dogmatic slumber by putting me into question. Thus, it is the nonepistemic, ethical encounter with the Other which disturbs the subject in its tranquil primordiality, and makes possible both reflection and reduction (Lévinas 1991b, 61; 1982, 224; 1991a, 103).

31. *Hua* 19, 425; cf. 3, 76.

32. *Hua* 3, 78.

33. *Hua* 3, 166.

34. Kern 1975, 21–22.

35. Cf. *Hua* 4, 248.

36. Cf. *Hua* 4, 102; 3, 166.

37. *Hua* 10, 116, 161.

38. Fink 1987, 62, cf. *Hua* 8, 93; 4, 253. Frequently Husserl also speaks of recollection as a "*Mit-sich-selbst-in-Gemeinschaft-Sein*" (Ms. C 7 8a; cf. Ms. C 7 25a; *Hua* 14, 359; 15, 519, 398).

39. Fink 1987, 55–57, 62; cf. *Hua* 4, 212.

40. As I pointed out in chapter 8, this does not imply, however, that there are no interesting or profound connections between reflection and these pathological phenomena.

41. Cf. Lévinas 1991a, 102; 1982, 47, 50. For the very same reasons it constitutes a problem for Henry's understanding of the nature of self-awareness.

42. *Hua* 9, 478.

43. *Hua* 14, 29.

44. *Hua* 8, 412; 15, 484.

45. Brough 1987, 23.

46. *Hua* 10, 75, 371; Ms. C 3 4a; Ms. C 7 14a.

47. Ms. L I 20 4a–b.

48. *Hua* 24, 244–45.

49. *Hua* 14, 29; Ms. C 16 59a; Ms. C 10 5a; Ms. C 2 10a.

50. Merleau-Ponty 1945, 399; cf. 1945, 76, 397, 460.

51. Held 1966, 95, 103.

52. Cf. Zahavi 1996.

53. Cf. Derrida 1967b, 181.

54. *Hua* 1, 139 (1960, 109).

55. *Hua* 1, 144; 15, 631.

56. Lévinas 1979, 89.

57. Cf. Waldenfels 1989; Boehm 1969; Zahavi 1996.

58. *Hua* 15, 484; Ms. C 17 84b; Merleau-Ponty 1945, 404, 413; Held 1966, 152–53, 160.

59. Lévinas 1961, 61 (1979, 65–66).

60. Lévinas 1979, 9, 53, 78; 1949, 194, 206, 214; 1961, 209; 1982, 183.

61. Lévinas 1961, 72; cf. 1949, 229.

62. Lévinas 1974, 158.

63. Henry 1990, 151–52.

64. Henry 1963, 477.

65. Henry 1963, 480–82, 490; 1990, 125, 164.

66. Henry 1963, 53 (1973, 41); cf. 1963, 549.

67. Henry 1963, 53, 57, 550, 555.

68. This title evokes Heidegger's remarks in *Sein und Zeit* concerning the necessity of analyzing that which *"zunächst und zumeist"* remains hidden from view, namely Being. It is exactly because there are phenomena which do not reveal themselves immediately that we need a phenomenology (Heidegger 1986a, 35; cf. Marion 1989, 90–97, Marion 1996). Much later, in a conference from 1973, Heidegger explicitly spoke of a "phenomenology of the inapparent [*Unscheinbaren*]" (Heidegger 1986b, 399). The moment Henry starts to speak of the condition of manifestation in terms of a radical invisibility, it also becomes hard to overlook some striking resemblances between his theory and Derrida's—in spite of all the fundamental discrepancies which certainly also abound. Both of them are trying to pass beyond a surface phenomenology occupied with act-intentionality and object-manifestation. According to Derrida, the ultimate condition of manifestation is not intuitively graspable. It cannot become the object of a reflection, it does not offer itself to vision, but remains forever the nocturnal source of light itself (Derrida 1972b, 297; 1989, 137). This ultimate condition is not itself present. But this does not entail that it is merely absent or hidden. Absence is simply

a modification of presence, namely an absent or delayed presence, and it does not carry us beyond the metaphysics of presence (Derrida 1972a, 24–25, 37, 77, 206; 1967a, 98). But if the condition of presence is neither present nor absent, neither visible nor concealed, what other possibilities are there? The condition of presence refuses to appear in person or present itself to a phenomenological gaze. It withdraws, or to use a Derridean and Lévinasian term, it *traces* (Derrida 1972a, 24; Gasché 1986, 149–50). The "trace" is the term used to designate the mode of being of that which conditions visibility without offering itself to vision. It cannot be presentified, but leaves an emptiness in its wake (Lévinas 1949, 201, 208, 230). In traditional metaphysical thinking, the trace has been taken to be derived. A trace is understood to point beyond itself. It is a trace by referring to something that has been present. It refers to that of which it is a trace. Thus, traces are understood as temporally delayed signs of the existence or movement of a being that has been present (Lévinas 1949, 200; 1972, 66; Strasser 1978, 206). But when Derrida and Lévinas speak of trace (or arche-trace) they are talking about a nonphenomenal trace which is more basic and more original than the presence which it has traditionally been taken to be the trace of. Both trace and presence and the difference between the two are constituted and conditioned by an infrastructural *différance*, which is the origin and condition of all difference between self and Other. It is this *différance* which permits self-presence, it is the retentional fold that permits the self to become present to itself. Both of the traditional categories—trace and presence—are erasures of the original trace, which is never itself present. They are the result of a suppression and concealment of *différance* (Derrida 1967b, 303; 1967c, 236; 1972a, 25, 76–77). As Derrida points out, it would have been better if one could avoid the entire distinction between original and derived, since it belongs to a framework which has consistently tried to conceal *différance*, and to exclude nonpresence as pure exteriority, as simple addition. But ultimately it is impossible to avoid metaphysical concepts altogether. It is impossible to criticize metaphysics without making use of it, since no other language is available (Derrida 1967b, 412; 1967c, 25, 38, 92, 237; 1972a, 73, 78).

69. In his book *Le tournant théologique de la phénoménologie française,* Janicaud has recently criticized the very notion of a "phenomenology of the invisible." As he writes, is it not absurd to speak in such terms, is it not misleading to call a thinking that abandons the visible in favor of the obscure and invisible for phenomenological? In response, I think one should distinguish two different questions. The first question is whether the move from the visible to the invisible is phenomenologically motivated. Is there, so to speak, something in the analysis of the visible that calls for an investigation of a more fundamental dimension? The second question is whether the very investigation of this invisible can be taken care of by phenomenology itself, or whether it should rather be left to a metaphysical or even theological thinking. As for the first question, it should be emphasized that practically all of the major phenomenological thinkers eventually realized that it would be necessary to transcend a mere analysis of act-intentionality and object-manifestation if they were to answer *the* phenomenological question concerning the condition of possibility for manifestation. Thus, I do not think that there is

any reason to deny that the move is phenomenologically motivated. And again let me emphasize that to speak of the invisible is not to speak of that which forever remains hidden; it is not to speak of that which never manifests itself, but simply to speak of something that manifests itself in a radically different way than the visible. As for the second question, it might very well be that there are aspects concerning the nature of manifestation which phenomenology cannot explore and answer itself. But to admit that is definitely not to accept a narrow definition of "phenomenology" that equates it with "surface-phenomenology" (a narrow conception which one occasionally encounters in both Lévinas and Derrida [Lévinas 1949, 199; 1979, 87; Derrida 1967c, 99]). As my analysis of self-awareness has, I hope, shown, phenomenology is in fact quite capable of investigating forms of manifestation other than the visible.

70. Held 1966, 77, 160.

Chapter 11

1. Lévinas 1961, 113, 121, 135.
2. Lévinas 1991b, 36, 50, 52; 1979, 21; 1982, 212, 239; 1961, 26, 129.
3. Lévinas 1961, 26–28.
4. Lévinas 1979, 83 (1987, 90).
5. Lévinas 1949, 172, 174, 187.
6. Lévinas 1949, 188.
7. Lévinas 1961, 28 (1979, 39).
8. Lévinas 1961, 211.
9. Lévinas 1961, 104–5.
10. Lévinas 1961, 233.
11. Lévinas 1949, 190, 142, 193.
12. Lévinas 1961, 33, 89, 215, 231; 1991b, 57–58.
13. Lévinas 1982, 243.
14. Cf. Grue-Sørensen, who suggests that self-awareness should be understood as a kind of feeling (1950, 70–71).
15. Cf. Zahavi 1996 and the contributions in Zahavi 1994b and in Depraz and Zahavi 1998.
16. Cf. Heidegger 1979, 149; Frank 1990, 54, 56. For a discussion of the resemblances between Husserl's analysis of the inner time-consciousness and Heidegger's analysis of Being, see Sokolowski 1978; Prufer 1988; and Hart 1996b.
17. Derrida 1967a, 9; 1972a, 36–37, 187, 207.

Appendix

1. Cf. Natsoulas 1989.
2. Freud 1945, 431 (1958, 260).
3. Freud 1945, 434 (1958, 263).
4. Freud 1940, 243 (1961, 16).

5. Freud 1946, 271.

6. Freud 1946, 264–65; cf. Brentano 1874, 147.

7. Cf. *Hua* 6, 192.

8. Freud 1941, 147.

9. Freud 1944b, 76–77 (1964, 70); cf. Freud 1941, 81.

10. Freud 1946, 270 (1957, 171); cf. 1946, 272.

11. *Hua* 6, 474 (1970, 386).

12. Freud 1942, 616–17 (1953, 612); cf. Freud 1946, 265.

13. Searle 1992, 152.

14. Cf. Freud 1944a, 304; 1946, 267.

15. Ricoeur 1950, 362, 367; Bernet 1996a, 46; Bernet 1996b. According to Kern, Freud himself in his most lucid moments rejected the notion of unconscious representations, acts, and affects, and restricted the unconscious to the drives, energies, and impulses (Kern 1975, 266–72).

16. To quote Hegel: "Quite generally, the familiar, just because it is familiar, is not cognitively understood" (Hegel 1988, 25 [1977, 18]). And Heidegger: "What is ontically nearest and familiar is ontologically the farthest, unrecognized and constantly overlooked in its ontological significance" (Heidegger 1986a, 43 [1996, 41]).

17. Henry 1965, 140 (1975, 101).

18. *Hua* 4, 338 (1989, 350); cf. 1, 101; 14, 36; Ricoeur 1950, 368.

19. Cf. Drüe 1963, 302.

20. *Hua* 13, 295.

21. *Hua* 9, 514; 4, 276–77.

22. Mishara 1990, 35; cf. *Hua* 11, 125.

23. *Hua* 11, 165.

24. *Hua* 11, 154. For some of Husserl's rare references to psychoanalysis, see *Hua* 4, 222; 6, 240.

25. *Hua* 4, 38; cf. 4, 100; 11, 416.

26. Ms. C 10 2b–3a.

27. *Hua* 11, 169–70; Ms. L I 15 17a.

28. *Hua* 11, 171.

29. *Hua* 11, 420.

30. *Hua* 11, 179.

31. *Hua* 24, 251; 17, 318–19.

32. *Hua* 9, 486; 11, 149, 160; Ms. C 8 5a–b. Cf. Binswanger 1953, 474–75; Montavont 1994.

33. Hart 1993, 39.

34. *Hua* 11, 167; 14, 156. We are after all capable of waking up, be it because our sleep is disturbed or because it happens to be the customary hour in the morning. That many people are able to wake up at the same time day after day, or even to wake up at an unusual hour, if they decide to do so before going to sleep, is revealing, since it seems to indicate that people have an ability to register the passing of time when asleep. I find that I usually wake up a few minutes before the alarm clock goes off if I have to get up early. And if it is important that I get

up at a specific time, I almost always wake up several times during the night, to check that the alarm clock is still functioning. Thus, it seems likely that sleep and sensibility do not exclude each other completely. A well-known example of this is presented by the parents who are able to sleep through a good deal of noise, but will awaken the moment their child cries. Perhaps we do in fact have experiences continuously during dreamless sleep, but experiences which we simply neglect to attend to, just as we during our waking hours may be insensible to habitual sounds. To quote Linschoten:

> [T]his means that we never sleep through and through. But then perhaps "complete sleep" is a mere theoretical construction, a limit-idea. When in my sleep I-in-my-origin have slid back into an almost plantlike mode of existence, then still a last, extremely vague kernel remains ready to unfold itself again into a living center of interests at the slightest signal. In my sleep I have not disappeared; *I* am sleeping, and in so doing remain ready to show my originality. Sleep is a state in which I, *anonymously,* just merely live, but am continuously ready to wake up as I-myself. . . . While sleeping I "deal" with a number of disturbances as being unimportant; they reach me vaguely because I am still "somewhere" awake in an anonymous way; but I *disinterest* myself from them and that means that I renewedly fall asleep. (Linschoten 1987, 110; cf. Flanagan 1997, 103)

Our ability to wake up seems to require the persistence of some core of consciousness. Thus, to repeat, sleep does not appear to present us with the total suspension of experiencing subjectivity, but rather with a fundamentally altered state of consciousness.

35. Ms. C 10 16a.

36. *Hua* 14, 53–54.

37. *Hua* 11, 380.

38. *Hua* 11, 424.

39. Klawonn argues that the very claim that subjectivity sleeps, and that its self-givenness is thereby interrupted, is unjustified based as it is on an external third-person description, made in objective time. From the first-person perspective, the only relevant one when it comes to self-manifestation, there is in fact no sleep, and no interruption, but one continuous unbroken field of presence (Klawonn 1991, 139–40; cf. James 1890 I, 238). Although I can only agree with his rejection of the view that subjectivity is interrupted every time the person goes to sleep or is otherwise "unconscious," I think Klawonn's suggestion is too insensitive to the diverse modes of consciousness. After all, when I wake up, I am usually aware of having slept. It is not only something that I infer because the sun has risen, or because I feel invigorated. And although a period of dreamless sleep might only be given to me as a felt gap, as an empty time, it is still experienced as my time, as a part of *my life* (cf. Linschoten 1961, 103). I think that Husserl's suggestion can account for this. For further discussions of the relationship between sleep and self-awareness, see Linschoten 1987; Hart 1993; and Zahavi 1997b.

40. Ricoeur 1950, 354–55.
41. According to Sartre, it is exactly because of its transcendent character that we can be in error about its nature.
42. Klawonn 1991, 89–92.
43. Tugendhat 1979, 142; Merleau-Ponty 1945, 436.
44. As Frank writes:

> Wenn ich verliebt bin, so bin ich zweifellos irgendwie gestimmt; aber es kann mir völlig unbekannt sein, daß "Verliebtheit" der richtige Klassifikationsterm für meinen Zustand ist. Es kann mir sogar passieren, daß alle, die mit mir zusammen sind und mich beobachtet, *wissen, was* mir widerfährt, während ich selbst es nicht weiß. Aber *wenn* ich mich, aus der Distanz einer *prise de conscience,* ihrer Deutung meines Zustandes anschließe, so tue ich es aus Evidenzen, über die *sie* nicht verfügt haben und die einzig entscheiden. Mithin muß eine Kontinuität des Bewußtseins zwischen dem *Wissen, wie* und dem *Wissen, daß* vermitteln, und das letztere muß seinen Erkenntnisgrund im ersteren haben. (Frank 1991a, 246)

45. Cf. the classical reflections by James 1890 I, 162–76; and Brentano 1874, 143–70.
46. Sartre 1943, 380–81.
47. Sartre 1943, 383 (1956, 334).
48. Sartre 1943, 385–86.
49. Sartre 1943, 405–7.
50. To quote Lewis: "Pain is a feeling. Surely that is uncontroversial. To have pain and to feel pain are one and the same. For a state to be pain and for it to feel painful are likewise one and the same. A theory of what it is for a state to be pain is inescapably a theory of what it is like to be in that state, of how that state feels, of the phenomenal character of that state" (Lewis 1980, 222).
51. Cf. Searle 1992, 172; Smith 1989, 95; Chalmers 1996, 4; Strawson 1994, 71.
52. Strawson 1994, 208–9.
53. Strawson 1994, 167. Cf. 1994, 171, 211.
54. Klawonn suggests that one might at most classify them as *psychoid* (cf. Klawonn 1991, 16, 105). Flanagan has recently introduced a distinction between "*experiential sensitivity*" and "*informational sensitivity.*" Somebody may be experientially insensitive but informationally sensitive to a certain difference. When we are merely informationally sensitive to something, we are not conscious of it, that is, pure informational sensitivity, or to use a better expression, pure informational pickup and processing is nonconscious. It is a processing without phenomenal awareness, without qualia (Flanagan 1992, 55–56, 147). Subjectivity has to do with experiential sensitivity, and it is only the latter that let us have phenomenal access to the object. Although it might be appropriate to operate with a notion of nonconscious informational processing, I think one should be careful not to assume that the informational sensitivity provides us with a nonphenomenal version of the *same* information as the experiential sensitivity.

55. Cf. Eagle 1988, 101–2; Moore 1988, 144.

56. Armstrong 1993, 94, 323–26, Armstrong and Malcolm 1984, 120. Since introspective consciousness is to be compared to perception, Armstrong suggests that it will be natural to say that the objects of introspection, i.e., our first-order mental states, act within our mind so as to produce our introspective awareness of these states (1981, 62). But since our introspective consciousness is also a mental state, and one that can itself become the object of a higher-order introspection, there is an obvious danger of initiating an infinite causal chain.

57. Cf. Wider 1993b.

58. Kleitman 1939, 282–83, 289; Farthing 1992, 246–47; Étévenon 1987, 202; Borbély 1986, 96–97; Pélicier 1985, 16, 19.

59. Armstrong and Malcolm 1984, 119–20.

60. Armstrong 1993, 93.

61. Hilgard 1977, 158; Kihlstrom 1984, 180.

62. Beaunis 1887, 118; James 1890 I, 201.

63. Pélicier 1985, 20.

64. James 1890 I, 208.

65. Hilgard 1977, 185, 236.

66. Hilgard 1977, 201.

67. Beahrs 1982, 61; Hilgard 1977, 18. In contrast, Freud claimed that the dissociation did not present us with the phenomenon of coconsciousness, but with two psychical complexes which were alternately conscious (cf. Freud 1945, 434–35.

68. Beahrs 1982, 183–84. This dissociation can also occur voluntarily. If one concentrates intensively on a particular topic, one might become oblivious to the surroundings. That is, through a selective attention one can force everything else, including pain, out on the margin. It might merely persist as an atmospheric disturbance.

69. James 1890 I, 209.

70. James 1890 I, 211. As Hilgard points out, however, the terms "hidden observer" and "secondary personage" are metaphors for cognitive processes which have become inaccessible for the normal consciousness of the hypnotized person. It does not mean that there is a secondary personality with a life of its own—a kind of homunculus lurking in the shadows of the conscious person (Hilgard 1977, 188). Rather than assigning the dissociated processes to distinct agents, they should be assigned to the subsystems of a single agent.

71. Hilgard 1977, 190. Insofar as hypnosis seems to involve a dissociation or vertical splitting, it is little wonder that attention has often been drawn to the striking similarities between the hypnotic state and the even more fundamental splitting observed in patients suffering from multiple personality disorder. It has been suggested that children who have been subjected to repeated traumatic experiences might use a form of self-hypnosis or dissociation to distance themselves from the painful experience. A presentation of some of the truly puzzling phenomena encountered in this disorder would lead too far, but for an introduction, see Braude 1991.

Works Cited

Anscombe, G. E. M. 1981. *Metaphysics and the Philosophy of Mind*. Oxford: Blackwell.

Aristotle. 1984. *The Complete Works of Aristotle*. 2 vols. Ed. J. Barnes. Princeton, N.J.: Princeton University Press.

Armstrong, D. M. 1981. *The Nature of Mind*. Brighton: Harvester.

———. 1993. *A Materialist Theory of the Mind*. London: Routledge.

Armstrong, D. M., and N. Malcolm. 1984. *Consciousness and Causality: A Debate on the Nature of Mind*. Oxford: Blackwell.

Ayer, A. J. 1956/1990. *The Problem of Knowledge*. New York: Penguin Books.

Barbaras, R. 1991. "Le sens de l'auto-affection chez Michel Henry et Merleau-Ponty." *Epokhè* 2: 91–111.

Bateson, G. 1972. *Steps to an Ecology of Mind*. New York: Ballantine Books.

Beahrs, J. O. 1982. *Unity and Multiplicity: Multilevel Consciousness of Self in Hypnosis, Psychiatric Disorder and Mental Health*. New York: Brunner/Mazel.

Beaunis, H. 1887. *Le somnambulisme provoqué*. Paris.

Behnke, E. A. 1984. "World without Opposite—Flesh of the World." Paper presented at the meeting of the Merleau-Ponty Circle, Montréal.

Benoist, J. 1994. *Autour de Husserl*. Paris: Vrin.

Bergson, H. 1927/1993. *Essai sur les données immédiates de la conscience*. Paris: PUF.

———. 1971. *Time and Free Will: An Essay on the Immediate Data of Consciousness*. Trans. F. L. Pogson. London: Georg Allen and Unwin.

Bernet, R. 1983. "Die ungegenwärtige Gegenwart. Anwesenheit und Abwesenheit in Husserls Analyse des Zeitbewußtseins." *Phänomenologische Forschungen* 14: 16–57.

———. 1985. "Einleitung." In *Texte zur Phänomenologie des inneren Zeitbewußtseins, 1893–1917*, by E. Husserl, xi–lxvii. Hamburg: Felix Meiner.

———. 1994. *La vie du sujet*. Paris: PUF.

———. 1996a. "The Unconscious between Representation and Drive: Freud, Husserl, and Schopenhauer." In *The Truthful and the Good*, ed. J. J. Drummond and J. G. Hart, 81–95. Dordrecht, Boston, London: Kluwer.

———. 1996b. "L'analyse husserlienne de l'imagination comme fondement du concept freudien d'inconscient." *Alter* 4: 43–67.

Binswanger, L. 1953. *Grundformen und Erkenntnis menschlichen Daseins*. Zürich: Max Niehans.

Blankenburg, W. 1979. "Phänomenologische Epoché und Psychopathologie." In *Alfred Schütz und die Idee des Alltags in den Sozialwissenschaften,* ed. W. Sprondel and R. Grathoff, 125–39. Stuttgart: Enke.

Boehm, R. 1969. "Zur Phänomenologie der Gemeinschaft. Edmund Husserls Grundgedanken." In *Phänomenologie, Rechtsphilosophie, Jurisprudenz,* ed. Thomas Würtenberger, 1–26. Frankfurt am Main: Klostermann.

Borbély, A. 1986. *Secrets of Sleep.* New York: Basic Books.

Brand, G. 1955. *Welt, Ich und Zeit.* The Hague: Martinus Nijhoff.

Braude, S. E. 1991. *First Person Plural.* London: Routledge.

Brentano, F. 1874/1973. *Psychologie vom empirischen Standpunkt.* Vol. 1. Hamburg: Felix Meiner.

———. 1928/1985. *Kategorienlehre.* Hamburg: Felix Meiner.

———. 1973. *Psychology from an Empirical Standpoint.* Trans. A. C. Rancurello, D. B. Terrell, and L. L. McAlister. London: Routledge and Kegan Paul.

Brough, J. B. 1972. "The Emergence of an Absolute Consciousness in Husserl's Early Writings on Time-Consciousness." *Man and World* 5: 298–326.

———. 1975. "Husserl on Memory." *Monist* 59: 40–62.

———. 1987. "Temporality and the Presence of Language: Reflections on Husserl's Phenomenology of Time-Consciousness." In *Phenomenology of Temporality: Time and Language,* ed. A. Schuwer, 1–31. Pittsburgh: Duquesne University.

———. 1991. "Introduction." In E. Husserl, *On the Phenomenology of the Consciousness of Internal Time, 1893–1917,* xi–lvii. Dordrecht: Kluwer Academic Publishers.

———. 1993. "Husserl and the Deconstruction of Time." *Review of Metaphysics* 46: 503–36.

Butterworth, G. 1995. "An Ecological Perspective on the Origins of Self." In *The Body and the Self,* ed. J. L. Bermúdez, A. Marcel, and N. Eilan, 87–105. Cambridge, Mass.: MIT Press.

Cabestan, Ph. 1996. "La constitution du corps selon l'ordre de ses apparitions." *Epokhè* 6: 279–98.

Castañeda, H.-N. 1966. "He, a Study in the Logic of Self-Consciousness." *Ratio* 8: 130–57.

———. 1967. "The Logic of Self-Knowledge." *Nous* 1: 9–2.

———. 1968. "On the Phenomeno-Logic of the I." *Proceedings of the Sixteenth International Congress of Philosophy* 3: 260–66.

———. 1970. "On Knowing (or Believing) That One Knows (or Believes)." *Synthese* 21: 187–203.

———. 1979. "Philosophical Method and Direct Awareness of the Self." *Grazer Philosophische Studien* 7, no. 8: 1–58.

———. 1987a. "The Self and the I-Guises, Empirical and Transcendental." In *Theorie der Subjektivität,* eds. K. Cramer et al., 105–40. Frankfurt am Main: Suhrkamp.

———. 1987b. "Self-Consciousness, Demonstrative Reference, and the Self-

Ascription View of Believing." In *Philosophical Perspectives*. Vol. 1, *Metaphysics*, ed. James E. Tomberlin, 405–54. Atascadero, Calif.: Ridgeview.

———. 1989a. "Self-Consciousness, I-Structures and Physiology." In *Philosophy and Psychopathology*, ed. M. Spitzer and B. A. Maher, 118–45. Berlin: Springer Verlag.

———. 1989b. "The Reflexivity of Self-Consciousness: Sameness/Identity, Data for Artificial Intelligence." *Philosophical Topics* 17, no. 1: 27–58.

Chalmers, D. J. 1996. *The Conscious Mind: In Search of a Fundamental Theory*. New York: Oxford University Press.

Chisholm, R. M. 1981. *The First Person*. Brighton: Harvester.

Claesges, U. 1964. *Edmund Husserls Theorie der Raumkonstitution*. The Hague: Martinus Nijhoff.

Cobb-Stevens, R. 1998. "James and Husserl: Time-Consciousness and the Intentionality of Presence and Absence." In *Self-Awareness, Temporality, and Alterity*, ed. D. Zahavi, 41–57. Dordrecht: Kluwer Academic Publishers.

Cole, J. 1991/1995. *Pride and a Daily Marathon*. Cambridge, Mass.: MIT Press.

Cole, J., and J. Paillard. 1995. "Living without Touch and Peripheral Information about Body Position and Movement: Studies with Deafferented Subjects." In *The Body and the Self*, ed. J. L. Bermúdez, A. Marcel, and N. Eilan, 245–66. Cambridge, Mass.: MIT Press.

Costa, V. 1994. "Derrida og Husserl—Problemet om Ursyntesen." In *Subjektivitet og Livsverden i Husserls Fænomenologi*, ed. D. Zahavi, 75–88. Aarhus: Modtryk.

Cramer, K. 1974. " 'Erlebnis'. Thesen zu Hegels Theorie des Selbstbewußtseins mit Rücksicht auf die Aporien eines Grundbegriffs nachhegelscher Philosophie." In *Stuttgarter Hegel-Tage 1970*, ed. H.-G. Gadamer, 537–603. Bonn: Hegel-Studien, Beiheft 11.

Cutting, J. 1997. *Principles of Psychopathology: Two Worlds—Two Minds—Two Hemispheres*. Oxford: Oxford University Press.

Depraz, N. 1995. *Transcendance et incarnation*. Paris: Vrin.

———. 1998. "Can I Anticipate Myself? Self-Affection and Temporality." In *Self-Awareness, Temporality, and Alterity*, ed. D. Zahavi, 85–99. Dordrecht: Kluwer Academic Publishers.

Depraz, N., and Zahavi, D. eds. 1998. *Alterity and Facticity: New Perspectives on Husserl*. Dordrecht: Kluwer Academic Publishers.

Derrida, J. 1967a. *La voix et le phénomène*. Paris: PUF.

———. 1967b. *L'écriture et la différence*. Paris: Éditions du Seuil.

———. 1967c. *De la grammatologie*. Paris: Les Éditions de Minuit.

———. 1972a. *Marges de la philosophie*. Paris: Les Éditions de Minuit.

———. 1972b. *La dissémination*. Paris: Éditions du Seuil.

———. 1973. *Speech and Phenomena and Other Essays on Husserl's Theory of Signs*. Trans. D. B. Allison. Evanston, Ill.: Northwestern University Press.

———. 1976. *Of Grammatology*. Trans. G. C. Spivak. Baltimore: Johns Hopkins University Press.

————. 1989. *An Introduction to Edmund Husserl's 'Origin of Geometry.'* Lincoln: University of Nebraska Press.

————. 1990. *Le problème de la genèse dans la philosophie de Husserl.* Paris: PUF.

Drummond, J. J. 1979–80. "On Seeing *a* Material Thing *in* Space: The Role of Kinaesthesis in Visual Perception." *Philosophy and Phenomenological Research* 40: 19–32.

Drüe, H. 1963. *Edmund Husserls System der phänomenologischen Psychologie.* Berlin: de Gruyter.

Duval, R. 1990. *Temps et vigilance.* Paris: Vrin.

Eagle, M. 1988. "Psychoanalysis and the Personal." In *Mind, Psychoanalysis, and Science,* ed. P. Clark and C. Wright, 91–111. Oxford: Blackwell.

Étévenon, P. 1987. *Du rêve à l'éveil.* Paris: Albin Michel.

Evans, G. 1982. *The Varieties of Reference.* Oxford: Clarendon Press.

Ey, Henry. 1973. *Consciousness: A Phenomenological Study of Being Conscious and Becoming Conscious.* Bloomington: Indiana University Press.

Farthing, U. W. 1992. *The Psychology of Consciousness.* Englewood Cliffs, N.J.: Prentice-Hall.

Fichte, J. G. 1797/1920. *Erste und Zweite Einleitung in die Wissenschaftslehre.* Leipzig: Felix Meiner.

————. 1994. *Introductions to the Wissenschaftslehre and Other Writings (1797–1800).* Trans. D. Breazeale. Indianapolis: Hackett.

Fink, E. 1957. "Operative Begriffe in Husserls Phänomenologie." *Zeitschrift für philosophische Forschung* 11: 321–37.

————. 1966. *Studien zur Phänomenologie 1930–1939.* The Hague: Martinus Nijhoff.

————. 1987. *Existenz und Coexistenz.* Würzburg: Königshausen and Neumann.

————. 1992. *Natur, Freiheit, Welt.* Würzburg: Königshausen and Neumann.

Flanagan, O. 1992. *Consciousness Reconsidered.* Cambridge, Mass.: MIT Press.

————. 1997. "Prospects for a Unified Theory of Consciousness or, What Dreams Are Made Of." In *The Nature of Consciousness,* ed. N. Block, O. Flanagan, and G. Güzeldere, 97–109. Cambridge, Mass.: MIT Press.

Franck, D. 1984. "La chair et le problème de la constitution temporelle." In *Phénoménologie et métaphysique,* ed. J.-F. Courtine, 125–56. Paris: PUF.

Frank, M. 1984. *Was ist Neostrukturalismus?* Frankfurt am Main: Suhrkamp.

————. 1986. *Die Unhintergehbarkeit von Individualität.* Frankfurt am Main: Suhrkamp.

————. 1989. *Das Sagbare und das Unsagbare.* Frankfurt am Main: Suhrkamp.

————. 1990. *Zeitbewußtsein.* Pfullingen: Neske.

————. 1991a. *Selbstbewußtsein und Selbsterkenntnis.* Stuttgart: Reclam.

Frank, M., ed. 1991b. *Selbstbewußtseinstheorien von Fichte bis Sartre.* Frankfurt am Main: Suhrkamp.

Freud, S. 1940. *Gesammelte Werke.* Vol. 13, *Jenseits des Lustprinzips: Massenpsychologie und Ich-Analyse—Das Ich und das Es.* Frankfurt am Main: S. Fischer.

————. 1941. *Gesammelte Werke.* Vol. 17, *Schriften aus dem Nachlass.* Frankfurt am Main: S. Fischer.

————. 1942. *Gesammelte Werke.* Vols. 2–3, *Die Traumdeutung: Über den Traum.* Frankfurt am Main: S. Fischer.

————. 1944a. *Gesammelte Werke.* Vol. 11, *Vorlesungen zur Einführung in die Psychoanalyse.* Frankfurt am Main: S. Fischer.

————. 1944b. *Gesammelte Werke.* Vol. 15, *Neue Folge der Vorlesungen zur Einführung in die Psychoanalyse.* Frankfurt am Main: S. Fischer.

————. 1945. *Gesammelte Werke.* Vol. 8, *Werke aus den Jahren 1909–1913.* Frankfurt am Main: S. Fischer.

————. 1946. *Gesammelte Werke.* Vol. 10, *Werke aus den Jahren 1913–1917.* Frankfurt am Main: S. Fischer.

————. 1953. *The Standard Edition of the Complete Psychological Works of Sigmund Freud.* Vol. 5, *The Interpretation of Dreams (Second Part) and on Dreams.* Trans. J. Strachey. London: Hogarth Press.

————. 1957. *The Standard Edition of the Complete Psychological Works of Sigmund Freud.* Vol. 14, *On the History of the Psycho-Analytic Movement: Papers on Metapsychology and Other Works.* Trans. J. Strachey. London: Hogarth Press.

————. 1958. *The Standard Edition of the Complete Psychological Works of Sigmund Freud.* Vol. 12, *The Case of Schreber: Papers on Technique and Other Works.* Trans. J. Strachey. London: Hogarth Press.

————. 1961. *The Standard Edition of the Complete Psychological Works of Sigmund Freud.* Vol. 19, *The Ego and the Id and Other Works.* Trans. J. Strachey. London: Hogarth Press.

————. 1964. *The Standard Edition of the Complete Psychological Works of Sigmund Freud.* Vol. 22, *New Introductory Lectures on Psycho-Analysis and Other Works.* Trans. J. Strachey. London: Hogarth Press.

Gallagher, S. 1986. "Body Schema and Body Image: A Conceptual Clarification." *Journal of Mind and Behavior* 7: 541–54.

Gallagher, S., and J. Cole. 1995. "Body Image and Body Schema in a Deafferented Subject." *Journal of Mind and Behavior* 16, no. 4: 369–89.

Gallup, G. G. 1977. "Self-Recognition in Primates." *American Psychologist* 32: 329–38.

Gasché, R. 1986. *The Tain of the Mirror.* Cambridge, Mass.: Harvard University Press.

Gibson, J. J. 1966. *The Senses Considered as Perceptual Systems.* London: George Allen and Unwin LTD.

————. 1979/1986. *The Ecological Approach to Visual Perception.* Hillsdale, N.J.: Lawrence Erlbaum Associates.

————. 1982. *Reasons for Realism: Selected Essays of James J. Gibson.* Ed. E. Reed and R. Jones. Hillsdale, N.J.: Lawrence Erlbaum Associates.

Goldman, A. I. 1997. "Consciousness, Folk Psychology, and Cognitive Science." In *The Nature of Consciousness,* ed. N. Block, O. Flanagan, and G. Güzeldere, 111–25. Cambridge, Mass.: MIT Press.

Graham, G., and G. L. Stephens. 1994. "Mind and Mine." In *Philosophical Psychopathology,* ed. G. Graham and G. L. Stephens, 91–110. Cambridge, Mass.: MIT Press.

Grue-Sørensen, K. 1950. *Studier over Refleksitivitet.* Copenhagen: J. H. Schultz.

Gurwitsch, A. 1966. *Studies in Phenomenology and Psychology.* Evanston, Ill.: Northwestern University Press.

———. 1974. *Das Bewußtseinsfeld.* Berlin: de Gruyter.

———. 1985. *Marginal Consciousness.* Athens: Ohio University Press.

Habermas, J. 1988. *Theorie des kommunikativen Handelns.* Vols. 1–2. Frankfurt am Main: Suhrkamp.

———. 1989. *Nachmetaphysisches Denken.* Frankfurt am Main: Suhrkamp.

———. 1991. *Der philosophische Diskurs der Moderne.* Frankfurt am Main: Suhrkamp.

Hart, J. G. 1989. "Constitution and Reference in Husserl's Phenomenology of Phenomenology." *Husserl Studies* 6: 43–72.

———. 1992. *The Person and the Common Life.* Dordrecht: Kluwer Academic Publishers.

———. 1993. "Phenomenological Time: Its Religious Significance." In *Religion and Time,* ed. J. N. Mohanty and A. N. Balslev, 18–45. Leiden: Brill.

———. 1996a. "Agent Intellect and Primal Sensibility." In *Issues in Husserl's Ideas,* ed. T. Nenon and L. Embree, vol. 2, 107–34. Dordrecht: Kluwer Academic Publishers.

———. 1996b. "Being and Mind." In *The Truthful and the Good,* ed. J. J. Drummond and J. G. Hart, 1–16. Dordrecht: Kluwer Academic Publishers.

———. 1998. "Intentionality, Phenomenality, and Light." In *Self-Awareness, Temporality, and Alterity,* ed. D. Zahavi, 59–83. Dordrecht: Kluwer Academic Publishers.

Heckman, H.-D. 1991. "Wer (oder was) bin ich? Zur Deutung des Intentionalen Selbsbezuges aus der Perspektive der ersten Person Singularis." In *Dimensionen des Selbst: Selbstbewusstsein, Reflexivität und die Bedingungen von Kommunikation,* ed. B. Kienzle and H. Pape, 85–136. Frankfurt am Main: Suhrkamp.

Hegel, G. W. F. 1977. *Hegel's Phenomenology of Spirit.* Trans. A. V. Miller. Oxford: Clarendon Press.

———. 1988. *Phänomenologie des Geistes.* Hamburg: Felix Meiner.

Heidegger, M. 1979. *Gesamtausgabe.* Vol. 20, *Prolegomena zur Geschichte des Zeitbegriffs.* Frankfurt am Main: Vittorio Klostermann.

———. 1986a. *Sein und Zeit.* Tübingen: Max Niemeyer.

———. 1986b. *Gesamtausgabe.* Vol. 15, *Seminare (1951–1973).* Frankfurt am Main: Vittorio Klostermann,

———. 1990. *Kant and the Problem of Metaphysics.* Trans. R. Taft. Bloomington: Indiana University Press.

———. 1991. *Gesamtausgabe.* Vol. 3, *Kant und das Problem der Metaphysik.* Frankfurt am Main: Vittorio Klostermann.

———. 1996. *Being and Time.* Trans. J. Stambaugh. Albany, N.Y.: SUNY Press.

Held, K. 1966. *Lebendige Gegenwart.* The Hague: Martinus Nijhoff.

———. 1981. "Phänomenologie der Zeit nach Husserl." *Perspektiven der Philosophie* 7: 185–221.

Held, R., and A. Hein. 1963. "Movement-Produced Stimulation in the Development of Visually Guided Behavior." *Journal of Comparative and Physiological Psychology* 56, no. 5: 872–76.

Henrich, D. 1966. "Fichtes ursprüngliche Einsicht." In *Subjektivität und Metaphysik. Festschrift für Wolfgang Cramer,* ed. D. Henrich and H. Wagner, 188–232. Frankfurt am Main: Klostermann.

———. 1970. "Selbstbewußtsein, kritische Einleitung in eine Theorie." In *Hermeneutik und Dialektik,* ed. R. Bubner, K. Cramer, and R. Wiehl, 257–84. Tübingen: Mohr.

———. 1971. "Self-Consciousness: A Critical Introduction to a Theory." *Man and World* 4: 3–28.

———. 1982a. *Fluchtlinien.* Frankfurt am Main: Suhrkamp.

———. 1982b. *Selbstverhältnisse.* Stuttgart: Reclam.

———. 1989. "Noch einmal in Zirkeln. Eine Kritik von Ernst Tugendhats semantischer Erklärung von Selbstbewußtsein." *Mensch und Moderne. Beiträge zur philosophischen Anthropologie und Gesellschaftskritik,* ed. C. Bellut and U. Müller-Schöll, 93–132. Würzburg: Königshausen and Neumann.

Henry, M. 1963. *L'essence de la manifestation.* Paris: PUF.

———. 1965. *Philosophie et phénoménologie du corps.* Paris: PUF.

———. 1966. "Le concept d'âme a-t-il un sens?" *Revue philosophique de Louvain* 64: 5–33.

———. 1969. "Does the Concept 'Soul' Mean Anything?" *Philosophy Today* 13, no. 2: 94–114.

———. 1973. *The Essence of Manifestation.* Trans. G. Etzkorn. The Hague: Martinus Nijhoff.

———. 1975. *Philosophy and Phenomenology of the Body.* Trans. G. Etzkorn. The Hague: Martinus Nijhoff.

———. 1985. *Généalogie de la psychanalyse.* Paris: PUF.

———. 1989. "Philosophie et subjectivité." In *Encyclopédie Philosophique Universelle, Bd. 1. L'univers philosophique,* ed. A. Jacob, 46–56. Paris: PUF.

———. 1990. *Phénoménologie matérielle.* Paris: PUF.

———. 1994. "Phénoménologie de la naissance." *Alter* 2: 295–312.

———. 1996. *C'est moi la vérité.* Paris: Seuil.

Hilgard, E. R. 1986. *Divided Consciousness: Multiple Controls in Human Thought and Action.* New York: John Wiley and Sons.

Holenstein, E. 1971. "Passive Genesis: Eine Begriffsanalytische Studie." *Tijdschrift voor Filosofie* 33: 112–53.

———. 1972. *Phänomenologie der Assoziation: Zu Struktur und Funktion eines Grundprinzips der passiven Genesis bei E. Husserl.* The Hague: Martinus Nijhoff.

Hume, D. 1888. *A Treatise of Human Nature.* Oxford: Clarendon Press.

Husserl, E. 1952. *Husserliana.* Vol. 4, *Ideen zu einer reinen Phänomenologie und phänomenologischen Philosophie II.* The Hague: Martinus Nijhoff.

———. 1956. *Husserliana.* Vol. 7, *Erste Philosophie I (1923–24).* The Hague: Martinus Nijhoff.

———. 1959. *Husserliana.* Vol. 8, *Erste Philosophie II (1923–24).* The Hague: Martinus Nijhoff.

————. 1960. *Cartesian Meditations*. Trans. D. Cairns. The Hague: Martinus Nijhoff.

————. 1962. *Husserliana*. Vol. 6, *Die Krisis der europäischen Wissenschaften und die transzendentale Phänomenologie*. The Hague: Martinus Nijhoff.

————. 1962. *Husserliana*. Vol. 9, *Phänomenologische Psychologie*. The Hague: Martinus Nijhoff.

————. 1966. *Husserliana*. Vol. 11, *Analysen zur passiven Synthesis*. The Hague: Martinus Nijhoff.

————. 1966. *Husserliana*. Vol. 10, *Zur Phänomenologie des inneren Zeitbewußtseins (1893–1917)*. The Hague: Martinus Nijhoff.

————. 1969. *Formal and Transcendental Logik*. Trans. D. Cairns. The Hague: Martinus Nijhoff.

————. 1970. *The Crisis of European Sciences and Transcendental Phenomenology*. Trans. D. Carr. Evanston, Ill.: Northwestern University Press.

————. 1971. *Husserliana*. Vol. 5, *Ideen zu einer reinen Phänomenologie und phänomenologischen Philosophie III*. The Hague: Martinus Nijhoff.

————. 1973. *Husserliana*. Vol. 1, *Cartesianische Meditationen und Pariser Vorträge*. The Hague: Martinus Nijhoff.

————. 1973. *Husserliana*. Vol. 16, *Ding und Raum*. The Hague: Martinus Nijhoff.

————. 1973. *Experience and Judgment*. Trans. J. S. Churchill and K. Ameriks. London: Routledge and Kegan Paul.

————. 1973. *Husserliana*. Vol. 13, *Zur Phänomenologie der Intersubjektivität I*. The Hague: Martinus Nijhoff.

————. 1973. *Husserliana*. Vol. 14, *Zur Phänomenologie der Intersubjektivität II*. The Hague: Martinus Nijhoff.

————. 1973. *Husserliana*. Vol. 15, *Zur Phänomenologie der Intersubjektivität III*. The Hague: Martinus Nijhoff.

————. 1974. *Husserliana*. Vol. 17, *Formale und transzendentale Logik*. The Hague: Martinus Nijhoff.

————. 1976. *Husserliana*. Vol. 3/1–2, *Ideen zu einer reinen Phänomenologie und phänomenologischen Philosophie I*. The Hague: Martinus Nijhoff.

————. 1977. *Phenomenological Psychology*. Trans. J. Scanlon. The Hague: Martinus Nijhoff.

————. 1980. *Husserliana*. Vol. 23, *Phantasie, Bildbewußtsein, Erinnerung*. Dordrecht: Kluwer Academic Publishers.

————. 1980. *Phenomenology and the Foundations of the Sciences—Third Book of Ideas Pertaining to a Pure Phenomenology and to a Phenomenological Philosophy*. Trans. T. E. Klein and W. E. Pohl. The Hague: Martinus Nijhoff Publishers.

————. 1984. *Husserliana*. Vol. 19/1–2, *Logische Untersuchungen II*. The Hague: Martinus Nijhoff.

————. 1984. *Husserliana*. Vol. 24, *Einleitung in die Logik und Erkenntnistheorie*. The Hague: Martinus Nijhoff.

————. 1985. *Erfahrung und Urteil*. Hamburg: Felix Meiner.

————. 1989. *Ideas Pertaining to a Pure Phenomenology and to a Phenomenological*

Philosophy—Second Book. Trans. R. Rojcewicz and A. Schuwer. Dordrecht: Kluwer Academic Publishers.

———. 1991. *On the Phenomenology of the Consciousness of Internal Time (1893–1917)*. Trans. J. B. Brough. Dordrecht: Kluwer Academic Publishers.

———. 1993. *Husserliana*. Vol. 29, *Die Krisis der europäischen Wissenschaften und die transzendentale Phänomenologie: Ergänzungsband*. Dordrecht: Kluwer Academic Publishers.

———. 1997. *Thing and Space: Lectures of 1907*. Trans. R. Rojcewicz. Dordrecht: Kluwer Academic Publishers.

———. The text contains references to the following places in Husserl's unpublished manuscripts. Manuscripts to be found in the Husserl-Archieves in Leuven, Belgium.

A V 5 (1933)	A VI (1930)
A V 4b	A VI 14a
A V 5a	A VI 45a
A V 5 7a	
A V 5 8a	

B I 14 (1932)	B III 9 (1931–34)
B I 14 138a	B III 9 8a
B I 14 138b	B III 9 14a
	B III 9 14b
	B III 9 18a
	B III 9 23a
	B III 9 79a
	B III 9 79b
	B III 9 105b

C 2 (1931–32)	C 3 (1930–31)
C 2 3a	C 3 4a
C 2 8a	C 3 8a
C 2 10a	C 3 8b
C 2 11a	C 3 26a
	C 3 32a
	C 3 41b
	C 3 42a
	C 3 62a
	C 3 69a
	C 3 76a

C 5 (1930)	C 6 (1930)
C 5 6a	C 6 4b
C 5 7a	C 6 5a

C 7 (1932)
C 7 6b
C 7 8a
C 7 14a
C 7 14b
C 7 25a

C 10 (1931)
C 10 2a
C 10 2b
C 10 3a
C 10 3b
C 10 5a
C 10 7a
C 10 9b
C 10 10a
C 10 13a
C 10 15a
C 10 15b
C 10 16a
C 10 17a

C 15 (1931)
C 15 3b

C 17 (1930–32)
C 17 15b
C 17 63a
C 17 63b
C 17 84b
C 17 88b

C 8 (1929)
C 8 5a
C 8 5b

C 12 (1931)
C 12 3b

C 16 (1931–33)
C 16 7b
C 16 10a
C 16 28a
C 16 30b
C 16 33b
C 16 42a
C 16 46b
C 16 49a
C 16 49b
C 16 59a
C 16 68a
C 16 68b
C 16 69b
C 16 78a
C 16 81b
C 16 82a

D 10 (1932)
D 10 11a
D 10 IV 11
D 10 IV 15

D 12 (1931)
D 12 III 14
D 12 III 15
D 12 III 24
D 12 III 37a

D 13 (1921)
D 13 I 4a

E III 2 (1921)
E III 2 5a
E III 2 12b
E III 2 22a
E III 2 22b
E III 2 23a
E III 2 24b

E III 3 (1933–34)
E III 3 3a

E III 9 (1931–33)
E III 9 16a

L I 1 (1917–18)
L I 1 3a

L I 2 (1917)
L I 2 16a

L I 12 (1917)
L I 12 3b

L I 13 (1918)
L I 13 3a

L I 15 (1917)
L I 15 2b
L I 15 3a
L I 15 4a
L I 15 17a
L I 15 22a
L I 15 22b
L I 15 35a
L I 15 35b
L I 15 36a
L I 15 36b
L I 15 37b

L I 16 (1917)
L I 16 12a

L I 17 (1917–18)
L I 17 9a
L I 17 9b

L I 19 (1917–18)
L I 19 3a
L I 19 3b
L I 19 10a

L I 20 (1917–18)
L I 20 4a
L I 20 4b

L I 21 (1917)
L I 21 5b
L I 21 34b

M III 3 II I (1900–14)
M III 3 II I 29–30
M III 3 II I 95

Jackson, F. 1982. "Epiphenomenal Qualia." *Philosophical Quarterly* 32: 127–36.

James, W. 1890/1918. *The Principles of Psychology.* 2 vols. London: Macmillan.

Janicaud, D. 1991. *Le tournant théologique de la phénoménologie française.* Combas: Éditions de l'éclat.

Jaspers, K. 1965. *Allgemeine Psychopathologie.* Berlin: Springer Verlag.

Jones, J. R. 1956. "Self-Knowledge." *Aristotelian Society Supplementary Volumes* 30: 120–42.

Kant, I. 1923. *Werke VIII.* Ed. E. Cassirer. Berlin: Bruno Cassirer.

———. 1971. *Kritik der reinen Vernunft.* Frankfurt am Main: Felix Meiner.

———. 1983. *What Real Progress Has Metaphysics Made in Germany since the Time of Leibniz and Wolff?* Trans. T. Humphrey. New York: Abaris Books.

Kapitan, T. 1997. "The Ubiquity of Self-Awareness." *Grazer Philosophische Studien.* Forthcoming.

Kern, I. 1975. *Idee und Methode der Philosophie.* Berlin: de Gruyter.

———. 1989. "Selbstbewußtsein und Ich bei Husserl." In *Husserl-Symposion Mainz 1988,* 51–63. Stuttgart: Akademie der Wissenschaften und der Literatur.

Kienzle, B., and H. Pape. 1991. *Dimensionen des Selbst: Selbstbewußtsein, Reflexivität und die Bedingungen von Kommunikation.* Frankfurt am Main: Suhrkamp.

Kihlstrom, J. F. 1984. "Conscious, Subconscious, Unconscious: A Cognitive Perspective." In *The Unconscious Reconsidered,* ed. K. S. Bowers and D. Meichenbaum. New York: John Wiley and Sons.

Kimura, B. 1997. "Cogito et Je." *L'Évolution Psychiatrique* 62, no. 2: 335–48.

Klawonn, E. 1990. "On Personal Identity: Defence of a Form of Non-Reductionism." *Danish Yearbook of Philosophy* 25: 41–59.

———. 1991. *Jeg'ets Ontologi.* Odense: Odense Universitetsforlag.

———. 1994. "Kritisk Undersøgelse af Kritikken." In *Kritisk Belysning af Jeg'ets Ontologi,* ed. D. Favrholdt, 129–89. Odense: Odense Universitetsforlag.

Kleitman, N. 1939. *Sleep and Wakefulness.* Chicago: University of Chicago Press.

Kühn, R. 1994. *Studien zum Lebens- und Phänomenbegriff.* Cuxhaven: Junghans-Verlag.

Laing, R. D. 1960/1990. *The Divided Self.* Harmondsworth: Penguin Books.

Landgrebe, L. 1963. *Der Weg der Phänomenologie.* Gütersloh: Gerd Mohn.

———. 1982. *Faktizität und Individuation.* Hamburg: Felix Meiner.

Larrabee, M. J. 1994. "Inside Time-Consciousness: Diagramming the Flux." *Husserl Studies* 10: 181–210.

Lee, N. 1998. "Edmund Husserl's Phenomenology of Mood." In *Alterity and Facticity: New Perspectives on Husserl,* ed. N. Depraz and D. Zahavi. Dordrecht: Kluwer Academic Publishers.

Lévinas, E. 1949/1988. *En découvrant l'existance avec Husserl et Heidegger.* Paris: Vrin.

———. 1961/1990. *Totalité et infini.* Dordrecht: Kluwer Academic Publishers.

———. 1972. *Humanisme de l'autre homme.* Paris: Fata Morgana.

———. 1974. *Autrement qu'être ou au-dela de l'essence.* The Hague: Martinus Nijhoff.

———. 1979a. *Totality and Infinity.* Trans. A. Lingis. The Hague: Martinus Nijhoff.

———. 1979b. *Le temps et l'autre.* Paris: Fata Morgana.

———. 1982/1992. *De Dieu qui vient à l'idée.* Paris: Vrin.

———. 1987. *Time and the Other.* Trans. R. A. Cohen. Pittsburgh: Duquesne University Press.

———. 1991a. *Entre nous: Essais sur le penser-à-l'autre.* Paris: Grasset.

———. 1991b. *Cahier de l'Herne.* Ed. C. Chalier and M. Abensour. L'Herne.

Lewis, D. 1979. "Attributions 'De dicto' and 'De Se.' " *The Philosophical Review* 88: 513–43.

———. 1980. "Mad Pains and Martian Pains." In *Readings in Philosophy of Psychology*, ed. N. Block, vol. 1, 216–22. Cambridge, Mass.: Methuen.

Lewis, M., and J. Brooks-Gunn. 1979. *Social Cognition and the Acquisition of Self.* New York: Plenum Press.

Linschoten, J. 1961. *Auf dem Wege zu einer phänomenologischen Psychologie.* Berlin: de Gruyter.

———. 1987. "On Falling Asleep." In *Phenomenological Psychology: The Dutch School*, ed. J. J. Kockelmans, 79–117. Dordrecht: Kluwer Academic Publishers.

Locke, J. 1975. *An Essay concerning Human Understanding.* Ed. P. H. Nidditch. Oxford: Clarendon Press.

Lycan, W. G. "Consciousness as Internal Monitoring." In *The Nature of Consciousness*, ed. N. Block, O. Flanagan, and G. Güzeldere, 754–71. Cambridge, Mass.: MIT Press, 1997.

McGinn, C. 1983. *The Subjective View.* Oxford: Clarendon Press.

———. 1997. "Consciousness and Content." In *The Nature of Consciousness*, ed. N. Block, O. Flanagan, and G. Güzeldere, 295–307. Cambridge, Mass.: MIT Press.

Mahler, M. S., F. Pine, and A. Bergmann. 1975. *The Psychological Birth of the Human Infant.* New York: Basic Books.

Malcolm, N. 1988. "Subjectivity." *Philosophy* 63: 147–60.

Marbach, E. 1974. *Das Problem des Ich in der Phänomenologie Husserls.* The Hague: Martinus Nijhoff.

Marion, J.-L. 1989. *Réduction et donation: Recherches sur Husserl, Heidegger et la phénoménologie.* Paris: PUF.

———. 1996. "The Saturated Phenomenon." *Philosophy Today* 40, no. 1: 103–24.

Mead, G. H. 1962. *Mind, Self and Society: From the Standpoint of a Social Behaviorist.* Chicago: University of Chicago Press.

Meltzoff, A. N., and M. K. Moore. 1995. "Infants' Understanding of People and Things: From Body Imitation to Folk Psychology." In *The Body and the Self*, ed. J. L. Bermúdez, A. Marcel, and N. Eilan, 43–69. Cambridge, Mass.: MIT Press.

Merleau-Ponty, M. 1945. *Phénoménologie de la perception.* Paris: Éditions Gallimard.

———. 1947. "Le primat de la perception et ses conséquences philosophiques." *Bulletin de la Société Française de Philosophie* 41: 119–53.

———. 1960a. *Signes.* Paris: Éditions Gallimard.

———. 1960b. *Les relations avec autrui chez l'enfant.* Paris: Centre de Documentation Universitaire.

———. 1962. *Phenomenology of Perception.* Trans. C. Smith. London: Routledge and Kegan Paul.

———. 1964. *Le visible et l'invisible.* Paris: Tel Gallimard.

———. 1966. *Sens et non-sens.* Paris: Les Éditions Nagel.

———. 1969. *La prose du monde.* Paris: Tel Gallimard.

———. 1988. *Merleau-Ponty à la Sorbonne.* Paris: Cynara.

Michalski, K. 1997. *Logic and Time: An Essay on Husserl's Theory of Meaning.* Dordrecht: Kluwer Academic Publishers.

Mishara, A. 1990. "Husserl and Freud: Time, Memory and the Unconscious." *Husserl Studies* 7: 29–58.

Mohanty, J. N. 1972. *The Concept of Intentionality.* St. Louis: Green.

Mohr, G. 1988. "Vom Ich zur Person. Die Identität des Subjekts bei Peter F. Strawson." In *Die Frage nach dem Subjekt,* ed. M. Frank, G. Raulet, and W. van Reijen, 29–84. Frankfurt am Main: Suhrkamp.

Montavont, A. 1993. "Passivité et non-donation." *Alter* 1: 131–48.

———. 1994. "Le phénomène de l'affection dans les *Analysen zur passiven Synthesis* (1918–1926) de Husserl." *Alter* 2: 119–40.

———. 1999. *De la passivité dans la phénoménologie de Husserl.* Paris: PUF.

Moore, M. 1988. "Mind, Brain and Unconscious." In *Mind, Psychoanalysis, and Science,* ed. P. Clark and C. Wright, 141–66. Oxford: Blackwell.

Nagel, T. 1965. "Physicalism." *The Philosophical Review* 74: 339–56.

———. 1974. "What Is It Like to Be a Bat?" *The Philosophical Review* 83: 435–50.

———. 1986. *The View from Nowhere.* Oxford: Oxford University Press.

Natorp, P. 1912. *Allgemeine Psychologie.* Tübingen: Mohr.

Natsoulas, T. 1989. "Freud and Consciousness: III. The Importance of Tertiary Consciousness." *Psychoanalysis and Contemporary Thought* 12: 97–123.

———. 1991–92. " 'I Am Not the Subject of This Thought': Understanding a Unique Relation of Special Ownership with the Help of David Woodruf Smith: Part 1." *Imagination, Cognition and Personality* 11: 279–302.

———. 1991–92. " 'I Am Not the Subject of This Thought': Understanding a Unique Relation of Special Ownership with the Help of David Woodruf Smith: Part 2." *Imagination, Cognition and Personality* 11: 331–52.

Neisser, U. 1988. "Five Kinds of Self-Knowledge." *Philosophical Psychology* 1, no. 1: 35–59.

Noonan, H. 1991. *Personal Identity.* London: Routledge.

Nozick, R. 1981. *Philosophical Explanations.* Oxford: Clarendon Press.

Parfit, D. 1987. *Reasons and Persons.* Oxford: Clarendon Press.

Pélicier, Y., ed. 1985. *Somnambules et Parasomniaques.* Paris: Economica.

Perry, J. 1979. "The Problem of the Essential Indexical." *Nous* 13: 3–21.

———. 1993. *The Problem of Essential Indexicals and Other Essays.* Oxford: Oxford University Press.

Pfänder, A. 1904. *Einführung in die Psychologie.* Leipzig: Verlag von Johann Ambrosius Barth.

Piaget, J., and B. Inhelder. 1969. *The Psychology of the Child.* New York: Basic Books.

Pothast, U. 1971. *Über einige Fragen der Selbstbeziehung.* Frankfurt am Main: Vittorio Klostermann.

Prufer, T. 1988. "Heidegger, Early and Late, and Aquinas." In *Edmund Husserl and the Phenomenological Tradition: Essays in Phenomenology,* ed. R. Sokolowski, 197–215. Washington, D.C.: Catholic University of America Press.

Richir, M. 1989. "Synthèse passive et temporalisation/spatialisation." In *Husserl,* ed. E. Escoubas and M. Richir, 9–41. Grenoble: Millon.

Rickert, H. 1915. *Der Gegenstand der Erkenntnis.* Tübingen: Mohr.

Ricoeur, P. 1950/1988. *Philosophie de la volonté I. Le volontaire et l'involontaire.* Paris: Aubier.

———. 1966. *Freedom and Nature: The Voluntary and the Involuntary.* Trans. E. V. Kohák. Evanston, Ill.: Northwestern University Press.

———. 1990. *Soi-même comme un autre.* Paris: Éditions du Seuil.

Rohr-Dietschi, U. 1974. *Zur Genese des Selbstbewußtseins.* Berlin: de Gruyter.

Rosenberg, J. 1981. "Apperception and Sartre's Pre-Reflective Cogito." *American Philosophical Quarterly* 18: 255–60.

Rosenberg, M. 1987. "Depersonalisation: The Loss of Personal Identity." In *Self and Identity,* ed. T. Honess and K. Yardley, 193–206. London: Routledge and Kegan Paul.

Rosenthal, D. M. 1993. "Higher-Order Thoughts and the Appendage Theory of Consciousness." *Philosophical Psychology* 6: 155–66.

———. 1997. "A Theory of Consciousness." In *The Nature of Consciousness,* ed. N. Block, O. Flanagan, and G. Güzeldere, 729–53. Cambridge, Mass.: MIT Press.

Ryle, G. 1949. *The Concept of Mind.* London: Hutchinson.

Sacks, O. 1990. *The Man Who Mistook His Wife for a Hat.* New York: HarperPerennial.

Sartre, J.-P. 1936/1988. *La transcendance de l'ego.* Paris: Vrin.

———. 1943/1976. *L'Être et le néant.* Paris: Tel Gallimard.

———. 1948. "Conscience de soi et connaissance de soi." *Bulletin de la Société Française de Philosophie* 42: 49–91.

———. 1956. *Being and Nothingness.* Trans. H. E. Barnes. New York: Philosophical Library.

———. 1957. *The Transcendence of the Ego.* Trans. F. Williams and R. Kirkpatrick. New York: Noonday Press.

———. 1967. "Consciousness of Self and Knowledge of Self." In *Readings in Existential Phenomenology,* ed. N. Lawrence and D. O'Connor, 113–42. Englewood Cliffs, N.J.: Prentice-Hall.

———. 14 May 1971. "Un entretien avec Jean-Paul Sartre." In *Le Monde,* with M. Contat and M. Rybalka.

Sass, L. A. 1994. *The Paradoxes of Delusion.* London: Cornell University Press.

Scanlon, J. D. 1971. "Consciousness, the Streetcar and the Ego: Pro Husserl, Contra Sartre." *Philosophical Forum* 2: 332–54.

Scheler, M. 1916/1927. *Der Formalismus in der Ethik und die materiale Wertethik.* Halle: Max Niemeyer.

———. 1922/1973. *Wesen und Formen der Sympathie.* Bern and München: Francke Verlag.

————. 1954. *The Nature of Sympathy*. Trans. P. Heath. London: Routledge and Kegan Paul.

Schilder, P. 1951. *Psychoanalysis, Man, and Society*. Ed. Lauretta Bender. New York: Norton.

Schmalenbach, H. 1991. "Das Sein des Bewußtseins." In *Selbstbewußtseinstheorien von Fichte bis Sartre*, ed. M. Frank, 296–366. Frankfurt am Main: Suhrkamp.

Schmitz, H. 1982. "Zwei Subjektbegriffe. Bemerkungen zu dem Buch von Ernst Tugendhat: Selbstbewußtsein und Selbstbestimmung." *Philosophisches Jahrbuch* 89: 131–42.

————. 1991. "Leibliche und personale Konkurrenz im Selbstbewusstsein." In *Dimensionen des Selbst: Selbstbewusstsein, Reflexivität und die Bedingungen von Kommunikation*, ed. B. Kienzle and H. Pape, 152–68. Frankfurt am Main: Suhrkamp.

Schües, C. 1998. "Conflicting Apprehensions and the Question of Sensations." In *Alterity and Facticity: New Perspectives on Husserl*, ed. N. Depraz and D. Zahavi. Dordrecht: Kluwer Academic Publishers.

Searle, J. R. 1992. *The Rediscovery of the Mind*. Cambridge, Mass.: MIT Press.

Sebbah, F.-D. 1994. "Aux limites de l'intentionnalité: M. Henry et E. Lévinas lecteurs des *Leçons sur la conscience intime du temps*." *Alter* 2: 245–59.

Seebohm, T. 1962. *Die Bedingungen der Möglichkeit der Tranzendental-Philosophie*. Bonn: Bouvier.

Seel, G. 1995. *La dialectique de Sartre*. Lausanne: Editions L'Age d'Homme.

Shoemaker, S. 1963. *Self-Knowledge and Self-Identity*. Ithaca, N.Y.: Cornell University Press.

————. 1968. "Self-Reference and Self-Awareness." *The Journal of Philosophy* 65: 556–79.

————. 1996. *The First-Person Perspective and Other Essays*. Cambridge: Cambridge University Press.

Shoemaker, S., and R. Swinburne. 1984. *Personal Identity*. Oxford: Blackwell.

Smith, D. W. 1983. "Is This a Dagger I See before Me?" *Synthese* 54: 95–114.

————. 1989. *The Circle of Acquaintance*. Dordrecht: Kluwer Academic Publishers.

Sokolowski, R. 1970. *The Formation of Husserl's Concept of Constitution*. The Hague: Martinus Nijhoff.

————. 1974. *Husserlian Meditations*. Evanston, Ill.: Northwestern University Press.

————. 1976. "Ontological Possibilities in Phenomenology: The Dyad and the One." *Review of Metaphysics* 29: 691–701.

————. 1978. *Presence and Absence*. Bloomington: Indiana University Press.

Soldati, G. 1988. "Selbstbewußtsein und unmittelbares Wissen bei Tugendhat." In *Die Frage nach dem Subjekt*, ed. M. Frank, G. Raulet, and W. van Reijen, 85–100. Frankfurt am Main: Suhrkamp.

Spitz, R. A. 1983. *Dialogues from Infancy: Selected papers*. Ed. R. N. Emde. New York: International Universities Press.

Stern, D. N. 1983. "The Early Development of Schemas of Self, Other and 'Self with Other.'" In *Reflections on Self-Psychology*, ed. J. D. Lichtenberg and S. Kaplan, 49–84. Hillsdale, N.J.: Analytical Press.

————. 1985. *The Interpersonal World of the Infant.* New York: Basic Books.

Strasser, S. 1978. *Jenseits von Sein und Zeit.* The Hague: Martinus Nijhoff.

Straus, E. 1956. *Vom Sinn der Sinne.* Berlin: Springer-Verlag.

————. 1958. "Aesthesiology and Hallucinations." In *Existence: A New Dimension in Psychiatry and Psychology,* ed. R. May et al., 139–69. New York: Basic Books.

————. 1966. *Phenomenological Psychology: Selected Papers.* London: Tavistock Publications.

Strawson, G. 1994. *Mental Reality.* Cambridge, Mass.: MIT Press.

Strawson, P. F. 1959. *Individuals.* London: Methuen.

————. 1966. *The Bounds of Sense.* London: Methuen.

Taylor, C. 1989. *Sources of the Self.* Cambridge, Mass.: Harvard University Press.

Theunissen, M. 1977. *Der Andere.* Berlin: de Gruyter.

————. 1984. *The Other.* Trans. C. Macann. Cambridge, Mass.: MIT Press.

Tugendhat, E. 1979. *Selbstbewußtsein und Selbstbestimmung.* Frankfurt am Main: Suhrkamp.

————. 1986. *Self-Consciousness and Self-Determination.* Trans. P. Stern. Cambridge, Mass.: MIT Press.

Van Gulick, R. 1997. "Understanding the Phenomenal Mind: Are We All Just Armadillos?" In *The Nature of Consciousness,* ed. N. Block, O. Flanagan, and G. Güzeldere, 559–66. Cambridge, Mass.: MIT Press.

Waldenfels, B. 1989. "Erfahrung des Fremden in Husserls Phänomenologie." *Phänomenologische Forschungen* 22: 39–62.

Wider, K. 1989. "Through the Looking Glass: Sartre on Knowledge and the Prereflective *Cogito.*" *Man and World* 22: 329–43.

————. 1993a. "The Failure of Self-Consciousness in Sartre's 'Being and Nothingness.'" *Dialogue* 32, no. 4: 737–56.

————. 1993b. "Sartre and the Long Distance Truck Driver: The Reflexivity of Consciousness." *Journal of the British Society for Phenomenology* 24, no. 3: 232–49.

Wilkes, K. V. 1988. *Real People: Personal Identity without Thought Experiments.* Oxford: Clarendon Press.

Wittgenstein, L. 1958. *The Blue and Brown Books.* New York: Harper and Row.

Yamagata, Y. 1991. "Une autre lecture de *L'essence de la manifestation*: Immanence, présent vivant et altérité." *Études philosophiques* 2: 173–91.

Zahavi, D. 1992. *Intentionalität und Konstitution. Eine Einführung in Husserls Logische Untersuchungen.* Copenhagen: Museum Tusculanum Press.

————. 1994a. "The Self-Pluralisation of the Primal Life: A Problem in Fink's Husserl-Interpretation." *Recherches Husserliennes* 2: 3–18.

————. 1995. "Intentionalitet og Fænomen hos Aristoteles, Thomas Aquinas og Brentano." *Filosofiske Studier* 15: 211–30.

————. 1996. *Husserl und die transzendentale intersubjektivität. Eine Antwort auf die sprachpragmatische Kritik.* Dordrecht: Kluwer Academic Publishers.

————. 1997a. *Husserls Fænomenologi.* Copenhagen: Gyldendal.

————. 1997b. "Sleep, Self-Awareness and Dissociation." *Alter* 5.

WORKS CITED

Zahavi, D., ed. 1994b. *Subjektivitet og Livsverden i Husserls Fænomenologi.* Aarhus: Modtryk.

———. 1998a. *Self-Awareness, Temporality, and Alterity.* Dordrecht: Kluwer Academic Publishers.

Zahavi, D., and N. Depraz, eds. 1998b. *Alterity and Facticity: New Perspectives on Husserl.* Dordrecht: Kluwer Academic Publishers.

Index